CAMBRIDGE STUDIES
IN ENGLISH LEGAL HISTORY

Edited by
D. E. C. YALE
Fellow of Christ's College
and Reader in English Legal History at the University of Cambridge

WILLIAM SHEPPARD, CROMWELL'S LAW REFORMER

William Sheppard is best known as one of the most prolific legal authors of the seventeenth century. His twenty-two books on the law include studies of conveyancing, actions on the case, tithe collection, several guides for local law enforcement and the first three legal encyclopedias to be written in the English language. His most interesting book, *England's Balme*, contains the most comprehensive set of law reform proposals published in that century.

This study presents the first full account of Sheppard's employment under Oliver Cromwell's Protectorate as well as an examination of his family background and education, his religious commitment to John Owen's party of Independents and his legal philosophy. An appraisal of all Sheppard's legal works, including those written during the civil war and the restoration period, illustrates the overlapping concerns with law reform, religion and politics in his generation. Sheppard had impressively consistent goals for the reform of English law and his prescient proposals anticipate the reforms ultimately adopted in the nineteenth century, culminating in the Judicature Acts of 1875–8. Dr Matthews examines the relative importance of Sheppard's books to his generation and to legal literature in general, assessing such bibliographical problems as the allegation that Justice Dodderidge was the original author of the *Touchstone of Common Assurances*. The study provides a full bibliography of Sheppard's legal and religious works and an appendix of the sources Sheppard used in the composition of his books on the law.

Nancy L. Matthews has been a Lecturer at University of Maryland and George Mason University and is now employed by the Smithsonian Institution Libraries, Washington, D.C.

WILLIAM SHEPPARD, CROMWELL'S LAW REFORMER

NANCY L. MATTHEWS

The right of the
University of Cambridge
to print and sell
all manner of books
was granted by
Henry VIII in 1534.
The University has printed
and published continuously
since 1584.

CAMBRIDGE UNIVERSITY PRESS

CAMBRIDGE

LONDON   NEW YORK   NEW ROCHELLE
MELBOURNE   SYDNEY

PUBLISHED BY THE PRESS SYNDICATE OF THE UNIVERSITY OF CAMBRIDGE
The Pitt Building, Trumpington Street, Cambridge, United Kingdom

CAMBRIDGE UNIVERSITY PRESS
The Edinburgh Building, Cambridge CB2 2RU, UK
40 West 20th Street, New York NY 10011–4211, USA
477 Williamstown Road, Port Melbourne, VIC 3207, Australia
Ruiz de Alarcón 13, 28014 Madrid, Spain
Dock House, The Waterfront, Cape Town 8001, South Africa

http://www.cambridge.org

First published 1984
First paperback edition 2004

A catalogue record for this book is available from the British Library

Library of Congress catalogue card number: 84-5832

ISBN 0 521 26483 9 hardback
ISBN 0 521 89091 8 paperback

CONTENTS

PREFACE

This study was originally undertaken for a master's thesis at the University of Maryland. Without the critical assistar.ce and advice I have received from my adviser, J. S. Cockburn, and from D. E. C. Yale, the editor of this series, and from J. H. Baker, the appraisal of Sheppard's contributions to legal literature would have been sorely inadequate. All have generously offered many helpful suggestions and it is a pleasure to express my thanks to each of them. Professor Cockburn has been unfailingly supportive, from the first seminar paper to the final reading of this manuscript. I would also like to express my appreciation to G. E. Aylmer for the helpful information he provided on details of the political and administrative history of the interregnum, and for the guidance given by Laurence E. Miller, Jr, on the intricacies of Calvinist theology. Throughout this project I have benefited immeasurably from many discussions with Charles M. Cook on the difficult problems connected with law reform. All of the individuals mentioned above provided substantial help by commenting on early drafts, saving me from misleading statements and outright mistakes. Any remaining errors in fact or judgment are, naturally, my own.

Most of the initial research was done at The Folger Shakespeare Library, Washington, D.C., where I received invaluable assistance from the members of the capable staff and from other readers at that congenial institution. I would also like to express my appreciation to the staff of the Library of Congress, Washington, D.C., with particular thanks to the Rare Book Division of the Law Library; to the staff at McKeldin Library, University of Maryland in College Park; and of the Treasure Room, Harvard Law School, and The Houghton Rare Book Library, both of Harvard University. During my research trips to England, courtesies were extended to me in London by the archivists and librarians of the British Library, Dr Williams's Library, Dulwich College Library, the Guildhall Library, the Institute of Historical Research, Lincoln's Inn Library, The

Middle Temple Library and the Public Record Office, Chancery Lane. I also consulted books and manuscripts held by Cambridge University Library and the libraries of Caius and Trinity Colleges of that university, the Bodleian and Worcester College Library of Oxford University, and the Gloucester Public Library. The Marquess of Bath granted me permission to consult the Whitelocke Papers at Longleat House. The staff of the Gloucestershire Records Office was very patient with my requests for countless records of parishes and of the city corporation, the consistory court, local manors and various family papers. I wish to thank all the individuals of those institutions for their helpful assistance and courtesy. Staff members of several libraries and repositories answered my letters requesting information, for which I am also grateful. They include the staff at Yale University working on the revision of Donald Wing's Short-title catalogue, Wadham College, Oxford, Dr Williams's Library, London, and the Wiltshire Record Office, as well as all the libraries holding copies of *England's balme*.

I would like to thank the American Bar Foundation and the William Randolph Hearst Foundation for the research grants that assisted me in the completion of this study. The History Department of the University of Maryland cooperated by allowing me to finish a project that took much longer to complete than any of us first suspected. I am particularly grateful to the late Walter Rundell, Jr, and Emory G. Evans, successive chairmen of the department, for their encouragement and support. The friendship and hospitality of British friends too numerous to list here made my working trips to England even more delightful than I had expected. Shelagh Weir especially has my deep gratitude. At home, I am greatly indebted to my children, Leslie, Diane, Josh and David Arnson, for coping with the household during my absences, and even more thankful for their encouragement and cooperation when I was working at home. Finally, it is a pleasure to extend my thanks for the countless ways my mother, Edna Matthews, my family, friends and colleagues have assisted me in the time it has taken to complete this work.

NOTES ON STYLE AND ON BIBLIOGRAPHY

American spelling has been used throughout including, for the sake of consistency, words within quotations. The only exceptions are the titles of books which appear as they were first published, with occasional punctuation added for clarity. All citations to Sheppard's books refer to the first edition unless otherwise noted. The place of publication has been provided only for those books printed outside London. Cambridge publications refer to England unless Massachusetts is specified.

Dating has been adjusted to the extent that the new year is reckoned to begin on 1 January rather than 25 March. In all other respects the seventeenth-century calendar has been followed.

Quotations have been modernized in capitalization, spelling and punctuation and it is hoped that greater clarity will compensate for what has been lost in contemporary flavor. Sheppard's penchant for capitalizing words for emphasis was as pronounced as his indifference to uniform spelling. Indeed, he had little regard for consistency in spelling his own name. I hope that the fervency of the curious mixture of his idealism and pragmatism still reaches the reader, lower case notwithstanding.

Page numbers appearing in square brackets indicate actual sequence of unpaginated pages while those in single inverted commas denote an error in the printed pagination.

The bibliography at the close of the text is in two parts. In the first, Sheppard's books have been listed in chronological order and include both subsequent editions by the author and posthumous editions by later editors. The second part lists the sources Sheppard cited in his works. The decision to include this unconventional listing was made with the hope that the sources Sheppard relied upon in the composition of his works on the law will be of interest to students of legal history three centuries later.

Primary and secondary sources used for this study are found in the footnotes. Printed sources cited in more than one chapter are listed with the abbreviations.

ABBREVIATIONS

AJLH	*The American journal of legal history* (as cited)
Allibone, *Critical dictionary*	S. A. Allibone, *A critical dictionary of English literature and British and American authors* (Philadelphia, 1807)
A & O	C. H. Firth & R. S. Rait, eds., *Acts and ordinances of the interregnum 1642–1660* (3 vols., 1911)
ASLH	The American Society for Legal History
Aylmer, *Interregnum*	G. E. Aylmer, ed., *The interregnum: the quest for settlement 1646–1660* (1972)
Aylmer, *King's servants*	G. E. Aylmer, *The king's servants, the civil service of Charles I 1625–1642* (1961)
Aylmer, *State's servants*	G. E. Aylmer, *The state's servants, the civil service of the English republic 1649–1660* (1973)
B.	Baron of the exchequer
Baker, *Legal history*	J. H. Baker, *An introduction to English legal history*, 2nd edn (1979)
Baker, *Legal records*	J. H. Baker, ed., *Legal records and the historian* (RHS, 1978)
Baker, *Spelman*	J. H. Baker, ed., *The reports of John Spelman* (2 vols., Selden Society, 1977)
Bassett, *Catalogue*	T. Bassett, *A catalogue of the common and statute law books of the realm* (as cited)
Bib. Coop.	*Bibliotheca Cooperiana, legal and parliamentary collection. A catalogue of a further portion of the library of Charles Purton Cooper, Esq.* (1856)
Bigland, *Gloucester*	R. Bigland, *Historical, monumental and genealogical collections, relative to the county of Gloucester* (2 vols., 1792)

BL

British Library

Add. MS

Additional Manuscript

Harl. MS

Harleian Manuscript

Lansd. MS

Lansdowne Manuscript

Sloane MS

Sloane Manuscript

Stowe MS

Stowe Manuscript

Black, *'Coram Protectore'*

S. F. Black, *'Coram Protectore*: the judges of Westminster Hall under the protectorate of Oliver Cromwell', *AJLH*, XX (1976), 32–64

Bridgman, *Legal bibliography*

R. W. Bridgman, *A short view of legal bibliography* (1807)

Burton's *diary*

Diary of Thomas Burton, Esq, ed. J. T. Rutt (4 vols., reprint, New York, 1974)

Burton's *diary*, Index of speakers

Diary of Thomas Burton, Esq, 'Annotated index of speakers in the parliament of 1656 and 1658/9', ed. P. Pinckney and P. H. Hardacre, vol. IV, 1–30

Busch, 'Lisle'

A. J. Busch, 'The interregnum court of chancery: a study of the career and writings of John Lisle, lord commissioner of the great seal (1649–1659)', Univ. of Kansas Ph.D. thesis 1971

C.

Chancery commissioner

CCAM

M. A. E. Green, ed., *Calendar of the proceedings of the Committee for the Advancement of Money* (1888)

CCC

M. A. E. Green, ed., *Calendar of the proceedings of the Committee for Compounding 1643–1660* (5 vols., 1889–92)

CJ

The journals of the house of commons (as cited)

C. J.

Chief justice of king's (upper) bench or common pleas

Clarke, *Bibliotheca legum*

J. Clarke, *Bibliotheca legum: or a complete catalogue of the common and statute law-books of the United Kingdom, with an account of their dates and prices* (1810)

Clarke papers

C. H. Firth, ed., *The Clarke papers, selec-*

tions from the papers of William Clarke, vol. III, Camden Society, new series, LXI (RHS, 1899)

CL*J* The Cambridge Law *Journal* (as cited)

C. P. Court of common pleas

CSPD Calendar of State Papers, domestic, Commonwealth period (13 vols., as cited)

CSPD, CI Calendar of State Papers, domestic, reign of Charles I (23 vols., as cited)

Cockburn, *Assizes* J. S. Cockburn, *A history of English assizes 1558–1714* (Cambridge, 1972)

Cockburn, *Crime in England* J. S. Cockburn, ed., *Crime in England 1550–1800* (1977)

Collection of orders B. Whitelocke, R. Keble & W. Lenthall, *A collection of such of the orders heretofore used in chauncery with such alterations and additions thereunto, as the right honorable the lords commissioners of the great seal of England, by and with the advice and assistance of the honorable the master of the rolls, have thought fit at present (in order to a further reformation now under their lordship's consideration) to ordain and publish, for reforming the several abuses of the said court, preventing multiplicity of suits, motions and unnecessary charge to the suitors, and for their more expeditious and certain course for relief* (1649)

Cook, 'Congregational Independents' S. G. Cook, 'The Congregational Independents and the Cromwellian constitutions', Church History, XLVI (1977), 335–57

Cotterell, 'Law reform' M. Cotterell, 'Law reform during the interregnum', Univ. of Sydney M.A. thesis 1967

DAB Dictionary of American Biography (as cited)

DNB Dictionary of National Biography (as cited)

Douthwaite, *Gray's Inn* W. R. Douthwaite, *Gray's Inn, its history and associations* (1886)

EcHR Economic History Review (as cited)

EHR English Historical Review (as cited)

Everitt, *Kent*

A. Everitt, *The community of Kent and the great rebellion* (Leicester, 1966)

Firth, *Protectorate*

C. H. Firth, *The last years of the protectorate 1656–1658*, 2nd edn (2 vols., New York, 1964)

Fletcher, *Pension book*

R. J. Fletcher, ed., *The pension book of Gray's Inn 1569–1669* (1901)

Foss, *Judges*

E. Foss, *The judges of England* (6 vols., 1857)

Foster, *Register to Gray's Inn*

J. Foster, *The register of admissions to Gray's Inn 1521–1889* (1889)

Gardiner, *History*

S. R. Gardiner, *History of the commonwealth and protectorate 1649–1660* (3 vols., 1897–1901)

Glouc. visit.

T. Fenwick & W. Metcalfe, eds., *The visitation of the county of Gloucester 1682–83* (Exeter, 1884)

GNQ

Gloucestershire Notes and Queries (as cited)

GPL

Gloucester Public Library

Hockaday abstracts

Typescript of Gloucestershire parish records taken from MSS of the Gloucester Consistory Court by F. S. Hockaday

GRO

Gloucester Records Office

GCR

Gloucester City records

GDR

Gloucester Diocesan records

Haller, *Liberty and reformation*

W. Haller, *Liberty and reformation in the puritan revolution* (New York, 1955)

Haller, *Puritanism*

W. Haller, *The rise of puritanism* (New York, 1957)

Harl. Soc.

Harleian Society publications (as cited)

Haskins, *Early Massachusetts*

G. L. Haskins, *Law and authority in early Massachusetts, a study in tradition and design* (reprint, Hamden, Conn., 1968)

Haydn, *Dignities*

J. T. Haydn, *The book of dignities*, 3rd edn (1894)

HEL

W. S. Holdsworth, *A history of English law* (16 vols., 1923–37)

Hill, *God's Englishman*

C. Hill, *God's Englishman, Oliver Cromwell and the English revolution* (1972)

Hill, *World upside down*

C. Hill, *The world turned upside down; radical ideas during the English revolution* (1972)

HLQ	*Huntington Library Quarterly* (as cited)
Hoffman, *Legal study*	D. Hoffman, *A course of legal study*, 2nd edn (Baltimore, 1836)
Ind. Lib.	The Index Library, British Record Society (as cited)
Ingram, 'Communities'	M. J. Ingram, 'Communities and courts: law and disorder in early-seventeenth-century Wiltshire', in Cockburn, *Crime in England*
J.	Justice of king's (upper) bench or of common pleas
James, *Social problems*	M. James, *Social problems and policy during the puritan revolution 1640–1660* (New York, 1966)
Jones, *Politics and the bench*	W. J. Jones, *Politics and the bench: the judges and the origins of the English civil war* (1971)
K. B.	Court of king's bench
Keeler, *Long Parliament*	M. F. Keeler, *The Long Parliament 1640–1641: a biographical study of its members* (Philadelphia, 1954)
Knafla, 'Inns of court'	L. A. Knafla, 'The matriculation revolution and education at the inns of court in renaissance England', in A. J. Slavin, ed., *Tudor men and institutions* (Baton Rouge, La., 1972), 232–55
Knafla, *Law and politics*	L. A. Knafla, *Law and politics in Jacobean England, the tracts of Lord Chancellor Ellesmere* (Cambridge, 1977)
LJ	*Journals of the house of lords* (as cited)
Longleat MS	Whitelocke papers, Longleat House
Lowndes, *Bibliographer's manual*	W. T. Lowndes, *The bibliographer's manual of English literature*, 2nd edn (6 vols., 1885)
LQR	*Law Quarterly Review*
Maitland, *Forms of action*	F. W. Maitland, *The forms of action at common law* (reprint, Cambridge, 1968)
Marvin, *Legal bibliography*	J. G. Marvin, *Legal bibliography, or a thesaurus of American, English, Irish and Scottish law* (Philadelphia, 1847)

Matthews, *Calamy*	A. G. Matthews, *Calamy revised: being a revision of Edmund Calamy's account of the ministers and others ejected and silenced, 1660–2* (Oxford, 1934)
Merc. pol.	*Mercurius politicus*
Milsom, *Foundations of the common law*	S. F. C. Milsom, *Historical foundations of the common law* (1969)
M. R.	Master of the rolls
M. T. Ad. Reg.	H. F. Macgeagh & H. A. C. Sturgess, eds., *Register of admissions to the honourable society of the Middle Temple 1501–1781*, I (1949)
M. T. Cal.	C. H. Hopwood, ed., *A calendar of Middle Temple records* (1903)
M. T. Min.	C. H. Hopwood, ed., *Middle Temple records, minutes of parliament* (3 vols., 1904)
Niehaus, 'Law reform'	C. R. Niehaus, 'The issue of law reform in the puritan revolution', Harvard Univ. Ph.D. thesis 1957
Nourse, 'Law reform'	G. B. Nourse, 'Law reform under the commonwealth and protectorate', *LQR*, LXXV (1959), 512–29
Pennington, 'County committee'	D. H. Pennington, 'The county committee at war', in E. W. Ives, ed., *The English revolution 1600–1660* (New York, 1971), 64–75
Playne, *Parishes*	A. T. Playne, *History of the parishes of Minchinhampton and Avening* (Gloucester, 1915)
Plomer, *Booksellers*	H. R. Plomer, *A dictionary of the booksellers and printers who were at work in England, Scotland & Ireland from 1641 to 1667* (Oxford, 1968)
P & P	*Past and Present* (as cited)
Prest, *Inns of court*	W. Prest, *The inns of court under Elizabeth and the early Stuarts 1590–1640* (1972)
PRO	Public Record Office
ASSI	Assizes
C	Chancery
E	Exchequer

PROB	Probate
SP	State Papers
Pub. intell.	*The publicke intelligencer*
RHS	The Royal Historical Society
Roots, 'Cromwell's ordinances'	Ivan Roots, 'Cromwell's ordinances: The early legislation of the protectorate', in Aylmer, *Interregnum*
'Salisbury charter'	Hubert Hull, ed., 'The Commonwealth Charter of the City of Salisbury', *Camden Miscellany*, XI, Camden Society, 3rd Series, XIII (RHS, 1907), 167–98
Shapiro, 'Law reform'	B. Shapiro, 'Law reform in seventeenth-century England', paper delivered at ASLH meeting, Williamsburg, Va., 1972
Shaw, *English church*	W. A. Shaw, *A history of the English church during the civil wars and under the commonwealth 1640–1660* (2 vols., 1900)
STC	A. W. Pollard & G. R. Redgrave, eds., *A short-title catalogue of books printed in England, Scotland & Ireland, and of English books printed abroad 1475–1640* (1926); 2nd edn, W. A. Jackson, F. S. Ferguson & K. F. Pantzer, eds., vol. II (1976)
Sta. Reg.	*A transcript of the registers of the Worshipful Company of Stationers, from 1640 to 1708* (3 vols., 1913–14)
Statutes	*The statutes of the realm* (as cited)
TBGAS	*Transactions of the Bristol and Gloucestershire Archaeological Society* (as cited)
Term cat.	E. Arber, ed., *The term catalogues 1668–1709* (5 vols., 1903)
Thurloe state papers	T. Birch, ed., *Collection of the state papers of John Thurloe* (7 vols., 1742)
TRHS	*Transactions of the Royal Historical Society* (as cited)
TT	*Catalogue of the pamphlets, books, newspapers and manuscripts relating to the civil war, the commonwealth and restoration, collected by George Thomason, 1640–1661* (3 vols., 1908)

U. B.   Court of the upper bench, 1649–60

Underdown, *Pride's*   D. Underdown, *Pride's purge, politics in*
purge   *the puritan revolution* (Oxford, 1971)

Underdown,   D. Underdown, *Somerset in the civil war*
Somerset   *and interregnum* (Hamden, Conn., 1973)

VCH   *Victoria history of the counties of England*

Veall, *Movement for*   D. Veall, *The popular movement for law*
law reform   *reform 1640–1660* (Oxford, 1970)

Wallace, 'Owen'   D. D. Wallace, Jr, 'The life and thought of
                         John Owen to 1660: a study of the sig-
                         nificance of Calvinist theology in English
                         puritanism', Princeton Univ. Ph.D.
                         thesis 1965

Washbourne, *Bib.*   J. Washbourne, ed., *Bibliotheca Glouces-*
Glouc.   *trensis* (Gloucester, 1825)

Weinbaum, *Borough*   M. Weinbaum, *British borough charters*
charters   *1307–1660* (Cambridge, 1943)

Whitelocke,   B. Whitelocke, *Memorials of the English*
Memorials   *affairs from the beginning of the reign of King*
                         Charles the First to the happy restoration of
                         King Charles the Second (4 vols., 1853)

Willcox,   W. B. Willcox, *Gloucestershire 1590–1640*
Gloucestershire   (New Haven, Conn., 1940)

Williams, *Glouc. parl.* W. R. Williams, *The parliamentary history*
hist.   *of Gloucestershire* (Hereford, 1898)

Williams, *Great*   W. R. Williams, *The history of the great*
sessions   *sessions in Wales 1542–1830* (Brecknock,
                         1899)

Winfield, *Chief*   P. Winfield, *The chief sources of English*
sources   *legal history* (Cambridge, Mass., 1925)

Wing   D. G. Wing, ed., *Short-title catalogue of*
                         books printed in England, Scotland, Ireland,
                         Wales and British America and of English
                         books printed in other countries 1641–1700,
                         2nd edn, I (New York, 1972); 1st edn,
                         II–III (New York, 1945–51)

WMQ   *The William and Mary Quarterly* (as cited)

Wood, *Athenæ*   A. à Wood, *Athenæ Oxoniensis*, ed. P. Bliss
                         (reprint, 4 vols., 1969)

Worc. Coll. MS   Manuscript collection of the papers of

William Clarke, Worcester College, Oxford. Edited by C. H. Firth as *The Clarke papers* (as cited)

Worden, *Rump Parliament* B. Worden, *The Rump Parliament 1648–1653* (Cambridge, 1974)

W & S W. C. Abbott, ed., *The writings and speeches of Oliver Cromwell* (4 vols., Cambridge, Mass., 1945)

INTRODUCTION

The reform of the law was William Sheppard's continuing professional interest from his first legal writing of 1631 to the preparation of his last book, published posthumously in 1675. Law reform, a term used widely in the seventeenth century, could be broadly defined as an effort to achieve a greater degree of justice, an exercise that might be accomplished through procedural reform or by altering the laws themselves. It could also mean the endeavor to gain a better understanding of legal principles or to publicize what was known of the settled law. More practically, it could involve an effort to facilitate a greater efficiency in the administration of justice. A particular interest in law reform had developed by the turn of the seventeenth century because the manner in which the law had been evolving had created serious impediments to swift, certain justice. These developments were tied directly to the conventions and the structure of the court system, historical problems that were not resolved until the nineteenth century. The variety of jurisdictions that had developed by the late sixteenth century both allowed for and precipitated the adoption of procedural innovations, an increased use of fictions and a progressive decline in the usage of original actions in favor of more flexible procedures. These changes in turn produced multiple suits and increases in both costs and delays. The concomitant rise of new demands placed upon the courts by changing economic and social conditions in the society gave a boost to the jurisdictions exercised by star chamber and chancery. This situation exacerbated the competitive relations among the courts as well as adding to the increased volume of suits; consequently the problems evolving from and contributing to a confusion in litigation were circular in nature, with causes and effects inextricably intertwined. While the uncertainty, delay and higher costs caused by the lack of unity among the courts remained a concern of law reformers until the reorganization of the nineteenth century, the adoption of procedural innovations to accommodate the needs of litigants was a shift in legal practice that

1

was welcomed by Sheppard and his philosophical mentors, Edward Coke and John Dodderidge. The adaptations accepted by the courts from the late sixteenth century onwards required explanations, and law reform therefore involved efforts to publicize both the new and traditional procedures through published works. Sheppard, like Coke, Dodderidge, Finch and other legal authors before him, wrote books in the vernacular to explain changes in the substance and process of the law, believing that the content of the law must be organized and understood if it were to fulfil the functions for which it was intended.

In addition to clarifying the changes in the law as they developed, Sheppard and some of his older contemporaries also hoped that alterations could be made that would, in their views, improve the law's effectiveness. Law reform was therefore also defined as the endeavor to make specific changes in both customary and statute law. Since the mid sixteenth century reformers had expressed interest in editing and abridging the statute book in order to remove expired laws and to condense multiple acts. A further goal was to reform the criminal code, a common aim being to remove capital punishment from crimes against property. Sheppard and other lawyers also hoped to bring legal improvement by adopting provisions for more accurate record-keeping. Other areas of concern were corruption and ignorance, problems which had long been recognized to be endemic in both law enforcement and in the administration of the courts. Proposals to exert effective controls over officials entrusted with responsibilities had been formulated by government administrators and members of parliament from Elizabeth's reign up to the time of the civil war. Law reform was therefore a serious matter of official concern at the time Sheppard began his legal studies in 1620. From the 1590s through the 1630s privy councillors, judges and parliamentary committees all were raising questions about the state of the law and of law enforcement, initiating official enquiries into possible avenues of resolution for several perceived problems.

In 1641, when Sheppard had been practising law for twelve years, the Long Parliament decisively resolved several political grievances against the Caroline administration that resulted in permanent changes in the judicial structure. The simultaneous relaxation of censorship restrictions over the press contributed to an expanded popular interest in law reform as laymen, outside the professional community of lawyers and government officials, framed new complaints and proposals for further adjustments in the legal structure. The volume of published works increased nearly 9000 per cent between 1640 and 1642 as articulate citizens from all walks of life joined in a general critical appraisal of what was wrong with their troubled society. Christopher Hill has suggested that there 'must have been hundreds of men' who, like Henry Spelman and Simonds D'Ewes, 'deliberately refrained from publication before 1640' and who finally released their works to printers during that unique period of freedom of the press.[1] This observation about the response to the lifting of inhibiting constraints applies to Sheppard and his decision to publish his first book in 1641. Hundreds of printed works collected by the bookseller, George Thomason, between 1641 and 1660 provide an exceptional insight into the wide range of ideas that were in circulation in what has been characterized as a popular movement for law reform.[2] The demands, hopes and criticisms of men representing an uncommonly broad spectrum of the population have provided legal, political, social and theological historians with a mine of information about the ideas that proliferated in that disturbed but imaginative society. With this widening of popular interest, the definition of law reform as it had been considered by members of the profession changed, expanding far beyond its former dimensions to include millenarian programs, utopian plans and proposals to dismantle outright the English legal and judicial structure. Studies which have concentrated on the wealth of pamphlet literature and on the activities of the successive governments of the interregnum have contributed greatly to our understanding of the intensity and scope of the mid-seventeenth-century movement for law reform. A great number of problems with the law that were perceived by contemporaries have been identified, as have been the many writers in that disparate group of men who ventured to offer criticisms of the legal system. Historians writing about the period have usually placed Sheppard in the group of moderate reformers when classifying the critics into groups. That identification is accurate if the term moderate is taken to include those men who shared the assumption that the traditional legal system, based on common-law principles, must be preserved and that it would benefit from having archaic, redundant, barbaric and feudal features permanently removed.

---

[1] Christopher Hill, *Some intellectual consequences of the English Revolution* (Madison, Wisconsin, 1980), pp. 48–9.
[2] Veall, *Movement for law reform*.

Sheppard's contributions to the law-reform movement are, however, distinguished from those of other moderates because, when formulating his proposed reforms, he designed a comprehensive plan that resolved all the complaints in a single rational scheme. His cohesive philosophy of reform was in a continuum with that impressive generation of Jacobean scholars who exerted the strongest influences on the formation of his legal philosophy.

The habit of questioning and examination that Sheppard brought to his considerations of law reform was also a component of his puritan training, another important intellectual characteristic of early-Stuart society. His strong religious beliefs and his legal training combined to form his most pronounced characteristics: an intense dedication to his perceived responsibilities, a moral earnestness in the values he held, a personal commitment to legal and social improvement, and an enviable capacity for hard work. The outbreak of the civil war was the event that set the course of his career as a law reformer. The combination of his most profound interests – law, religion and politics – exemplifies the major concerns of his age, and his corpus of works illuminates many of the problems in government and society perceived by contemporaries that contributed to the remarkable changes of the period. Although Sheppard was known to his generation primarily through his published works, he also made important contributions to the protectorate government's program for law reform as Cromwell's legal adviser. His work therefore adds an important dimension to the evidence of Cromwell's reputation as an advocate of law reform.

1

BIOGRAPHY

Law is a rule for the governing of a civil society, to give every man that which doth belong to him. Our laws are divided into three sorts: common law, which is nothing else but common custom and that which is commonly used through the whole nation; and this is founded especially upon certain principles or maxims made out of the law of God and the law of reason. 2. Statute laws, which are certain acts and constitutions of parliament that have been made in all succeeding generations, to correct, abridge and explain the common law; and all these to give right to every man, and to preserve every man from wrong. 3. The customs of particular places, which are the laws of the places. There is also the civil law, martial law, ecclesiastical law, canon law, law of nations, law merchant, a part of the law of nations, and the law of chivalry, or title of honor. And of all these laws, our law taketh some notice.

'Of law', *Epitome* (1656), p. 683

My advice to men that go to law is as that to men that make war, to do it with good advice. A fee in the beginning of a suit to a learned lawyer is well bestowed; a fee then saved is ill saved, and oft times causeth the expense of many fees afterwards. The beginning is half the whole; lay the foundation sure, and expect a successful building.

Faithfull councellor, I (1651), sig. A3v

William Sheppard was one of the most prolific legal authors of the seventeenth century and certainly the most original. His diversified publications filled more space on booksellers' shelves than those of any other legal writer apart from Coke. Great landowners purchased his books on the law of real property while the stewards of their private courts relied upon one or more of the five contemporary editions of his book on manorial jurisdiction. Justices of the peace were familiar with his manuals on local government, a collection which extended to guides written expressly for constables, church-wardens and clerks of the market as well as magistrates. Sheppard also published books on specialized fields of contemporary law, including five editions of a tract on the law of tithes, three editions of a collection of warrants for keeping the peace, a summary of laws

5

relating to religious practice and an innovative abridgment on the law of corporations. His two treatises on actions on the case were used by students at the inns of court and by members of the legal profession and their clients, as were his four books on the law of real property. He also sent legal encyclopedias into print on three separate occasions, all written in English and introducing a format that included legal definitions, summaries of statute law and short treatises on both common-law and chancery practice. His career as a writer and compiler spanned more than half a century, beginning during his student days in the time of James I and continuing until his death in 1674, well into the reign of Charles II. His encyclopedias were later improved upon by the great eighteenth-century abridgers, but Sheppard is due the credit for his pioneering efforts to collect, digest and publish together a substantial amount of the common and statute law, bringing together a wealth of scattered knowledge from the oldest standard references to contemporary reports. The wide range of sources he cited in his works ensured their continued use into the eighteenth and nineteenth centuries by lawyers in search of precedents. In both volume and range of topics, Sheppard's contributions command a pre-eminent place in English legal literature.

Many of Sheppard's writings have been included in major legal bibliographies of the past two centuries, but the man himself has escaped the attention of most students of seventeenth-century England. Recently his major contribution to the law-reform literature of the interregnum, *England's balme*, has been noticed by legal historians,[1] but the fact that Cromwell's grant to him of a serjeant's writ was a direct consequence of his composition of that singular book has been overlooked. At the time Sheppard was called to the coif he had served as a salaried member of the protectorate administration for two-and-a-half years. Cromwell's determination to use the authority granted him by the Instrument of Government to introduce meaningful reform had led him to engage Sheppard's services as a legal consultant with the principal assignment of discovering and defining the complaints and grievances that had made law reform such a compelling public issue since the first days of the Long Parliament. During the period that Sheppard was developing the

---

[1] Busch, 'Lisle', pp. 194–201; Cotterell, 'Law reform', pp. 194–6; *HEL*, I, pp. 430–3; VI, pp. 415, 421–2; Knafla, *Law and politics*, p. 107n; Niehaus, 'Law reform', pp. 216–20; Nourse, 'Law reform', p. 525; Shapiro, 'Law reform', pp. 35n, 38n; Veall, *Movement for law reform*, pp. 113–15; T. Wolford, 'The laws and liberties of 1648', *Boston Univ. Law Review*, XXVIII (1948), 426–63.

details of a comprehensive law-reform program, he made other important contributions to government policy. He prepared several books which publicized contemporary law, devised a standard deed that could be used for the registration of land, and wrote the corporation charters that were issued under Cromwell's seal to more than a dozen English and Welsh boroughs in 1656–7. There are also strong inferential grounds to suggest that he was the draftsman of the Chancery Ordinance that Cromwell issued in 1654. The position Sheppard occupied in the administration was of a more specialized nature than other posts in the central government. He worked in relative seclusion at Whitehall, untroubled by the day-to-day assignments discharged by other members of the protector's staff. He was given assistants and sufficient time – more than two years – to work on his major law-reform project, devising the solutions he believed would be most effective in resolving the problems and conflicts that had beset English justice for so many years.

Sheppard was one of the few reformers of interregnum England who was an accomplished legal author. Other members of his profession had published suggestions for improvements in the legal system, but none had credentials comparable to Sheppard's in terms of the range of topics he had covered in his earlier publications. His practical experience and his legal philosophy qualified him as the most competent person Cromwell could have found to analyze critically the shortcomings of the legal system, and then suggest remedies that would strengthen the common-law and equity courts. Sheppard's professional contributions to the protectorate, culminating in the publication of *England's balme*, proved that he possessed not only the abilities of a legal technician, but also the creative ingenuity to devise solutions to the outstanding problems of delay and expense that had vexed would-be reformers for generations. In his approach to reform, he retained the social cement of both law and religion. Responding to Cromwell's appeal for stability and settlement after more than a decade of war and disruption, he prepared a plan of reform that would secure property and encourage the elevation of public standards of conduct as well as bring about a simplification of the law and legal process.

While Sheppard's books on the law were well known to contemporaries, he was essentially an outsider to the legal establishment. Having spent his professional life in the country, he had never developed a practice in the central courts and even his ties with his inn, the Middle Temple, had slackened after his call to the bar. He was also free of attachments to any political group. He had never been a member of parliament nor did he have ties with the army. He had, however, been a strong supporter of parliament's cause and an active member of the Gloucestershire county committee since 1643, but his stake in the post-war governments of the commonwealth and protectorate was religious and ideological. His only published political statements prior to joining the protectorate administration were endorsements of the commonwealth in two works of 1649 and 1651 and, in a more personal vein, a declaration of unabashed admiration for Cromwell as the ideal lay preacher in a tract printed in 1652. Sheppard's legal philosophy was inseparable from his religious conviction that the law of man should glorify God. He also believed that the law could be no better in its service than the men who enforced it, that equitable remedies must be available, that recourse to appeals was imperative in the light of the human fallibility of judges and juries and the corollary conviction that judgment could not be trusted to one man acting alone.

In Sheppard, Cromwell had found an ideal legal adviser, an experienced and mature practitioner four years older than the protector himself. Both men had been born in Elizabeth's reign and were of the generation that grew up under James I and came to maturity in the contentious years of the 1620s and 1630s. Both men were deeply pious and derived strength from an intense and unswerving faith in providence. Both were men of the country, as proud of their rustic backgrounds as they were devoted to their families. And both spent their lives in unflagging pursuit of reform. Compared with what we know of Cromwell, few personal details of Sheppard's life have survived, but there is enough contemporary evidence in state papers and local and institutional records to discern the outlines of his long and interesting life.

William Sheppard was born in the last years of the sixteenth century in a small Gloucestershire village on the Severn estuary. His family was of the lesser gentry in the area and its origins, though somewhat obscure, are not without distinction. He was named for his grandfather, a protestant minister of Frampton-on-Severn who was deprived of his benefice by authorities of the Marian church in 1554.[2] The ousted preacher subsequently married Margaret Brom-

---

[2] William Sheppard, priest of Frampton parish, was deprived of his living on 3 Sept. 1554: GRO, GDR, 2A, fol. 98.

wich (née Codrington), a widow from his forfeited parish, and fathered two sons, Philip and Francis. The family settled in a village some twelve miles south of Frampton and, apparently, the preacher Sheppard never returned to his pastoral calling. As a 'gentleman of Titherington', he assisted in arbitrating a dispute for the Elizabethan Commission of Ecclesiastical Causes in 1575 and the same year is mentioned in a decree concerning testamentary goods.[3]

The minister's son, Philip, was given some lands inherited by his mother from her grandfather, Sir Nicholas Poyntz, and the young man returned to the Frampton area to settle on the property. There, in 1594, Philip Sheppard married Elizabeth Tyrrell in the parish church of St Andrew, Whitminster. The following year their first child was born and, at the baptism on 14 December 1595, the infant was christened William after his paternal grandfather.[4] The size of Philip's family grew quickly as four more children – Sarah, Rebecca, John and Samuel – were born in the next few years.[5]

A small woollen industry had developed around the fulling mill at Whitminster towards the end of the century, but the local economy suffered a series of reversals as periodic flooding of the Severn washed away farming and grazing land. Early in the second decade of the seventeenth century, Philip Sheppard moved his young family to the more prosperous Cotswold region south of Stroud.[6] They settled in Horsley, a fourteenth-century stone-built village where the growth of an active cloth-making industry had been stimulated by the construction of several mills. The Sheppard family prospered, acquiring more land for sheep to supply the flourishing wool market and, despite the economic depressions that followed in that turbulent century, the Sheppard's eventually entered the circle of the more affluent gentry of the Stroud area. Philip's younger sons, John and Samuel, acquired estates near Horsley and their descendants joined

---

[3] GPL, Hockaday abstracts, XLVI, pp. 97, 119; *GNQ*, IV, p. 250; W. A. Sheppard, *A brief history of the Sheppard family ... in the county of Gloucestershire, England; compiled from authentic sources* (Calcutta, 1891), pedigree fold-out pasted in back cover, dated 9 Dec. 1887; *TBGAS*, LIX, pp. 61, 184; LXIV, p. 135.

[4] GRO, P 362 IN 1/1, fols. 5v, 6r; J. Smyth, *History of the hundred of Berkeley* (Gloucester, 1885), III, pp. 246, 331–2.

[5] Parish records list the baptisms of Sarah in 1597, Rebecca in 1600, John in 1602 and Samuel in 1605: GRO, P 362 IN 1/1, fols. 6r–7v.

[6] J. Smyth, *Men of armour for Gloucestershire 1608* (1902), p. 305; *GNQ*, I, p. 464; *VCH Glouc.*, X (1972), pp. 139–43, 296.

the local ruling class.[7] William, the eldest son, left the Cotswolds to prepare for a career in the law and then he, too, returned to spend most of his life in Gloucestershire, following his profession and attending to the management of his estate.

Philip Sheppard's decision to educate his heir in the law may have been made partly for reasons of economic necessity. In that litigious age it was an incalculable benefit to have a trained barrister to assist, as William was to do, in the management of family business ventures. The legal profession had been growing in numbers and wealth over the previous generation and enrolments at the inns of court rose dramatically in the years of Sheppard's adolescence.[8] When the considerable investment of a legal education was weighed against its advantages, the decision was finally made to send the eldest son off to London. Sheppard was almost twenty-five years old, several years older than most of his fellow students, when he was first admitted to an inn of court.[9] Having married young, he had already fathered two children by that time, John born in 1618 and Mary in 1620, and the evidence indicates that his first wife died at Mary's birth or shortly thereafter.[10] In November 1620, when his daughter was only six months old, Sheppard left his young family behind in the Cotswolds and set off for London to begin his legal education.

Sheppard entered the Middle Temple, the inn selected by almost half the Gloucestershire men seeking a legal education. It was also the inn that enrolled the largest percentage of gentry eldest sons.[11] His choice was undoubtedly encouraged by Nathaniel Stephens, lord of Horsley Manor and Sheppard's friend and future employer. Six

---

[7] T. D. Fosbrooke, *Abstracts of records and manuscripts respecting the county of Gloucester* (Gloucester, 1807), I, p. x; *GNQ*, II, pp. 508–9; Playne, *Parishes*, pp. 113, 125; *TBGAS*, LXVI, pp. 49–50, 113–14, *VCH Glouc.*, II (1907), pp. 157–69; X (1972), pp. 29, 139; XI (1976), pp. 154–5, 161, 175–7, 180–1, 194.

[8] W. Prest, 'Counsellers' fees and earnings in the age of Sir Edward Coke', in Baker, *Legal records*, pp. 165–84; *Inns of court*, pp. 5–11.

[9] Sheppard was admitted to the Middle Temple on 25 Nov. 1620: *M. T. Ad. Reg.*, I, p. 111. Years later his widow wrote to Anthony à Wood that her husband had attended New Inn as well, the only remaining inn of chancery connected with the Middle Temple in the 1610s: Wood, *Athenæ*, IV, p. 340; W. Herbert, *Antiquities of the inns of court and chancery* (1804), p. 281. Dr Prest estimated that £40 p.a. was a conservative figure for a law student's expenses in the early seventeenth century: Prest, *Inns of court*, pp. 27–8.

[10] John was baptised on 30 Aug. 1618 at Horsley parish and Mary on 7 May 1620 at Winkfield parish, Wilts., home of her mother's family: GRO, P 181, IN 1/1, fol. 29; D 149/F13, fol. 140.

[11] Knafla, 'Inns of court', p. 245; Prest, *Inns of court*, pp. 6, 33, 37, 245.

years Sheppard's senior, Stephens had been admitted to the Middle Temple in 1604 and, like his Gloucestershire cousins of the same name, maintained strong ties with his inn.[12] Upon admission to his inn, Sheppard was assigned to living quarters with William Hussey, son of a long-time family friend, and the two men perpetuated the ties between the two families for another generation. They shared lodgings for the eleven years Sheppard kept chambers there and later became partners in property ventures. During the civil war both Sheppard and Hussey served as active members of parliament's committees in their respective counties and many years later their paths crossed again in the law courts of Westminster.[13]

During Sheppard's years of training in the 1620s he and his fellow students at the inns became well informed about the nature of the religious and political controversies that developed with increasing intensity through that stormy decade. When Charles I succeeded his father, theological issues became more sharply defined as influential preachers came into conflict with the religious leaders of the new regime. Two of the leading puritan theologians, John Preston and Richard Sibbes, held lecturing posts at Lincoln's Inn and Gray's Inn respectively, while Sheppard's own Temple church had funds to provide for both a preacher and a minister through most of the period he was in attendance.[14] The sermons Sheppard heard during those formative years in London made indelible impressions that were observable years later in his writings on both religious philosophy

---

12 Nathaniel Stephens (1589–1660) named Sheppard steward of Horsley Manor no later than 1630, and Sheppard retained the office for at least 25 years: GRO, D 547 A/M29; 547a/*E2; *M. T. Ad. Reg.*, I, p. 82.
13 Hussey's father was remembered in Philip Sheppard's will: PRO, PROB 11/142, fol. 121. The younger Hussey entered the Middle Temple in 1612, was called to the bar in 1620, was named bencher and reader in 1642 and treasurer in 1649–50. He served on the Dorset county committee during the war and remained active in Middle Temple affairs until his death in 1673. In 1639 he and Sheppard sold some land they had owned jointly: A. R. Bayley, *The civil war in Dorset 1642–1660* (Taunton, 1910), pp. 314, 375, 389, 396, 415; *CSPD*, VI, p. 275; X, pp. 123–4; J. S. Cockburn (ed.), *Western circuit assize orders 1629–1648*, Camden, Fourth Series, XVII (RHS, 1976), pp. 237, 251, 286; *M. T. Ad. Reg.*, I, p. 99; *M. T. Cal.*, pp. 79, 160; *M. T. Min.*, II, pp. 658, 670, 723, 778; C. H. Mayo (ed.), *Dorset standing committee 1646–1650* (Exeter, 1902), pp. xi, xxviii, 136, 198, 205, 226, 245, 248, 318, 412, 445, 448, 493, 506; *Wiltshire Inquisitions*, Index Lib., XXIII (BRS), pp. 332–5.
14 The 'puritan lay presence' at the inns is discussed by Prest, *Inns of court*, pp. 204–19. For Preston and Sibbes see Haller, *Puritanism*, pp. 70–4, 80, 161; C. Hill, *Puritanism and revolution* (1964), pp. 239–45; Prest, *Inns of court*, pp. 189–90.

and law reform. In the political field, too, grievances touching law, administration, the system of justice and social welfare were raised and debated by the five contentious parliaments that met in that decade. Many of the reform issues that Sheppard first heard articulated by the politicians of the 1620s he formulated into concrete proposals for legal and social reform in his own publications of the 1650s.[15]

During his years at the Middle Temple Sheppard returned many times to his Cotswold village. In 1621, within a year of his admission to his inn, he married for a second time, taking as his bride Anne, daughter of George Worth of Buckington Manor, Wiltshire. She settled in Horsley while her husband divided his time between his London inn and his country home. Before the end of the decade Anne gave birth to at least five children, four of whom were baptised in the Horsley church of St Martin.[16] In June 1623 Sheppard was called home to attend his ailing father and, as heir apparent and executor, received verbal instructions when Philip signed his will. Three months later William returned again to bury his father and attend to the dispositions of his estate.[17] With his large family, soon grown to include seven children, and an inherited estate to manage, Sheppard's roots were firmly established in the country long before he had completed his legal education.

His wife Anne had two sisters whose marriages cemented close relationships between Sheppard and their husbands. Her sister Isabel married William's brother Samuel in 1628 and this additional

---

[15] For Sheppard's law-reform proposals, see ch. 4. A great number of the issues he dealt with had been considered by parliaments of the 1620s.

[16] The four children baptised in Horsley during the 1620s were Elizabeth in June 1623, Sarah in June 1624, Samuel in Mar. 1627 and Anne in June 1628: GRO, P 181, IN 1/1, fols. 37, 38, 41, 43. Another son, William, junior, was born during this decade. In a record of the marriage of William Sheppard, junior, and Eleanor Hayward on 16 Mar. 1651 at the church of St Michael in Gloucester the groom is identified as an attorney in the court of common pleas: GRO, P 154/14, IN 1/1, fol. 77v. In 1655 William Sheppard, junior, was named an attorney of the Gloucester tolsey court and in 1659–60 he was appointed a militia commissioner and an assessment collector by the restored Rump Parliament: GRO, GCR 1425/1547; A & O, II, pp. 1324, 1369; CJ, VII, p. 734. The Horsley parish register records baptisms of three more children born to William Sheppard later: Dorothy in Sept. 1637, Jonathan in Dec. 1639 and Judith, who was married there in Sept. 1654: GRO, P 181, IN 1/1, fols. 54, 65, 89.

[17] Philip Sheppard's will is dated 16 June 1623 and Elizabeth, Anne's first child and William's second daughter and third child, was baptised on 22 June. Philip was buried at Horsley on 20 Sept. 1623: PRO, PROB 11/142, fol. 121; GRO, P 181, IN 1/1, fols. 8x, 37.

tie between the two brothers strengthened their life-long friendship.[18] The marriage of Anne's sister Margaret to Robert Nicholas in 1622 made Sheppard brother-in-law to a fellow Middle Templar. Nicholas, who later sat for Devizes in the Long Parliament and was made a judge of the central courts during the interregnum, was second cousin to Oliver St John and therefore part of that alliance of illustrious families that linked, either by birth or by marriage, Oliver Cromwell, John Hampden, Bulstrode Whitelocke and John Desborough. Sheppard's connections through Nicholas with the sprawling network of leading families in the legal and political establishment of the 1640s and 1650s can be reckoned as one of the many contributing factors in Sheppard's call to serve the protectorate thirty years later.[19]

Sheppard's call to the bar of his inn on 19 June 1629 after nine years of study marked the end of his active participation in the society.[20] Although he continued to keep chambers with Hussey for another two years, there is no evidence that he made any effort to maintain connections with his inn or to establish a Westminster practice.[21] Already thirty-four years old, Sheppard was finally at liberty to return to his large family and embark upon a promising career as a country lawyer.[22]

As he set about establishing his practice in the 1630s, the diverse nature of his clients' affairs broadened his knowledge of the law. Continuing a custom he had followed in his student days, he kept

[18] Samuel married Isabel Worth in Horsley on 21 Mar. 1628: GRO, P 181, IN 1/1, fol. 85. The brothers owned land jointly in Wilts. and served together on the Glouc. county committee during the war: GRO, D 547A/T36; PRO, PROB 11/346, fol. 117; *GNQ*, II, p. 508; *A & O*, II, pp. 299, 664.

[19] Nicholas was admitted to the Middle Temple in 1613 and called to the bar in 1621. In Apr. 1622 he married Margaret Worth in Salisbury. He was appointed recorder of Devizes in 1639 and had an active career in parliament from 1640 until 1649 when he was raised to the bench. In 1654 he was transferred from the upper bench to the exchequer bench: *DNB*: sub Robert Nicholas; Keeler, *Long Parliament*, p. 285; *M. T. Ad. Reg.*, I, p. 101; G. W. Marshall (ed.), *The visitation of Wiltshire 1623* (Harl. Soc., CV–CVI, 1882), pp. 39, 41; *VCH Wilts.*, VII (1953), p. 271; X (1975), pp. 271, 312.

[20] Most Middle Templars spent eight or more years at the inn before achieving this distinction and Sheppard was no exception: *M. T. Ad. Reg.*, I, p. 111; *M. T. Min.*, II, p. 752; Prest, *Inns of court*, p. 55, table 9.

[21] Dr J. H. Baker has informed me that he has not noticed Sheppard's name in contemporary law reports. Sheppard did not attend the autumn reading of 1631, a default for which he was fined: *M. T. Min.*, II, pp. 757, 778. See n. 40.

[22] There were few lawyers in the Severn-basin region of Gloucestershire: *GNQ*, I, p. 139.

systematic records of his own observations and of decisions delivered, organizing and supplementing the information with material found in printed works. References to cases heard locally that Sheppard later cited in his publications indicate that his practice carried him to a number of local courts. He referred to opinions delivered and decisions made at local general sessions, at assizes on the Oxford and Western circuits and at the great sessions of Wales.[23] His work also took him to the diocesan consistory court[24] and later, he described himself as steward of a surviving hundred court in Stroud. His account of the jurisdiction claimed by that court and the sheriff's county court, including a comprehensive listing of fees for each, testified to his familiarity with the procedures of those two ancient institutions.[25] For many years Sheppard also served as one of the six attorneys of the Gloucester tolsey court, held monthly at the shire hall.[26] Another major sphere of his practice was the stewardship of a number of manorial courts in Gloucestershire.[27] Frequent meetings

---

[23] Sheppard cited Gloucester general sessions in his *Whole office*, pt 2, p. 127 and Wiltshire quarter sessions in *Constables* (1655), ch. 12. Decisions delivered at Gloucester assizes, Oxford circuit, were cited in *Actions upon the case for deeds*, pp. 82, 98, 114, 141, 144, 308; *Constables*, p. 299; *Epitome*, pp. 248, 993; *Faithfull councellor*, I, pp. 143, 155, 156; II, pp. 112, 320; *Law of common assurances*, pp. 50, 248, 251, 554; and *Touchstone*, pp. 39, 166, 271. Also on the Oxford circuit, Hereford assizes, *Sure guide*, p. 242; Worcester assizes, *Sure guide*, pp. 255, 258, 290. Cases from Salisbury assizes, Western circuit, are found in *Actions upon the case for deeds*, pp. 82, 92, 102; *Constables*, pp. 37, 228; *Epitome*, pp. 706, 985; *Faithfull councellor*, I, pp. 132, 204, 285, 290; II, p. 269; *Grand abridgment*, I, p. 536; *Law of common assurances*, pp. 50, 86, 193, 248, 251, 554; *Parson's guide*, p. 29. Cases heard in the Welsh courts are cited in *Epitome*, p. 762; *Faithfull councellor*, I, pp. 153, 258; and *Touchstone*, pp. 378, 387, 769.

[24] GPL, Hockaday abstracts, CCXLVI, fol. 117.

[25] In *A survey of the county judicatures* (1656), pp. 72–6, 90–2.

[26] The Gloucester city court, known as the tolsey court, had a jurisdiction encompassing the recovery of debts worth less than 40s. and debts to any amount by writ of *justicies*. During the period Sheppard served as an attorney the court limited to six the number of attorneys with the right to plead: GRO, GCR 1424/1546 (1651–3); 1425/1547 (1653–7); 1426/1548 (1668–73). Sheppard mentioned the 'court of the tolsey in Gloucester' in his *President of presidents* (1677 edn), pp. 343–4.

[27] Sheppard presided as steward over the manorial courts of Nathaniel Stephens in Alkerton, Eastington and Horsley: GRO, D 149/F13, fol. 129; D 547a/*E2; D 547A/M29. Other Gloucestershire courts he served as steward were the manors of Cheltenham, Longney, Lower Slaughter, Salmonsbury and Slaughter Hundred: GRO, D 855, D 149/B3, fols. 53–5; D 45, D 1099; D 1395, series 3. It is likely that he was steward in the courts belonging to his brother Samuel in Avening, Blaisdon, Minchinhampton, Nailsworth, Rodborough and Stroud, all in Gloucestershire, and at Buckington Manor, Wilts.: PRO, PROB 11/346,

and a wide jurisdiction over misdemeanors and copyhold assured a large volume of business on a regular basis and the broad knowledge of local custom that Sheppard acquired was incorporated into one of his most successful books.[28] His instinct to reform, a trait apparent in most of his legal works, can be traced back to 1630 when, as steward of Horsley Manor, he drafted a set of by-laws for the 'better government' of the community for his friend and neighbor, Nathaniel Stephens.[29]

Within the compass of Sheppard's varied professional activities, the complex land law of England attracted his particular interest and he eventually published four books on that topic alone.[30] During his first years of practice, his understanding of property law was broadened by the knowledge he gained from John Bridgman, an elderly judge who lived in Nympsfield, a village neighboring Horsley. From the late 1620s until the judge's death in 1638 Sheppard apparently visited him frequently, noting his professional comments which were later incorporated into Sheppard's published legal studies. Bridgman's influence was most pronounced in Sheppard's first major book on the law, The touchstone of common assurances. The habit Sheppard developed of collecting the opinions of Bridgman and other west-country judges along with other case material served him well, for the memoranda he kept formed the core of information in the manuals, monographs and encyclopedias he published over a thirty-year period.[31]

The decade of the 1630s was also important for the development

---

fol. 117 (courts listed in the will of Samuel Sheppard). I am grateful to Dr Andrew Foster for providing information about Sheppard's stewardships in Cheltenham, Lower Slaughter, Salmonsbury and Slaughter Hundred.

[28] See ch. 2, Sheppard, The court-keepers guide (1649).

[29] The by-laws, dated 25 May 1630, were agreed to and signed by Stephens, Sheppard and fourteen of the more substantial inhabitants, including Sheppard's brother-in-law Christopher Hillier. The by-laws provided for regulating enclosures, maintaining gates and hedges, keeping sheep out of the commons and containing pigs, horses and cattle. The inhabitants were required to give sureties for strangers who came to the parish as tenants, parish officers were to account for all their receipts and disbursements, and two haywards and six sheeptellers were to be elected and sworn to their offices: GRO, D 547 A/M29 (ii fols.).

[30] Sheppard's four books on the law of real property were The touchstone of common assurances (1648), The president of presidents (1655), The law of common assurances (1669) and The practical counsellor in the law (1671).

[31] See ch. 2 for discussion of Bridgman's influence on the composition of the Touchstone and other works.

of Sheppard's religious philosophy. His system of beliefs, based upon the precepts of orthodox Calvinism, can be correlated with his views about the functions of law and authority in society. The proposals for legal change he published during the protectorate cannot be fully understood without an appreciation of how his faith permeated his assumptions of a reformed and improved society that would be governed by laws enacted to help bring about God's providential plan. His advocacy of criminal-law reform, abolition of primogeniture, and the establishment of an integrated court system with jurisdiction in both law and equity and with provisions for appeal all derive from his theological beliefs as did his views on a 'saved' magistracy serving society in cooperation with the spiritual leadership of a professional ministry. Sheppard became a follower of John Owen and his colleagues, Thomas Goodwin and Philip Nye, of the conservative branch of the religious Independents in the late 1640s, and it is possible to identify some of the influences that contributed to his commitment to that group.[32] A tradition of piety had undoubtedly been established in the Sheppard family two generations earlier by William's grandfather, the preacher of Frampton, who had received his clerical training during the reign of

[32] John Owen assumed leadership of the conservative branch of the religious Independents in 1649, the year he became Cromwell's personal chaplain. The movement for English Independency took its name from the theologians' desire to be free (independent) from the superior authority of a national synod. Its founders were the five 'dissenting brethren', Thomas Goodwin, Philip Nye, Sydrach Simpson, Jeremiah Burroughs and William Bridge, who, as members of the Westminster Assembly of Divines, had filed a 'dissent', and published it as *An apologeticall narration* in early 1644. In it they requested toleration for the continuation of their own kind of preaching in the face of the probable adoption of a Presbyterian form of church government. The development of their ideas owed most to John Cotton, doyen of the New England way. Their 'middle way' between liberty and order in gathered congregations was to be achieved by giving the 'key of rule' to duly constituted church officers who would control the sacraments and discipline of the congregation while allowing the members the 'key of liberty' to interpret and expound on the scriptures. Differences of opinion could be tolerated so long as heresy and error did not lead to notorious sin and civil order was not disturbed. As the Independent movement grew in England, Owen and the surviving dissenting brethren (Burroughs had died in 1646) came to represent the right-wing, or conservative branch of the movement with their insistence upon maintaining Calvinist orthodoxy and suppressing heresy. Others who called themselves Independents, particularly radical sectarians in the army, favored complete toleration. I wish to thank Dewey D. Wallace, Jr, for the helpful information he provided about the influence of John Owen and the conservative Independents in the years 1649–57. Haller, *Liberty and reformation*, pp. 116–28; G. Nuttall, *Visible saints* (Oxford, 1967), pp. 11–13; Wallace, 'Owen', pp. 137–44, 195–205.

Edward VI. Later in the Tudor century influences of continental protestantism were brought to Gloucestershire by Flemish refugees who came to find employment as weavers.[33] By the third decade of the seventeenth century there were strongholds of puritanism scattered around the Cotswolds and, due to the efforts of Nathaniel Stephens, one of those centers was Horsley. The election of Stephens as county member to the Long Parliament has been credited to the support generated on his behalf by the puritan clergymen of the county,[34] and his identification with the movement for religious reform can be traced back almost a decade earlier. In the early 1630s, after Sheppard had established his practice in his country village, Stephens, as patron of Horsley church, had appointed Edward Norris as curate. In 1635, when the religious climate became tense on the eve of Laud's metropolitical visitation, Norris left the Horsley pulpit for Bristol. There, as a leading activist in arranging for the migration of puritan families to Massachusetts, he sent members of his own congregation off to New England in 1636. His publication of three anti-Antinomian tracts and his outspoken defense of Calvinist orthodoxy became increasingly irritating to church authorities and by 1639 Norris and his wife had fled to the New World. Within a year Norris was called to the pulpit at Salem where he remained until his death in 1659. In his last years Norris earned a reputation for toleration, an uncommon trait in Massachusetts, by opposing accusations of witchcraft and fanaticism against Baptists and Quakers.[35] Many principles that guided Norris's career were later espoused by Sheppard and the two men may well have corresponded with one another after the preacher's departure for the New World, a possibility that would account for Sheppard's knowledge of the Massachusetts experiment in civil government.

[33] GRO, GDR 2A, fol. 98; Keeler, *Long Parliament*, pp. 46–8; *VCH Glouc.*, XI (1976), pp. 154–60.
[34] Keeler, *Long Parliament*, p. 351; Williams, *Glouc. parl. hist.*, pp. 53–4.
[35] Norris was curate of Horsley church until 1634: GRO, GDR 185, fol. 27v; 189, fol. 38v; Matthews, *Calamy*, p. 255. For more on Norris see: *DAB: sub* Edward Norris; *DNB: sub* Edward Norris; J. Eliot, *A biographical dictionary containing a brief account of the first settlers...in New England* (Boston, 1809), p. 336–8; J. B. Felt, *The ecclesiastical history of New England* (Boston, 1855), I, pp. 387, 414; J. F. Jameson (ed.), *Winthrop's journal* (New York, 1908), I, p. 331; II, pp. 60, 227, 268; L. A. Morrison, *Lineage and biographies of the Norris family in America from 1640 to 1892* (Boston, 1892), pp. 12–13; *VCH Glouc.*, XI (1976), p. 259; J. Winthrop, *The history of New England from 1630 to 1649*, ed. J. Savage (Boston, 1853), I, p. 397.

During Norris's last autumn in Horsley, in 1634, Sheppard's eldest son, John, matriculated at Magdalen, Norris's Oxford college, to begin his education for the ministry. The following year Sheppard transferred his son to Wadham, one of the two Oxford colleges most critical of the new archbishop, William Laud. John received his bachelor's degree from Wadham in 1638 and a master's degree in divinity from St Edmund Hall in 1641.[36] A few years later John was made rector of the church and chapel of Saints John and Mary in Devizes, a benefice in the gift of the city corporation of which his uncle, Robert Nicholas, was recorder.[37] The same year that John completed his divinity studies, Sheppard published his first book, a manual for constables, in which he commented on his son's new profession.

The ministry (and service whereabout this officer is most of all conversant) is a worthy work, and the greatest of all other, tending and serving to the immediate worship of the great God and the salvation of men's souls; so is their calling and office one of the most high and honorable of all others... These men come nearest to God of any other, and (as it were) wait about His person and are of His privy chamber. They are styled angels of the churches and stars in Christ's right hand. As therefore (in respect of their calling) they are the men whom God hath honored, and worthy of double honor; so I wish that no man may despise them, seeing that to despise them is to despise Christ that doth send them.[38]

The respect and esteem Sheppard accorded the clerical profession was a major contributing factor in his decision to educate his heir as a clergyman. A generation earlier William himself, also an eldest son, had been sent to study law, and his resolve to have his own heir follow the ministerial calling marks an interesting shift in the priorities of this seventeenth-century Gloucestershire family. In the four religious works Sheppard published during the interregnum he elaborated

---

[36] Norris was still in Horsley in Sept. 1634 and John Sheppard entered Magdalen on 10 Oct. of the same year: GRO, GDR 185, fol. 27v; J. Foster, *Alumni Oxoniensis 1500–1714* (1968), IV, p. 1345; R. B. Gardiner (ed.), *The registers of Wadham College, Oxford* (1889), I, p. 125; L. Stone, 'The educational revolution in England 1560–1640', *P & P*, XXVIII (1964), p. 49.

[37] BL, Add. MS 15670, fol. 116 (20 June 1646); A. G. Matthews, *Walker revised* (Oxford, 1948), p. 370; Shaw, *English church*, II, pp. 358, 547; *VCH Wilts.*, X (1975), p. 285; Willcox, *Gloucestershire*, p. 125. Nicholas maintained an interest in the church of SS John and Mary. In Apr. 1650 when travelling as an assize judge on the Western circuit he donated £30 to the poor of that parish: *A history military and municipal of the ancient borough of the Devizes* (1859), p. 189.

[38] W. Sheppard, *The offices and duties of constables* (1641), pp. 251–2.

further upon the crucial role the ministry played in local society and in his major reform *opus*, *England's balme*, he held that the godly reformation of English society was dependent upon the leadership and authority of the clergy and a select magistracy working in cooperation with one another.[39]

Sheppard remained in the Cotswold village of Horsley until 1637 when, on the occasion of his final marriage, he moved to the environs of Gloucester. After his second wife, Anne, had died in the late 1620s he had married a widow whose surname was Fisher and this third wife, too, predeceased her husband. His fourth and last marriage, which took place in August 1637, was to Alice Coney and at that time he resettled his family in Hempstead, a parish bordering the county town.[40] The Hempstead home where he and Alice raised their own children as well as Sheppard's children and grandchildren from his earlier marriages remained a busy household for the rest of their lives. Although the decision to move his residence had been made for personal and professional reasons, his proximity to Gloucester proved to have important political consequences when civil war broke out four years later.

Sheppard preserved strong ties to his Cotswold home after the move, continuing to be retained by clients from Horsley and serving as steward of the manor court.[41] His personal attachments to the village were equally constant and, just a year after his own marriage, he returned to Horsley to celebrate the wedding of his eldest daughter, Mary.[42] Her husband, John Clifford, inherited the principal family estates in Frampton-on-Severn which was the original home of William's paternal grandfather and adjoined William's own birthplace at Whitminster. The close friendship and business ties Sheppard shared with his son-in-law Clifford were cemented by their mutual political allegiance to parliament during the 1640s[43] and

---

[39] The religious works are discussed below in this chapter.

[40] Marriage allegation of Sheppard and Alice Coney, 12 Aug. 1637: GRO, Q 3/1, fol. 46. His prior marriage to the widow Fisher is cited in *Glouc. visit.*, p. 167, and in a nineteenth-century pedigree compiled by a descendant, William Albert Sheppard: see n. 3. A local source noted Sheppard's residence in Horsley between 1623 and 1637: F. A. Hyatt and R. Austin, *Bibliographer's manual of Gloucestershire literature*, Biographical supplement, II (Gloucester, 1916), p. 401.

[41] GRO, D 547a/*E2; GPL, Hockaday abstracts, CCXLVI, p. 117.

[42] GRO, P 181, IN 1/1, fol. 87; D 149/F 13, fol. 140 (4 Aug. 1638).

[43] GRO, D 149/xi, xii; BL, Add. MS 5494, fol. 94; *VCH Glouc.*, X (1972), p. 143.

endured long after Mary's death in 1651.[44] Sheppard's close bonds
with his brother Samuel, who remained in nearby Minchinhampton,
and Nathaniel Stephens, lord of Horsley Manor, similarly took on
new dimensions as the three became politically allied years before the
civil war. As early as 1627 the crown's fiscal policies had aroused
resistance from the gentry of the nation and Stephens joined the
sheriff and members of other prominent families in his county in
refusing to pay the forced loan demanded by Charles I. His opposition
enhanced his local political standing and he was elected county
member to the 1628 parliament. Through the 1630s, as the tensions
provoked by Charles I's personal rule mounted, Stephens allied
himself with the growing number of gentry who nursed grievances
against not only the extra-parliamentary taxation schemes but also
Laud's ecclesiastical policies.[45] By 1635 as patron of Horsley church
he had named another puritan to replace Edward Norris who had left
for New England.[46] The following year he refused to obey the royal
order to pay ship money and was removed from the peace commission
for his defiance. When in 1636 the sheriff complained to the privy
council that 'the chiefest gentlemen of the county of Gloucester
have paid nothing towards the shipping business', Stephens's name
again appeared on the list of defaulters along with that of Samuel
Sheppard.[47] Through this difficult decade the political tensions
fostered a growing alienation between William and Samuel Sheppard
on the one hand and their brother John on the other. John Sheppard,
who held a royal appointment during the 1630s, remained loyal to
the crown when civil war came and the division along political lines
in the family developed into a permanent estrangement. Even after

[44] The Clifford family papers, now held in the Gloucestershire Records Office,
include many legal documents naming William Sheppard: GRO, D 149/E 29,
fol. 166; F/3; T 1188; xi. Mary Clifford had four daughters, the eldest of whom
inherited the Clifford estate and arms. I am very grateful to Mrs Peter Clifford
of Frampton Court, a direct descendant of William Sheppard and his daughter
Mary, who permitted me to see and photograph a decorated parchment pedigree
of the Clifford family that names Sheppard and displays the Sheppard arms.
The pedigree was proved in 1673 by Robert Cooke, Clarenceux King of Arms:
see n. 225.

[45] Bigland, Gloucester, I, p. 537; Willcox, Gloucestershire, pp. 35, 117, 119, 128;
Williams, Glouc. parl. hist., pp. 51, 53–4.

[46] Norris left sometime after Sept. 1634 and by 1635 Stephens had named as his
replacement Samuel Heiron who aligned himself with the Presbyterians in the
1640s: GRO, GDR 185, fol. 27v; 189, fol. 38v.

[47] PRO, C 181/4, fol. 81v; E 179/273/7, fol. 6 (arrears of Ship Money); SP 16/345,
fol. 66; CSPD CI, IX, p. 246 (Feb. 1636).

the restoration, William and Samuel were never reconciled to their brother.[48]

In the spring of 1640 the gentry of the nation was given the opportunity to express their political sentiments when writs went out for the first parliamentary election in eleven years. Nathaniel Stephens again stood for the county seat he had won in 1628 but, while he attracted some local support, the contested seat went to a royalist, Robert Tracy. The second county seat was filled by a puritan barrister, Robert Cooke, who claimed the distinction of having aroused the enmity of the government and been summoned before Laud's High Commission for questioning.[49] Within weeks the members had been dismissed and the abortive episode of the Short Parliament cost the king dearly in political support from Gloucestershire. In October, when elections were held for the Long Parliament, the puritan party made significant gains and a majority of the ten Gloucestershire members were opponents of the royal administration. On his second try of the year and with the help of the county's puritan clergy, Nathaniel Stephens secured one of the county seats although Robert Cooke, the other knight of the shire, lost his seat to a royalist, John Dutton. Dutton acknowledged the animosity felt between the parties when, after the election, he swore he 'would never more trust any man that wore his hair shorter than his ears'.[50] The following year his defeated opponent, the puritan Robert Cooke, won a seat for Tewkesbury in a by-election. Other puritan acquaintances of Sheppard who were elected in the autumn of 1640 were his brother-in-law Robert Nicholas for Devizes and one of Nathaniel Stephens's cousins for Tewkesbury.[51]

From the first meetings of the Long Parliament until the opening campaigns of the civil war, constitutional changes of a magnitude undreamed of by previous generations were made in the name of reform. While the politicians at Westminster drove ahead under

---

[48] From 1633 to 1640 John Sheppard served intermittently as royal escheator. By 1647 John was named royalist under-sheriff for the county and compounded to Goldsmith's Hall the same year. In 1650 he served as private secretary to Prince Maurice, nephew to Charles I. He was the only immediate member of the Sheppard family not mentioned in Samuel's will: PRO, PROB 11/346/117; CCC, IV, p. 2618; Glouc. visit., p. 167; Ind. Lib., IX, pp. 178, 183–4, 186, 189.

[49] Keeler, Long Parliament, pp. 46–8, 141; Williams, Glouc. parl. hist., p. 53.

[50] GNQ, I, pp. 410–14.

[51] Edward Stephens was elected for Tewkesbury. For other members of the Long Parliament, see Keeler, Long Parliament, pp. 46–8, 316, 350–1; Underdown, Pride's purge, pp. 381, 386; Williams, Glouc. parl. hist., pp. 53–4.

Pym's guidance to redress the most blatant grievances against the displaced Stuart regime, armies rallied to meet the military challenge of Charles I's raised standard at Nottingham. The grass-roots support given by men in the localities under parliament's control, particularly in the collection of taxes, was crucial to the success parliament claimed over the royalists four years later. In the spring of 1643 parliament named Sheppard to his county's committee to collect assessments for 'the speedy raising... of money to maintain the new army'. That first Gloucestershire committee was headed by the governor of the garrisoned city, the mayor and recorder of the town, the five county and borough members of parliament and a small group of ten citizens, including Sheppard, all of the rank of esquire. The strategic importance of Gloucester (Prince Rupert captured nearby Bristol two months later) called for men of undoubted loyalty as well as an acknowledged status in the local community. The following year an ordinance appointing a committee for the defense of the besieged Gloucester garrison again named Sheppard, and throughout the first and second civil wars he remained active in the local ruling establishment.[52] Between 1643 and 1649 Sheppard served concurrently on the committees of Sequestration, Assessment, Compounding and Advance of Monies as well as on the county militia committee. These groups of men, known collectively in each county as 'the committee', also alleviated the hardships of war where they could.[53]

The confusion created by having a number of different taxes collected by the same, small group of individuals acting under several sets of orders allowed for a variety of ad hoc collection arrangements. General supervision of the county committees by the central administration through the war years was lax and local committeemen like Sheppard had more autonomy in handling public revenues than formal instructions would indicate. In the autumn of 1647 when the military threat to Gloucester had subsided, Sheppard took advantage

---

[52] Sheppard's name was undoubtedly suggested by Nathaniel Stephens, M.P. *A & O*, I, pp. 169, 428; W. S. Baddeley, *A Cotteswold manor, being the history of Painswick* (1929), p. 192; Pennington, 'County committee', p. 68; Underdown, *Pride's purge*, p. 29; *VCH Glouc.*, XI (1976), p. 177.

[53] Gloucestershire endured heavier losses during the civil war than most other communities (war losses estimated at £34,000 and losses due to burning at £26,000): James, *Social problems*, p. 51. For Sheppard's committee activities: *A & O*, I, pp. 168–9, 428, 966, 1083, 1136, 1237; *CCC*, I, p. 133; GPL, MS 16069, fols. 9–11; *TBGAS*, XVI, p. 77.

of this flexibility and proposed in a letter he wrote to his royalist neighbor, John Smyth, to advance a local project.[54] The events leading to Sheppard's proposition were commonplace after four years of civil war, but the details claim our attention for what they reveal about Sheppard's personal and community interests. The citizens of Nibley had asked Sheppard, as a member of the county committee, for a £30 reimbursement they claimed was due them for having quartered some army horses on their properties. Another official had already agreed to support the request but Sheppard, objecting that the bill to the state had been submitted too late for repayment to be considered, wrote to Smyth, a prominent citizen of that small community. In his letter Sheppard began by explaining that the only county revenues available at that time were the rents from sequestered estates which were specifically reserved for the use of the army. He then pointed out that Nibley parish had failed to pay the previous month's assessment and, moreover, that the people of that neighborhood were well over £100 in arrears of taxes owed to the Committee for the Advance of Monies. If, therefore, the citizens of Nibley wanted the state to repay them for the quartering charges, it was only 'exact justice that we [the committeemen] must needs levy it of them first'. As an alternative arrangement, Sheppard proposed to cancel the debt owed the state on the condition that the parishioners denote money for the support of the college and library of Gloucester cathedral. If this charitable 'offering' were made, Sheppard would arrange for the money to be recorded as a gift. If, on the other hand, the men of Nibley did not make a donation, Sheppard would see to it that legal proceedings were brought to recover the unpaid taxes owed by the community.[55] It is not known if Sheppard's bargaining in 1647 was successful, but several years later his goal was furthered when Gloucester city officials successfully petitioned the government for funds to support their college and library. And by 1657 an act of parliament had opened the cathedral buildings to public worship, the education of children and 'other public uses'.[56]

---

[54] Sheppard had been collecting delinquency fines from Smyth since at least July 1645: GPL, MS 16069, fols. 9–11. Smyth and his father both served the Berkeley family as stewards and the younger Smyth was one of the most prominent royalists in western Gloucestershire in this period. In 1660 he was knighted by Charles II along with twelve other men of the county and named to the Order of the Royal Oak: GNQ, II, p. 12.
[55] BL, Add. MS 33588, fol. 61 (Smyth of Nibeley papers).
[56] CSPD, IX, p. 98; X, p. 3. See below, n. 144.

As the 1640s drew to a close, Sheppard published his second and third books, both based on the knowledge he had gained from his twenty years of legal practice. *The touchstone of common assurances* was published in 1648 and in the next year *The court-keepers guide* was issued in its first edition. These two studies were later republished without revision and both remain among his most well-known and enduring contributions to English legal literature.[57]

By 1648 enthusiasm for parliament's cause against the king was on the wane and all around the war-weary nation local committeemen who had worked for parliament through the war years now drew back in hopes of a negotiated peace with the king. As many officials, particularly those from the old ruling families, withdrew their support, the concentration of local authority in the hands of only a few became more pronounced. Sheppard was one of the few in his area who continued to discharge his duties and on one occasion he notified the authorities in London that the burden of collecting the most recent assessment had fallen unfairly on himself and only two others of the thirty-man Gloucestershire committee.[58] Yet he willingly stayed at his post because he believed that it was imperative for men of property like himself to remain in positions of local authority in the face of the increasingly disruptive activities of radical groups. Moreover, his unswerving faith in the providential course of events and his stalwart advocacy of legal and social reform convinced him that national leaders, particularly Cromwell, could be relied upon to guide the country along the path towards a national regeneration.

There were two occasions in 1648 when Sheppard could have met Oliver Cromwell, and while a personal encounter remains a matter of conjecture, the likelihood is so great that they met at least once that those opportunities should be noted. The first came in early May when Cromwell visited Gloucester and was entertained at the tolsey court in which Sheppard served as one of the six attorneys. The second and equally probable moment was when Cromwell and Ireton stayed at Horsley as guests of Nathaniel Stephens on a mission to persuade their host to ally himself with the party opposed to negotiating a truce with the king.[59]

---

[57] See ch. 2 for details of the books and the *Chronological Bibliography* for subsequent editions.
[58] *CCC*, p. 133.
[59] See above, n. 26. *TBGAS*, XXII, p. 12; David Verey, *Gloucestershire, I, The Cotswolds*, ed. N. Pevsner, The Buildings of England series (1970), p. 278; *W & S*, I, p. 606; Washbourne, *Bib. Glouc.*, p. cxviii.

The events leading to the establishment of the commonwealth, from the purge of parliament in December 1648 until the execution of the king and the organization of the new state early in 1649, threw Englishmen into political confusion. Sheppard aligned himself with the fragment of constitutional government that remained at Westminster and his support of the Rump Parliament marked the beginning of a more intensely political period in his life. His belief in the providential nature of the constitutional cataclysm led him to compose two religious works in 1649, and he dedicated the first to the Rump Parliament. *Of the foure last and greatest things: death, judgement, heaven and hell* was released in April, one month before the commonwealth was declared, and while the text contained only instructions for pious behavior according to strict Calvinist theology, Sheppard wrote a strong declaration of political support for the members remaining in parliament in his introduction.[60] The Rump's legitimacy, as the single remaining vestige of *de jure* authority after the abolition of the monarchy, was of great consequence to Sheppard, the lawyer; and the spiritual well being of those men who held the reins of government was of crucial concern to Sheppard, the puritan. With guarded optimism he wrote that his object was to remind the politicians that they were accountable for the consequences of their public decisions and their private behavior. 'We need not tell you that it is a double crime which is committed under the sacred name of authority and greatness, that the sins of great ones in the politique are as dangerous as pestilent fevers to the natural body', but this admonishment and the sober message of the text did not conceal his underlying hope for improvement and confidence in the future. 'Now England is distracted, and her foundations out of course, He hath raised you up (the unwearied worthies of the nation) to repair the breaches and settle the foundations thereof...You have the blessing of many thousand prayers upon you; you are engaged in as acceptable a service to God and man as ever any assembly was; as great expectation there is from you as ever was from any parliament of England, and as likely you are to have the opportunity to render your names renowned to succeeding generations as ever any parlia-

---

[60] The book collector, George Thomason, dated his copy 20 Apr. 1649 and the commonwealth was declared in an act passed on 19 May: *TT*, I, p. 739. The publisher was Thomas Brewster who also published Sheppard's *Catechism* that year, and a second edition of *Foure last things* was brought out later in 1649 by Giles Calvert. Both men specialized in religious tracts and both were named printers to the council of state in 1653: Plomer, *Booksellers*, pp. xix, 43, 47–8.

ment of ours had.'[61] The other religious publication of that year was a short catechism which Sheppard wrote, published at his own expense and distributed to the people of Gloucester.[62] The theological doctrines he advanced were again the orthodox Calvinist tenets of the 'protestant core' and he recommended its study to his fellow townsmen as a 'suitable sabbath pastime'. It was his hope that the head of each household would call regular catechizing sessions to teach family members, domestic servants and apprentices the basic theological precepts he had had printed so 'that the servants of men would also be the servants of God'. The primary nucleus of the Christian family was the basic unit upon which a godly, reformed society would be built and Sheppard reminded his readers, 'is not the reformation of church and commonwealth from the reformation of families?'.[63] The counterpart to the father's authority in the family was the magistrate's power in the community and Sheppard championed magistracy as 'an ordinance of God by which some men are set up and authorized by a law to rule over the rest for the preservation of the whole'. He wrote that that ordinance of God continues and that Christians were to submit to it, 'magistrates being in all times alike needful and useful in the commonwealth'.[64] Sheppard's views on the authority of magistrates and the importance of orthodox teachings had a great measure of political importance in the chaotic climate of 1649. The Long Parliament had issued an ordinance in August 1645 enforcing the use of the Presbyterian *Directory for the publique worship of God* and the following year abolished the Anglican hierarchy.[65] But the members of that parliament never adopted any of the other recommendations of the Westminster Assembly of Divines and, with the questions both of doctrine and of church structure still unsettled after years of debate by politicians and theologians, Sheppard prepared his catechism as a suggested profession of faith for the citizens of Gloucester.

The auspicious year of 1649 that, for Sheppard, promised reform in government and hope for the settlement of the religious question was a happy year for members of his family. His wife Alice gave birth to a daughter they christened Rebecca, and in April the family celebrated a doubly joyous occasion when two of Sheppard's

---

[61] W. Sheppard, *Foure last things*, sigs. A2v–3r, A2r–v.
[62] W. Sheppard, *A new catechism* (1649). The only discovered surviving copy of this 56-p. catechism is held by the Bodleian Library.
[63] Ibid., sigs. A3v–4r.   [64] Ibid., pp. 20–1.
[65] *A & O*, I, pp. 582, 879.

daughters from his second marriage applied on the same day for wedding licenses to marry Gloucestershire men. Sarah married Anthony Andrewes, the minister and 'constant preacher' of Haresfield parish and Anne was wed to Richard Pitt, a gentleman of Rudford parish.[66] The same year the Rump awarded William's eldest son, John, a substantial augmentation to his Wiltshire parish living. A few years earlier the Long Parliament had registered John as a 'godly and well affected preacher' after he had been ejected from his pulpit during the civil war. By July 1648 John had been restored to his benefice in Devizes and the augmentation he received in the spring of 1649 was determined by parliament's policy of providing an average allowance of £100 a year per clergyman.[67]

For Sheppard's support of the Rump Parliament, he was rewarded with a place on the Gloucestershire peace commission in the first year of the commonwealth.[68] The new government, in its administrative reorganization, returned the rule of the countryside to the traditional local rulers, the justices of the peace, taking it from the hands of the powerful county committees that had held sway during the civil war years. A partial purge of the peace commissions assured that outright enemies of the commonwealth were removed from positions of authority and replaced with trusted supporters, like Sheppard.[69]

---

[66] Sarah was 25 years old and Anne, 21: GRO, GDR 207 B, fol. 27 (18 Apr. 1649); *GNQ*, II, p. 215. In 1664 Andrewes was still possessed of Haresfield parish and was serving as chaplain to the earl of Bedford: GPL, Hockaday abstracts, CCXXXIII.

[67] BL, Add. MS 15670, fol. 116; Shaw, *English church*, II, pp. 193–4, 214, 216, 224, 358, 547.

[68] PRO, C 193/13/3, fol. 26v; *The names of the justices of peace in England and Wales...*(1650). Sheppard's name does not appear in the pre-1650 peace-commission lists consulted: PRO, C 181/4, fol. 81 (1631); SP 16/212 (1632); C 181/4, fol. 114v (1632), fol. 136 (1633); C 193/13/2, fol. 28 (1634–5); C 181/5, fols. 13r–v (1635); SP 16/405, fols. 28–9 (1638); C 181/5, fols. 369–70 (1640); C 231/6, fols. 50, 97, 109, 115, 116, 130, 142, 174, 177 (1646–9). While Sheppard's gentry background and legal training qualified him for a place on the local bench, it appears that he did not have sufficient local standing to be named until his political activities of the civil-war period were taken into account. From the beginning of the war until July 1646 no peace commissions were named and no assizes were held and local government was entrusted to the county committees, of which Sheppard was an active member in Gloucestershire. From 1646 to 1650 Sheppard may have been sitting on the local bench with justices who had been named in the early 1640s, but the surviving records of that period are not complete.

[69] In the political reorganization of 1650, 19 new names (including Sheppard's) were added to the Gloucestershire peace commission and only four of the 45 incumbent justices were removed: Underdown, *Pride's purge*, p. 311.

Within weeks of his appointment to the local bench Sheppard took the Engagement to the Commonwealth, a loyalty oath statutorily enjoined on all office-holders to preserve the political revolution that had taken place.[70] The more efficient and assertive central government of the commonwealth called upon local justices of the peace to perform specific duties in keeping the peace of their communities. Sheppard's orders included prosecuting enclosure rioters[71] and examining witnesses about public statements that had been made by a Socinian preacher.[72] He also headed a local chancery commission that made recommendations for redrawing parish boundaries in the interest of equalizing church revenues.[73] He and Nathaniel Stephens were called to testify at an indemnity hearing[74] and, throughout the commonwealth period, he continued to serve on the restructured local committees for assessment, compounding and the militia.[75]

The adjustments in local power structures made by the newly organized central committees in London brought many unexpected changes in personnel[76] and Sheppard, who had enjoyed a steady advancement in his political fortunes since 1643, met with a temporary reversal when the central Committee for Compounding removed him from a local office he had held for several years. In May 1650 a fellow-magistrate, John Dorney, was appointed to succeed Sheppard as steward of the estates belonging to royalist delinquents. Unwilling to surrender the authority of the office, Sheppard refused to deliver the official records over to his replacement. Dorney

[70] A certificate attesting to his subscription was sent to London with the comment that Sheppard and another magistrate had 'always been very active for parliament' and 'are both very fit for places of trust': CCC, I, pp. 278–9 (23 July 1650).
[71] PRO, SP 25/64, fol. 489 (27 June 1650).
[72] PRO, SP 25/13, fol. 31 (19 Nov. 1650).
[73] BL, Stowe MS 577, fol. 22 (1651–2); PRO, C 193/13/4, fol. 39r (1652–3); C 231/6/256, fol. 25 (1653); GNQ, II, p. 215; Aylmer, State's servants, p. 268; Shaw, English church, II, pp. 248–55; Underdown, Pride's purge, p. 272.
[74] PRO, SP 24/12, fol. 114v (31 Dec. 1652); Aylmer, State's servants, pp. 13–14.
[75] A & O, II, pp. 35, 299, 467, 664; CCC, I, pp. 224, 245, 262; GPL, MS 16069, fols. 18–19; Washbourne, Bib. Glouc., pp. 389–91.
[76] In the interest of economy and efficiency the central government of the commonwealth gave full control of a coordinated taxation program to seven full-time commissioners selected from outside parliamentary ranks. With a salaried staff to assist them, they instituted a structural reorganization of the systems of revenue collection. For the effects of these changes on the localities, see Aylmer, State's servants, pp. 12–13; Everitt, Kent, pp. 286–91; Pennington, 'County committee', pp. 72–3; Underdown, Pride's purge, pp. 316–18; Somerset, pp. 163–4.

complained to London and the controversy was still boiling in July when the central committee sent a third notice that Dorney was to have the court rolls and deeds of the delinquent estates and another commanding Sheppard to deliver the documents to Dorney. A year and a half later the London committee was still trying to compel Sheppard to turn over £800 worth of bonds under threat of a £40 fine.[77] The dispute appears to have ended at this point and the absence of further information would seem to indicate that Sheppard finally conceded his claim. He and Dorney continued to work together for several more years and while Sheppard's contrary behavior in this episode may have interfered with Dorney's collection of the steward's fees, the controversy did not damage Sheppard's local reputation nor hinder his steady climb in the ranks of power. His position in the Gloucestershire political establishment remained secure even through the unpredictable fluctuations in government during 1653, from the forced dismissal of the Rump in April through the summoning of the Barebones Assembly in July and beyond the self-dissolution of that hapless body six months later.

In 1652 Sheppard published his third religious work, supporting a position that placed him squarely in the philosophical camp of the conservative wing of the religious Independents, a group that held distinct opinions about lay preaching, church government and Calvinist orthodoxy.[78] *The people's priviledge and duty guarded against the pulpit and preachers' incroachment* was written during a pamphlet war that was being conducted around the question of whether laymen should be permitted to preach. Sheppard contended in his tract that 'gifted men' should be permitted to expound on the scriptures under certain conditions if safeguards were provided to protect the minister's office from 'encroachment' and he proposed that the Rump repeal the two ordinances that forbade lay preaching.[79]

---

[77] *CCC*, I, pp. xiv–xv, 224, 262, 275, 516.

[78] See above, n. 32 for the conservative Independents John Owen, Thomas Goodwin and Philip Nye. Lay preaching was an important tenet of the conservative Independents' 'middle way' and public professions of faith were encouraged. Sheppard specifically cited Goodwin and Nye as well as other writings of these Independents on pp. 45–8 of his book.

[79] W. Sheppard, *The people's priviledge* (1652), pp. 27, 63, 66–7. Sheppard granted ministers their full professional prerogatives to administer sacraments and advocated full legal protection for property rights, including the exclusive privilege of being paid wages for preaching. The ordinances Sheppard wanted repealed were one limiting preaching to ordained ministers passed on 26 Apr. 1645 and a proviso added on 31 Dec. 1646 prohibiting laymen from expounding

The attacks against lay preachers by conservative clergymen had begun in earnest when, with the partial demobilization of forces in 1651, many unordained radical chaplains and 'mechanic' preachers left the army and began to carry their messages of universal salvation through the countryside. The dangers of both heresy and notions of lawless democracy that could be spread had led several clergymen of more traditional persuasion to publish tracts claiming that preaching be exclusively reserved to members of their profession.[80] Sheppard entered the debate defending the 'free and open exposition of the scriptures' by responsible laymen and also reaffirming the need for a professional class of ministers, 'for the opinion denying ministry is as bad as the opinion denying magistracy; and both of them are heretical, dangerous and damnable'.[81] He acknowledged that the spread of heresy must be controlled but insisted that 'gifted men, not preachers by office, may exercise their gifts by preaching in a constituted church' and, with an adroit touch of political style, he dedicated the book to his ideal of the lay preacher, 'Oliver Cromwell, Lord General of all the forces of parliament in England'.[82] This dedication combined with an exposition of the fundamental principles held by John Owen, Thomas Goodwin and Philip Nye was a strong political statement in 1652.[83] These conservative Indepen-

---

on scripture. The latter had passed on a division of 105 yeas to 57 noes, with Oliver Cromwell acting as a teller for the negative: *A & O*, I, pp. 677, 749; *LJ*, VII, p. 337; *CJ*, V, pp. 34–5.

[80] In 1651 tracts arguing that only ordained ministers should be permitted to preach were published by two ministers, Thomas Hall who wrote *The pulpit guarded* and John Collinges, who published *Vindiciae ministerii evangelici: a vindication of the great ordinance of God, viz. a gospel ministry*. Within months of the time they were distributed, a radical army chaplain turned preacher, Thomas Collier, attacked the positions taken by Hall and Collinges in his book, *The pulpit-guard routed*. Collier's censure of the clerical profession was in turn refuted by John Ferriby in *The lawful preacher* and the pamphlet debate continued into 1652 with controversialists writing on both sides of the issue. Sheppard cited and commented on all of these writings in his work, *The people's priviledge and duty guarded against the pulpit and preachers' encroachment* (23 Mar. 1652). See *Chronological Bibliography* for the full title. Within four weeks of its release Collinges responded with a 180-page rejoinder entitled *The shepheard's wanderings discovered...by way of reply and answer to the late book called The people's priviledges* [sic]...*by William Sheppard*. Collinges signed his preface on 26 Apr. and George Thomason dated his copy 28 July: *TT*, I, p. 880.   [81] W. Sheppard, *People's priviledge*, p. 2.

[82] Ibid., p. 21. He wrote a four-page Dedicatory Epistle to Cromwell.

[83] Owen had been Cromwell's personal chaplain since 1649 and, in 1650, the council of state made Owen its preacher and gave him lodgings at Whitehall. The conservative Independents continued to gain influence through 1652: Wallace, 'Owen', pp. 195–202.

dents had established themselves as the most influential group of advisers to the Rump Parliament and their plan for church settlement was even then under committee consideration.[84] The Independents' platform was to promote puritan piety under a policy of broad toleration, allowing all non-heretical groups to practise their faith under the supervisory authority of the state. And although the Rump failed to adopt a definitive settlement, two years later Cromwell instituted those principles by ordinance with the help of Owen, Goodwin and Nye.

The establishment of the protectorate in December 1653 brought a momentous change in Sheppard's life when, in the first months of the regime, he was called from his country home to serve the government in London. Summoned to act as Cromwell's legal adviser, Sheppard accepted a salaried position on the staff of the reorganized administration with the principal assignment of designing a comprehensive program of law reform.[85] His mandate was to cast a critical eye over every facet of English law and to advise Cromwell precisely which laws should be repealed, which required

[84] Sheppard's book was out by 23 Mar. 1652: *TT*, I, p. 865. A month earlier, on 10 Feb., parliament appointed a committee of 14 to consider a plan for a religious settlement that had been drawn up by Owen and his group and presented in a petition which also called for the suppression of a Socinian tract, *The Racovian catechism*. A second parliamentary committee was ordered to investigate the heretical tract and subsequently ordered that it be burned. Cromwell served on both committees and eight of the ten ministers who signed the petition were self-proclaimed Independents. On 18 Feb. a larger group of ministers submitted a detailed proposal for a church polity based upon the retention of fundamentals, the suppression of heresy and the toleration of non-heretical churches. This was published as *The humble proposals of Mr Owen, Mr Tho. Goodwin, Mr Nye, Mr Simpson and other ministers* and it included the signature of the fourth surviving 'dissenting brother', William Bridge. This group favored a state-supported church, controlled by triers to test for heresy and scandal, and ejectors, to remove unfit ministers. The Rump did not begin debate on these proposals for another year and it was not until 1654 that Cromwell instituted Owen's plan by executive ordinance: P. Toon, *God's statesman, the life and work of John Owen* (Exeter, 1971), pp. 83–4; *W & S*, II, pp. 517–20; Wallace, 'Owen', pp. 195–205; Worden, *Rump Parliament*, pp. 137, 296, 326–7.

[85] Another 'Mr Sheppard' who worked in the protectorate administration is mentioned in state papers. Matthew Shepherd, an alderman of London and a colleague of the recorder of London, William Steele, accepted assignments from the central administration and was named to the high court of justice on 13 June 1654: *A & O*, II, p. 917. Therefore, references in state papers designating only 'Mr Sheppard' (including all spellings of the name) have not been incorporated in this study unless internal evidence established that the reference was to William and not Matthew. Law-reform consultants had been engaged by the Barebones Assembly in 1653, but only on an *ad hoc* basis, not on a long-term salaried contract: *CSPD*, IX, p. 587.

more stringent enforcement and what sort of reforms could be devised to correct existing injustices and inequities.

From the first days of the Long Parliament there had been a consensus among politicians that the reform of English law was of the first importance, and yet after the revolutionary enactments of 1641–2, efforts to resolve even the most universal grievances had been piecemeal. The war years had brought little progress towards reform, the commonwealth period had been disappointing, and the most recent government, the Barebones Assembly, had attempted a couple of major legal reforms with near disastrous results. Until the establishment of the protectorate no central executive had been sufficiently determined or powerful enough to implement reform by fiat. But in the spring of 1654 Cromwell had signalled his determination to develop and implement a long-range plan for remodelling the legal structure when he hired Sheppard, an experienced and seasoned lawyer, to work exclusively on proposals for legal change and improvement. Just as Lambert's Instrument of Government had furnished a constitutional foundation and John Owen's 'fundamentals' promised a resolution to outstanding religious issues, a viable legal base for the anticipated godly commonwealth would be provided by the administration's legal expert. The strategy of employing a reliable legal technician to design a workable blueprint for reform was a two-edged sword, for Cromwell had not only publicly committed himself to the cause of reform, but he was also politically impelled to satisfy the public clamor for law reform that since 1640 had grown into a major national issue. On both grounds – of strong executive desire and popular demand – Sheppard's charge to prepare a sound program of comprehensive reform was not only politically expedient but imperative to the success of the new administration.

The selection of Sheppard for this onerous task was due as much to his legal philosophy and religious convictions as to his professional skills. The nine books he had already published had included in their prefaces statements that accorded well with the aspirations of the protectorate. Those published since 1649 contained high optimism for the future of the country as well as praise for Cromwell. His published religious works expounded crucial aspects of the conservative Independents' philosophy so faithfully that Cromwell's personal chaplain, John Owen, may have been the individual who directed the protector's attention to this pious barrister. Sheppard was also an 'intimate acquaintance' of John Owen's former tutor, Thomas Barlow, clearly another positive factor in his selection, and Anthony à Wood wrote years later that Sheppard had been 'much frequented for his counsel and advice by the godly party in the time of the grand rebellion'.[86] Middle Templars of Sheppard's generation who held positions of power in the protectorate were probably also instrumental in bringing Sheppard to Cromwell's attention, the most likely possibilities being Sheppard's brother-in-law Robert Nicholas, J.U.B., and John Lisle, the chancery commissioner.[87]

Sheppard was settled at Whitehall possibly by mid March and certainly sometime prior to June 1654. The specialized nature of his assignment usually permitted him to work at one remove from the daily concerns of government. His unique position commanded an annual salary of £300, a substantial sum for a civil servant in a fiscally depressed regime.[88] The decision to accept this appointment was not, however, dictated by the monetary compensation. He had earned

[86] Thomas Barlow (1607–91), provost of Queen's College, Oxford, and librarian of the Bodleian collection from 1642 to 1660, became bishop of Lincoln in 1675. He collaborated with Sheppard on a book, *Sincerity and hypocrisy*, which was published in Oxford in Apr. 1658. Both Sheppard and Barlow were singularly devoted to Calvinist orthodoxy and both were bibliophiles. With the exception of the years Sheppard spent in London working for Cromwell (1654–7), the two men lived at no great distance from one another from 1630 until Sheppard's death in 1674. Barlow may have introduced Sheppard to Owen during the latter's tenure as vice-chancellor of Oxford University, 1652–8. The information about Sheppard's 'intimate' friendship with Barlow comes from Anthony à Wood, who corresponded with Sheppard's widow: Wood, *Athenæ*, IV, pp. 339–40. For Barlow: *DNB*: *sub* Barlow; Wallace, 'Owen', pp. 14–15. See below, n. 203.

[87] The Middle Temple dates for admission and call to the bar for the three men are Sheppard, 1620, 1628; Nicholas, 1613, 1621; Lisle, 1626, 1633. Bulstrode Whitelocke was also a contemporary Middle Templar, admitted 1619 and called to the bar 1626: *M. T. Ad. Reg.*, I, pp. 101, 109, 111, 117.

[88] Sheppard was paid £300 a year in full during his first three years with the government, though the payments were usually late. Warrants for payments of £150, half-year salary: *CSPD*, X, pp. 589 (June–Dec. 1654), 591 (June–Dec. 1655); PRO, SP 25/77, fol. 216 (Jan.–July 1656); *Thurloe State Papers*, VI, pp. 593–4 (1656–7); *CSPD*, XI, p. 555 (1657). Members of the council of state and the judges of the central benches earned £1000 a year, the council's secretary Thurloe was paid £800 a year, but most of the salaried personnel in the central administration were paid more modest sums. Only Sheppard's unique position as Cromwell's legal adviser explains his unusually high salary. The state's chaplains and members of the council's staff were paid £200 a year, the council's legal advisers were paid £100 and £110, the registrar £150 and the auditors £175: Aylmer, *State's servants, passim*; *CSPD*, VII, pp. 447, 455; VIII, pp. 97–8; X, p. 591; XI, p. 556. For the judges' salaries, see Cockburn, *Assizes*, p. 56.

much more in his country practice and later complained of the financial hardships he and his family suffered for having accepted this call to the protector's service. His work at Whitehall entailed the loss of his country practice, temporary separation from his family and, in the end, a discredited professional reputation.[89] He accepted the assignment for the challenge it offered and the period of his official tenure proved to be the most creative and productive in his long career as an author of legal works.

At the time Sheppard entered the administration, Cromwell and the council were in the midst of pursuing an impressive agenda of reform. Two provisions in the written constitution, the Instrument of Government, gave the protector and council authority to promulgate ordinances carrying the full strength of law until such time as parliament took further action upon them.[90] Although every order issued would have to withstand the scrutiny of the parliament scheduled to meet in September 1654, a great deal of progress was accomplished in the first months of the regime. More than eighty ordinances were issued under the executive authority in that time, many of them executing policies that had been initiated or considered by earlier governments, others inaugurating new programs that were distinctive to the protectorate, and a few reversing actions that had been introduced by previous governments, including the repeal of the Rump's Engagement to the Commonwealth.[91] A likely time for Sheppard's arrival at Whitehall was just before 16 March, because on that day the council referred consideration of a problem inherited from the previous regime, the Barebones' act for small-debt courts, 'to the commissioners named by the protector for the regulation of the law'.[92] While Sheppard's precise contributions are impossible

---

[89] He listed his sacrifices in a letter to the council of state citing the separation from his family; see n. 199. Apart from short visits to his home, he seems to have spent all his time in London and during the years he worked at Whitehall, his name was temporarily removed from the Gloucestershire peace commission: PRO, C 181/6, fols. 91–3 (1654); fols. 119–21 (1655); fols. 140–2, 163–4 (1656); C 193/13/6, fols. 34v–37v (1656–7).

[90] Articles VI and XXX, The Instrument of Government. The 42 articles of the constitution are printed in *A & O*, II, pp. 813–23.

[91] This impressive legislative record has not yet been studied exhaustively, but excellent summaries can be found in Aylmer, *State's servants*, pp. 47, 334, and Roots, 'Cromwell's ordinances', pp. 143–64.

[92] The Barebones' act 'For the relief of poor prisoners and creditors' was suspended the following month by Cromwell, acting on the recommendation of his legal adviser. A substitute ordinance prepared by Justice Atkins and Baron Thorpe was also amended by Cromwell and his adviser before it was issued: *CSPD*, VII, pp. 31, 65, 93, 134–5, 174, 202; *A & O*, II, p. 911.

to trace completely, the commencement of his regular salary payments, his unique position as Cromwell's personal legal adviser, and
the similarity of the proposals he later published to the reforms
undertaken by Cromwell and the council imply that he was deeply
involved in reform efforts from the time he entered the
administration.

Cromwell and the council followed the customary legislative
process in their ordinance-making activities. Proposals, treated as
parliamentary bills, were introduced to the council with two readings,
referred to a conciliar sub-committee and then returned to the council for debate, amendment and a final reading before being referred
to the protector for approval. This process therefore demanded that
individual council members take on specific committee responsibilities for ordinances under consideration even as they dispatched
the routine and extraordinary business of government as members
of the council as a whole. Although the council met several times a
week and many of its members were prodigiously energetic, it was
necessary to call on assistance from its staff and from outside
consultants to help with the business of state, just as Cromwell had
engaged Sheppard's help, particularly in matters involving legal
technicalities.[93]

Of the seventeen men who sat on the council in this period, twelve
had served in at least one parliament and eleven (perhaps twelve) had
spent some time at an inn of court.[94] However, until Humphrey

[93] Peter Brereton and John Reading served as legal counsel to the council of state:
CSPD, VIII, p. 98. There were undoubtedly others, including Gabriel Beck,
who performed services of a legal nature for the council, too: Aylmer, State's
servants, pp. 276, 418–19.

[94] The fifteen named by the Instrument of Government were Anthony Ashley
Cooper, John Desborough, Charles Fleetwood, Philip Jones, John Lambert,
Henry Lawrence, Richard Major, Edward Montagu, Gilbert Pickering, Francis
Rous, Philip Sidney (Viscount Lisle), Philip Skippon, Walter Strickland,
William Sydenham and Charles Wolseley. All these men sat on the council at
least occasionally except for Fleetwood who was serving in Ireland as lord deputy
and commander-in-chief until mid 1655. Three men were added to the council
in the first year, Humphrey Mackworth in Feb., Nathaniel Fiennes in Apr., and
Edmund Sheffield (Earl of Mulgrave) in June, 1654. All had parliamentary
experience except for Desborough, Lambert, Mackworth, Major and Sheffield.
Those who had spent some time at an inn of court were Cooper, Desborough,
Fiennes, Lawrence, Montagu, Pickering, Rous, Sidney, Skippon and Strickland.
Fleetwood, though not in London at this time, had attended Gray's Inn. The
twelfth who might possibly have attended an inn was Lambert. John Thurloe,
the council's secretary, had attended Lincoln's Inn from 1646 to 1653, and was
called to the bar in the latter year, but he had held many public appointments
during the years he was enrolled, most of the positions acquired with the help
of his patron, Oliver St John. Those responsibilities allowed him little time for

Mackworth joined the council on 7 February, not one member was a fully trained lawyer.[95] Mackworth's legal skills were immediately put to use preparing ordinances dealing with technical matters and in his first six months on the council he was responsible for producing at least fifteen ordinances.[96] But the government needed a great deal more legal advice than Mackworth alone could provide and as early as January, judges, serjeants, Westminster lawyers and a former chancery commissioner all were enlisted to assist in drafting ordinances in the campaign for reform.[97] One ordinance was actually drafted by two judges, and even that was amended by 'his highness's counsellor at law',[98] but the usual procedure was for one of the council's committees to meet and consult with outside advisers, members of its own staff or with Cromwell's legal adviser when drafting the ordinances.

By September when parliament met, Cromwell spoke with pride of the many reforms he and the council had instituted by ordinance.[99] Since the first month of the regime the protector's overriding concerns had been to establish a religious settlement and to reform the courts, especially chancery. His determination to accomplish those goals was announced in a letter Thurloe had written to Whitelocke in Sweden. 'My lord's first and chief care is to settle the courts of justice...His highness takes the like care of the ministry, providing equally for its reformation as for its establishment.'[100]

The religious settlement had been undertaken first. On 1 March Philip Nye and Thomas Goodwin, two theologians associated with Owen's party of conservative Independents, met with a committee

---

the inn's learning exercises and readings which, in any case, had fallen far below their former standards in these years of disruption. For Thurloe, see Aylmer, *State's servants*, pp. 165–7, 258; *DNB*: *sub* Thurloe.

[95] Mackworth had entered Gray's Inn in 1621, was made a bencher of his society in 1645 and an ancient in 1651. R. J. Fletcher, *The Pension book of Gray's Inn, 1569–1669* (1901), I, pp. 354, 380; Williams, *Great sessions*, pp. 37–8.

[96] *CSPD*, VI, pp. 282, 404, 411, 414; VII, pp. 13, 54, 67, 76, 175, 190, 208, 212, 252 (2x), 281, 322. Mackworth's death in Dec. 1654 was a great loss to the council.

[97] Assignments given to judges, serjeants and lawyers: *CSPD*, VI, pp. 360, 373, 385, 404, 407, 412, 419, 425; VII, pp. 1, 6, 124, 214; to civil lawyers and admiralty judges: ibid., VI, p. 360; VII, p. 33; to Thomas Widdrington, former chancery commissioner: ibid., VI, pp. 387, 419.

[98] Atkins, J. and Thorpe, B.: see above, n. 92. It was Aug. before the ordinance was ordered to be printed: *CSPD*, VII, pp. 262, 295.

[99] *W & S*, III, p. 439 (4 Sept. 1654).

[100] John Thurloe to Bulstrode Whitelocke: Longleat MS, XV, fols. 27r–v (21 Jan. 1654).

of the council and within three weeks the first of the three ordinances of the religious settlement was promulgated.[101] As for the nation's courts, Cromwell began filling the benches 'with the best and most learned men he can find in England' and on 21 January had the notice given that 'the court of chancery is put under a regulation, which is committed to the care of Sir Thomas Widdrington, Mr Attorney General and Mr Chute. The law will be considered by the learned of that profession and sober in their spirits so that through the blessing of God the breach will be repaired and the people governed by the good old laws and all arbitrariness in government laid aside.'[102] In fact, two more months elapsed before Cromwell was ready to let his judges and lawyers try their hands at reform. First, he re-established the judiciary, confirming the chief justices in their places, replacing and transferring others and creating a new chancery commissioner (Widdrington) as well as new judges and serjeants to fill out the ranks.[103] By April Cromwell was ready to proceed with 'a solid and good reformation of the law and the proceedings in the courts of equity and law...[still] being resolved to give the learned gentlemen of the robe the honor of reforming their own profession'.[104] Cromwell and the council closed the courts for Easter Term and the protector met personally with two committees he had appointed to devise new rules for the courts.[105] On the day of Cromwell's first meeting with the two committees, Thurloe wrote to Whitelocke, the absent chancery commissioner, that 'the great things his highness sets himself to are the reformation of the law and the ministry'. The committee appointed to regulate the law courts,

101 *CSPD*, VII, p. 6; *A & O*, II, p. 855 (20 Mar. 1654).
102 The attorney-general was Edmund Prideaux and Challoner Chute was a prominent barrister whose practice was primarily in chancery. Thurloe to Whitelocke: Longleat MS, XV, fol. 27v (21 Jan. 1654).
103 In Jan. five judges were confirmed under new patents, four were removed and one, Robert Nicholas, was transferred to the depleted exchequer bench: PRO, C 231/6, fols. 276–7; Black, '*Corem protectore*', p. 38. Thurloe wrote to Whitelocke on 27 Jan. that Widdrington was to replace Richard Keble as chancery commissioner, but that action was not taken until Apr.: Longleat MS, XV, fol. 31; *CSPD*, VII, p. 83. Eight new serjeants were called in Jan. and Feb. and one, Matthew Hale, was raised to the bench within a week of his call: PRO, C 231/6, fols. 276–8.
104 Thurloe to Whitelocke: Longleat MS, XV, fol. 117 (7 Apr.).
105 *TT*, II, p. 61 (ordinance to close the courts). Cromwell met on 12 Apr. with John Lisle and Widdrington, C.C., William Lenthall, M.R., Challoner Chute and the committee to reform the law courts, Matthew Hale, Hugh Wyndham and John Glynne: Thurloe to Whitelocke, Longleat MS, XV, fols. 117r, 135v (7, 13 Apr.).

which included reform-minded men who had just been placed in the judicial establishment, produced new sets of orders for common pleas and the upper bench that were published later in the year.[106] But the members of the chancery committee, all of whom had previously had the opportunity to work on a reform of that court, failed to produce a reform in the six weeks that elapsed before the courts reopened at the end of May.[107]

Cromwell may have anticipated this outcome, given the past performances on reform by the members of the chancery committee and, although he had amended the adjournment ordinance by shortening the time of the courts' closures, he apparently had been determined to let his judiciary have a genuine opportunity to devise a reform themselves. One contemporary observer was surprised that the courts had been permitted to reopen 'even though the regulation of the law is not yet completed'.[108] But Cromwell had a contingency plan ready to put into operation: to have a reform ordinance drafted by someone else for consideration by the council of state exclusively that would be returned to him for approval and promulgation. Every surviving account of the events surrounding the preparation of the 1654 Chancery Ordinance agrees on two points: that the judges failed to produce a reform for chancery ('For what reason I know not', wrote one contemporary) and that Cromwell and his council subsequently issued an ordinance of their own making in August.[109] A

---

[106] Longleat MS, XV, fol. 135v (13 Apr.); Hale, Wyndham and Glynne wrote *The rules and order for the regulation of the common bench* that were registered for publication on 18 Nov. 1654: *Sta. Reg.*, I, p. 460. They were signed by Oliver St John, C.J., and Atkins, J. At the time the rules were composed St John was in the country, suffering from ague, and Atkins was working on new ordinances for the council of state: Thurloe to Whitelocke, Longleat MS, XV, fol. 135v (13 Apr.). The *Rules and orders for the court of upper bench at Westminster* followed the model prepared for common pleas and were published in Dec.: *Sta. Reg.*, I, p. 461 (4 Dec.).

[107] Busch, 'Lisle', pp. 190, 225, 310–11; *CJ*, IV, pp. 701, 703, 708, 710 (Oct. 1646); *Collection of orders*; Longleat MS, XV, fol. 13; Whitelocke, *Memorials*, III, p. 89. Subsequently, Lisle was the only chancery commissioner who agreed to enforce the reform Cromwell issued in 1654.

[108] George Cockaine to Whitelocke, Longleat MS, XV, fol. 195v (26 May). Cockaine had written on 14 Apr. about the committees' meeting 'about reforming the law which must be done before they have another term': ibid., fol. 138v.

[109] E. Leigh, *Second considerations concerning the high court of chancery and the most excellent ordinance for the regulation and limitation of that court* (1658), pp. 2–3. In June 1655 Nathaniel Fiennes, C., speaking from the bench, explained 'the reasons which hath induced the lord protector and the council to draw up a new regulation and order touching the proceedings in the said court of chancery':

review of what is known of the activities at Whitehall and Westminster after the courts reopened for Trinity Term at the end of May supplies an answer to the genesis of this controversial ordinance. Hindsight makes it clear that Cromwell was determined to have chancery reformed and the religious question settled before parliament was due to meet. After the failure of the judges' committee in April and May and with only three months remaining before the scheduled legislative gathering, Cromwell apparently turned to his own legal adviser, Sheppard, and entrusted him with the task of drafting an ordinance with constructive and compulsory provisions.

A week after the judges opened Trinity Term at Westminster Hall, Cromwell's counsellor-at-law returned to the council the amended ordinance for small-debt courts that had been altered by the protector.[110] On the same day, 8 June, the council of state enlarged its own committee 'for the regulation of the law', adding Wolseley as its new member to join Mackworth and Strickland.[111] A week later, on 15 June, Sheppard registered with the Stationers' Company two books he had just completed for Cromwell, both composed to assist in law-enforcement and one directly related to the implementation of the religious settlement.[112] On 18 June Cromwell met with the council's law-regulation committee to discuss what provisions they would recommend for inclusion in an ordinance to reform chancery, the one court that to date had proved immune to reform.[113] After determining on that day and the next the broad lines of reform to be incorporated in the ordinance, the council members returned to their busy schedule of normal duties. It was at this time that Cromwell must have authorized his own legal adviser to draft a detailed and comprehensive document according to his personal instructions and at his explicit request that included the provisions he and the council committee had determined were necessary. Three-and-a-half weeks later, on 13 July, a sixty-seven article draft had been completed and was returned to the council.[114] The routine

Thurloe State Papers, III, p. 570 (2 July 1655). The most detailed contemporary evidence of the chancery commissioners' objections is found in Whitelocke, *Memorials*, IV, pp. 192–201, 204–7.

[110] *CSPD*, VII, p. 202 (8 June). See above, n. 92.
[111] Ibid., pp. 202, 215 (8, 20 June).
[112] *Sta. Reg.*, I, p. 449 (15 June). See ch. 3 for details of these first two books Sheppard wrote for the protectorate.
[113] *CSPD*, VII, pp. 214–15 (19 June); *W & S*, III, p. 338 (18, 19 June).
[114] *CSPD*, VII, p. 252 (13 July).

procedure that was employed for major ordinances began immediately. After two readings, the lengthy draft was referred to a
conciliar committee.[115] At the same meeting, *after* the draft ordinance
had been safely committed, the council gave the order for Bulstrode
Whitelocke to be summoned the very next day and sworn to his office
of chancery commissioner.[116] Whitelocke, who had served continuously in that capacity since 1648, had been in Sweden for the
previous ten months negotiating a commercial treaty and, although
Thurloe had assured him through regular correspondence that
Cromwell intended to retain him in his office, his absence since
November 1653 had prevented him from taking the oath to the new
regime.[117] Whitelocke had returned to London on 1 July and
although he had had two private interviews with Cromwell, the
government had not called him to be sworn.[118] This deliberate
postponement of permitting Whitelocke to assume his office points
to Cromwell's determination to allow the draft ordinance to be
completed without any outside interference. The other two commissioners who had already been given the opportunity to participate
in a reform effort posed no threat at this point. Widdrington tended
to vacillate when put to any sort of test in public office and Cromwell
undoubtedly knew his man well enough to assume that he would take
no decisive action without prodding. Lisle did not have the same
passive nature, but he had just taken a new, temporary post on the
High Court of Justice that had been established under the authority
of the Treason Ordinance.[119] In the event, it is unlikely that any of
the three chancery commissioners had any notion that an ordinance
concerning their court was under consideration at that very time. So
Cromwell and his council were free to devise their own reform,

115 The standing committee for the regulation of the law was enlarged to include
Lambert, Desborough and Fiennes to assist in the consideration of this major
ordinance: ibid.   116 Ibid.
117 Lisle and Widdrington had been sworn to their offices on 4 Apr. See above,
n. 103.
118 Whitelocke was bitterly aware of the 'slighting and ingratitude' of being made
to wait to be sworn to his office: B. Whitelocke, *Swedish Embassy*, ed. H. Reeve
(1855), II, pp. 432–57, 463; *W & S*, III, pp. 353, 359, 361.
119 Widdrington had resigned as commissioner of the great seal in Jan. 1649 because
of 'some scruples and conscience' that prevented him from serving a regicide
regime: Whitelocke, *Memorials*, II, p. 532. He resumed the office under the
protectorate only with the greatest reluctance: Widdrington to Whitelocke,
Longleat MS, XV, fol. 137 (14 Apr. 1654). Lisle was elected president of the
court on 15 June, and presided over a trial that lasted until the fourth week of
July: *CSPD*, VII, pp. 209, 212, 233–40; *W & S*, III, p. 351.

calling only upon advisers they specially selected for assistance. During the weeks that the Chancery Ordinance was being reviewed and amended by Cromwell and the council, the three chancery commissioners, Whitelocke, Widdrington and Lisle, were all approved for new appointments by the council, to serve concurrently as treasury commissioners along with the two chief justices and three other individuals. The appointments carried salaries of £1000 a year and may have been made partly to appease the chancery officers when they discovered that their court had been reformed without their having been consulted on the details.[120] The Chancery Ordinance was finally issued on 21 August, five weeks after it had first been presented to the council, and was published on 30 August.[121] In the few weeks remaining before the first protectorate parliament met, the second and third ordinances of the religious settlement were issued, thereby fulfilling the two goals Cromwell had first vowed to accomplish in January 1654.[122]

The mandates of Sheppard's appointment as Cromwell's legal adviser were to serve as a personal consultant on matters 'tending to the regulation of the law' and, second, to frame a comprehensive program of law reform.[123] In the course of performing these services Sheppard composed nine books on legal topics, three specifically advancing proposals for legal improvement. The master proposal, *England's balme*, was not published until October 1656 but two other recommendations that appeared in print were brought to the attention of the council of state towards the end of 1655. These two proposals, to establish deed registries and to incorporate county courts into the national system of justice, were favorably received and in early January 1656 the council voted to renew his salary.[124] A month later the council asked Sheppard to present other details of his plan to a committee of its own membership, and Thurloe notified General Monck in Scotland, 'The council have ordered this week that Mr Sheppard do prepare some thing to be offered about the law.'[125] The

---

[120] *A & O*, II, p. 918; *CSPD*, VII, p. 284 (2 Aug.).
[121] *A & O*, II, pp. 949–67; *CSPD*, VII, p. 317; *Sta. Reg.*, I, p. 455.
[122] *A & O*, II, pp. 968, 1025 (28 Aug., 2 Sept.).
[123] W. Sheppard, *England's balme*, sigs. A7r–v.
[124] See ch. 3 for details of the two books, *The president of presidents* and *County judicatures*. *CSPD*, IX, p. 107 (9 Jan. 1656); Worc. Coll. MS, xxvii, fol. 147v (1 Dec. 1655).
[125] PRO, SP 25/76, fols. 531–2 (8 Feb. 1656); Worc. Coll. MS, xxvii, fol. 167v (26 Feb. 1656).

committee charged with reviewing Sheppard's proposals was composed of members of the standing committee on the regulation of the law, Strickland, Jones, Wolseley and Fleetwood; a commissioner of the great seal, Fiennes; and six other council members, Lambert, Montagu, Mulgrave, Pickering, Rous and Sidney. In just over a week's time the committee authorized Sheppard to present his program to the council at large and two days later, on 21 February 1656, Cromwell approved the order.[126]

With the stamp of official approval on the details presented to date, Sheppard continued to work out further features of his scheme for another three months. At the end of May when the council summoned him back to report on his progress, his proposals were so extensive and touched on so many politically sensitive areas that an extra-conciliar committee was appointed to review them in depth. The instructions given the five-man committee were 'to consider of some things relating to the laws which are prepared by Mr William Sheppard, and confer with him therein, and so prepare the same for the consideration of the council'.[127] With plans to call a new parliament being formulated at that very time, it was imperative for the government to determine which, if any, of Sheppard's proposals could be incorporated into the legislative agenda. A contemporary news-writer who noticed this development wrote that members of the outside committee had been 'appointed to consider of those things prepared by Mr Sheppard relating to the law and report their opinions to the council'.[128] This account, which was sent to army headquarters in Scotland, implied that the report returned by the five outsiders would be taken under advisement by the council as opinions only and not necessarily recommendations.

All five of the men appointed to consult with Sheppard were qualified by their legal backgrounds to comment knowledgeably upon proposed changes in the system. However, the likelihood that any one of them would give a full and unqualified endorsement to Sheppard's entire program was decidedly slim. One member of this screening committee was Samuel Wightwick, chief clerk of the upper bench and the sole representative of the current judicial establish-

---

126 After Mackworth's death in Dec. 1654 Philip Jones had taken his place on the standing committee for the regulation of the law. Fleetwood must have been added after his return from Ireland in late 1655: PRO, SP 25/76, fols. 547, 552, 562 (15, 19, 21 Feb. 1656).
127 PRO, SP 25/77, fol. 150 (29 May 1656).
128 Worc. Coll. MS, xxviii, fol. 36r (3 June 1656).

ment. Wightwick had succeeded to his office at the beginning of the protectorate, having served for many years as deputy to Robert Henley, his predecessor. His interests were assuredly with preserving the traditional court structure and its perquisites intact to protect the fortune in vested interests he had at hand.[129] The committee of review also included Thomas Manby and Peter Brereton. Like Sheppard, both were barristers with experience of working in the government. Manby, who had the more distinguished career, had already been involved in efforts to reform the law. In January 1652 he had been, along with Matthew Hale, William Steele and Charles Cocke, among the first appointees to the law-reform commission approved by the Rump's selection committee. His contributions to the Hale Commission included drafting the amendments to the bill establishing small-debt courts and his service with that body won him the position of probate judge in 1653 with an annual salary of £300, a sum equalling that earned by Sheppard.[130] Peter Brereton, a third member of the committee, was an ancient of Gray's Inn and a cousin to John Bradshaw. In March 1655 he had accepted employment as counsel to the council of state at a salary of £5 a week and his most recent assignment had been service on a task force directed to revise the fees of an officer in the court of chancery.[131] Brereton's associates on that fee-revision committee appointed just four weeks earlier were also the fourth and fifth members of the group appointed to consult on Sheppard's program, Bulstrode Whitelocke and Thomas Widdrington. The attachments that existed between Brereton and Manby on the one hand and Whitelocke and Widdrington on the other were soon to become official connections. Sometime in the ensuing two years the former two aligned themselves directly with the latter pair when they secured positions as counsels-at-law to the two lords

[129] This chief clerk's office was one of the most lucrative in the entire judicial establishment: Aylmer, *King's servants*, pp. 305–8; *State's servants*, pp. 97–8. I am grateful to Prof. Aylmer for providing information about Wightwick.

[130] Manby was called to the bar of Lincoln's Inn in 1640 and was made a bencher in the late 1650s. He was created a Welsh judge after the restoration and later edited Wingate's *Abridgment* of statutes (1670, 1674, 1675): *CSPD,*.VII, pp. 343, 455; VIII, pp. 113, 117, 155, 178, 259; IX, pp. 30, 320; Cotterell, 'Law reform', pp. 48, 55, 77; Williams, *Great sessions*, pp. 173–4.

[131] PRO, SP 25/77, fol. 338; *CCC*, I, p. 463; *CSPD*, VIII, pp. 98 (the Christian names of Peter Brereton and John Reading are reversed in the printed calendar), 259; IX, pp. 221, 337, 340, 364; X, pp. 24, 46; Douthwaite, *Gray's Inn*, pp. 71–3; Fletcher, *Pension book*, pp. 283, 317, 354; Foster, *Register to Gray's Inn*, p. 160.

treasurers.[132] To designate Manby and Brereton as retainees of Whitelocke and Widdrington in mid 1656 would be to overstate the connections at the time. However, the association that was soon to be made official indicates that the lords treasurers found these two legal associates sufficiently agreeable and compliant to name them their assistants. Working together on Sheppard's program, Manby and Brereton could be expected to defer to any strongly held judgments about Sheppard's proposals that would be voiced by either Whitelocke or Widdrington, both of whom occupied positions of authority substantially superior to their own.

As for Whitelocke and Widdrington, they were the two individuals still in the protectorate establishment least likely to agree to a program of the innovative dimensions that Sheppard had drawn.[133] And yet, paradoxically, Cromwell could not afford to ignore them because of the influence they commanded in the political arena. Although the agenda for parliament included compelling matters of foreign policy and finance, members of the administration were planning to introduce a program of law-reform bills based upon Sheppard's proposals. If any backing for the government's legislative plans could be won from the two wavering revolutionaries, the enactment of a meaningful program of reform would be decidedly more promising given the support Whitelocke and Widdrington could attract from other members of parliament. Both men had extensive experience as legislators, their careers dating back to the Long Parliament. They had served in the 1654 parliament and both were to play leading roles in the upcoming legislature, with Widdrington elected speaker and Whitelocke named his *pro tempore* replacement for a while.[134] The political support of these two well-known members of the legal establishment had lent an air of respectability useful to politicians in power on several occasions, but Cromwell's attempt to engage their support at this early stage of policy formulation was definitely a calculated risk. Experience had proved that their reactions to legal change were unpredictable. Although they were currently serving as treasury commissioners, just

---

[132] *CSPD*, IX, pp. 281–2. Manby and Brereton marched in Cromwell's funeral procession as counsels-at-law to the lords treasurers, Whitelocke and Widdrington: *Burton's diary*, IV, pp. 523–7.

[133] Henry Rolle, C.J.U.B., had resigned in June 1655 over George Cony's case involving the legality of custom duties: Cockburn, *Assizes*, p. 291.

[134] *CJ*, VII, p. 482 (27 Jan. 1657).

a year earlier, in June 1655, the two men had surrendered the great seal as a direct consequence of their refusal to preside over the reformed court of chancery under the new regulations of Cromwell's ordinance.[135] Whitelocke later claimed that his conscience prevented him from administering the terms of the ordinance because of his objections to most of its provisions, but his career and Widdrington's showed that only a few, particular innovations were distasteful to them. Since the commonwealth had been established almost eight years earlier, there had been no consistency in the pattern of their objections to change. Widdrington, for example, had refused to stay in office as chancery commissioner in a regicide regime in 1649, but had retained his seat in its ruling body, the Rump Parliament.[136] And Whitelocke, who took exception to the constitutional authority by which the Chancery Ordinance had been promulgated, had no compunction about remaining in office as a treasury commissioner, a post created by the identical authority.[137]

The circumstances surrounding the drafting and promulgation of the Chancery Ordinance suggest an explanation for the two former commissioners of the great seal being named to the committee assigned to review Sheppard's law-reform designs in mid 1656. Cromwell and the council had deliberately avoided consulting with the principal officers of the court when the ordinance was being prepared in June through August 1654.[138] While the government may have hoped that the court's officers would abide by the new regulations once they were published, that expectation was not realized and Whitelocke and Widdrington had yielded up their offices rather than implement the provisions of reform. The resentment felt by the two who left office at having been ignored during the preparation of the reform had been explicitly expressed by White-locke to the council and the insult they felt they had suffered at having been left out and their opinions left unsolicited can go a long way

---

[135] Although the parliament of 1654 had suspended the ordinance, after the parliament had been dissolved and the suspension had elapsed, the council notified the chancery officers that the ordinance was to be put into effect at Easter Term 1655. After preparing a list of objections, Whitelocke and Widdrington finally resigned their offices after a confrontation with Cromwell on 6 June: *CSPD*, VIII, pp. 137 (23 Apr.), 200 (6 June); Whitelocke, *Memorials*, IV, pp. 192–201 (Apr. 1655), 205–6 (6, 8 June 1655).

[136] For Widdrington, see above, n. 119; Worden, *Rump Parliament*, pp. 34, 65, 393.

[137] *A & O*, II, p. 918; *CSPD*, VII, p. 284; *Thurloe State Papers*, III, p. 370; *W & S*, III, pp, 393, 476; Whitelocke, *Memorials*, IV, p. 204.

[138] See above, pp. 39–41, nn. 113–16.

towards explaining their peeved resignations.[139] It is therefore quite possible that the council was, in May 1656, attempting to mollify the two when they were invited to review this new set of reform proposals, to make amends for having wilfully ignored them in 1654 and overruled their objections in 1655. If Cromwell and the council could discover any particular objections they might have to Sheppard's plan, there was enough time remaining before parliament met to neutralize potential opposition by adjusting the government's legislative program. The attempt to win the cooperation of Whitelocke and Widdrington was not unrealistic because several of Sheppard's proposals were familiar to them, having been considered by previous parliaments. In fact, Whitelocke himself had helped to draft the Rump's bill for registering land titles, one of the principal components of Sheppard's scheme.[140] It therefore seems likely that the government solicited their opinions in an attempt to gain the support of potential allies.

In the same week the council delegated Whitelocke, Widdrington, Manby, Brereton and Wightwick to assess the master design for legal reform, Sheppard returned to Gloucestershire to visit briefly with his family. His brother Samuel's success in the woollen industry had enabled him to acquire more extensive land holdings. Having purchased manor lands in 1649 and 1651, he was preparing to expand his holdings in May 1656 to include the property and lordship rights of two more estates adjacent to the family home in Horsley. William was with him on the 28th and 30th of that month to witness the conveyance of Gatcombe Abbey to his brother by Thomas, Lord Windsor.[141] Since Sheppard was away from London on 29 May, the

---

[139] Whitelocke, *Memorials*, IV, pp. 188, 191 (Mar. 1654, Apr. 1655). An historian of the court of chancery wrote, 'If Whitelocke had been honest and consistent, and not impressed by an inordinate love of antiquity and self-interest, much effective reformation of the court of chancery might have been accomplished, notwithstanding the perpetual changes of parties and policy; but he was consistent only in his irresolution, inconsistencies and desire of pleasing all parties; and his character is admirably summed up by Clarendon who says that "he had a nature that could not bear or submit to be undone"': J. Parkes, *A history of the court of chancery; with practical remarks* (1828), p. 181.

[140] A copy of the Rump's bill for land registration listed in a nineteenth-century catalogue reads, 'Copy of a draft of an act prepared in the time of the commonwealth, 1653, by Bulstrode Whitelocke, Esq, and John Lisle, Esq, two of the parliamentary commissioners of the great seal, Chief Baron Lane, Mr Prideaux and Sir Anthony Ashley Cooper, for a registry of conveyance and incumbrances of lands': *Bib. Coop.*, p. 125.

[141] Playne, *Parishes*, pp. 124–5.

day the council named the committee, he probably did not learn of its appointment until he returned to Whitehall. With the major outlines of his reform program completed and in the hands of the council of state, Sheppard and his brother had every reason to enjoy their visit and their respective accomplishments.

Sheppard was back in London by 12 June to accept an assignment working directly under the authority of the council of state.[142] While this new responsibility carried some degree of political urgency, he still found time to continue refining his law-reform program. Official records reveal nothing more about the committee appointed to review Sheppard's proposals and no evidence has been found of the committee conferring with Sheppard, as it had been directed to do. Nor do state papers contain any reference to the report the council had requested the committee to submit. No record of the opinions of Manby, Brereton or Wightwick to Sheppard's program has been discovered, but the proceedings of the 1656 parliament contain unmistakable evidence of the stands taken by Whitelocke and Widdrington on the issue of comprehensive legal reform. The most generous comment that can be made concerning Whitelocke's attitudes to reform bills is that his support was vacillating at best, while Widdrington's performance as speaker in managing the reform bills that were introduced must be termed incompetent if not deliberately obstructionist. And yet Sheppard continued to retain the confidence of the council of state. Three weeks after Sheppard assumed his new assignment, Cromwell and the council ordered immediate payment of some back wages due to him, a telling sign of approval from a financially pressed regime that was notoriously slack in meeting its salary commitments.[143] And it may be no coincidence that on the day Sheppard was paid, Cromwell and the council approved the transfer of Gloucester cathedral with its school and library to the city corporation with the understanding that the property be used for education and other public benefits. Sheppard had been promoting the use of the Gloucester cathedral library for public education for nine years, and the realization of that project was one of the many gratifications he enjoyed in 1656.[144] Of the other

---

[142] The assignment of preparing corporation charters is described below, pp. 52–8: PRO, SP 25/77, fol. 175 (12 June 1656).

[143] PRO, SP 25/77, fol. 216 (1 July 1656).

[144] Ibid. See above, n. 56. The Gloucester transfer was approved by parliament on 9 June 1657: A & O, III, p. ci.

rewards in store for him, the most meaningful must have been the number of bills adapted from his proposals that were introduced in the 1656 parliament by members of the council of state. During the autumn months while parliament was considering those bills, the public finally learned the details of Sheppard's comprehensive program of reform from the text of his most interesting book, released in October, to which he had given the soothing title, *England's balme*.

Sheppard had postponed the publication of *England's balme* until parliament had convened so that he could use all the available time to complete his proposals, never satisfied that he had discovered every deficiency and abuse in the law. At one point in the late summer he had gone to the legal quarter of London to solicit recommendations from professional colleagues. At Lincoln's Inn he found the indefatigable William Prynne, who categorically rejected Sheppard's appeal for assistance. Prynne also used the occasion as a pretext to publish yet another of his vituperative pamphlets that voiced the eloquent but embittered author's objections to the constitutional disruption of the interregnum. This disagreeable encounter with Prynne might have been predicted since the famous dissident of the 1630s had maintained a consistently antagonistic attitude towards every government that had succeeded the Long Parliament and many of his writings expressed the underlying frustration and anger he suffered because of his eclipsed political career.[145] Prynne began his privately published pamphlet, *A summary collection...*, with the statement that he had been 'importunately solicited by Mr William Sheppard, a lawyer especially employed by some swordmen and grandees at Whitehall' to offer suggestions for legal improvement, 'which I then informed him I had no time to do', and that others 'had written so much in the justification of our laws as would satisfy and silence all soldiers and others that ignorantly censured them'.[146] Prynne did concede grudgingly in the conclusion to his pamphlet that 'there are some few grievances [and] abuses, not in the theory, but

---

[145] W. M. Lamont, *Marginal Prynne, 1600–1669* (1963), pp. 181, 188–9; Underdown, *Pride's purge*, pp. 144, 194–5; *Somerset*, pp. 156, 162, 173. He published more than 200 tracts between 1627 and the 1660s, most of them dealing with constitutional issues and many financed by the author himself: see Wing.

[146] W. Prynne, *A summary collection of the principal fundamental rights, liberties, proprieties of all English freemen* (Printed for the author, 1656), sig. A2r. At least two, and possibly four editions were printed that autumn, the first was registered on 22 Sept.: *Sta. Reg.*, II, p. 86. The first edition had 32 pages; the second, which was enlarged to 64 pages, retained every invective against Sheppard and the slurs against the 'swordmen' at Whitehall were even more strident.

practice of our laws...fit to be redressed', adding sardonically, 'which I myself had many years since reformed (as I told Mr Sheppard upon his aforementioned motion to me) had not those army-men violently pulled me with other members out of the house, and interrupted the settlement, peace, liberty...and good government of the kingdom'. His contempt for Cromwell and the 'grandees' and military men in the government extended to include judges as well and he named several officials, charging them and 'others in the greatest present powers for their exhorbitant, tyrannical proceedings in...disofficing, disfranchising and sequestering all sorts of men in corporations at their pleasure'.[147] The 'disfranchising' mentioned by Prynne – a breach of a traditional liberty correlative to his own expulsion from parliament in 1648 – was a very topical issue when he wrote in the election summer of 1656. The Instrument of Government had introduced a new franchise that eliminated a number of small boroughs and reduced the representation of others. By this reapportionment the number of borough members fell from 419 (the number elected to the Long Parliament) to an insignificant 136. Prynne, who had opposed parliamentary reapportionment since the 1640s, could not let pass the opportunity to champion the cause of the 283 disenfranchised burgesses who had lost representation in both the parliament of 1654 and the approaching legislature of 1656.[148]

The second censure Prynne levied against Cromwell and his political advisers, the 'disofficing' of men in corporations, was based upon a recent administrative policy that had been adopted in the spring of 1656 and was entering its most active phase of implementation in the summer when Prynne wrote. Moreover, it was a charge aimed directly at Sheppard, condemning his part in the council's project. Since 12 June 1656 Sheppard had been drafting for the administration charters of municipal incorporation that, in several instances, replaced civic officers of questionable reputation or of doubtful loyalty with trusted supporters of the protectorate.[149] The council's interest in local government began when problems in two

---

[147] Prynne added a note that he had taken the trouble to publish the pamphlet only to 'gratify Mr Sheppard and discharge my bounden duty to my profession and country': Prynne, *Summary collection*, p. 32. For the quotations, see ibid., pp. 20–1, 23, sigs. A2v, A3r, A4r, p. 11 in that order.

[148] Worden noted that Prynne and others in the Rump Parliament opposed reapportionment 'on the ground that it constituted a threat to the ancient rights and charters of boroughs': Worden, *Rump Parliament*, p. 156.

[149] PRO, SP 25/77, fol. 175.

areas were brought to its attention. In Colchester, where two factions of the governing body had been quarrelling since the first civil war, an expelled officer had taken his grievance to the upper bench, a move that exacerbated a difficult situation.[150] The government also had cause to be concerned about Salisbury and Blandford, both of which had been implicated in the abortive Penruddock rebellion of March 1655. Although these three locales were extremely volatile centers of civic distress, internal political frictions in many other towns also called for the attention of the central government.

On 21 September 1655, the same day that the major-generals were commissioned, Cromwell issued a proclamation that all royalists and delinquents were to be barred from parliament and corporation offices and deprived of their voting rights. The order, which extended an act of 1652, included a supplemental clause stipulating that all officials, including corporation officers and justices of the peace, must be not only loyal to the regime but also 'of pious and good conversation and well qualified with discretion, fitness and ability to discharge the trust committed to them'.[151] Within two months of Cromwell's proclamation both Colchester and Salisbury as well as Chipping Wycombe sent petitions to the government protesting local political conditions and requesting Cromwell to ensure, in the words of one, that 'godliness may be encouraged and good government settled'.[152] During the last months of 1655 Major-General Whalley sent the council a report of 'wicked magistrates' setting up ale-houses in Lincoln and Coventry while Desborough wrote from Bristol of corporation officers 'discountenancing the godly and upholding the loose and profane', adding the warning that this was 'indeed...a disease predominating in most corporations'. In Tewkesbury and Gloucester, Desborough, acting on his own initiative, discharged a total of thirteen corporation officers.[153] In

---

[150] For Arthur Barnardiston's suit, see Aylmer, *State's servants*, pp. 95, 303; *CSPD*, VIII, p. 202 (9 June 1655).

[151] A month earlier, on 22 Aug., the major-generals had been instructed to 'keep a strict eye on...the disaffected' and 'to promote godliness'. In July royalists had been ordered to leave London and report to the local officers of their home parishes: *CSPD*, VIII, pp. 232–3 (6 July), 296 (22 Aug.), 343 (21 Sept.); Gardiner, *History*, III, p. 261.

[152] Colchester, 26 Sept.: J. H. Round, 'Colchester during the commonwealth', *EHR*, XV (1900), pp. 653–4; Salisbury, 29 Nov.: *CSPD*, IX, p. 41; Chipping Wycombe, 14 Nov.: Gardiner, *History*, III, p. 266. The quotation is from the Salisbury petition.

[153] Gardiner, *History*, III, pp. 160–7.

January 1656 petitioners from Carlisle notified the council of their objections to a recently elected royalist mayor and some aldermen, including in their petition the ubiquitous complaint against alehouses. The council president responded with a strong directive to enforce Cromwell's proclamation but allowed four royalist councilmen to remain in office for the sake of political stability.[154]

With Cromwell's proclamation a matter of record – that only fit men should be entrusted with office – the council considered the problem of how to implement its declared policy and satisfy the complaints of petitioners in aggrieved boroughs. A series of investigations into the issues raised in the three pending petitions from Colchester, Salisbury and Chipping Wycombe were conducted by conciliar committees and by 20 February 1656 a course of action had been decided upon for one of the three. On that day Cromwell assumed another prerogative of his royal predecessors and ordered the city of Chipping Wycombe to surrender its charter. The next day the Salisbury petition was referred for consideration to council members Desborough, Sydenham, Wolseley and Sidney with instructions to consult with Cromwell's legal adviser. After a week of deliberations with this unnamed consultant – undoubtedly Sheppard in view of subsequent events – the committee for the Salisbury petition was charged with the more general assignment of considering grants of new charters to all municipalities, a much more effective and traditional method of ensuring good government in boroughs than had been the enforcement of Cromwell's proclamation by conciliar directives or direct action by the major-generals.[155] The decision to issue new charters, a suggestion which appears to have been recommended by Sheppard, seems to have been based upon Cromwell's desire to govern according to traditional methods as far as possible. The renewal of municipal charters by a new supreme magistrate was unquestionably sound English practice and, by accepted custom, the reissued charters would include the names of men selected by the central administration to form the governing body.

In the weeks following the decision of 29 February, the council's

[154] Ibid., p. 291.
[155] Desborough's interest in many of these towns can be traced to his appointment as major-general for Gloucestershire, Wiltshire, Dorset, Somerset, Devon and Cornwall on 27 Mar. 1655. J e had chosen Salisbury as his headquarters: *CSPD*, IX, pp. 192–3, 195, 204 (20, 21, 29 Feb. 1656).

interest in reviewing charters intensified. On 10 March Colchester submitted another petition, this one requesting a new charter that would place more power in the magistrates' hands.[156] The next day the council appointed a committee 'to consider and confer with what persons they please touching the renewal of charters',[157] as another step was taken towards instituting a generalized policy. On 4 April the council decided to send the Colchester petition to committee along with a recently received petition from the town of St Albans.[158] Three days later Reading applied for confirmation of its charter.[159] Towards the end of May the council, acting upon the committee's recommendation, ordered a new charter to be issued to Salisbury.[160]

On 10 June the council received a petition from Blandford, the town that, along with Salisbury, had shared complicity in the Penruddock rising of the previous year, and the petition was referred to the conciliar committee for charter renewal.[161] On 12 June the committee, with Desborough as its spokesman, recommended that the Colchester charter be called in for revision and the council formalized its new policy of reviewing municipal charters by establishing a standing sub-committee composed of Sheppard and three others to prepare new municipal charters. The instructions given to Sheppard that day indicate that the council anticipated a full-fledged campaign to encourage towns throughout the country to petition the regime for charter renewal. The council's charge to Sheppard was

To consider all charters of corporations the renewing whereof shall be prayed. And...any two of them are hereby empowered to revise such charters and the several alterations that shall be proposed to be made...and to draw them up in such form and with such variations as they shall find most convenient having respect in the whole to the countenancing of religion and good government and the discouraging of vice in the respective corporations.[162]

Of the three men appointed to work with Sheppard on charter revision, only one, Gabriel Beck, actually participated in the project. A Gloucestershire man who had attended Lincoln's Inn, Beck had

[156] Gardiner, *History*, III, pp. 289–90; Round, 'Colchester', p. 656.
[157] Worc. Coll. MS, xxviii, fol. 6r (11 Mar. 1656).
[158] *CSPD*, IX, p. 255 (4 Apr. 1656).
[159] B. L. K. Henderson, 'The commonwealth charters', *TRHS*, Third Series, VI (1912), p. 136.
[160] *CSPD*, IX, p. 330 (22 May 1656).
[161] Gardiner, *History*, III, pp. 137–8.
[162] PRO, SP 25/77, fol. 175 (12 June 1656).

held a number of minor legal posts in the government since 1643 and during this period his salary was £200 *per annum*. He continued to be assigned to other responsibilities through the summer and it was only after October 1656, when the charter activity increased, that Beck began to assist Sheppard on a regular basis. Eventually, in the spring of 1657, Beck succeeded Sheppard as chairman of the charter committee.[163] The other two men named to the charter committee in June 1656 never became actively involved. Thomas Manby and Peter Brereton had only two weeks earlier been assigned to the committee to comment on Sheppard's law-reform proposals with Whitelocke, Widdrington and Wightwick. Their legal backgrounds account for their appointment to the charter committee but there is no evidence that either Manby or Brereton made any contribution to the preparation of the dozen or more municipal charters that were drafted in 1656–7.

The adoption of the council's charter-review policy was the second stage of the protectorate's program to bring godly reform to the countryside and to maintain domestic security throughout the nation. Nine months earlier, in September 1655, the simultaneous release of Cromwell's proclamation and the delivery of the major-generals' commissions had signalled the beginning of those efforts. In March 1656 Cromwell spoke to the governing body of London assembled at Whitehall to explain that the institution of rule by the major-generals and of the decimation tax was for 'the security of the peace of the nation, the suppressing of vice and encouragement of virtue, the very end of magistracy'.[164] Three months later the government had succeeded in shifting part of the responsibility for enforcing local reforms from the major-generals to the hands of the magistrates in self-governing corporations. Once this return to traditional governance was adopted as a formalized policy, the work of charter revision was not undertaken in haste.

As Sheppard set to work preparing drafts for the several charters already surrendered, the council took more petitions under advisement. In July the charters of King's Lynn and Woodstock were referred to Desborough's committee while Guernsey's charter was sent directly to Sheppard for revision.[165] In mid August the names

---

[163] PRO, SP 25/77, fol. 335 (18 Aug.); *CSPD*, IX, p. 312; X, p. 591; XI, p. 354. For other details, see Aylmer, *State's servants*, pp. 418–19, n. 3.
[164] Worc. Coll. MS, xxviii, fols. 5r–6r.
[165] PRO, SP 25/77, fols. 217, 300 (3, 31 July 1656).

selected by Secretary Thurloe for insertion in the Colchester charter were turned over to Wolseley and two other council members for approval. The same day the council agreed to order the preparation of a new charter for Woodstock.[166] From mid August until the beginning of October there was a hiatus in charter activity as council members prepared for the impending parliament. At the time elections were held only the revised charter for Colchester had been issued.[167]

Two weeks after parliament had convened the council resumed deliberations on charter renewal. From October 1656 until January 1657 the pending petitions from Chipping Wycombe, Blandford, Reading and Woodstock were considered. In the same period six more charters were called in for renewal, those for Maidenhead, Chepstow, Abergavenny, Leeds, Marlborough and Gateshead. Of these ten, plus the four that had been issued by August, at least nine are known to have been prepared by Sheppard and it is safe to assume that in the last months of 1656 Sheppard, the chief assistant to the council's charter committee, prepared most, if not all, of the draft charters himself.[168] The unrivalled familiarity with the English law of corporations that he acquired during those months provided the material for his last book of the protectorate period, *Of corporations, fraternities and guilds*, the first English book on this specialized branch of the law.[169]

The grievances embodied in the requests for charter renewal illustrate the sort of problems the central government faced in its quest for stability. Like the signatories of the first three borough petitions to win the attention of the council (Colchester, Chipping Wycombe and Salisbury), many civic representatives had long-

---

[166] PRO, SP 25/77, fols. 305, 328–9, 343 (1, 14, 21 Aug. 1656).

[167] The new charter had a definite political effect in Colchester where the parliamentary election was delayed until after the new charter was issued. The Colchestrian representatives were Henry Lawrence, president of the council of state, and John Maidstone, steward of Cromwell's household: Paul J. Pinckney, 'A Cromwellian parliament: the elections and personnel of 1656', unpublished Ph.D. dissertation, Vanderbilt University, 1962, pp. 186–9, 346. Burton's contemporary account names John Biscoe (or Briscoe) as the second Colchestrian representative along with Lawrence, but the only B(r)iscoe found by Ellen Goldwater was William Briscoe who sat for Cumberland: Goldwater, 'Two Cromwellian parliaments: politics, patronage and procedure', unpublished Ph.D. dissertation, City University of New York, 1973, p. 379; *Burton's diary*, Index of Speakers, pp. 4–30.

[168] PRO, SP 25/77, fols. 175–6, 300; *CSPD*, X, pp. 121, 149, 161, 181, 191.

[169] See ch. 3 for discussion of Sheppard's *Of corporations*.

standing complaints to lodge. Leeds and Marlborough both submitted petitions in December 1656 complaining of economic, political and/or legal problems that had originated in the civil-war period or earlier.[170] The council responded by ordering Sheppard to prepare new charters for both towns. The same month the bailiff of Leominster, disturbed by 'alehouses, vice and wickedness', petitioned the protector to reduce the number of corporation officers in his town 'because there are few well-affected'.[171] The council's interest in municipalities, grounded in both pragmatism and idealism, therefore extended to replacing disaffected officers with allies of the puritan cause in some cases for the purpose of stabilization. Hence, Prynne's charge against Cromwell and Sheppard for 'dis-officing' men in corporations.[172] It is noteworthy that almost a third of the charters issued by Cromwell went to towns that had been granted charters by Charles I.[173] This allows for the possibility that at least some of the corporation officers replaced by Cromwellian appointees might well have been placed in office originally by the Stuart regime. While the new municipal charters of the protectorate corrected defects in previous patents or made amends for wrongs suffered in the civil war, Cromwell and his council followed the traditional forms for granting patents that had been observed by earlier monarchs.[174] With his assertive executive council and a skilled draftsman of Sheppard's ability, Cromwell made full use of the means and machinery he had at his disposal to consolidate the goals of his political victory.

The protectorate administration followed a traditional procedure in its consideration of municipal petitions.[175] Each petition, addressed to Cromwell as chief of state, was sent to the council for one reading and was then referred to the council's committee for charters. Desborough, Sydenham, Wolseley, Lambert and Jones remained the

170 *CSPD*, X, pp. 181, 208, 224, 241.
171 Ibid., p. 220 (n.d.); Henderson, 'Charters', p. 158 (16 Dec. 1656).
172 See above, n. 147.
173 Six of the twenty-two municipalities petitioning Cromwell had been granted new charters by Charles I, Abergavenny (1638), Carlisle (1637), Colchester (1635), Leeds (1626), St Albans (1632) and Salisbury (1631): 'Salisbury charter', p. 173; Weinbaum, *Borough charters*, pp. xxx–liv.
174 In his study of protectorate charters Henderson noted that 'it is beyond dispute that he [Cromwell] employed well known and perfectly understood machinery for his scheme': Henderson, 'Charters', p. 131.
175 The council also adhered to traditional procedure in its consideration of ordinances. See Roots, 'Cromwell's ordinances', pp. 148–50.

most active members.[176] After committee deliberation the petition was returned to council with recommendations. The next stage was to send the petition to Sheppard with instructions for the revisions to be included in his draft. When Sheppard's work was completed the draft would be returned either to the council committee or, occasionally, to the council itself for further consideration. At some point in the course of these stages an individual or a group of persons would be assigned the politically sensitive task of assembling a list of names for proposed corporation officers to be included in the new charter. Usually that person was either council secretary Thurloe or a member of the council's charter committee but occasionally outside suggestions were sought from the major-general in charge of the locality. Once the council had agreed to all the amendments and the names, the last stage would be to send the draft to Cromwell for final approval, whereupon the charter would be issued to the town either by letters patent or under the recently revived privy seal.[177] The entire process was time consuming and many months could elapse between the time the petition was first read and the moment the new charter was issued. The citizens of Chipping Wycombe and Reading waited more than a year for their new charters, and the grants to Salisbury, Colchester, Blandford and Woodstock were all more than six months in preparation. On the other hand, the charters for Abergavenny, Leeds, Gateshead and Marlborough, which were turned over to Sheppard in November and December 1656 respectively, were drafted and returned to the council for approval by the third week of January 1657.[178]

When in the year following the June 1656 establishment of the council's committee for charters, it became known that the government was willing to grant and confirm charters to municipalities, the volume of petitions for privileges submitted to Cromwell and the council increased appreciably. Records of special requests survive for

---

[176] PRO, SP 25/77, fols. 220–1; *CSPD*, IX, p. 204; Round, 'Colchester', p. 657.
[177] Examples of each of these stages is found in PRO, SP 25/77, fols. 220, 328–9; *CSPD*, X, pp. 191, 241.
[178] Chipping Wycombe: Gardiner, *History*, III, pp. 266–7; *CSPD*, IX, pp. 192–3; X, pp. 149, 224–5. Reading: Henderson, 'Charters', p. 136. Colchester and Salisbury: see above, nn. 155, 158. Blandford: PRO, SP 25/77, fol. 175; *CSPD*, X, p. 164. Woodstock: PRO, SP 25/77, fol. 220; *CSPD*, X, p. 241. Abergavenny, Leeds, Gateshead and Marlborough: *CSPD*, X, pp. 161, 181, 191, 224, 234, 241, 284.

six hospitals and eleven schools and colleges.[179] Several of these were attached to petitions requesting the renewal of a municipal charter, while other towns made application only for a specific benefit, like the Gloucester petition for the grant of the cathedral school to the city, or that of Wells, which asked that the cathedral be authorized for public worship.[180] In the economic sphere petitions were submitted for no fewer than seventeen fairs and markets and from fourteen groups of craftsmen, tradesmen and merchants. Some of these non-municipal petitions were either approved or rejected at the council meeting where they were first read but in most cases a decision was deferred pending further investigation. Several were sent to the trade committee for study while others went to the attorney- or solicitor-general.[181] Only the petitions for municipal charters, those that received the greatest amount of attention, followed a formalized course of several stages of consideration.[182]

As for the charters themselves, the protectorate grants that Sheppard prepared were very traditional in both form and content. The lengthy Salisbury charter, reproduced by Sheppard in his 1659 book, *Of corporations, fraternities and guilds*, was a model recital of customs and conventions that had developed through the medieval centuries and into the early-modern period.[183] All of Sheppard's charters embody a deep-seated respect for traditional conventions in their confirmations of former privileges, especially local customs that a town might claim by traditional right. He also followed the contemporary trend of granting additional privileges of local juris- diction and supplemental offices, particularly that of recorder. His pronounced concern for social welfare in the granting of hospitals and

---

179 The appendix to Henderson's article lists 68 petitions or grants for local privileges, most of them dating from 1656–7: 'Charters', pp. 155–61.
180 Gloucester cathedral school: PRO, SP 25/77, fols. 175–6, 216, 220; *CSPD*, X, p. 23.
181 PRO, SP 25/78, fol. 374; *CSPD*, IX, pp. 69, 260–1, 374.
182 The political implications of the Cromwellian charters have been commented on by Gardiner, *History*, ch. 42; Goldwater, 'Two parliaments', Henderson, 'Charters', Pinckney, 'Cromwellian parliament', Round, 'Colchester'; as well as James R. Davis, 'Colchester, 1660–1662: politics, religion and office-holding in an English provincial town', unpublished Ph.D. dissertation, Brandeis University, 1980; J. H. Plumb, *The growth of political stability in England, 1675–1725* (1967), p. 52; J. H. Round, 'Cromwell and the electorate', *The Nineteenth Century*, XLVI (1899), pp. 947–56; Underdown, *Pride's purge*, pp. 324–5.
183 See ch. 3 for a full description of Sheppard's charters.

schools place the charters Sheppard wrote for Cromwell in the mainstream of the progressive development of charter-granting practice through the Tudor and Stuart centuries. The seventeenth-century tendency to narrow the franchise is also observable in Sheppard's charters, but an observer seeking an example of ruthless political manipulation or the flouting of tradition must look to the charters issued by the later Stuarts after the restoration. Cromwell's charters are the embodiment of tradition. Many of Sheppard's charters have been lost, some from the normal attrition of historical records and others from the deliberate destruction of 'rebel' documents at the time of the restoration.[184] The survival of his book on the law of corporations has therefore become all the more valuable as a key to the aspirations of the protectorate administration with respect to local-government policy.

Two weeks after the second protectorate parliament convened at Westminster, Sheppard signed the preface to *England's balme* at Whitehall. The book was entered in the registers of the Stationers' Company on 11 October 1656 and by 23 October George Thomason, the book collector, had received his copy.[185] The government's decision to permit Sheppard's program for law reform to be published and distributed to the public implies that the protectorate administration was prepared to back both the philosophy and the details of the plan.[186] Although the book did not carry an official endorsement, the contemporary censorship policy overseen by Secretary Thurloe would not have allowed for this bold program to be published at such a politically sensitive time unless it had won the tacit approval of the protector and a majority of the council.[187] The government's

---

[184] The new Salisbury charter was revoked even before the restoration by the restored Rump Parliament in 1659: *CJ*, VII, p. 745. Henderson wrote in 1912, 'Of the Cromwellian charters, possibly only those granted to Chester, Swansea, Gloucester, Newport and perhaps that for the College of Durham remain in existence at the present time. In addition, one may probably add the charter granted to Gateshead': Henderson, 'Charters', pp. 144, 146–7. The charters for Maidenhead, Salisbury and Colchester, all written by Sheppard, may be added to Henderson's list. See discussion of *Of corporations*, ch. 3.

[185] The introductory remarks to the reader, signed at Whitehall, concluded at sig. A3v; the registration is listed in *Sta. Reg.*, II, p. 90. Thomason's copy is dated on the title page in his own hand, as was his custom: W. Sheppard, *England's balme* (1656), BL, shelfmark E 1675 [2].

[186] See ch. 4, pt II.

[187] A censorship policy had been in effect since Sept. 1655: *CSPD*, VIII, p. 319 (5 Sept. 1655).

approbation of Sheppard's work was also manifested by a signal honor awarded to this faithful servant.

The supreme moment of Sheppard's career in Cromwell's service arrived on 25 October 1656 when the government for which he had labored honored him with a serjeant's writ.[188] Five days later he was sworn as a member of the order of the coif in the court of chancery. He was presented at the bar of common pleas a few days later to receive seisin of his new profession as a pleader before that court. The patrons named in the writ were two fellow Middle Templars, William Hussey and Nicholas Lechmere, both readers of his inn.[189] Hussey, who had shared chambers with Sheppard from 1620 to 1631, had remained active in the inn's affairs, serving as both reader and treasurer, but his legal activities had little political color.[190] Lechmere, the other patron, was one of the many reluctant revolutionaries of the legal establishment in parliament during the interregnum. Although he accepted appointment as attorney of the Duchy of Lancaster under Cromwell and served in both the 1654 and 1656 parliaments, he had earlier distinguished himself as an opponent of law-reform bills when he sat in the Rump.[191] Therefore, no ideological

[188] Sheppard was one of fourteen serjeants called by Oliver Cromwell's protectorate. By comparison, 23 serjeants were called by parliament in 1648–9. I am grateful to J. H. Baker who located both the writ and remembrance: PRO, C 202/40/1, return immediately (serjeant's writ); Record of serjeant's writ: PRO, C 231/6, fol. 350; Sheppard called: PRO, SP 25/78, fols. 83, 248, 303. The motto he used for his rings is not known, but the two serjeant's rings mentioned in his brother Samuel's will were undoubtedly those fashioned by Sheppard when he was made a member of the order of the coif: PRO, PROB 11/346, fol. 117 (Samuel Sheppard's will, 1672).

[189] Remembrance of Sheppard's creation: writ for count, 14 Oct., return *cras. Anim.* (3 Nov.), *Praecipe in capite*, William Hussey, Esq., and Nicholas Lechmere, attorney-general for the Duchy of Lancaster, patrons: PRO, CP 45/404, m. 4. Both of the official newspapers carried the news of Sheppard's creation: *Merc. pol.*, no. 334, p. 7356; *Pub. intell.*, LC, microfilm 147, p. 956.

[190] See above, n. 13.

[191] The similar backgrounds of Lechmere and Sheppard permit the speculation that the men were personally acquainted. Lechmere was born in Gloucestershire and educated at the cathedral school in which Sheppard took such an interest. He took a degree at Wadham College, Oxford, the college of Sheppard's son, John, and then entered the Middle Temple. Because he blocked reform legislation in the Rump, Dr Worden believes that one of his major political concerns was 'to protect his own profession from the demands of reformers': Worden, *Rump Parliament*, p. 65. Lechmere served in both protectorate parliaments and on the eve of the restoration received a patent to be counsellor-at-law to the commonwealth: PRO, C 231/6, fol. 452 (3 Feb. 1660); J. W. Bund, *The civil war in Worcestershire 1642–1646* (Birmingham, 1905), pp. 226–7, 233, 250; *CSPD*, X,

sympathy with the details of Sheppard's reform program can be attributed to either patron.

As for Sheppard himself, there is every indication that he accepted the distinction of the coif only as an honor. His name with the new title was included in the list of honorific officers leading the Gloucestershire peace commission in 1657 and 1658[192] and his rank as serjeant was mentioned on the title pages of the three books he published in 1658–9,[193] but there is no evidence that he ever took advantage of the primary privilege of pleading before the common bench. Nor is there any indication that he rode as an assize judge.[194] His work on the corporation charters for the council of state kept him occupied through the remainder of 1656 and into the early months of the following year, apparently continuing at his post at Whitehall.

In addition to Hussey and Lechmere, a third Middle Templar was connected with the events surrounding the publication of *England's balme*. Dawbeney Williams, a young barrister of that inn, published an eighteen-page pamphlet on 5 November 1656 that referred to Sheppard's reform proposals. Williams' tract was called *A perspicuous compendium of several irregularities and abuses in the present practice of the common law of England* and the thrust of his argument was that many abusive aspects of the court system could be corrected by administrative edict and enforced by the bench. This, of course, was precisely the manner by which the government had reformed the court of chancery, but Williams did not note that. He

---

p. 251; Cockburn, *Assizes*, pp. 278–80, 289; *DNB*: sub Lechmere; Prest, *Inns of court*, p. 114n; Underdown, *Pride's purge*, pp. 218n, 224, 238–9; Worden, *Rump Parliament*, pp. 30, 65, 109, 110n, 203–4, 313n.

[192] PRO, C 193/13/6, fols. 34–7 (1657); 193/13/5, fol. 41 (1658). His title is also listed with the assessment commissioners of 1657 for Glouc.: *A & O*, II, p. 1069 (1657); *GNQ*, p. 91 (1657). Minutes of the council of state also include Sheppard's title in references to him: PRO, SP 25/78, fols. 83, 248, 303 (Aug., Oct., Nov. 1657).

[193] All of Sheppard's books prior to and including *England's balme* describe the author as 'esquire'. The same holds true for all published after the restoration. The three published with his title were *Sincerity and hypocrisy* (1658) and *A new survey of the justice of peace, his office* (1659), and *Of corporations* (1659).

[194] See above, n. 21. Cockburn's study of assizes confirms that Sheppard received a commission to ride the Oxford circuit in the early months of 1659, but the winter circuits were subsequently cancelled: Cockburn, *Assizes*, pp. 272, 284, n. 29 cites PRO, Index [now C 231] 4213. That commission would have been issued by Richard Cromwell's government prior to the fall of that regime in Apr. 1659. Lists from other assize circuits from 1657 through 1659 do not include Sheppard's name: PRO, C 181/6, fols. 230, 273, 290–1, 369.

closed his short essay with the comment that he need add no more because 'this subject being since undertaken (though unknown to me) by a reverend sage of our law, the learned Mr Serjeant Sheppard, whose labors are very great in its reformation'. The pamphlet was dedicated to council-member Sydenham and, while Williams' advocacy of reform by executive decree accurately echoed the approach that had been taken by Cromwell and the council since 1654, the pamphlet's muted tone and its brevity as well as the reference to Sheppard's law-reform efforts seem to indicate that the author was prepared to defer to the administration's current plans to work through parliament.[195] Few other contemporary references to Sheppard's program have been found. The most tangible evidence of the protector's desire to introduce legal reform into practical politics through legislative channels can be found in the parallels between bills presented to the parliament that autumn and the proposals printed in *England's balme*.

At the time Sheppard received his coif he had spent a quarter of a century working towards the improvement of English law and it is particularly fitting that his elevation to the rank of serjeant can be credited directly to the publication of his most creative effort as a legal scholar. The fate of his law-reform proposals now lay with parliament. However, as the session progressed, the prospect of their enactment became less and less promising. In the spring of 1657 conservative members of the house joined together to support the return to a traditional bicameral legislature headed by a hereditary dynasty. While Cromwell contemplated accepting the Humble Petition and Advice, a hundred soldiers confronted him with a warning to reject the kingship offered him. Members of parliament reworded the petition with terms Cromwell was able to accept and in the subsequent turmoil of constitutional and foreign-policy deliberations, all hopes for the enactment of meaningful legal reforms vanished.

[195] D. W., *A perspicuous compendium* (1656), sig. A2r. Williams (*c*. 1630–85?) was of the Isle of Purbeck, Dorset, and he dedicated the pamphlet to William Sydenham, captain-governor of the nearby Isle of Wight. Williams had spent some time at New Inn, was admitted to the Middle Temple on 14 Feb. 1649, and was called to the bar just three years later, on 8 Feb. 1652, an unusually short amount of time but perhaps not unique in this disruptive period. He kept his chambers at the Middle Temple at least through 1656. On 26 Mar. 1655 state papers name him 'present solicitor of the state' with a salary of £100 p.a. I am grateful to Professor G. E. Aylmer for providing me with this information on Williams: *CSPD*, VIII, p. 97; *M. T. Ad. Reg.*, I, p. 147; *M. T. Min.*, II, p. 974; III, pp. 1033, 1053, 1068, 1071, 1088, 1103.

The adoption of the Additional and Explanatory Petition in June 1657 had the effect of shelving much of the pending legislation until the next parliamentary session, scheduled for 1658. The abandonment of Sheppard's program coincided with his retirement from the central administration. Thereafter no major policy programs were entrusted to him and the decline in his public career was apparent early in 1657. His assistant, Gabriel Beck, gradually took over the drafting of charters[196] and Sheppard was given no new assignments, nor was he paid his allotted wages. By August he was in such dire financial straits that he appealed in person to the council of state for the payment of his back salary. The request was granted immediately with the order that the arrears 'be satisfied and paid out of the council contingencies', but the directive added that the annual stipend was to end at Michaelmas, in only a few weeks' time. Cromwell was present at the meeting and gave his assent to the order. In the margin of the council's minutes where the protector's 'approval in person' was noted, another comment was written in the same hand: '£3000 should be allowed to Serjeant Sheppard'.[197] The marginal figure in the council's minute book, ten times Sheppard's annual salary, is unmistakable and while it may be a clerical error, there remains the possibility that Cromwell meant Sheppard to have that large sum as severance pay, in gratitude for his loyal services. Two weeks later his back salary was paid in full, but no record of an accompanying bonus has been discovered.[198] With his official duties terminated, Sheppard left Whitehall and returned home with the intention of resurrecting his private law practice. His reception in Gloucestershire was disappointing and three months later, on 24 November, he wrote plaintively to the council of state:

To his highness the lord protector and his honorable council. The humble petition of William Sheppard, serjeant-at-law. That your petitioner hath to the neglect of his own family spent most of his time in the service of his generation. That by that unexpected call which your petitioner had unto your service and engagement, so far therein as to print here, is become distasteful to many. That your petitioner by this service hath lost his [law] practice utterly in his country and is put into an incapacity of recovering

---

[196] Beck began to work with Sheppard in late Dec. 1656. By Mar. 1657 Beck was preparing the charter for Aylesbury alone: *CSPD*, X, pp. 224, 234, 241, 300, 308; XI, p. 354.

[197] Appearance before the council, 14 Aug. 1657: PRO, SP 18/156/31. Order for payment of arrears and termination of salary: PRO, SP 25/78, fol. 83.

[198] *CSPD*, XI, pp. 66, 555; *Thurloe State Papers*, VI, pp. 593–4.

it again. That your petitioner's charge is great, having five children of his own and a widow and three children of one of his sons, a minister, left upon him, all as yet unprovided for. That [by] the charge of his removal and the loss of his practice he is out much more than he hath received of his salary for his service. Your petitioner therefore humbly prayeth that your highness and your honorable council will be pleased to bestow upon him some office or place to continue some part of his salary for the maintenance of him and his family in his old age.[199]

The council referred Sheppard's petition to a committee that reported back the very next day, recommending that Sheppard receive an annual pension of £100 'in respect of the loss of his practice by his being called out of the country for a public service',[200] advising Cromwell to issue a warrant for the pension to be paid out of the exchequer. No record has been discovered of any payments actually being made to Sheppard and, apart from including him in the Gloucestershire peace commissions, there is no evidence that the protectorate administration took any further notice of this devoted servant after it became apparent that his law-reform proposals were not politically viable.[201]

By the close of 1657 Sheppard had retired to his Gloucestershire home in Hempstead, rejoining his wife, Alice, and those of his children and grandchildren who were still part of the household.[202] In the first months after resettling in Hempstead he turned away from the worldly concerns of politics and legal improvement and devoted his attention to the religious questions that had first inspired his commitment to the puritan cause. He entered upon his retirement by composing a 400-page essay that commented upon some crucial issues of his theology, disputing a point that had been made by Richard Baxter in one of the most popular spiritual books of that generation, *Saint's everlasting rest*. Taking exception to Baxter's

[199] PRO, SP 18/157/131, fol. 150 (14 Nov. 1657).
[200] PRO, SP 25/78, fols. 301–3 (24–5 Nov. 1657). The council members sitting on the committee that made the recommendation were Jones, Mulgrave, Wolseley, Fleetwood, Sydenham, Sidney and Fiennes.
[201] Sheppard was not mentioned in 'disbursements to several pensioners', 1 Nov. 1657–1 Nov. 1658: *Thurloe State Papers*, VII, pp. 481–2. Sheppard's name was listed in Glouc. peace commissions until the restoration: PRO, C 193/13/4, fol. 42r (1657); C 193/13/6, fols. 34v–37 (1657); C 193/13/5, fol. 41 (1657–8); C 181/6, fols. 355, 374, 402 (1659).
[202] His daughter Rebecca and John's widow and children were certainly among those mentioned in the petition. Rebecca lived in the family home until her marriage on 28 Oct. 1675, 18 months after her father's death: *Glouc. visit.*, p. 69 (Futter pedigree). Which four of William's other children might still have lived with him cannot be said with certainty: see above, n. 16.

discourse on the singularly important tenet of a Christian's saving grace, Sheppard completed his longest and final religious study in a few months' time. His close friend, Thomas Barlow, provost of Queen's College, Oxford, collaborated with him and the work, *Sincerity and hypocrisy*, was published in Oxford in April 1658.[203]

There were spiritual comforts to accompany his theological studies in the first years of his retirement. In August 1658 Jonathan Smith, a young Independent preacher, was appointed rector of Hempstead church. His tenure was relatively short-lived and he was ejected in the first year of the restoration and replaced with a conforming minister who subscribed to every clause of the stringent 1662 Act of Uniformity. Smith stayed on in the parish for at least another ten years. Sharing an earnest dedication to the same theological system, Sheppard and Smith surely found compatibility and solace in their agreement upon matters of faith.[204]

Just a year after Sheppard's retirement the first protectorate came to an end when Oliver Cromwell died on 3 September 1658. Both sympathizers and enemies of the regime acknowledged the enormous loss sustained by the puritan cause at the death of the man who had inspired hundreds like Sheppard to work tirelessly for the cause of godly reformation. Two months after his death, a great funeral *cortège* gathered at Somerset House on the Strand to pay tribute to the valiant leader and an impressive array of officials, convened according to rank, formed a procession to Westminster Abbey. The assembly included representatives of the household, the administration, the judiciary, the religious establishment and the diplomatic corps in order of precedence, following royal custom. The men there and the offices they held afford a glimpse of the conservative direction the first protectorate had taken in the last year of Oliver Cromwell's life. The presence of those who stood for resistance to change and a propensity to return to a familiar status quo with regard to the constitution, the legal structure and the social establishment was matched by the noticeable absence or reduced ranks of the more

---

[203] Barlow wrote the last chapter of the book. See above, n. 86.
[204] Smith, a minister's son, was made rector of St Swithin's church, Hempstead, on 4 Aug. 1658 when he was 24 years old. In 1672 he was licensed under the Declaration of Indulgence as a Congregationalist (i.e. Independent) teacher in both Hempstead and at his second home in Ross-on-Wye, Herefordshire. He died in 1678. After the enforcement of the Act of Uniformity, St Swithin's was served by George Wall (1662–9): GPL, Hockaday abstracts, CCXL; GRO, GDR, CCVIII, fol. 40 (16 Aug. 1662, George Wall subscribed to Act of Uniformity): Matthews, *Calamy*, p. 447; Shaw, *English church*, II, p. 588.

stalwart proponents of reform. Of Cromwell's serjeants, Sheppard, who had retired to his Gloucestershire home, did not attend. The order of the coif was represented instead by two of the most conservative Cromwellian appointees, Erasmus Earle and John Maynard. Of the men who had urged Cromwell to reject the Humble Petition and Advice, Lambert's absence was the most notable. And John Owen marched as a commissioner of approbation rather than in his former position as Cromwell's chaplain, from which he had been removed after his fall from favor. The shift towards retrenchment rather than further reform was mirrored in the presence of many who had consistently thwarted legislative and executive programs for change. Whitelocke and Widdrington, who had been the most prominent and perhaps the most effective obstructionists to Sheppard's reform designs, were both there, still serving in the offices they had occupied even before resigning the great seal in the spring of 1655. Those two treasury commissioners were attended in the procession by Thomas Manby and Peter Brereton, two other members of the committee appointed to review Sheppard's reform proposals, now serving officially as counsels-at-law to Whitelocke and Widdrington.[205]

The altered political mood that prevailed at Westminster at the time of Cromwell's death was discernible in the country as well. Members of the traditional ruling families who a decade before had been fined as delinquents and stripped of political power had in some areas begun to reassume their former influence after the establishment of the protectorate. In Sheppard's community, where the Berkeleys had always held sway, the current head of that family, George Berkeley, had resumed his political predominance[206] and in the autumn of 1658 Sheppard took a part in a conciliatory effort to make amends for the political frictions of the past. In November, 1658, Berkeley, as patron to a Leicestershire church, presented Thomas Audley as minister to the parish. Audley, who had been ejected from

---

[205] In June 1658 Widdrington was named chief baron of the exchequer, retaining concurrently his post as treasury commissioner. Whitelocke returned to the great seal after Cromwell's death. The account of Cromwell's funeral procession by John Prestwick can be found in an appendix to the 1974 reprint of *Burton's diary*, IV, pp. 523–7. Sheppard's former assistant, Gabriel Beck, marched as 'solicitor to the council of state'.

[206] Berkeley was renamed to the Gloucestershire peace commission on 27 Mar. 1655 and was elected county member to parliament in 1656. He was the younger, but sole surviving son and succeeded to his inheritance as lord Berkeley in Aug. 1658: PRO, C 213/6, fol. 307 (Mar. 1655); *Burton's diary*, Index of speakers, p. 6; Williams, *Glouc. parl. hist.*, p. 56.

a Gloucestershire rectory during the civil war by Sheppard and
others on the county committee for his enmity to parliament,
petitioned the protectorate government for permission to take the
pulpit to which Berkeley had presented him. In his petition Audley
gave the history of his ejection, claiming that he had been removed
only for 'differing in judgement' at a time when political loyalties
were of the highest priority, and not for 'scandal in life, doctrine or
conversation', and Sheppard added his name to a certificate of
support for Audley.[207] While Sheppard's reversal about Audley's
suitability was completely compatible with his personal religious
philosophy of toleration for all but the disruptive and scandalous
religious leaders and groups given a stable political climate,
Sheppard's sensitivity to the loss of reputation he had suffered
among his neighbours who were critical of his political activities in
the 1640s must be kept in mind as well.

In the summer of 1659 William Sheppard's retirement was
temporarily interrupted when for a short time he was once again
called back into the national arena. Oliver Cromwell's death in 1658
had thrown England into a political turmoil that lasted until the
restoration a year and a half later. Cromwell's mantle as head of state
had fallen on the shoulders of his elder surviving but less gifted son,
Richard. This continuity in the Cromwellian dynasty had been
brought about by the skillful manoeuvring of Whitehall politicians
and the second protectorate had been launched with the tractable but
unpromising Tumble-down Dick at the helm. The council of state
summoned a parliament in Richard's name on the old, pre-
Instrument-of-Government franchise in January 1659 and this
legislative session had been even less successful than its predecessors
of 1654 and 1656. A small but well-organized party of republicans
in the assembly refused to recognize either the new head of state or
the 'other' (upper) house that had assembled in accordance with the
provisions of the Humble Petition and Advice. By April, Richard had
succumbed to pressure from army officers and had been persuaded
to dissolve the parliament and to step down from the position he had
inherited from his father.[208] The collapse of the second protectorate
created a constitutional vacuum that paved the way for the recall of
the Rump Parliament. From May until October 1659 that body sat

[207] Audley had been ejected from Cromhall parish, Glouc., in 1646: *CSPD*, XII,
p. 188 (18 Nov. 1658).
[208] E. M. Hause, *Tumble-down Dick, the fall of the house of Cromwell* (New York,
1972), chs. 1 & 2, p. 430.

again at Westminster and, with the assistance of yet another council of state, attempted to discharge the responsibilities of government. Military security and financial solvency took immediate priority on the Rump's agenda and once again parliament approved the names of trusted men around the country to serve as militia commissioners. In Gloucestershire, Sheppard's name headed the local list.[209] The seasoned group of politicians sitting in the Rump felt secure in their power through the summer months and, taking responsibility for preserving continuity in the administration of justice, appointed assize commissions and issued orders for palatine and Welsh jurisdictions. The dispatch of business was, however, hampered by the revival of unresolved issues that had been set aside for the six years since the Rumpers had last met. Quarrelsome disputes over conflicting philosophies among the activists of this leaderless state continued through the summer and autumn and in the maelstrom of nominations, patents and circuit orders, William Sheppard was three times proposed for a judgeship.

His first nomination, as judge assistant to Lancaster, came early in July. The county palatine of Lancaster, abolished by the Long Parliament, had been revived in 1654 under the protectorate. On 8 July the Rump's Committee for Nomination of Persons to Places of Public Trust was ordered by the council of state to recommend Sheppard to replace Thomas Fell who had died in 1658. Parliament accordingly ordered the patent to be issued.[210] At this point serious disagreement arose among members of the Rump as to whether this ancient but once-abolished jurisdiction should be allowed to continue its privileged existence, and so no further action was taken on the Lancastrian vacancy at the time. On 1 August a bill to continue the palatine jurisdiction and privileges of Lancaster failed to receive a second reading on a division of sixteen ayes to twenty-three noes, so the house ordered another bill to be drafted for taking away the regalities of not only Lancaster, but Chester and Ely as well. At the end of the week the house passed an act to extend the assize circuits to Lancaster, then ordered that the palatine seal be surrendered to the house by 1 November and used no more, the profits of the seal to be sequestered to the commonwealth.[211]

[209] *A & O*, II, pp. 1324–5 (26 July); *CJ*, VII, pp. 719, 734; PRO, E 1074 (15).
[210] PRO, SP 25/127, fol. 46 (Sheppard in place of Fell, 8 July); Williams, *Great sessions*, pp. 58–9. The palatine privileges and jurisdiction of Lancaster had been revived by ordinance in Feb. 1654: *CSPD*, VI, p. 415.
[211] *CJ*, VII, pp. 744–5, 748–9 (1, 2, 5 Aug.).

Just days before the palatine jurisdictions met their fate for the second time in twenty years, the house heard nominations for vacancies on the Welsh circuits and Sheppard's name was put forward for a judgeship for the second time on 5 August. Since 1646 the chief justice of Chester, traditionally regarded as head of the Welsh bench, had been John Bradshaw, the regicide. His assistant had been the same Thomas Fell who had served concurrently as assistant to both benches of Chester and Lancaster from 1655 until his death in 1658, and after that time Bradshaw had presided alone in Chester.[212] When Bradshaw fell ill in London in the spring of 1659 he deputed a substitute, John Radcliffe, to preside in his place for Easter Term, *pro hac vice tantum*.[213] On 5 August, the same day the Rump abolished the palatine privileges of Lancaster and with them the judge assistant's position to which Sheppard had been nominated, the house resolved that Sheppard be appointed in place of Radcliffe to the office the deceased Fell had held as judge assistant to Chester. Parliament ordered that Sheppard be issued a patent under the great seal so that he could preside over the summer circuit, but no record of that patent has been located and it is unlikely that the Chester summer circuit was held so late in the season in 1659.[214]

In September, while the Rump continued to make changes in the personnel of the nation's benches, Sheppard was nominated for a third time.[215] On this occasion his appointment passed the great seal and on 3 October he received a patent to be chief justice of the North Wales circuit of Anglesey, Caernarvon and Merioneth. He was sworn the same day in the Whitehall lodgings of the dying John Bradshaw, head of the Welsh bench.[216] The appointment carried a salary of £250 *per annum*, a figure commensurate with his previous income as the protector's legal adviser.[217]

Sheppard's career as a judge was as ill-fated as his membership of the order of the coif. Just as his patent as serjeant-at-law was held to be invalid by the restored Rump, the government to which he owed

---

[212] Bradshaw retained his position despite a quarrel with Cromwell about his patent in Aug. 1656; P. J. Pinckney, 'Bradshaw and Cromwell in 1656', *HLQ*, XXX (1967), pp. 233–40; Williams, *Great sessions*, pp. 1–30.

[213] 'For this one particular occasion'. Williams, *Great sessions*, p. 101.

[214] *CJ*, VII, pp. 735, 749 (27 July, 5 Aug.). The English summer assizes that year were held between 18 July and 5 Aug.: PRO, ASSI, 35/100/2–7.

[215] *CJ*, VII, p. 788 (29 Sept.).

[216] PRO, C 231/6, fol. 442 (3 Oct.). Whitelocke noted, 'Sept. 1659. Serjeant Sheppard made a judge in Wales': *Memorials*, IV, p. 362.

[217] Williams, *Great sessions*, p. 17.

his appointment as judge was swept away in a military coup ten days after he was sworn to the bench. For the next two-and-a-half months England was governed by a committee of safety. On 26 December General Monck recalled the Rump for the last time and on 21 February 1660 the once-purged remnant of the Long Parliament was restored. The members who had been excluded in 1648 were invited to resume their places in the house and the long period of rebel government had ended. When the Long Parliament made new appointments to the Welsh bench on 14 March another of Cromwell's serjeants, Evan Seys, was named chief justice of the Anglesey circuit in Sheppard's place.[218] Two days later the Long Parliament dissolved itself after nineteen years of continuous constitutional existence and the path was cleared for the return of a Stuart monarch.

The inexorable flow of events towards a Stuart restoration washed away all possibility that Sheppard might again serve his state in a high official capacity. In January 1660 Sheppard was named to a tax-collection committee for his city and his county, so ending his public career as he had begun it seventeen years earlier.[219] But March his fall from power was so complete that he was excluded from the Gloucestershire militia committee, a group that included many of his interregnum colleagues.[220] When the Act of Indemnity was issued, Sheppard's name was not listed with those incapacitated from holding office, nor was it included among those to whom Charles II issued pardons.[221] He was one of the few serjeants of the interregnum not recalled by the restored monarchy, an ironic fate to befall one of the most prolific legal authors of his age.[222]

Sheppard, who was sixty-four years old at the time of the restoration, spent his remaining years with his family in Hempstead.

---

[218] Ibid., pp. 101–3.   [219] *A & O*, II, p. 1369 (26 Jan. 1660).
[220] Ibid., p. 1431 (Mar. 1660).
[221] PRO, C 231/7, fols. 36, 92, 125 (pardons for Glouc.); *Statutes*, V, p. 232 (12 Car. II, c. 11, s. 38: names of those excepted from Act of Indemnity).
[222] Of the 39 serjeants called between 1648 and 1659, only eight of that number who were still alive in the summer of 1660 were not recalled to their offices by Charles II. Besides Sheppard the others were Roger Hill, John Glynne, Robert Nicholas (Sheppard's brother-in-law), Oliver St John, William Steele, Francis Thorpe and Peter Warburton. I wish to express my thanks to J. H. Baker who provided me with this information from his studies of the order of the coif. The peace commissions also omitted his name, but at 64 years, his age exempted him from public service. BL, Lansd. MS, II, 232, fols. 48, 51 (1670, 1671 peace commissions); GRO, Q/SI b (Quarter sessions records 1660–68); PRO, ASSI 5/1/1, fol. 33 (1661 peace commission); C 220/9/4, fols. 32–4 (1660); 193/12/3 (1662).

Settling into that quiet community, he turned again to his legal studies. Even after the collapse of the government he had supported so ardently he did not despair of improving the law, a pursuit to which he had devoted his energies throughout his writing career. He published another seven books in the next fourteen years, all of them further attempts to classify and abridge the unwieldy mass of the common law. Although he never again engaged in public activities, some of his political attitudes to politics and legal philosophy were inserted parenthetically into his later works. All his optimism of the commonwealth and protectorate years was gone and Sheppard shared with his readers a grim prediction in a 1662 publication: 'It is not improbable but we are now fallen into the last age ، ‾ the world, foretold by our blessed savior, wherein...iniquity shall abound.'[223]

Hearth-tax returns imply that Sheppard and his family lived comfortably though not grandly in his last years.[224] In those surprisingly productive years he remained as devoted to his family as he was dedicated to his legal studies. In 1670 he presented his son-in-law John Clifford with a newly published copy of his fourth book on land law.[225] He also maintained ties with the Cotswold country around Horsley, particularly with his brother Samuel who still lived in the Minchinhampton home he had purchased in 1656. The close relationship between the brothers which had been strengthened by their respective marriages to the Worth sisters and their service together on the county committee during the civil war remained fast through the years. Their mutual affection was expressed by William's gift to his brother of his serjeant's rings and by Samuel's bequests to William's children.[226]

Sheppard continued to work tirelessly at his legal research until the end of his life. He died on 26 March 1674[227] at the age of

---

[223] W. Sheppard, *Action upon the case for slander* (1662), sig. a1v.

[224] Hearth-tax returns for 1672 record Sheppard paying the second highest rate of the 34 assessments in Hempstead: GRO, D 383, pt 2, fol. 131.

[225] Clifford's gift copy of Sheppard's *Law of common assurances* (1670) is held by the Middle Temple library. The fly-leaf inscription, dated 12 Mar. 1670, reads '*ex dono authoris*'.

[226] The 1672 hearth-tax returns show Samuel still living at Gatcombe Abbey near Minchinhampton, the year he died: GRO, D 383, pt 1, fol. 42. William's serjeant's rings were bequeathed to Samuel's heir, Philip, who had also been trained as a barrister at the Middle Temple: PRO, PROB 11/346, fol. 117. Samuel died in Mar. 1672, two years before William.

[227] His will has not been located. It is not with the Canterbury probate records (PRO, PROB) nor with those in the diocese of Gloucester (GRO, *GDR* 218A, fols. 175–252: acts and administrations 1668–76). I would like to thank Father Michael Sheehan for his helpful suggestions towards efforts to locate it.

seventy-eight and was buried in the nave of St Swithin's, Hempstead's fourteenth-century parish church. The inscription on his burial place read *William Sheppard, Ar*[migerous], with the date of his death below. Above the lettering an escutcheon bearing his arms was cut in the stone.[228] His last and most ambitious study, *A grand abridgment*, was accepted for publication by the imprimatur, John Vaughan, in the year after he died and was published in April 1675 by the crown's patentee for legal publications, the Atkins family.[229]

Sheppard's widow, Alice, lived on in Hempstead for nearly two decades after her husband's death and in her will she bequeathed a 20*s.* gold piece that had been minted during the commonwealth almost half a century earlier.[230] That parliamentary coin and the serjeant's rings that provided the family with nostalgic souvenirs were important symbols of Sheppard's commitment to the puritan undertaking. But his legacy to the nation endures in the twenty-seven books he composed and published.

[228] He was buried on 30 Mar. 1674: GRO, P 173, Acc. 3097, IN 1/1, fol. 43v. The flat stones of his burial place can still be seen in the center aisle of the church near the entrance and the baptismal font. The left side is so worn that it is barely legible today and only the outline of the coat of arms is discernible (ermine on a chief embattled sable, three battles axes argent). The church was restored in 1885 and at that time the lower stone with his widow's name was replaced. The full inscription on Sheppard's stone was noted in one of the more reliable eighteenth-century antiquarian studies: Bigland, *Gloucester*, II, p. 67.

[229] Sheppard's *Grand abridgment* was in the press before he died.

[230] Alice Sheppard died on 29 July 1693 and was buried on 31 July with her husband in the Hempstead church: GRO, P, Acc. 3097, IN 1/1, fol. 50v. Her will was probated in the Gloucester Consistory Court: GRO, GDR wills, 1693/13.

2

EARLY LEGAL WORKS, 1641–1654

Everyone, no matter of what rank, should do their duty and so rest assured that the fulfillment of each traditional task was part of the work of justice which rendered it a work of God. 'Cursed is he that doth the work of God negligently.' And what you find here, you have warrant to do; do it, and fear not, for it is written, 'He shall give his angels charge concerning thee, to keep thee in thy ways.'

Introduction, *Constables* (1641), sig. A8r

Let able and fit men be chosen to and kept in these offices. And truly (if I be not mistaken) herein lieth almost the whole work of reformation in church and commonwealth, to make and keep the officers thereof good... Had our bishops and officers about them been chosen out of the best men of the time, doubtless Episcopacy had not been so grievous and odious; and exchange it for Presbytery, and let the Presbyters be ambitious, covetous and contentious, and may not this model be more grievous and odious? The like may be said of the Independent model...[but] 'when the righteous are in authority the people rejoice' (Proverbs 29.2)...Let our justices of the peace then be curiously chosen out of the fittest of men.

Introduction, *The whole office of the country justice of the peace* (1650), sigs. A5r–v

The first ten of Sheppard's twenty-seven books were published in the troubled times between 1641 and 1654 when the nation was learning to cope with the dislocations of the civil war and the uncertainties of the commonwealth. Ten others were written within the concentrated period of four years when he was employed by the protectorate government. The remaining seven went into print after Oliver Cromwell's death, when Sheppard had retired from government service. His subjects were law and religion, reflecting two of the major concerns of that beleaguered generation. The twenty-three books on legal topics spanned a wide range of subjects, including the fields of property law, local law-enforcement, the law of borough corporations, laws relating to religious observance, treatises on the common law and encyclopedic abridgments. His religious compositions have historical interest in that the first three may have brought to Cromwell's notice a country lawyer whose religious convictions accorded well with the goals of the protectorate government.[1]

Sheppard was forty-six years old when he embarked upon his career as an author with the publication of *The offices and duties of constables, borsholders, tythingmen, treasurers of the county stock, overseers of the poore and other lay-ministers : whereunto is adjoyned the severall offices of church-ministers and church-wardens*, the first in a series of instructional handbooks he was to write for the multitude of local law-enforcement personnel.[2] He introduced the book with a thirteen-page 'Epistle' containing an important part of his philosophy of government. Addressing all his 'loving countrymen', Sheppard explained that while there was a plethora of handbooks for magistrates, court stewards and sheriffs, the most recent manual for lesser local officials was outdated, having been published more than twenty years earlier.[3] His hopes that his modernized handbook would reach a large audience were explicitly stated at the outset:

Taking into consideration how commonly (necessity so requiring) the most of you are called and enjoined to take upon you the offices of constables, churchwardens, and the like offices, that there is scarce a man amongst you (at least of the meaner rank) but sooner or later he is forced to serve in some or all of them... and the most of you are very unskillful in the points and matters belonging to the duty of your places: whence it happeneth sometimes (on the right hand) too confidently you exceed your authority and adventure to do that for which you have no warrant; by means whereof the honest officer is sometimes punished and falleth into the hands of the evil man, the lewd and malicious malefactor, hereby escaping his deserved punishment. And more commonly, on the left hand (for he that goeth in the dark knoweth not where he goeth), too fearfully, you go not so far as your authority, nor do so much as you have charge to do; so that albeit these offices be daily executed by many amongst you, yet few of you know the extent of the authority and duties thereof.[4]

So for want of information, the delinquent was encouraged and justice neglected. Sheppard's ideal of a moral and orderly society

[1] For a complete listing of titles, editions and publication dates, including his four religious works, see *Chronological Bibliography*.
[2] Borsholders and tithingmen were archaic terms for officers whose duties coincided with the constabulary. W. Sheppard, *The offices and duties of constables*...(1641, 1652, 1655[?], 1657).
[3] Sheppard was mistaken about the most recent edition of that work. An enlarged version of Lambarde's *Duties of constables, borsholders and tithingmen* was released in 1631.
[4] Sheppard, *Constables*, sig. A2v.

served by well-informed, conscientious, Christian men who would enforce the time-honored law of England became a major theme throughout all his works. All levels of the citizenry had duties and so required a guide to assist them in the execution of their civic responsibilities, especially the 'meaner sort' who filled the lower echelons of the local hierarchies. In summary, Sheppard admonished his audience to read the book over and over again, to keep it always at hand (it was published in a portable octavo edition) and to consult the annexed table of contents for quick reference.[5]

While the greater part of the text concerned constables, the other parish officers mentioned in the title were also described.[6] In each instance, the office was defined, the method of selection stated and the duties delineated, always with marginal notes citing the author's authority. Sheppard relied heavily on the works of Fitzherbert, Kitchin, Lambarde and Dalton and cited relevant statutes and cases in his expositions.[7] Throughout the text he reminded his reader many times of his principal object in preparing the manual: the good order and spiritual well being of each community depended upon the character and ability of the individuals selected to hold positions of authority in the parish and upon the knowledge they had of their responsibilities. This was a theme to which Sheppard returned continually in his writing career. The 1630 *Book of Orders*, which he cited frequently, had directed that constables be chosen from the 'abler sort'. Yet, Sheppard observed, a decade later the tendency continued to 'put these offices upon the meaner sort of men; [and] the more able sort do think themselves thereby exempted, [yet] they are therein much deceived'.[8] According to Sheppard, the reformation of English law must begin with an improvement in the quality of law-enforcement personnel and the dissemination of full and correct information.

Some of Sheppard's religious politics are also found in *Constables* where, in his closing remark in the section on spiritual officers, he advocated supplemental financial support for ministers in parishes

---

[5] The 16-page table of contents included cross-references. Sheppard, *Constables*, sig. A8r.

[6] The distribution of the 359 pages was constables, 78 pp.; ministers, 64 pp.; churchwardens, 45 pp.; overseers of the poor, 37 pp.; surveyors of highways, 12 pp.; treasurers of the county stock and the relief of poor, maimed soldiers and mariners, 4 pp.; treasurers of the county stock for relief of prisoners of the king's bench and marshalsea, 2 pp.

[7] See below, *Sheppard's Sources*.   [8] Sheppard, *Constables*, p. 17.

where tithes did not provide a 'competent allowance and maintenance'. He also referred the reader to a book published in 1620
which had championed the continuance of parish tithes, 'for if none
be, farewell religion; and what then can ensue but the abomination
in the highest places of this kingdom? Which God forbid.'[9]
Sheppard's religious and political philosophy was more precisely
defined in later books and pamphlets, but the major outlines can be
found in *Constables*: ignorance, corruption and the disorderly state
of the common law had all contributed towards creating the
deplorable conditions of his age. If the reformation of English society
were to proceed, justices of the peace and an adequately endowed
ministry, the indispensable mainstays of local government, must
themselves be knowledgeable about the law. Since the effectiveness
of their work depended upon the assistance of reliable subordinates,
Sheppard would put his talents to work sorting out the laws so that
minor public officials would be educated to the extent of their public
responsibilities.

Eleven years later, in 1652, Sheppard published a much shorter
version of *Constables*. Modifying the structure of this commonwealth
edition, he divided it into two separately sold parts, 'for the more
conveniency of purchase and portage'.[10] Book One treated only the
constabulary and was half the length of the corresponding section in
the 1641 edition. Cutting the verbosity meant sacrificing considerable
historical and jurisdictional detail, but the short, seventy-three-page
handbook was more likely to be used because of its compactness.
Some recent laws concerning sabbath observance and prohibitions
against stage plays and maypoles were incorporated into the text, but
most of the duties described were of earlier origin. The second part
of the book eliminated the long section on ministers and dealt only
with seven lesser local officials, again in half the compass of the first
edition. Here, Sheppard apprised his readers of some recent reforms
of legal inadequacies of which he had complained in the earlier
volume. The exigencies of the civil wars and the conflicts in Ireland
and Scotland had led the government to reverse some severe
Elizabethan penalties and to make provisions for returning military
men, an improvement in the law which did not escape Sheppard's
notice. One chapter described the mechanics of pension distribution
with the fee scales for injured combatants as well as the provisions

[9] Ibid., p. 314; Thomas Ryves, *The poore vicars plea* (1620), p. 151.
[10] Sheppard, *Constables* (1652), sig. A4v.

for widows and orphans as established by an ordinance of 1647.[11] Such advances in social services were appreciated by Sheppard but his keen eye noted other flaws in the system that called for improvement. In the first chapter on constables' duties, he expressed the hope that justices of the peace 'may devise some way...to relieve' the constable from the financial burden of personal expenses incurred when on official travel and, in a later work, he introduced the more positive proposal that all officials be paid regular salaries as well as expenses by the state from a county fund.[12] In most respects the second part of this 1652 publication was a condensed version of the first edition although some rewritten parts brought a finer degree of precision to descriptions of the obligations and legal liabilities of the offices discussed. This two-part version was reissued in 1657.

In 1655, when Sheppard was employed by Cromwell, he wrote a third version of *Constables*, expanding the text to twenty chapters and returning to his original one-volume format. Published in the year of Penruddock's rebellion, a time when it was essential that the government reassert its authority in every community, Sheppard revised this edition to accommodate descriptions of virtually all public officials at the local level. To facilitate peace-keeping efforts in the countryside, he added summaries of six offices not included in the earlier volumes. The origins of four lay in common-law tradition: the hayward, responsible for maintaining the hedges of enclosed grounds and seeing that they not be 'broken down or levelled'; the watchman, ordered to arrest and secure suspicious persons under statutory mandate; the bailiff of the manor, who had duties for keeping order; and fair owners.[13] The two new civil offices Sheppard introduced had been created by statute during the war years to supply needs arising from the abolition of the ecclesiastical

---

[11] In the first edition he had protested that poor soldiers and shipwrecked sailors were liable to be accounted felonious rogues under the provisions of 39 Eliz. I, c. 17 if they were, by circumstance, driven to beg or to counterfeit a certificate of passage. He had proposed that the state assume responsibility for these veterans, particularly if they were hurt or maimed, and to assure that they 'be relieved with money' in each county they crossed on their return home: Sheppard, *Constables* (1641), pp. 93–5; *Constables* (1652), pp. 62–7; Ordinance of 28 May 1647: *A & O*, I, p. 938.

[12] Sheppard, *Constables* (1652), ch. 2; *England's balme*, p. 32.

[13] Internal evidence establishes that this was a protectorate edition, the date tentatively established as 1655: see the Ordinance of 1654 cited in ch. 13 and allusions to the powers of the lord protector in ch. 1. The publisher however noted it to be the 'second [sic] edition, with divers additions and alterations agreeable to the late acts and ordinances [n.d.]'. The four common-law officers were discussed in chs. 16, 17, 18 & 20.

establishment. The parish clerk, whose duty was the general maintenance of the church, was made a salaried officer by an act of 1647
and the registrar of the parish had in 1644 been delegated the
responsibility of keeping all church records.[14] The government's
compelling interest in maintaining internal security was underscored
by Sheppard's printing in full the consolidating Highway Ordinance
of 31 March 1654 in the chapter on the surveyor of highways.[15] Apart
from these changes, most of the book reproduced *verbatim* passages
from the 1652 edition.

Seven years after Sheppard published the first edition of *Constables*,
his second book, *The touchstone of common assurances*, appeared in the
London bookshops.[16] Released in 1648, this collection of twenty-three
essays on conveyancing became his most enduring and best-known
work. Sheppard's introductory remarks explained that the book was
the product of notes and observations begun during his student days
at his inn. Over the twenty years of his country practice he had
enlarged upon the original material, developing a reference guide for
his own use until, at the urging of a friend, he decided to make public
his detailed studies of the complex laws of conveyancing. Realizing
that the work would be valuable to law students and practising
lawyers alike, he dedicated the *Touchstone* to 'the benchers of the
Middle Temple and to the rest of the gentlemen of that society' in
a gesture of appreciation for the learning he had acquired in his eight
years of study there.[17]

---

[14] For the parish clerk and the registrar respectively, see W. Sheppard, *Constables*
(1655), chs. 15 & 14; *A & O*, I, p. 1065 (Act of 9 Feb. 1648), p. 582 (Act of
4 Jan. 1645).

[15] W. Sheppard, *Constables* (1655), ch. 13; *A & O*, II, p. 861.

[16] Some 1648 editions carried the title *The learning of common assurances*.
Seventeenth-century publishers would frequently release manuscripts in their
possession to more than one printer with the result that the title pages in different
copies of the same edition could be at variance. When the book was reissued
in 1651 the title was established as the *Touchstone*. The book was first registered
on 12 July 1648 although George Thomason, the book collector, had received
his copy on 26 Mar. 1648: *Sta. Reg.*, I, p. 298; *TT*, I, p. 603. The publication
date has been incorrectly noted as 1641 by a number of legal bibliographers. The
initial date of publication was, however, acknowledged to be 1648 by the editor
of the 1820 London edition: R. Preston (ed.), *Touchstone* (9th edn, 1820–1), sig.
A4v.

[17] Having allowed his connections with his inn to lapse since *c.* 1630, he wrote, 'I
may perhaps have been so long out of your sight that I may be also by this time
out of your minds. Nevertheless, it is not out of my mind that I, having received
that seed of growth of that little knowledge in the laws of this kingdom which
God hath given me in the seedplot of your ancient and honorable society,
do...owe the fruit thereof to you': Sheppard, *Touchstone*, sig. A2r.

Each chapter opened with a definition of one type of conveyance and was followed by a description of the rules, principles and legal maxims that governed the conveyance. His comments were supported by textual authorities and case examples and he included variations and specific conditions as well as limitations. The detailed expositions were necessarily lengthy and in the preface Sheppard explained that even after three decades of study, 'For my own part I must ingenuously profess that I can scarce look into a title or meddle with a conveyance of weight wherein I cannot make and move more doubts and questions than I am able to resolve and answer.' Every known circumstance of conveyancing that might serve as a precedent had therefore been searched out by the author and included with a citation to his source until he was satisfied that his extensive investigations were accurate and not misleading.[18] Sheppard extracted information from more than a score of fifteenth- and sixteenth-century sources, bringing together scattered cases, legal maxims and definitions from abridgments, Year Books, books of entries, reports and other early legal literature. He relied most heavily upon contemporary printed works, particularly Coke's *Reports* (1600–16) and the *First Institute* (1628). The same penchant for modern material was seen in his selection of cases. More than 175 Jacobean decisions are reported, as compared to seventy-five from Elizabeth's reign and a smaller sampling dating back to the thirteenth century. No fewer than twenty-five cases date from the years of his country practice after he left the Middle Temple.[19] The pioneering monograph that Sheppard brought into print was an unusual type of book for its day and it remained highly valued by the profession for two centuries. He later duplicated the approach used in its composition in his encyclopedic collections and in his two treatises on actions on the

---

[18] Ibid., sig. A3v. In the preface, Sheppard had assured his readers, 'There are few material things as touching this subject to be found anywhere dispersed in the volumes of law but they are not found somewhere herein and that there shall not happen one case in a hundred but a hundred to one the diligent reader may here find the case itself, or some case that by good inference may apply to it': ibid., sig. A4v.

[19] Cases heard between 1628 when Sheppard was about to be called to the bar and 1648, the date of publication, are found in ibid. pp. 67, 81, 115, '138', 165, 166, 171, 181, 226 (twice), 239, 246, 262, 264, 271, 272, 282, 323, 324, 369, 387, 394, 447, 464, 516.

[20] The *Faithfull councellor*, I & II (1651, 1654), the *Epitome* (1656), and the *Grand abridgment* (1675); *Action upon the case for slander* (1662) and *Actions upon the case for deeds* (1663).

case.[20] And yet this book which typifies so well Sheppard's method and style as a legal author has, since the eighteenth century, been attributed by many to John Dodderidge, J.K.B. (1612–28).

The allegation that Sheppard did not write the *Touchstone* can be traced to an incriminating report written by J. Booth of Lincoln's Inn on the title page of his personal copy of the book in about 1760. Twenty years later, when the first posthumous edition of the *Touchstone* was printed, Hilliard, the editor, reproduced in its entirety the inscription in Booth's copy.

No part of this work is Sheppard's but the title, for it was originally wrote by Justice Dodderidge, whose library Sheppard purchased, where, among other books, he found the original manuscript of this treatise, and afterwards published it as his own. Sir Creswell Levinz had seen the manuscript in Justice Dodderidge's hands, and from him Mr Pigott, who was my author, had this information.[21]

Hilliard was convinced by the charge of Sheppard's plagiarism for he added his own comment that 'a report, propagated by persons so respectable, amounts almost to a certainty'.[22] Subsequent editions of the *Touchstone* reprinted Hilliard's accusation, and by the turn of the nineteenth century the charge against Sheppard had grown from Booth's hearsay report into well-established legend.[23]

The *Touchstone* is, nonetheless, filled with evidence of Sheppard's authorship. In addition to the method and the style, both character-istic of Sheppard's later works, and with its frequent citations to sources published after Dodderidge's death, the subject matter itself bears the mark of Sheppard's hand. The *Touchstone* is the work of a practising conveyancer while Dodderidge's works, on the other hand, are either historical studies or of a more theoretical nature. The

---

[21] Quoted by Hilliard in W. Sheppard, *Touchstone* (1780), ed. Edward Hilliard, pp. 503–4.

[22] Quoted in 'Mr Hilliard's Address' by Richard Preston (ed.), *Touchstone* (1820), sig. c1r.

[23] Sheppard was not the only Cromwellian retainer to have his reputation blackened in the mid eighteenth century. John Milton was accused in 1749 of plagiarizing the entire text of *Paradise lost* from a number of sixteenth- and seventeenth-century neo-Latin authors: J. L. Clifford, 'Johnson and Lauder', *Philological Quarterly*, LIV (1975), 342–56; M. J. Marcuse, 'The pre-publication history of William Lauder's "An essay on Milton's use and imitation of the moderns in his *Paradise lost*"', *The papers of the Bibliographical Society of America*, LXXII (1978), 37–57. I am grateful to Dr Jason P. Rosenblatt for this information about the eighteenth-century attack on Milton and for the sources cited above.

early-Stuart judge wrote on the origins and powers of parliament;[24] a scholarly study on the royal prerogative and another on the Anglo-Scottish union projected by James I;[25] a history of the governments of Wales, Cornwall and Chester;[26] and a treatise on legal study prepared as a guide to an English lawyer's education.[27] He also 'perused and enlarged upon' a treatise by William Bird on 'the several degrees of nobility in this kingdom'.[28] His 1602 reading on advowsons at New Inn which was published in 1630 had circulated in manuscript before publication.[29] Two other works which have been ascribed to Dodderidge are an essay on the legal rights of women and a treatise on executors' responsibilities.[30] None

[24] J. Dodderidge et al., The several opinions of sundry learned antiquaries : viz. Mr Justice Dodderidge, Mr Agar, Francis Tate, William Canden [sic] and Joseph Holland : touching the antiquity, power, order, state, manner, persons and proceedings of the high-court of parliament in England, ed. John Dodderidge (the younger) (1658).

[25] A treatise on the royal prerogative 'A breefe project', BL, Harl. MS 5220, fols. 3–21), and another on the Anglo-Scottish union, 'A brief consideration of the union of twoe kingdomes in the handes of one kinge' (BL, Sloane MS 3479, fols. 59r–67v), are mentioned by Knafla, Law and politics, pp. 71, 184.

[26] John Dodderidge, A history of the ancient and moderne estate of the principality of Wales, the dutchy of Cornewall and earldome of Chester (1630).

[27] John Dodderidge, The English lawyer, describing a method for the managing of the lawes of this land (1631). The third section of this treatise, 'Methodus studendi', circulated in manuscript before 1631 and it is quite possible that it was in circulation even before Dodderidge's death in 1628. One surviving manuscript copy held by The Folger Shakespeare Library has 66 pages at the beginning of a student's commonplace book entitled 'Judge Dodderidge his method for the study and practise of the common law of England': Folger Shakespeare Library, MS v.b. 184, pt I, 66 fols. From internal evidence in the latter part of this commonplace book it appears that the material following Dodderidge's treatise was entered prior to 1624. The last date recorded in the book is 1624 and Lionel Cranfield is mentioned as master of the wardrobe, a position Cranfield held from 1618 to 1624: ibid., pt II, fols. 128, 146. Dodderidge's 'Methodus studendi' was also published in 1629 as The lawyer's light : or, a due direction for the study of the law; see below, n. 39.

[28] William Bird, The magazine of honour : or, a treatise of the severall degrees of the nobility of this kingdome, with their rights and priviledges, ed. John Dodderidge (1642).

[29] John Dodderidge, A compleat parson (1630). J. H. Baker has located surviving manuscript copies of Dodderidge's reading in BL, Add. MS 32092; Inner Temple, MS Misc. 37; Harvard Law School, MS 2025. I am grateful to Dr Baker for this information.

[30] John Dodderidge, The lawes resolutions of women's rights (1632); The office and duty of executors : or, a treatise of wills and executors, directed to testators (1641, 1676). This short treatise on executors, first published anonymously, has since been attributed to both Dodderidge and Sir Thomas Wentworth: DNB: sub Wentworth.

of these known works resembles in subject, style or length the 529-page guide for conveyancers that Booth credited to him.

The opinion that Dodderidge and not Sheppard was the author of the *Touchstone* remained publicly undisputed for twenty years until two legal bibliographers challenged it in the first decade of the nineteenth century. R. W. Bridgman and John Clarke both noted that the work could not possibly have been written by the Stuart judge because a great part of the text was founded upon Coke's *First Institute* which was first published in 1628, the year of Dodderidge's death.[31] Yet other cataloguers and bibliographers continued to give Dodderidge credit for the work and Sheppard's reputation remained besmirched. The story of Sheppard's purchase of Dodderidge's library also persisted and, as with all rumors, changed through the years so that by the 1850s a book collector could record that there had been a sale of the deceased judge's library at which Sheppard had purchased the manuscript of the *Touchstone*.[32]

No record has been found of a public sale of Dodderidge's library, but fragments of information when pieced together suggest a plausible account of the events surrounding the dispersal of Dodderidge's personal legal papers. Justice John Dodderidge was, like Sheppard, a Middle Templar and over the course of his seventy-three years had served as a member of parliament, reader of his inn, solicitor-general, and ultimately as a puisne judge of king's bench. His last eight years on the bench coincided with the period when Sheppard was studying at the Middle Temple and attending the central courts during law terms. The fact that Dodderidge and other contemporary judges had an important influence on the development of Sheppard's legal thought is attested to in Sheppard's later legal writings.[33] The childless Dodderidge died in 1628 and his estate was inherited by his brother Pentecost of Barnstaple, Devon. In the

---

[31] Bridgman, *Legal bibliography*, p. 344; Clarke, *Bibliotheca legum*, p. 237. However, in the 1920s, Holdsworth suggested that Dodderidge might have used the manuscript of Coke's *First Institute* when writing the *Touchstone* and that Sheppard, when editing the manuscript later, inserted the references to the printed edition: *HEL*, V, p. 391.

[32] Charles Purton Cooper's note in the fly-leaf of his copy of Sheppard's *Parson's guide*, printed in annotated publication of Sotheby's sale of 1852: *Bib. Coop.*, p. 85.

[33] Sheppard cited eight of Dodderidge's decisions in the *Touchstone*: Sheppard, *Touchstone*, pp. 7, 36, 124, 130, 163, 345, 383, 419. Dodderidge's decisions were also cited in the *Faithfull councellor*, I, the *Epitome* and *Actions upon the case for deeds*. For influence of other contemporaries, see below, nn. 50 & 52.

following year, 1629, Pentecost Dodderidge sent his nineteen-year-old son John to study law at the Middle Temple, the inn to which the young student's illustrious uncle had been attached. Subsequent events lead to the conjecture that the judge's professional collection of manuscripts and books may have been given to his nephew and namesake by the legal heir, Pentecost.[34] Thirty years later the younger Dodderidge published his only book, a collection of tracts on parliament which included an essay written by his uncle.[35] The younger Dodderidge's regard for this tract apparently did not extend to the judge's other learned studies because Judge Dodderidge's manuscripts were dispersed between 1629 and 1632 and London booksellers brought into print five posthumous books from manuscripts acquired from the estate.[36] The fact that the younger Dodderidge was studying at the Middle Temple after 1629 (he was called to the bar in 1637), during the same years his uncle's works were first published, suggests that the law student was responsible for the dispersal of at least part of Dodderidge's library. In any event, the individual who released the Dodderidge manuscripts to printers, whether it was the nephew or someone else, might have sold other of the judge's papers as well. In 1629, when Sheppard was called to

---

[34] The Middle Temple admitted the young John Dodderidge under a special fine on 26 June 1629, 'being nephew and heir to John Dodderidge, knt, late judge of the king's bench': *M. T. Ad. Reg.*, I, p. 122; *M. T. Min.*, II, pp. 754–5. See also *DNB*: *sub* J. Dodderidge (1555–1628); Foss, *Judges*, VI, pp. 306–10; Haydn, *Dignities*, pp. 372, 401, 409; Williams, *Glouc. parl. hist.*, p. 116.

[35] The younger Dodderidge had a strong personal interest in parliament. He sat for Barnstaple in the Long Parliament from 1646 until he was ejected by Pride's purge in 1648; he represented Devonshire in the parliament of 1654 and was again elected county representative in 1656 and, although he was excluded from the first session by the council of state, he was permitted to take his seat at the second session: *Burton's diary*, II, pp. 418, 436, 457; *Index of speakers*, p. 11; Underdown, *Pride's purge*, p. 371. He signed the preface to *Several opinions touching parliament* on 3 Dec. 1657, prior to being admitted to the second session of the 1656 parliament: Dodderidge (ed.), *Several opinions*, p. [23].

[36] Judge Dodderidge's first three posthumous books were published by three different publishers: *The lawyer's light* (1629) by Benjamin Fisher; *A history of Wales, Cornwall and Chester* (1630) by Godfrey Edmondson and Thomas Alchorne; and *A compleat parson* (1630) by John Grove. Of these men, only Grove is known to have specialized in law books: R. B. McKerrow (ed.), *A dictionary of printers and booksellers in England, Scotland, Ireland, and of foreign printers of English books 1557–1640* (1910), pp. 4, 104–5, 118–19. The fourth and fifth books. *The English lawyer* (1631) and *The lawes resolutions of women's rights* (1632), were published by the assigns of John More who held the king's patent for the monopoly of all law-book publications. The 1632 book was sold by Grove.

the bar of the Middle Temple, he was preparing to return to Gloucestershire to establish a country practice. If there had been a Dodderidge manuscript dealing with basic principles of conveyancing which he had the opportunity to purchase, it is only reasonable to conclude that he would have done so. Given the sparse evidence, it must remain a matter of conjecture whether or not the *Touchstone* was founded upon a Dodderidge manuscript Sheppard acquired between 1629 and 1632, the year he left London.

There are further observations that must be considered in relation to the charge that Sheppard plagiarized Dodderidge's work. According to Booth, Pigott had been told by Levinz that he, Levinz, had seen a manuscript copy of the *Touchstone* 'in Justice Dodderidge's hands'. This report, if true, could not possibly mean that Levinz had seen the manuscript in Dodderidge's possession since Levinz was born in 1627 and Dodderidge died in 1628.[37] Pigott's allegation (according to Booth) of Levinz's report of a Dodderidge manuscript may have been a reference to holograph notes written in the judge's hand that were in circulation in 1655 when Levinz first entered Gray's Inn. Although this would have been seven years after Sheppard first published the *Touchstone*, it is possible that a short treatise on conveyancing by Dodderidge was still in circulation in the legal community (as his reading on advowsons and his '*Methodus studendi*' had been) and that Sheppard may have copied the same treatise years before in his student notes without knowing it was the work of Dodderidge. Sheppard was scrupulous about citing his authorities in his published works and advocated the passage of a stern law of copyright in *England's balme*, his compendium of law reform proposals.[38] But he was also curiously uninformed about Dodderidge's works and the *Touchstone* itself contains two errors in attribution. Sheppard ascribed both *The lawyer's light* and *The use of the law* to Dodderidge and although the two treatises were published in a single volume in 1629, the latter was not by Dodderidge.[39] Moreover, Sheppard cited *The lawes resolutions of*

---

[37] *DNB*: *sub* Dodderidge (1555–1628); *sub* Levinz (1627–1701).

[38] W. Sheppard, *England's balme*, p. 182.

[39] Benjamin Fisher, the publisher, wrote in an introduction to the volume that *The lawyer's light* was the work of the deceased 'reverend and learned professor [of the law], J. D.' and while he could not identify the author of *The use of the law*, he suggested that the two treatises were 'so like as if they were *gemini horoscope uno*'. He also explained that he was publishing the two essays 'not as *proximiores sanguinis* or proper executors of the will of the deceased, but as creditors to whom

women's rights as one of his sources in the *Touchstone* and was unable to identify the author although knowledgeable contemporaries might have attributed it to Dodderidge.[40] If the *Touchstone* could be shown to be an enlargement of a Dodderidge manuscript on conveyancing, then it would have to be described thenceforward as *Sheppard on Dodderidge's Touchstone*.[41] And if a Dodderidge manuscript on conveyancing is ever discovered, the credit will still be Sheppard's

---

the administration of their [the two authors] good intentions for the public is committed': *The lawyer's light* (1629), 3 unsignatured leaves at the beginning of the book. Sheppard mistakenly assumed that the pair had been written by Dodderidge and, throughout his writing career, always referred to *The lawyer's light* as 'Justice Dodderidge's treatise' and to *The use of the law* as 'the appendix to Just. Dodderidge's treatise': W. Sheppard, *Touchstone*, pp. 266, 475, 485, 501. Sheppard used the same citations in his *Faithfull councellor*, I, and his *Epitome*. See below, *Sheppard's Sources*, sub Bacon and n. 1.

Fisher's confession that his acquisition of the two essays was not due to his being either a close relative or an executor lends credence to the theory that he knew Dodderidge's personal papers had been or still remained in the custody of a legal executor. The Dodderidge essay that Fisher did acquire and publish was in general circulation at the time and is identical to MS V.b. 184 in The Folger Shakespeare Library collection. See above, n. 27. Two years after Fisher published the two treatises, in 1631, the assigns of John More, the patentee who held the monopoly for legal publications, published the complete Dodderidge treatise in three sections under the title *The English lawyer* (1631). The publishers named Dodderidge as the author and stated in the introduction, 'the later part of this volume [sect. 3, '*Methodus studendi*'] was heretofor obscurely printed by an imperfect copy from a then unknown [sic] author under the title, *The lawyer's light*: we now reimprint it in a fair light, by the author's own copy, written (for the most part) with his own hand; we vouch his name and entitle it, as he himself did, *The English lawyer*. The other part hereof which was not formerly printed we now also put forth according to the author's own copy': Dodderidge, *The English lawyer* (1631), sig. A2r. The added parts were the first section on the natural abilities required for the study of the law (pp. 1–26); and the second section on the intellectual virtues and the areas of knowledge necessary for legal study (pp. 27–148); the third section, '*Methodus studendi*', was printed on pp. 149–271. The publishers' claim of having the 'author's own copy' was undoubtedly true, because they included in the table of contents detailed descriptions of two additional treatises projected by Dodderidge which the publishers explained were either not written or 'not found as yet'. The second treatise was to have been on 'a counsellor, or practiser of the laws' and the third on 'a judge'. The publishers' claim that their book was the official version implies that they had acquired the rights to this official version from the Dodderidge estate: ibid., sigs. A2r–A4r; Plomer, *Booksellers*, p. 131.

40 W. Sheppard, *Touchstone*, pp. 279, 281; cited again without the author's name in the *Faithfull councellor*, I, and in the *Epitome*.

41 Or, *Sheppard on Dodderidge's common assurances*, in the sense that Coke's *First Institute* was also known as *Coke on Littleton*['*s Tenures*].

for bringing into print a long monograph illustrated with cases that was valued by the legal community for more than two centuries. Any consideration of the charge of plagiarism against Sheppard must take into account the credibility of his detractors as they were quoted by Booth a century after the initial publication of the *Touchstone*. Preston, a nineteenth-century editor of the book, ventured an explanation for the persistent slur on Sheppard's reputation when he conceded 'the name of Sheppard had not any charms for the profession'.[42] The personal discredit Sheppard suffered at the time of the restoration had a brutally damaging impact on his professional reputation. Levinz (1627–1701), who purportedly was the original source of the allegation, established strongly royalist connections after being called to the bar in 1661.[43] The second defamer, Nathaniel Pigott (1661–1737), who was said to have heard the story from Levinz, wrote a book on common recoveries and is said to have compiled an index to the *Touchstone*. His interest in the book explains his seeking information about its author from Levinz, a younger contemporary of Sheppard.[44] It takes little imagination to surmise that the royalist servant Levinz was capable of either perpetrating or repeating an accusation of plagiarism against a retainer of the despised Cromwell. Certainly both Levinz and Pigott would be inclined to give full credit for the *Touchstone* to a respected judge who had served the first Stuart king rather than to acknowledge a disgraced puritan politician as the author.

The *Touchstone* was reissued as a monograph only once in

---

[42] Preston also acknowledged that the *Touchstone* 'had, like the other works which bear the name of Sheppard, been neglected or discarded': R. Preston, ed., *Touchstone* (1820), sig. A2r, p. 1.

[43] Levinz entered Gray's Inn in 1655 and was called to the bar in 1661; he was knighted and served as counsel to the crown in 1678, was named attorney-general in 1679 and was raised to the bench the following year. He sat with Judge Jeffries at the 'Bloody Assizes' and presided at the Rye-House-plot trial of Lord Russell: *DNB*: *sub* Levinz. Levinz is also known for having 'assiduously promoted the king's political interests' when riding the Western assize circuit in 1685: Cockburn, *Assizes*, p. 253.

[44] Pigott was called to the bar of the Inner Temple in 1688: *DNB*: *sub* Pigott. His book was entitled *A treatise of common recoveries, their nature and use* (1739); 2nd edn, 'revised and corrected by a serjeant-at-law [G. Wilson]' (1770). J. Booth who recorded the Levinz–Pigott allegation against Sheppard was probably James Charles Booth who had been admitted to the bar of either the Middle Temple or the Inner Temple in 1721 and later, in Nov. 1740, was admitted to Lincoln's Inn: Lincoln's Inn, *The records of the honorable society of Lincoln's Inn, Admissions* (1896), I, p. 421.

Sheppard's lifetime and that edition of 1651 is identical to the original, save for the first leaf of the introduction.[45] Sheppard later republished the entire contents of the book in his encyclopedic abridgments of 1656 and 1675, inserting the chapters into the longer texts in alphabetical order.[46] The appearance of the first posthumous edition after a lapse of more than a century was due to the citation of Sheppard's book by Willes, C.J.C.P., in *Roe* d. *Wilkinson* v. *Tranmer* in 1758.[47] Willes' use of its authority from the bench prompted a revived interest in the work and it was reprinted in London in 1780, 1784, 1790, 1791, 1820–1 and 1826; in Dublin in 1785; and in American editions in 1808–10 and 1840–1. Eighteenth- and nineteenth-century editors reproduced the original text *verbatim*, enlarging the contents with recent decisions and notes from Blackstone's *Commentaries* and other works. It is a creditable testimonial to Sheppard that his *Touchstone* continued to draw high compliments from its editors two centuries after its first publication and the respect accorded the book (if not the author) assured its prominence among the classical legal texts of the modern Anglo-American tradition.[48]

[45] The headpiece on the first leaf was changed from a crown to a non-royal decoration in the 1651 commonwealth edition, but the 529 pages of text, the dedication and the table are identical. Even printers' errors (pp. 349–52, 376–8) were duplicated which suggests the type was not reset and that the second edition was merely a reissue of the 1648 copy with a new introductory page (sig. A2r). Seventeenth-century booksellers would often change a title page and re-date it to sell back stock. For another view of the small number of sales of the *Touchstone*, see ch. 3 for Sheppard's introduction to the 2nd edition of his *President of presidents*.

[46] See chs. 3 and 5 for discussions of the *Epitome* (1656) and the *Grand abridgment* (1675) respectively.

[47] *Willes's Reports*, pp. 684, 686; 2 *Wilson* at p. 28. Fourteen years earlier, in 1744, Willes had expressed dissatisfaction with Pigott's book on common recoveries. In his decision in *Martin* d. *Tragonwall* v. *Strachan*, he said when noting contradictions on pp. 18 and 21, 'I do not mention this to reflect on Mr Pigott, for he was certainly a very learned man in this part of the law, and a very good conveyancer. But I mention it only to show that when the greatest men endeavor to maintain points which are not maintainable, and to give reasons for things which are not founded in reason, they will necessarily be forced to talk inconsistently. And Mr Pigott has himself admitted on page 37 of the same book, where he says very truly of these recoveries... that the reasons given for the operation of recoveries favor a wonderful subtilty': *English Reports*, CXXV, p. 1263. It is an ironic coincidence that the judge who was responsible for the revived interest in Sheppard and his *Touchstone* was publicly critical of Sheppard's detractor.

[48] Hilliard called the *Touchstone* 'a very excellent and concise treatise' and in the 1791 edition added, 'The very speedy sale of a large impression of the last folio edition of this work hath confirmed the editor in the opinion he originally

The *Touchstone* also commands interest for the biographical details it provides about Sheppard's career and his professional contacts in the years prior to 1648. The impressive number of sources he called upon, both traditional and recent, indicates that he had either acquired or had access to a remarkable collection of books on the law at his home in Gloucestershire. His citations to recently published books were factors of considerable importance in his success as a compiler of new developments in the law.[49] A second characteristic of his writing which is first seen in the *Touchstone* is the number of cases of his own report which had been heard on the Oxford and Western assize circuits and in the courts of the Welsh Marches. His inclusion of cases decided by Jones, J. (Oxford circuit 1622–34), Whitelocke, J. (Oxford circuit 1625, 1629–32), Hutton, J. (Western circuit 1617–25) and Denham, B. (Western circuit 1617–25) indicate that he spent as much time as possible in the country even during his student years.[50] Conversely, he cited no Westminster cases of his own report after 1630 when his law practice was confined to the west country.

The strong personal influence of John Bridgman, Chief Justice of Chester (1626–38), on Sheppard's legal thought is also first observable in the *Touchstone*. There are eleven citations to the judge's opinions in the text and only one refers to a case decision. The first citation reads, 'Justice Bridgman, opinion in private' and nine subsequent references note simply, 'per Just. Bridgman' [n.d.]. The last attribution reads, 'and of this opinion were Sir John Walter and

---

entertained of the intrinsic merit of the *Touchstone*': W. Sheppard, *Touchstone* (1780), p. 503; (1791), p. vii. Preston wrote in the introduction to the 1820 edition, 'For the soundness of its propositions, its succinct method and its excellent arrangement, this book is not surpassed by any work on the law': *Touchstone* (1820), p. xviii. The *Touchstone* was cited in American cases even before the publication of the American editions: *Webster's lessee* v. *Hall*, 2 *Harris and M'Henry*, pp. 19, 23 (*Maryland Reports*, 1782).

49 See below, *Sheppard's Sources*.
50 Sheppard, *Touchstone*, cites Jones, pp. 271, 282, 299, 324, 453, 487; Whitelocke, p. 282; Hutton, pp. 246, 476; Denham, pp. 228, 230; cases heard at Gloucester assizes, pp. 39, 166, 299, 487; at Salisbury assizes, pp. 228, 230; and in Wales, pp. 378, 387. J. H. Baker has also noticed that 'Sheppard cited a number of west country cases in the *Marrow* [*Faithfull councellor*, I] and the *Grand abridgment*, which are quite possibly of his own reporting or recollection': J. H. Baker, 'Counsellors and barristers', *CLJ*, XXVII (1969), p. 227, n. 38. The information on judges riding assize circuits has been taken from Cockburn, *Assizes*, pp. 270–2.

Sir John Bridgman upon deliberate advise'.[51] The frequent citations to Bridgman's opinions in this and later works reveal that Sheppard enjoyed the privilege of personal access to the judge and the benefit of his studied views on various points of law. Bridgman's residence at Nympsfield was a few miles from Sheppard's home in Horsley. Twenty-seven years older than Sheppard, Bridgman was a bencher and reader of the Inner Temple who was created serjeant-at-law in 1623 and was appointed to head the Welsh bench in 1626, a position he held until his death in 1638. In the same twelve years he attended to his periodic duties at Chester, he served concurrently as recorder of Gloucester, Shrewsbury and Ludlow. Since none of these posts required residency, Bridgman kept his Nympsfield home and Sheppard evidently spent many hours with his eminent neighbor in the years 1629–37 when the two lived in such close proximity to one another. As mentor to the beginning lawyer, Bridgman had a wealth of knowledge to share which Sheppard duly transcribed into the *Touchstone* and later works.[52]

One of the basic tenets of Sheppard's legal philosophy that was first mentioned in the *Touchstone* was that the laws by which a society is governed should be in a language understood by its people, including all written laws, judicial proceedings and records and all books pertaining to the law. In the introduction he took pride in likening himself to Coke, Finch and Dodderidge, whose books in the vernacular had been well received. The popular demand that law French and Latin be abolished from all legal proceedings and records was satisfied within two years of the *Touchstone*'s publication and Sheppard made significant contributions towards 'turning the law into English' during the interregnum. Even after the restoration

---

[51] Sheppard, *Touchstone*, pp. 7, 63, 137, 153, 167, 169, 272, 274, 387, 398, 459. John Walter was solicitor-general in 1621 and shared chambers with Bridgman at the Inner Temple for many years.

[52] References to Bridgman's personal opinions are found in the *Faithfull councellor*, I & II, the *Epitome*, *Actions upon the case for deeds*, the *Law of common assurances* and the *Grand abridgment*. Sheppard's familiarity with the provisions of the *Book of orders* which he mentioned in *Constables* may be due in part to the fact that the enforcement of its rules in the eleven Welsh counties had been entrusted to Bridgman 'during the vacancy of the lord president of the council of the Welsh Marches': *Orders for the better administration of justice* (1630), sigs. K1v–K2r. Bridgman's only printed work was published posthumously in 1659 by 'J.H.' of the Middle Temple. It is an English translation of 55 reports by Bridgman, most of them common-pleas cases dating prior to 1626, when Bridgman's chief residence was still in London: [J. H., ed.], *Reports of Sir John Bridgman* (1659). For John Bridgman, see Foss, *Judges*, VI, p. 29; Haydn, *Dignities*, pp. 386, 409; Willcox, *Gloucestershire*, p. 207; Williams, *Great sessions*, pp. 34–5.

when the medieval languages were readopted by the courts and by many legal authors, Sheppard remained faithful to his own philosophy and continued to write all of his books in English.[53]

Another of Sheppard's convictions articulated in the *Touchstone* was his advocacy of a well-trained legal profession taking sole responsibility for the preparation of legal documents and the process of adjudication. Although he wrote this book as a reference guide primarily for the use of students and practitioners, he acknowledged that his second aim was to teach men of property 'to see by the view of an infinite variety of cases...how much there goes to making up of an able conveyancer'.[54] This purpose was set out in immediate conjunction with two caveats: when looking for any particular point of information, the reader was admonished to read the whole chapter surrounding the issue to gain a contextual understanding; and the author also warned against reliance upon the book's information unless it were complemented by advice from a trained lawyer. Published at a time when the legal profession was under attack for the responsibilities of its members in adding to the expenses and obfuscations of the law, the *Touchstone* contained its author's strong indictment of lay conveyancers. Sheppard wrote,

And considering withal the mischief arising everywhere by rash adventures of sundry ignorant men that meddle in these weighty matters, there being now in almost every parish an unlearned, and yet confident pragmatical attorney (not that I think them all to be such), or a lawless scrivener that

53 W. Sheppard, *Touchstone*, sig. B1v; *A & O*, II, p. 455 (22 Nov. 1650). In the introduction where Sheppard wrote, 'The wisdom of parliament hath thought to command all the statute laws to the people in English, and to appoint that pleadings should be in English', he could not have been referring (in 1648) to the Rump Parliament's decree of Nov. 1650 that ordered all pleadings and records to be translated into the vernacular. There was, however, a fourteenth-century statute (36 Edw. III, stat. 1, c. 15) that had ordered pleading, arguments and judgments to be delivered in English in all courts. Although this statute seems never to have been implemented, Coke quoted almost one-third of its text in his *First Institute* (1628), an authority which Sheppard cited extensively in the *Touchstone*. Coke's extraction from the original statute was essentially an *apologia* for his own translation from the law French and he was careful to quote only the most general phrases of the statute which mentioned that the 'laws and customs...be learned and used in the tongue of the country' so that every man might 'the better keep, save and defend his heritage and possessions': Edward Coke, *The first part of the institutes of the lawes of England* (1628), p. 2v. Coke's deliberate misrepresentation of the provisions of the fourteenth-century statute appears to have misled Sheppard, at least concerning an order for statutes to be turned into English. Sheppard's reliance upon Coke's authority was very marked throughout his writing career, but it should be noticed that this trait was not unique to Sheppard, either in the seventeenth century or subsequently.

54 W. Sheppard, *Touchstone*, sig. A4r.

may perhaps have some law book in their houses, but never read more law than is on the backside of *Littleton*; or an ignorant vicar, or it may be a blacksmith, carpenter or weaver, that have no more books of law in their houses than they have law in their heads; and yet is apt and able...to dispatch without any scruple any business whatsoever offered to their hands...(an evil fit for the consideration of a parliament)...[A]nd therefore these men have gotten the start of me much. And yet (much marvel it is to see) how these empirics of the law (if I may so call them) are sought unto and made use of...the which is not for lack of opportunity of finding more learned men in the law, for there is a sufficient store of them in all places; nor do those that employ these empirics of the law always save (if they think it saved) money hereby, for besides the great mischief which is oft times done by themselves by the unskilfullness of these workmen, some of them by reason of their much custom are grown more chargeable than an ordinary counsellor whose fee is certain and known.[55]

Sheppard called these amateur practitioners 'usurpers upon and intruders into other men's callings', charging that they 'thrust their sickles into other men's harvests and that they have not yet learned that rule of divinity, "to abide in the calling wherein they are called"'.[56] Sheppard's admonitions about the complexities involved in drawing conveyances were certainly justified, but his absolute dismissal of lay conveyancers was unwarrantably exaggerated. That non-professional class of notaries had practiced since the twelfth century and many of them were quite capable. Although there were many misfortunes that ensued from poorly drawn conveyances, lay conveyancers continued to practice until 1804 when all land-transfer business was restricted to members of the legal profession.[57] Sheppard's intractable position on his profession retaining a monopoly in the preparation of conveyances was, however, understandable given the lack of deed registries and the critical climate of 1648 when proposals were heard to abolish the legal profession altogether. A few years later Sheppard devised a simplified form for registering conveyances,[58] but throughout his career he continued to advocate the imperative need for a well-trained legal profession. The

---

[55] Ibid., sigs. A3r–A4r. C. W. Brooks has remarked that scriveners were the most numerous group of men performing legal services in the late sixteenth century and that the oath of the Scriveners' Company of London 'indicates that the writing of deeds was the main work of its members': 'The common lawyers in England, c. 1558–1642', in *Lawyers in early modern England and America*, ed. Wilfred Prest (1981), p. 49.

[56] W. Sheppard, *Touchstone*, sig. A4r.

[57] *HEL*, VI, p. 447.

[58] See ch. 3 for discussion of Sheppard's *President of presidents* (1655, 1656).

Touchstone was an ambitious undertaking, even for a barrister with twenty years experience. Its favorable reception encouraged Sheppard to venture further into the field of legal publications.

In 1649 he published his third book on the law and the subject matter was again drawn from a major aspect of his country practice. The *Court-keepers guide*, an instructional manual for manor lords and their stewards, was one of his most successful legal handbooks and his publishers sent five editions into print within thirteen years, all corrected and modernized by the author.[59] The continuing marketability of Sheppard's guide was the most telling indication of its popular acceptance since seventeenth-century publishers retained all rights respecting texts in their possession and the decision to reissue this type of book was made solely on commercial grounds. Handbooks for manorial courts were a conventional type of legal literature and the unusual success of Sheppard's manual can be credited to his maturing skill as a compiler and to the command he had over his material. At the time Sheppard's guide was published, he presided as steward over at least seven manor courts in Gloucestershire and it is likely that he held other courts in neighboring counties as well. His earliest traced appointment as steward was at his home in Horsley manor where he had drawn up a set of by-laws and orders 'for the better government' of the community in 1630, the year after he had been called to the bar.[60] Sheppard's considerable experience with these franchises made him keenly aware of the need for a well-organized guide because although many stewards were trained barristers, the customary law of these local courts was not included in the learning exercises at the inns of court. The increasing case loads carried by the central courts in the seventeenth century must not

---

[59] W. Sheppard, *The court-keepers guide* (1649, 1650, 1654, 1656, 1662). The publication date of the *Court-keepers guide* is listed as 1641 by Allibone, *Critical dictionary*, II, p. 2076; *DNB: sub* William Sheppard; *HEL*, IV, p. 121; F. J. C. Hearnshaw, *Leet jurisdiction in England* (Southampton, 1908), p. 36. A search of the Stationers' Registers, the *Thomason Tracts* and extant copies of the book fails to substantiate the 1641 date. The first edition of the book can be dated to 1649 on the strength of Sheppard's statement in the introduction, 'this is the third piece of our law...that I have put into English': sig. A1r. *Constables* (1641) and the *Touchstone* (1648) are known to be the earlier two. Furthermore, a reckoning from the numbers assigned to later editions corroborates 1649 as the date of the first edition (e.g. 1650 is noted as the second edition, 1654 as the third, etc.). Some forms in Latin are translated into English in the last three and the oath to the commonwealth has been changed to 'kingdom' in the 1662 edition.

[60] See ch. 1, nn. 27, 29.

obscure an appreciation of the important role these lesser franchises played in the routine daily life of the country population where stewards heard personal actions and the admittance and surrender of copyhold tenure.[61]

The first quarter of the book was an exposition of the court leet and the sheriff's tourn from which it had developed. These ancient courts of record continued to exist on privately owned manors and, in some cases, had been incorporated in the franchises of boroughs. Courts baron, discussed in the next part of the book, had a jurisdiction theoretically more limited than that of the leet and were not courts of record, but there were many around the country that could be called every third week and they controlled all forms of tenure but freehold, regulated local commerce and heard any civil action claiming damages of less than 40s. Like the leet, the court baron had powers to fine its suitors, and the steward's office in both courts was one of considerable profit. Sheppard enumerated the duties and responsibilities of the steward and of the suitors, including the forms for complaints and the oaths administered. He then listed the lord's dues from his customary and copyhold tenants as well as the few benefits owed to the tenant by the lord. The third and last part of the book was a 150-page essay on copyhold in which the various types of tenure were reviewed from an historical viewpoint and the remedies available to the lord for obligations not met were discussed.[62] The product of Sheppard's effort was an invaluable handbook for the efficient and profitable management of manors. It was brief, accurate and successful.

Sheppard's high regard for the services provided by courts leet and baron made him critical of the few illogical flaws in these local jurisdictions. His major objection was that the private nature of manorial courts exempted stewards from the standards governing public officials by common-law tradition. According to custom,

---

[61] Prest has suggested that a high percentage of barristers called between 1590 and 1640 did not practise at Westminster but spent their professional lives in the country, keeping manorial courts, attached to various provincial courts or acting as conveyancers. His educated judgment accurately reflects Sheppard's career as a country lawyer from 1629 to 1654, when he was called to London by Cromwell: Prest, *Inns of court*, pp. 51, 53–4, 152, 218. The significant services performed for local communities by manorial and other types of courts has been discussed by C. W. Brooks, 'The common lawyers in England, c. 1558–1642', pp. 42–3, 46, 49; Willcox, *Gloucestershire*, pp. 267–305.

[62] W. Sheppard, *Court-keepers guide*, introduction, pp. 1–2; courts leet, pp. 3–65; courts baron, pp. 66–95; copyhold, pp. 95–181; tenures, pp. 182–254.

tenure of the stewardship was at the discretion of the lord, the appointment made by word or by patent, and because the law did not stipulate to the contrary, any man was eligible to serve. 'Therefore...an infant, lunatic, *non compos mentis*, an outlawed or excommunicated person' could be entrusted with all the powers, including copyhold tenure, under a steward's command.[63] The issue of the integrity and ability of individuals exercising legal powers was one of Sheppard's major concerns as a reformer and his strongest appeal for honest, godly and capable men to fill all positions of public responsibility was made in *England's balme*, the most important of the books he was to write for Cromwell.

After Sheppard's death in 1674, two further editions of the *Court-keepers guide* were printed, in 1676 and 1685. The editor, William Browne, credited Sheppard as the original author and added an appendix of precedents of court rolls. The printer changed the chapter headings from arabic to roman numerals, but in every other particular the posthumous editions are merely reprints of the book Sheppard first sent into print in 1649.[64] A prefatory note in the 1685 edition stated that the work, which was 'no less judicious than laborious', had been well received and esteemed by practitioners because it was more accurate and briefer than any other of its genre.[65] The appearance of an eighth and final edition in 1791 can be explained by the legal profession's revived interest in Sheppard's works following the reprinting of the *Touchstone* in 1780, 1784, 1785, 1790 and 1791.

In 1650 Sheppard's first handbook for justices of the peace, *The whole office of the country justice of peace*, was printed as a two-volume set, and seventeenth-century purchasers usually had them bound together as a single unit. The first volume pertained to justices' powers on a daily basis and the second set down their duties in quarter and petty sessions, appending thirty-seven pages of indictment forms. The book was published in March and included acts and ordinances promulgated as recently as December 1649. Many anachronistic terms interspersed with recent legislative changes in

---

[63] Ibid., p. 115.
[64] Gabriel Bedell, one of the initial publishers, was dead by this time but his partner, Thomas Collins, is named with William Birch as co-publisher. The three printers of these last two editions are identified as 'the assigns of Richard and Edward Atkins', the same men responsible for printing Sheppard's posthumous book, the *Grand abridgment*, in 1675.
[65] Sheppard, *Court-keepers guide* (1685), sig. A4r.

both volumes indicate that this handbook of almost 400 pages had been initially compiled during the reign of Charles I.[66] Following the design he had used for his 1641 book on constables, Sheppard again relied heavily on the authorities of Dalton and Coke as well as statute and case law in presenting the myriad duties and responsibilities of the office.

Dedicated to all the magistrates of the commonwealth, a group with whom Sheppard was proud to be numbered, the book's introduction was a testimonial to the author's confidence in the new government and his zeal for a national regeneration. In his opening remarks, he noted that although the power of magistrates' authority was potentially very great, the full execution of their powers had in recent years been so neglected that he was determined to set the commonwealth on the right course by preparing this basic guide.

And truly I may say, we have been the most happy commonwealth for having, and the most unhappy for execution of good laws in the world. For the life of the law being in execution, who doth not see that most of our laws are but dead and breathless carcasses, and they themselves by their non-execution are executed.[67]

The recent history of slack enforcement was due partly to the county committees having assumed most of the responsibility for maintaining local order during the war years, but Sheppard also claimed that the problem stemmed from the unfitness of the men appointed to the local benches in the past and from their want of information about the full extent of their powers. He claimed that justices had frequently been ignorant of their duties 'and know not, cowardly and dare not, otherwise engaged and employed and cannot, or lazy and negligent and will not do the duty of their places'.

They have wanted will or skill. They have the price in their hand, but have no heart to it. Here's the disease, and grievous it is to the people: and the cure is obvious and already espied and begun by our state physicians. Let able and fit men be chosen to and kept in these offices. And truly (if I be not mistaken) herein lieth almost the whole work of reformation in church and commonwealth, to make and keep the officers thereof good.[68]

Sheppard had very concrete ideas about his requisite qualifications for magistrates and he listed nine, annotating each with marginal

---

[66] W. Sheppard, *The whole office of the country justice of peace* (1650, 1652, 1656, 1662). References to royal institutions and ecclesiastical laws are found in pt 1 on pp. 13, 14, 19, 182; and in pt 2 on pp. 38, 45, 63, 69, 76. Evidence that Sheppard attempted to modernize his material is in pt 1, p. 178 (Act of 24 Dec. 1649).

[67] Ibid., sig. A4v.   [68] Ibid., sig. A5r.

notes from the scripture and from legal philosophers. The justice of
the peace, according to his standards, must be a man able in body
and mind to serve the commonwealth, 'not an ignoramus, one that
can do nothing without his clerk'; a godly man who wished to reform
himself and so would take care to try to reform others; a man of
understanding and judgment who could distinguish between the
justice of a complaint and the malice of a plaintiff; 'a man of courage,
valiant for God' and for the execution of his office; 'a man of truth,
one that...counts it his duty and dignity to sift it out in all things,
and having found it, to embrace and maintain it'; an honest man who
would not take bribes nor 'punish the guiltless' for personal gain;
a man 'addicted and affected to justice'; 'an active, not a lazy man';
and finally, 'a known man'. By this last characteristic, Sheppard
meant an individual excelling others in reputation, power and rank.[69]

Not an obscure and mean man, for power will arm skill...I say not every
justice of the peace must have £1000 a year, or be a gentleman, &c. But
I say he had need to have enough to carry him through his office; and it
were fit he did excel other men, if not in these things, yet at least in wisdom,
piety, courage and better qualifications.[70]

A series of scriptural quotations followed; then Sheppard concluded
with this heartening promise:

Such men will consider that they execute the judgments of God, and not
of men, that He sits amongst them, and looks on them, and that there is
no iniquity in Him, respect of persons, nor taking of gifts. And therefore,
they laying aside all partiality, respect of persons, base fear, foolish pity,
sinful favor, and malice, unnecessary delay, precipitate rashness, and
self-seeking, will duly, indifferently and uprightly minister justice to
every man. And the God of order, the king of all government, give us
justices and grant us such an execution of judgment and justice that our
officers may be officers of the peace...according to the prophecy.[71]

It was an eloquent introduction bound to appeal to the political
leaders of the Rump who were faced with the task of effecting the
godly settlement for which parliament and the army had striven.
W. B. Willcox's study of Gloucestershire between 1590 and 1640
substantiates Sheppard's allegation that corrupt law-enforcement
practices were sufficiently commonplace to warrant the concern of
a puritan reformer. Bribery, illegal arrest, arbitrary behavior and
intimidation, contempt and even violence were not unusual occur-

---

[69] Ibid., A6r–A7r.
[70] Ibid., sig. A7r–v.   [71] Ibid., sigs. A7v–A8r.

rences in Sheppard's county or any other part of England and his plea for honest and competent magistrates had a true ring when it reached the ears of the politicians at Whitehall and Westminster.[72]

Sheppard's forty-seven chapters on magistrates' duties out of sessions gave convincing evidence of the pervasive control over society that could be exerted through traditional authority. Following a description of general powers, seven chapters discussed the enforcement of religious practices according to the common law and recent parliamentary ordinances, reflecting the priority Sheppard gave to devout behavior. Duties relating to the maintenance of public order and prosecution of disorderly members of society finally commenced in the eighth chapter. Eleven subsequent chapters of recent (1644–50) legislation apprised the reader of changes in the law.[73] The second part of the *Whole office* discussed magistrates' duties in petty and quarter sessions and these latter 200 pages of the book resemble in form the first part. Sheppard included traditional charges and duties, authority for warrants, recent modifications by ordinance or statute, writs and procedure, all with the omnipresent scriptural admonitions. Frequent references to royal institutions in this part, too, indicate that much of the text had been prepared long before Sheppard inserted the commonwealth alterations. The final thirty pages of this two-part handbook presented indictment forms, not yet in English translation as ordered by the Rump but still in the traditional Latin.

After three interregnum editions, the book was reissued in 1662, the first part by an editor who identified himself only as 'a lover of justice'. Three short chapters were added to introduce the volume and the eleven original chapters pertaining to commonwealth legislation were expunged. Apart from these modernizations, the book was identical to Sheppard's first edition. The second part of the 1662 edition was corrected and enlarged by Sheppard himself. He, too, deleted the voided laws of the preceding period and added as well a five-page description of recognizances, but essentially the book was the same as that first printed in 1650.[74]

Sheppard ventured into a third genre of legal literature in 1651.

---

[72] Willcox, *Gloucestershire*, pp. 55–62.
[73] At the closing of part one, a blank page was followed by an unpaginated leaf of text that discussed delinquent and scandalous ministers and powers of surveillance recently granted to justices of the peace concerning sabbath observance (Ordinance of 23 Aug. 1647).
[74] See *Chronological Bibliography*.

The faithfull councellor, or the marrow of the law in English, published 'By Authority',[75] was the first of his three efforts to compile a legal encyclopedia. The power sanctioning the publication was the Rump Parliament to which Sheppard had dedicated a religious work two years earlier.[76] That body had, towards the end of 1650, ordered that all legal records and literature be translated into English and Sheppard accommodated the edict with this 500-page abridgment written in the vernacular. Intending to show 'how any action may be warrantably laid in the...law for relief in most cases of wrong done', Sheppard set out in fifty-eight chapters short descriptions of legal process illustrated by cases. The last chapter, describing the court of chancery, was introduced by the author's note explaining, 'there being many cases...wherein a man hath wrong enough, and yet hath no action or remedy at all given him by the common law, but he is left to his remedy in chancery, in a way of conscience and equity. Therefore...we shall add a few things to this point.'[77]

Issued at a time when the popularity of the commonwealth was at a low ebb,[78] Sheppard's introductory remarks were a celebration of the new political state and the legal profession that would serve it. His dedication to the judges of the central courts affirmed his optimism in the future of the state 'that wants nothing but age to make it happy' and he encouraged the members of the bench to lead the transition towards a settlement in which the commonwealth would be 'crowned with religion, peace and plenty'.[79] He elaborated upon his faith in the law's potential to provide correctives to injustices in the progress towards general reform in his message to the reader where he wrote, 'Most men...speak too much of the maladies and distempers of the times; but give me a man that can...advise and give a remedy.' With the clarification of the law as Sheppard's object, he offered the work 'as friend of the common-wealth' in the hope that 'with all [the] faults [of both the author and the printer], the book might still be useful and profitable'.[80] Acts and ordinances as recent as October 1650 were included and it is clear

---

[75] W. Sheppard, *The faithfull councellor* (1651, 1653).
[76] The religious study Sheppard dedicated to the Rump Parliament, *Of the foure last and greatest things: death, judgement, heaven and hell*, was first released in Apr. 1649, one month before the commonwealth was declared. See ch. 1, n. 60.
[77] W. Sheppard, *Faithfull councellor*, I, p. '596' (ch. 59, 'Of chancery').
[78] See Worden, *Rump Parliament*, ch. 12.
[79] W. Sheppard, *Faithfull councellor*, I, sig. A2v.
[80] Ibid., sigs. A3r–A4v.

that the manuscript was rushed into print for immediate use without having been properly arranged by the author or provided with clear headings by the printer.[81] Although the information published was incomplete and poorly organized, the *Faithfull councellor* heralded a new type of legal literature.

This first encyclopedic work established a base upon which several more mature works rested. Chapters of this volume were later reproduced in more carefully prepared books published in 1656, 1662, 1663 and 1675. Sheppard's lengthy exposition of actions on the case, a subject of great contemporary importance, was developed into two full monographs which were published in the restoration period,[82] while other portions were reprinted with virtually no changes in later encyclopedic collections.[83] Many of the essays were rewritten and the table of contents was put into order for the publication of his *Epitome* in 1656.[84] The inclusion of chancery procedure in an abridgment of English law was another innovative characteristic of the *Faithfull councellor* and Sheppard continued to include sections on equity in later encyclopedias. When he published this work in 1651, the future of the great equity court was uncertain. Even as a dilemma in litigation had been created by the abolition of the ecclesiastical and prerogative courts, vociferous popular demands to abolish the court of chancery were raised. Stimulated by angry pamphlet literature, a large segment of the political public assumed an attitude of general revulsion against chancery as its powers – which were presumed to be discretionary – smacked of an arbitrary and unacceptable vestige of the Stuart monarchy. With its costly expenses and unreasonable delays, there was a unanimity of opinion that the equity court had to be reformed if it were to survive, but no consensus had been reached as to the most suitable way to accomplish this. Popular proposals ranged from outright abolition to the proposal

---

[81] Recent acts are cited on pp. 368 and '570'. The type was reset and the mispagination corrected in the 1653 edition.

[82] Sheppard devoted ten chapters (150 pages) to actions on the case in the *Faithfull councellor*, I. See ch. 5 for discussion of the two full-length works of 1662 and 1663.

[83] It was not unusual for authors to republish their own work under new titles in this period. Examples of essays reprinted with virtually no changes in the *Epitome* (1656) are those on conspiracy, nuisance, trover and conversion, deceit, bastardy and parts of tithes. The essay on conspiracy was used in *Action upon the case for slander* (1662) and the *Grand abridgment* (1675).

[84] Some of the essays revised between 1651 and 1656 were prohibition, distress, *habeas corpus* and libel.

in circulation since the Elizabethan period that a modified fee scale be posted. The court, which had not held sessions during the war years, began to schedule cases for hearing after the establishment of the commonwealth. In that first republican year the great seal had been put into commission with Bulstrode Whitelocke, John Lisle and Richard Keble serving as lords commissioners while William Lenthall, Speaker of the Rump, continued as Master of the Rolls, an office he had held since 1643. In order to expedite hearings in the court, Whitelocke, Keble and Lenthall published a manual of rules and orders which were to be followed until further reforms were made.[85] As the court began hearing the backlog of cases in 1649–50, two collections of chancery cases dating from the early seventeenth century were published.[86] Sheppard made use of all three of these timely publications in his 1651 essay on chancery in the *Faithfull councellor* and his endeavor provided an up-to-date summary of precedents and guidelines currently governing that controversial court.[87]

The *Faithfull councellor*, like the *Touchstone*, was written to be used as a reference guide for lawyers, students and potential litigants. Sheppard advised both clients and their attorneys to use it with care and for general information only. Furthermore, the author warned the general public against going to law without first engaging a learned lawyer, pointing out that poorly planned litigation was likely to become expensive, dilatory and aggravating. The legal descriptions in this and later encyclopedias were written to help simplify and clarify the law, but his systemizations were always presented with the caveat that there would be a continuing need for a trained professional class to ensure security of property and to guide litigation through the courts. A second edition of the *Faithfull councellor* was published in 1653. The reset type for the entire text indicates that the book had clearly been a popular success. An error in pagination had been corrected, but in all other respects the two editions were identical.

---

[85] *Collection of orders*. The chancery officials issued and published 103 orders under thirteen headings. There were no other comprehensive orders for chancery reform until Cromwell and the council of state issued the Chancery Ordinance of August 1654.

[86] See *Sheppard's Sources* for Carew and Tothill. Tothill had been one of the six clerks and his collection of cases heard between 1604 and 1614 was edited by Sir Robert Holborne: *HEL*, V, p. 277n; Knafla, *Law and politics*, p. 178.

[87] Throughout the book Sheppard cited the 1651 *Orders* 25 times and the reports of Tothill and Carew hundreds of times.

In 1654 an entirely new work by Sheppard was published under the title, *The second part of the faithfull councellour : or, the marrow of the law in English. In which is handled more of the useful and necessary heads of the common law.* The book was frankly an embarrassment to Sheppard who explained to his readers in an introduction which read like an *apologia* that his publishers had disappointed him. He wrote,

I have but this one word more to say to you. I have had lying by me for many years some few rude notes referring to many useful heads of the common law, being of my own collection and for my private use: the which some having espied would not rest till they had prevailed with me to make these common also; to satisfy their importunity, and because I was persuaded they might do some good, and could do no hurt; and finding my former labors have had so good acceptance among you, I was drawn to make these public also. And in order thereunto I delivered my papers (with this promise) that they should first be perused, corrected & methodized by some able man, I not having time nor strength my self to do it, but they are printed, and this is not so fully done as I could have wished.[88]

Sheppard's primary objection to the book was its lack of organization, although he also remarked that the publishers had failed to modernize his references to the abolished monarchy.[89] The publishers who had promised to find a competent editor had failed to do so and the book was printed with neither chapter divisions nor headings. Topic changes were noted only in the margins and the few long essays were difficult to locate. An index listed some of the subjects but the absence of separate units within the text severely limited the book's usefulness. The *Faithfull councellor*, II, was never republished in the same form. The only explanation as to why it was ever printed at all can be that there was a strongly felt need in the first year of the protectorate to print in English any available descriptions of the law in order to provide a stable legal base and to enhance the new government's appearance of legitimacy. Sheppard, as an established author of legal texts and a new member of the administration, was

---

[88] W. Sheppard, *Faithfull councellour*, II (1654), sigs. A2r–v. Sheppard probably began working for Cromwell in London at about this time or a bit earlier. The book was registered on 16 Mar. 1654: *Sta. Reg.*, I, p. 444. This spelling of the *Faithfull councellour*, Part II, which also appears in the *Chronological Bibliography of Sheppard's Books*, will hereafter be modified to conform to the spelling used in Part I for the sake of consistency.

[89] 'And instead of the name (king) where that word is used, it should have been the lord protector': *Faithfull councellor*, II, sig. A2v.

an obvious contributor to the growing body of legal literature translated into the vernacular. But the author himself recognized that the printing of this book in March 1654 in the form in which it appeared was foolishly premature. Two years later the contents were rearranged under alphabetical heads and the entire text of the *Faithfull councellor*, II, was incorporated into the *Epitome*.

The seven books on the law which Sheppard published between 1641 and March 1654 contain all the characteristics of his later legal works: his overriding concern with property law, his knowledge of local government, his desire to compile a definitive collection of definitions and treatises on common and statute law and equity procedure and, most important, his zeal to educate and to reform, where necessary, aspects of English law. A marked emphasis on matters with which provincial barristers were concerned can be seen in the handbooks on local government. All three were of middling to greater value in the legal literature of mid-seventeenth-century England. Judged by the longevity of continued editions, the *Court-keepers guide* was the most successful of the three while the work on constables occupied a relatively inferior position in the professional literature. Nevertheless, Sheppard's effort in 1652 to prepare a new two-part edition of the original *Constables* indicates that the book enjoyed some fame. While the constabulary might not have been as inclined to purchase an instructional guide as manorial stewards were, *Constables* was undoubtedly valued by justices of the peace as an aid in the supervision of their subordinates. The *Whole office*, Sheppard's manual for magistrates, met with reasonable success with its four editions, but it never seriously challenged the continuing popularity of Dalton's *Countrey justice* which was to appear in seven new editions by the end of the century.[90] The *Faithfull councellor*, I and II, were the weakest of his early books although they were of the most ambitious scope. The major failings were in organization, problems which were considerably corrected when the texts were republished, greatly enlarged, under the title of the *Epitome* in 1656. Although the value of both parts of the *Faithfull councellor* (1651 and 1654) was limited, Sheppard can be credited with having compiled one of the earliest legal encyclopedias. This species of professional literature did not achieve its fullest development until the mid eighteenth century when Comyns and Bacon brought to maturity the

---

[90] Michael Dalton's *The countrey justice* which had first been published in 1618 was re-issued in its sixteenth edition in 1655.

form which originated with Sheppard.[91] The shoddy editing of the *Faithfull councellor*, II, rather than the content may be responsible for this work having been frequently overlooked by legal bibliographers. The innovative *Touchstone* alone remains a landmark in the legal texts of the period. This work became a classic and represents one of Sheppard's three major contributions to his age and to subsequent generations.

The most notable traits apparent in Sheppard's first seven works are the author's irrepressible instinct to reform and his keen insight into the law's inadequacies. These early works were all published when Sheppard was in his late forties and early fifties, at a time when he had accumulated about two decades of experience as a practitioner. A combination of mature judgment, meticulous concern with proper forms, and impatience with archaic and inefficient hindrances in legal process prompted him to suggest improvements and alert his readers to existing shortcomings in the law. He had developed a wide diversity of interests and skills in his country practice and through his local governing responsibilities that allowed him to approach each facet of the law with a reformer's critical eye, seeking improvement through clearer definition, legislative enactment or creative actions taken on the private initiative of public officials. His concern for preserving and refining the customary laws of England made him an obvious candidate for the assignment he accepted in the spring of 1654: to formulate a general program of law reform for Cromwell's protectorate.

[91] Matthew Bacon, *New abridgment* (1737–66), 5 vols.; John Comyns, *Digest of the laws of England* (1762–1767), 5 vols.

3

THE PROTECTORATE PERIOD, 1654–1659

So that the law that was instituted for the quiet and defense of man is now by corruption abused to his vexation, charge and offense. I cannot say but woe and alas, that we are so miserably fallen and degenerated. And taking notice further that there is at this time upon the spirit of our present authority a deep sense of this and some other evils and pressures upon the nation; with a resolution, as far and as fast as it can, to cure them, if we ourselves do not obstruct it.

> *County judicatures* (1656), sigs. A3v–4r

And calling to mind the excellent invention of our common law (observed by an eminent judge of the nation, Coke *Second Institute*, fol. 311) that men should not be troubled for suits of small value in the great and remote courts of the nation, but that they might be heard and determined in the country, with small charge and little or no travel, it ordained county judicatures.

> *County judicatures* (1656), sig. A2v

I have taken the pains here in this work to contrive and make up one great precedent for common assurances by deed in a new and untrodden way and method ... the main design and labor thereof to show when a conveyance is good and wherein the defects thereof do lie.

> *President of presidents* (1656), sigs. A2v–3v

In the spring of 1654 Sheppard was called from Gloucestershire to serve the newly established protectorate government at Whitehall. His primary responsibilities were to advise Cromwell on legal matters and to prepare a comprehensive program for the reform of the law. His understanding of his assignment is best described in his own words.

When I was first called by his highness from my country to wait upon him to the end that he might advise with me and some others about some things tending to the regulation of the law, which I understood to have respect not only to the doctrine itself and the things amiss therein, but also to the grievances and complaints of the nation, the reformation whereof must be either by the making of new laws that are wanting, or the execution of old laws that are already made.[1]

[1] W. Sheppard, *England's balme*, sig. A7r.

Working at Whitehall independent of the council, Sheppard was undisturbed by the daily, routine affairs of government that claimed the attention of most members of the central administration. Given the freedom to focus on the policy aspects of legal problems, he set to work with the assistance of a small staff, assembling a collection of grievances and remedies and organizing his proposals ' as questions or cases to be debated only by such helpers as I expected in the work; and so by us to have been offered to the consideration of the next parliament'.[2] The abortive meeting of the 1654 assembly precluded consideration there of any law-reform scheme, and consequently Sheppard had another two years to complete his comprehensive program. That finished work, *England's balme*, was a compendium of law-reform proposals, many of which were drafted as bills and presented to the parliament of 1656.[3] Sheppard also wrote eight other books on legal topics in the three-and-a-half years of his official employment, the most productive period in his career as an author.[4] Two others contained proposals to supplement deficiencies in the law itself or in available legal remedies.[5] The remaining publications were expositions of existing law, written to facilitate enforcement, to promote government policies or to acquaint the public with recent changes in the law. The protectorate administration also put Sheppard's skills to use in rewriting charters of incorporation for boroughs.[6] There is, moreover, a convincing amount of circumstantial evidence to indicate that Sheppard was the draftsman of the Chancery Ordinance issued by Cromwell and the council of state in August 1654. For these extensive services, Sheppard was awarded the unusually high salary of £300 a year, a sum three times that earned by legal advisers to the council of state.[7]

Summoned to London by Cromwell himself, Sheppard probably arrived just before 16 March 1654. On that day the council referred a problem to Cromwell's law-reform adviser[8] and Sheppard regis-

---

[2] Ibid., sig. A7v.
[3] See below, ch. 4, pt I for his law-reform proposals, pt II for the bills presented to the 1656 parliament.
[4] For a complete listing, see the *Chronological Bibliography*. The tenth book of the protectorate period was a religious work, *Sincerity and hypocrisy*. See ch. 1, nn. 86, 203.
[5] *A survey of the county judicatures* (1656) and *The president of presidents* (1655/6) are both discussed in this chapter.
[6] Sheppard's contributions to charter writing are discussed in ch. 1.
[7] See ch. 1, n. 88.
[8] See ch. 1, n. 92.

tered his first new book on the law in more than three years.[9] The simultaneous occurrence of these two events suggests that Sheppard had just arrived in London to enter Cromwell's service. Four days later, Cromwell and the council issued the first ordinance of the religious settlement, the bellwether of an impressive agenda of reform undertaken by the government over the following several months.[10]

Two provisions in the written constitution, the Instrument of Government, gave the protector and council authority to promulgate ordinances carrying the full strength of law until such time that a parliament took further action upon them[11] and, in the time allowed before the first legislature was scheduled to meet in September 1654, Cromwell was determined to use this constitutional authority to its fullest extent and to decree reform by ordinance.[12] The religious settlement, the first major policy inaugurated, was constructed with the help of Cromwell's personal chaplain, John Owen, and his colleagues among the conservative Independents, Philip Nye and Thomas Goodwin,[13] and Sheppard was called upon to assist in its implementation. The settlement itself was based upon the fundamental principles of the small religious party of Independents that had been embodied in the written constitution and its successful execution was predicated upon the continued collection of tithes to provide an economic base of support for the preaching ministry. The program was launched by an ordinance of 20 March 1654 appointing commissioners of approbation (or triers) to select candidates for tithe-supported benefices. The settlement became fully operational within the next six months with the decrees of two more ordinances, the second appointing a commission of ejectors (with powers to disapprove ministerial appointments) and the third providing for a redistribution of parish boundaries.[14] Article XXXV of the Instru-

---

[9] W. Sheppard, *The faithfull councellor*, II (1654), was the poorly edited companion volume to Sheppard's 1651 legal encyclopedia of the same name: *Sta. Reg.*, I, p. 44 (16 Mar. 1654). It was the most disorganized book Sheppard ever published and he was compelled to apologize in the introduction that the book had been rushed into print prematurely. The government's interest in making practical use of his legal skills immediately explains the hasty and ill-advised registration and printing of Sheppard's collection of legal notes.

[10] *A & O*, II, p. 855 (20 Mar. 1654).

[11] See ch. 1, n. 90. [12] See ch. 1, n. 91.

[13] For Owen's support of 'fundamentals', see Worden, *Rump Parliament*, pp. 137, 296–7. Nye and Goodwin met with four council members on 1 Mar. to draft the first ordinance: *CSPD*, VII, p. 6.

[14] *A & O*, II, pp. 968, 1025.

ment which had ordered the continuation of tithe collections had also promised that another form of ministerial maintenance would be sought in the future and the conciliar committee charged in April with framing the second ordinance was accordingly instructed 'also [to] consider how to avoid the inconveniences of maintaining a ministry by receiving tithes, and how the same may by degrees be put into some other effectual way without impairing the maintenance'.[15] The consensus that tithe collections would have to continue in the immediate future therefore underlay the reassertion that a shift to a different financial source would be made when possible and Sheppard was called upon to compile a manual of laws on tithe payments at the time the second ordinance was under consideration. His handbook, *The parson's guide : or, the law of tithes*,[16] was ready for distribution by 15 June and before the year was out, the pamphlet was twice reprinted.[17]

Sheppard collected information which filled only thirty-one pages of a small pamphlet. He began by describing the nature of tithes, the season in which they were due, and exemptions, providing detailed information for parsons and lay impropriators throughout rural England.[18] Following the description of tithable property, he then commented on the place of tithes in the law since the abolition of the church courts. Possessing all the incidents of lay inheritance, tithes were recoverable in the courts of exchequer and chancery or before two justices of the peace, and the author cited precedents for recovery by actions of debt or trespass and explained the termination of tithe responsibility by custom, prescription, composition or by act of parliament.[19] Throughout the ten chapters, Sheppard followed his

[15] The committee appointed to prepare the ordinance for ejecting unacceptable ministers was selected on 5 Apr.: *CSPD*, VII, p. 76.

[16] W. Sheppard, *The parson's guide* (1654): *Sta. Reg.*, I, p. 449 (15 June 1654).

[17] The three editions of 1654 have different type-settings and misspellings vary among the texts of the three editions. The tables are different in all three and marginal notes were set on divergent parts of the pages. Copies of the three issues of 1654 all name the same printer and publishers, indicating that the book was printed on three separate occasions to ensure broad distribution. The Folger Shakespeare Library holds a copy of each edition: S 3204; S 3205 (bound with 10889.5); S 3205.2.

[18] Tithes were owed only for those things that were renewed yearly by act of God; exemptions included the fish of a river and a stand of timber.

[19] After the church courts were abolished, most tithes were recovered in the equity side of the exchequer. Sheppard also noted that some predial tithes could be sued for by action of debt in the common-law courts. For details of tithe jurisdiction, see W. H. Bryson, *The equity side of the exchequer* (Cambridge, 1975), pp. 11–12, 19, 31, 163, 200.

usual custom of reinforcing his text with citations of statute and case authorities.

The tithe system had been under attack since the early part of the century and, although Cromwell's decision to continue their collection until another source of funding for the ministry had been found touched off criticism from tithe abolitionists, it won the support of lay impropriators among the gentry class with its reassurance concerning Cromwell's intention to protect property rights.[20] Sheppard reminded the reader in his introduction that while a substitute source of funds was being sought by the government, tithe collections must continue for the time being to supply the revenues needed to support a preaching clergy. He explained that 'the strife there is everywhere about the payment of tithes' and 'the ignorance of the law in this matter' had led him to prepare this informational tract, 'hoping that when men know what the law is herein, the one will not demand more nor the other offer less than what the law sets down to be due [and] much of this trouble may be prevented and some peace procured'. Assuring his readers that his guide 'doth neither justify nor condemn tithes', he could not resist adding, 'I wish they were taken away, so that first of all a more convenient way of maintenance instead thereof be provided for the minister; but this I suppose will ask time'.[21] Sheppard subsequently addressed the problem of tithes in his investigation of grievances against the law and by 1656 he had formulated a plan for an alternative means of ministerial support which he presented in *England's balme*.[22] The three editions of *Parson's guide* published in 1654 undoubtedly helped to facilitate the flow of tithe payments needed for the smooth operation of Cromwell's religious settlement. Moreover, Sheppard's book proved to have durability as well as immediate political value since tithes continued to be collected until the nineteenth century. When tithe abolition was emphatically rejected by the restoration government, Sheppard enlarged his

---

[20] The Long and Rump Parliaments had ordered tithe collection to continue but Republicans, Baptists, Quakers and Fifth Monarchists all were opposed to tithes, sharing the sentiments of John Milton that a 'hireling ministry' of a national church was anathema to individual freedom. A majority of the Barebones' members took action to terminate the assembly's existence partly to prevent passage of a bill to abolish the tithe system: *A & O*, I, pp. 567, 996, 1117, 1226; *CJ*, VII, p. 128; Gardiner, *History*, II, pp. 240, 253, 275; *W & S*, II, pp. 536-7.

[21] W. Sheppard, *Parson's guide*, sigs. A3r–4r.

[22] W. Sheppard, *England's balme*, pp. 130-2.

pamphlet and published two new editions in 1670 and 1671.[23]

Sheppard's second publication for the protectorate was registered with the Stationers' Company on the same day as *Parson's guide*. The *justice of peace, his clerk's cabinet* was a short but crucial supplement to Sheppard's twice-published guide for magistrates.[24] While the parent work, the *Whole office*, described the full range of responsibilities devolving on justices of the peace, this short manual for their clerks gave precise instructions for drafting warrants correctly. Sheppard explained in the preface,

When we laid down and gave you the learning of the office of the justice of peace without warrants, we showed you what they might do but did not show you how they might do it. By the want whereof it hath been found in our own and other men's experience that justice hath sometimes been hindered...We have been therefore much pressed to make a supply herein.[25]

The book opened with an introductory chapter explaining how to prepare a warrant and the author set out twenty-four explicit directions for the clerk to follow concerning the style, the manner of address, the date, the names and places to be included and the clauses necessary to complete each order. The titles of the twenty-seven chapters that followed spelled out the wide administrative, regulatory and judicial powers entrusted to the justice of the peace, the officer Sheppard viewed as the mainstay of the peace of the realm. He also included explanations about how to enforce recently enacted

---

[23] The ten chapters of the enlarged editions followed the same topical format and the text was enlarged with recent cases. Sheppard also re-wrote the introduction, arguing that the origins of tithes were founded in English custom, dating to the ancient Saxon church, 'when Rome's religion was a stranger': *Parson's guide* (1671), sig. A2v. He made this point to assert the exclusive jurisdiction of the common-law courts in tithe disputes, implicitly condemning the jurisdiction of the ecclesiastical courts. The 1670 edition was issued by the original publishers of 1654, Lee, Pakeman and Bedell; the 1671 edition was published by the law patentees, Richard and Edward Atkins.

[24] The two books were registered on 15 June 1654; *Sta. Reg.*, I, p. 449. The publishers of both works, William Lee, Daniel Pakeman and Gabriel Bedell, had published Sheppard's *Whole office* (1650, 1652) and were, in 1656, to publish a 3rd edition of that work as well as his *Epitome*. These three men, with Matthew Walbancke, had also published the *Touchstone* (1648, 1651) and Bedell had published the *Court-keepers guide* (1649, 1650, 1654). See below, pp. 120–1 for Sheppard's dispute with these men.

[25] W. Sheppard, *The justice of peace, his clerk's cabinet* (1654), sigs. A2r–3r. The next edition of the parent work, *The whole office of the country justice of peace*, was not issued until 1656.

laws for sabbath observance and civil marriage and against blasphemy, heresy, maypoles, swearing, adultery and fornication.[26] The *Clerk's cabinet* which was, like the *Parson's guide*, written to educate the public about the enforceable law of the day, provided information that was indispensable to the good government of every community and yet was not generally available until Sheppard's book was published.[27] The author stressed throughout the importance of citing the correct authority for each warrant, notice or summons. He repeatedly warned against the pitfalls a justice of the peace and his clerk might encounter, 'especially in a case not common', in their efforts to preserve the peace of the community. Sheppard rejected the authority of some traditional warrants because of ambiguity or inadequacy and questioned the validity of others on the grounds of unproven authority. He included an example from his own experience concerning an alleged offender who had escaped for want of the correct warrant and, to avoid repetition of similar situations, offered an educated opinion on the 'safer way' to proceed against suspected criminals.[28]

Sheppard's handbook on warrants continued to be valued long after the government for which it had been written had collapsed. In 1660 he prepared a restoration edition, expunging all the warrants pertaining to interregnum legislation. Three chapters were deleted and eleven indictment forms added, but the text was not appreciably changed. A third and final edition appeared in 1672, again corrected by Sheppard himself and published this time by the crown's law patentee. In this final edition, too, there were slight variations, but the general format and most of the text of the first edition were preserved.[29]

---

[26] Sheppard, *Clerk's cabinet*, pp. 18, 126, 11, 94, 127, 96. A form for the enforcement of the Highway Ordinance of Mar. 1654 (*A & O*, II, p. 861) was printed on p. 88. Other legislation of the 1640s and 1650s was cited in chs. 3, 4, 8, 14, 15 and 23.

[27] J. S. Cockburn has noted that 'Even on matters as basic as the correct wording of criminal indictments there were before the mid-seventeenth century virtually no generally accessible sources of information': Cockburn, *Assizes*, p. 168.

[28] Sheppard, *Clerk's cabinet*, sig. A3r, pp. 47, 61–2.

[29] The 1660 edition, issued by the original publishers, Lee, Pakeman and Bedell, substituted the king's name for lord protector in the headings and modernized the dating of warrants to the year 1660. The chapters on blasphemy, churchwardens and tithes were omitted as were all textual references to civil war and interregnum legislation. The 3rd edition issued twelve years later was published by the assigns of the crown's patentee for law books, Richard Atkins and his son Edward. The Atkins family had just won a suit in chancery that had

While no concrete evidence has been discovered about the precise nature of Sheppard's daily activities in the year after he completed the *Parson's guide* and the *Clerk's cabinet*, it can be safely assumed that he began to work methodically on his principal assignment of formulating a general program of law reform. His publication of three major works between late 1655 and October 1656, books that involved a substantial amount of research and preparation, as well as the completion of two minor works and a completely rewritten earlier book, indicate that he made prodigious progress in his law-reform efforts.[30] In addition to his preliminary studies for the publications of 1655–6, there is evidence to suggest that in June 1654 Cromwell delegated Sheppard, his personal legal adviser, to prepare the draft of the Chancery Ordinance that was reviewed by the council of state on 13 July and issued under Cromwell's authority on 20 August.

The reform of the nation's largest and most criticized court numbers, along with the religious settlement, as one of the two innovative accomplishments of the protectorate. Both were designed by Cromwell and his personal advisers with the approval of the council of state and both were instituted by ordinances prior to the meeting of the first protectorate parliament in September 1654. The resolution of these two issues was a high priority for the new government because, during the preceding summer, the Barebones Assembly had taken steps to abolish the court of chancery and tithes, the traditional source of financial support for ministers, without providing alternatives for either.[31] While both institutions had been widely criticized for more than two generations, the attention

---

been pending since before the civil war in which their right to the monopoly to publish all law books had been upheld: Plomer, *Booksellers*, pp. 8–9, 131–2. Their 1672 edition of the *Clerk's cabinet* printed on the title page *Cum gratia & privilegio regiæ majestatis*. The text was a near reproduction of the 1654 edition. Only two copies of the 1672 edition have been located, both held by Dulwich College, London. I wish to thank the librarian of that college for permitting me to study them.

30   All five new books are discussed in this chapter. The rewritten book was his second one-volume version of *Constables*.

31   In Aug. 1653 the Barebones Assembly 'resolved that the high court of chancery shall forthwith be taken away' and ordered a committee to prepare a bill accordingly. The bill returned was rejected by the house, partly because it made no provision for the adjudication of pending and future suits in equity. A second bill to abolish chancery was read in Oct. and that also failed to pass the house: *CJ*, VII, pp. 296, 336, 338, 346 (5 Aug., 19 & 22 Oct., 3 Nov. 1653).

brought by the Barebones to the defects in each ensured that the future of both chancery and tithes would come under close scrutiny in the next parliament unless the executive arm took some decisive action before the scheduled meeting. Cromwell had first expressed his determination to resolve the religious questions and to have new regulations prepared for chancery and the other Westminster courts in January 1654.[32] At the time Sheppard entered the protector's service, there was another indication that chancery reform was on Cromwell's mind and that he was specifically determined to restrict its jurisdiction. On 20 March he removed from chancery's authority custody over lunatics and idiots, thereby reversing an action taken the year before by the Barebones. This order, made by executive decree, restored to the sovereign an authority customarily exercised by the head of state.[33] Two weeks later Cromwell took another decisive step towards mandating a new regulation of his courts when he and the council adjourned Easter Term to permit time for specially appointed committees that included the chancery commissioners to draw up orders to correct 'the abuses and corruptions crept into the ordinary course and administration of justice, both in law and equity, the reformation whereof hath not yet been attained'. At the end of May he permitted the courts to reopen even though no progress had been made on the reform of chancery.[34] With the first protectorate parliament due to meet in September, in just three months' time, Cromwell was therefore under pressure to get on with the business of chancery reform as expeditiously as possible. The still incompleted religious settlement had been entrusted to the hands of a committee of the council assisted by some Independent ministers, but the question of chancery reform was assuming a sense of urgency. The concern that both the future of tithes and the reform of chancery

---

[32] In Jan. 1654 the council's secretary Thurloe had written to the absent chancery commissioner Bulstrode Whitelocke in Sweden, 'My lord's first and chief care is to settle the courts of justice' and 'his highness takes the like care of the ministry, providing equally for its reformation as for its establishment' and, in Apr., 'the great things his highness sets himself to [are] the reformation of the law and the ministry': Longleat MS, XV, fols. 27v, 135v.

[33] The Barebones' act of 13 Oct. 1653 had given jurisdiction over idiots and lunatics to chancery in place of the abolished court of wards: A & O, II, pp. 767–8. On 16 Feb. 1654 the earl of Arundel was declared a lunatic and Cromwell's order claiming his own jurisdiction in such cases was issued on 20 Mar.: A & O, II, p. 854; Longleat MS, XV, fol. 25.

[34] The quotation is taken from the ordinance ordering the adjournment of Easter Term: A & O, II, pp. 869–70 (8 Apr. 1654). See ch. 1, pp. 37–8 for the appointment of the committees and their meetings and accomplishments.

be resolved before parliament met was shared by many supporters of the protectorate. Charles Fleetwood, a member of the council of state *in absentia*, wrote from Ireland to the council's secretary, John Thurloe, on 12 July.

It is much to be wondered at that the regulation of the law goes on so slowly, and the business of tithes not ascertained... I know your hands are full, and fear that we may be too hasty in expectation; but the eyes of all are upon my lord [Cromwell], and if ever these considerations come before a parliament, where there will be such a diversity of interests, I fear it may prove as fatal as both have been in the last two parliaments.[35]

But Fleetwood, at such a distance from London, was not aware of the progress already made on these two urgent political matters and on the very day after he wrote that letter in Ireland, a detailed, sixty-seven-article ordinance to reform the court of chancery was given its first two readings before the council of state.[36] Cromwell must have ordered the preparation of a draft document incorporating specific and compulsory reforms for his council to consider weeks before its first presentation, anticipating the lengthy deliberations he and the council would face in determining the final provisions of an effective reform of a court that had for so long appeared to be impervious to reform. The nature of the ordinance that was finally promulgated after five weeks of consideration indicates that Cromwell had turned to his own legal adviser to prepare the draft that was submitted to the council on 13 July.

The underlying assumption of the 1654 Chancery Ordinance corresponds to an important component of Sheppard's legal philosophy, that the courts of law and of equity must both be preserved. Acknowledging the importance of retaining principles of equity, Sheppard had written in 1651 that chancery had been established 'to allay, qualify and temper the rigor, severity and sharpness of the common law', noting too the corollary provision that its jurisdictional claims must be prevented from intruding into the authority of the law courts. 'And in cases tending to overthrow a maxim or fundamental point of the common law, this court is tender and will not easily admit any suit in it.'[37] Article LXVI of the 1654 ordinance

---

[35] Fleetwood remained in Ireland until late in 1655: Fleetwood to Thurloe, *Thurloe State Papers*, II, p. 445 (12 July 1654).
[36] *CSPD*, VII, p. 252 (13 July 1654).
[37] The quotations are taken from Sheppard's first legal encyclopedia, the *Faithfull councellor*, I (1653 edn), p. 374, 429.

confined chancery's jurisdiction strictly to cases where there was no relief at law, and six other articles specifically removed certain types of cases from the purview of the equity court.[38] This curtailment of jurisdiction was the one accomplishment Cromwell singled out when he opened his parliament in September 1654. 'The chancery hath been reformed – and I hope to the just satisfaction of all good men – and the things depending there, which made a burden of the work of honorable persons entrusted in those services beyond their ability, it hath referred many of them [pending suits] to those places where Englishmen love to have their rights tried, the courts of law at Westminster.'[39] Throughout the Chancery Ordinance there are specific provisions that correlate to proposals Sheppard included in his master design for law reform, *England's balme*. Interest in preserving as much traditional process as possible can be seen in the retention of the forms of procedure generally and the *subpoena* in particular, extended by Sheppard to common-law actions in his book of 1656.[40] A determination to avoid delays, reduce costs and eliminate corruption, all of which had detracted from chancery's effectiveness in dispensing justice, was found all the way through both the ordinance and *England's balme*. In both plans, the sale of office was forbidden and the accountability of every court officer in the discharge of his responsibilities was ensured by stern penalties for abuse. Also in both reforms, explicit provisions were made for accurate record-keeping, fixed time limits, following the proper sequence of cases and proceeding upon whatever information was available at the specified time of process. Provisions to amend and supplement the court's record at any time were also included in both plans. Vexatious suits were to be penalized by costs assigned and fees, bail and fines would be established by fixed rules and not left to the discretion of the court.[41] Article VIII of the ordinance authorized

---

[38] The Chancery Ordinance is printed in *A & O*, II, pp. 949–67. In the ensuing references only the article number will be cited. Articles XLIX–LIII limited chancery's jurisdiction in mortgage cases, article XLVII ordered that chancery could not issue a decree against an act of parliament and article XLVIII removed legacy suits from the equity court to the law courts. Four other articles severely restricted the court's use of injunctions.

[39] *W & S*, III, p. 439 (4 Sept. 1654).

[40] The ordinance did not change, but regularized the procedure of the court by introducing compulsory mechanisms of efficient administration that provided for the swift and open conduct of a suit: Articles IV–VII.

[41] See ch. 4, pt I, for details of Sheppard's law-reform proposals that were published in *England's balme*.

justices of the peace to take sworn answers from defendants in the capacity of masters of chancery extraordinary, a provision that raised objections from chancery officers charged with executing the reform. This trust and responsibility bestowed upon magistrates was an important and distinguishing characteristic of Sheppard's plan for reform and the proposals in *England's balme* extended the authority entrusted to justices of the peace far beyond the ordinance's provision for taking sworn answers.[42] The most distinctive parallel between the 1654 ordinance and the 1656 proposals was the provision for a superior bench. Article LXIII stipulated that an appellate court should re-hear cases upon petition of an aggrieved party against a chancery decree. The appellate bench, which consisted of the chancery commissioners and two judges from each of the common-law courts (at least one of whom must be a chief justice or chief baron) was identical to the high bench supplied in Sheppard's 1656 plan and was endowed with the same full powers to void, alter or confirm the original decree.[43] This singular innovation bore little resemblance to the appellate bench proposed by the Hale Commission in 1652. That plan, which had abolished the bill of review, provided for appeals of both common-law and equity cases to a bench composed of twenty persons from outside the legal profession nominated by parliament to serve one-year terms. One judge from the upper bench and another from common pleas were also to sit on the court, but other judges and lawyers were to be excluded from the other twenty seats.[44] That inexperienced and transient bench was the product of a compromise, designed to accommodate the few radical members of the extra-parliamentary commission and there was slim likelihood that it would have resolved any difficult appeal cases to the satisfaction of litigating parties accustomed to the trained bench that had served the system of justice for several centuries. On the other hand, the

[42] Chancery commissioners Whitelocke and Widdrington and Master of the Rolls Lenthall objected to article VIII and most other articles in the ordinance when Cromwell ordered them to enforce its provisions in the spring of 1655: Whitelocke, *Memorials*, IV, pp. 192–201.

[43] Under the provisions of Article LXIII a litigant could file a petition against a decree within three months of judgment. The decision reached by a majority of the appellate bench would be final. The appellate court Sheppard proposed in *England's balme* would consist of the judges of the three central law courts and chancery with the judge(s) who heard the case originally disqualified from the rehearing: W. Sheppard, *England's balme* (1656), pp. 81–2, 84, 198–9, 47–8, 51, 154, 198, 78–9.

[44] Cotterell, 'Law reform', pp. 81–2.

appellate bench proposed in both the 1654 ordinance and Sheppard's 1656 plan was completely professional in composition and, in fact, bore close resemblance to the supreme court of judicature that ultimately was established in the later nineteenth century.

The argument for Sheppard's authorship of the 1654 draft ordinance must take account of the fact that only a practising lawyer could have prepared the complex and detailed provisions and, apart from the members of the April committee that had failed to produce a reform, Sheppard was the only fully trained lawyer working actively in the administration in the early summer of 1654. Mackworth, the only lawyer on the council of state, undoubtedly made important contributions to the meetings of the council's committee for the regulation of the law that returned its recommendations back to the council at large later in July, but the demands of his conciliar responsibilities and the time element involved preclude the possibility that he had actually written the sixty-odd articles that were first presented to the council on 13 July.[45] Given all the available evidence of time, inclination and internal evidence, it appears that the detailed draft presented to the council in mid July was prepared by Sheppard at Cromwell's specific request.

A year elapsed before Sheppard published his third book for the protectorate administration. In *A view of all the laws and statutes of this nation concerning the service of God or religion* which was published 'by command' in 1655, he explored the legal ramifications of the religious settlement that had been promulgated by ordinance the previous year. The eighty-four-page duodecimo listed nullified laws, explained recently enacted orders and, most important, spelled out in practical terms the 'sense of the present authority' to provide clear guidelines on how the numerous laws in question were meant to be enforced.[46] Sheppard opened his investigation by paraphrasing the constitutional provisions that provided the framework for the settlement. Having asserted the primacy of scriptural authority, the principle of religious toleration and the state's responsibility for supporting a teaching clergy, he continued his discussion with an

---

[45] See above, ch. 1, nn. 95, 96.
[46] W. Sheppard, *A view of all the laws and statutes of this nation concerning the service of God or religion* (1655), p. 22. A three-page table of contents directed the reader to specific topics. The book was advertised officially in the following year in one of Marchamont Needham's two newsletters, the only two the government permitted to be published after Aug. 1655: *Pub. intell.*, no. 42, p. 718 (21–8 July 1654).

affirmation of several older laws governing sabbath observance that 'severely enjoin the sanctification and forbid all manner of profanation' of the Lord's day. He specified that the sanctity of the sabbath had been restored to its central position in public worship by an act of 1650 that abrogated feast days, and referred his reader to the *Whole office*, his handbook for magistrates, for fuller details of the laws governing sabbath observance.[47]

The most valuable passages in *Laws concerning religion* were those in which Sheppard brought his knowledge of the law and of current policy to bear on the practical application of the religious settlement. He described the mechanics of the new system of triers and ejectors and the provisions of the ordinance ordering the redistribution of parish boundaries, referring his reader to his *Parson's guide* for detailed instructions governing tithe payments and available legal remedies for the recovery of tithes.[48] He also attempted to reconcile the new constitutional principle 'that men not be punished for their opinions that...do not [sic] injury nor make disturbance' with the Blasphemy and Heresy Acts of 1648 and 1650 that were still in force. He concluded that only a very careful interpretation of the statutes would bring about the desired latitude in religious practice: ' It seems then necessary here to distinguish amongst these [heretical] opinions and to make these only punishable by these acts and ordinances which deny the Godhead in its essence or attributes, or Christ in his natures...And all those that tend to licentiousness...and those that are Popish (as free will, purgatory, images and the like), such are as against scripture...and those that are against magistracy and ministry altogether...that these only are to be punished. And that the lesser, and not dangerous opinions, denying Presbytery, baptising of infants, and affirming that men must be rebaptised and the like, that these are not punishable now by these laws.'[49] Sheppard's interpretation was a fair reflection of the spirit of the law agreed upon by the political and religious leaders of the protectorate for liberty of worship. The key institutions of the magistracy and the ministry were to be preserved and protected; orthodoxy to be maintained but liberty of conscience granted to all who held non-heretical beliefs which deviated from Calvinist guidelines. Sheppard's summary of

[47] W. Sheppard, *Laws concerning religion*, pp. 1–7, 23.
[48] Ibid., pp. 28–9, 66 (tithes); 32–4 (triers); 72–8 (ejectors); 68–72 (parish-boundary redistribution).
[49] Ibid., pp. 16–17.

Cromwell's policy, notwithstanding its limiting conditions, delineated and publicized the remarkable liberality of the protectorate settlement.

A related change introduced by the protectorate in the nation's religious laws concerned public worship. In 1645 the Long Parliament had ordered that the Directory be followed in all religious services under the penalty of a £5–£50 fine, but Sheppard observed in this book that 'this law seems now to be altered' by article XXXVII of the Instrument 'and that no man now is to be molested about forms of religion'. To substantiate that 'this is the sense of the present authority', he cited the ejectors' ordinance of August 1654.[50] He also reviewed the repeal of laws compelling religious uniformity and the abolition of the disciplinary arms of the ecclesiastical establishment as well as the abrogation of the Book of Common Prayer and the repeal of the Thirty-nine Articles. Following the philosophy of his fellow conservative Independents, Sheppard contended that any censures against individuals were 'now left to the regular and orderly churches to be used and ordered amongst themselves in Christ and his gospel's way. But for the national discipline by way of excommunication, suspension and the like, there can be none such used in these days, bishops being gone, for there is no law nor way for it.'[51] He wrote that churches were no longer 'capable of holiness' but instead were now places of 'covenant' and that 'parishioners are not now bound as heretofore to come to their own assemblies or parish or to any parish church to serve God, but...may [go to] what place they please'.[52]

The piecemeal character of the religious legislation between 1641 and 1655 had created legal problems arising from the abolition of the ecclesiastical court system and church authority in general and legislators had failed to formulate remedies for grievances relating to the remaining aspects of religious practice. The repair of a church left in a state of dilapidation by an ejected minister was a case in point and Sheppard, advocating that the state was obliged to provide some judicial recourse for aggrieved parishioners, suggested that complaints of this nature be taken to chancery.[53]

Cromwell's desire to educate the public in the letter and the spirit of the law upon which his religious settlement was grounded

---

[50] Ibid., pp. 22–3.
[51] Ibid., pp. 20–1, 25–6, 42–3, 51–2, 78–9, 82–3.
[52] Ibid., pp. 23, 25–6.   [53] Ibid., p. 53.

accounts for the printing 'by command' of *Laws concerning religion.* Sheppard's authoritative summary was a unique effort in the protectorate period, publicizing modifications that had been made by the Instrument and by ordinance and also identifying laws that had been repealed over the previous fourteen years as well as half-forgotten laws that were still in force. The book fulfilled its immediate purpose, but with the collapse of puritan rule five years later, it became an historical curiosity. This work which typified so well the function Sheppard performed for the protectorate government was, understandably, never republished.

In contrast, Sheppard's second book of 1655 which presented an original proposal to improve the legal system survived as an important contribution to English legal literature. *The president of presidents. Or, one general president for common assurances by deeds* was a guide to drawing conveyances on a uniform model.[54] In the introduction, Sheppard suggested that if his standardized form were adopted by property holders and their conveyancers, property rights would be better secured. One of the major efforts of the interregnum movement for law reform had been to establish public registers to record land holdings and in 1652 the Hale Commission had recommended that each county provide an official repository for such registration. When the Rump Parliament considered the proposal in the spring of 1653, the bill was blocked by a group of influential lawyers who stalled progress with a three-month debate on the advisability of registering encumbrances.[55] Under the protectorate when there was a new opportunity to consider business left unfinished by the Rump, Sheppard, as Cromwell's legal adviser, turned to the substance of the problem of securing property and devised this precedent to facilitate the registration of land holdings.

Sheppard's precedent for a standardized conveyancing form was completed by September 1655, fifteen months after he first entered the administration, and the first edition of the *President* was released in October. A few weeks later Sheppard presented a proposal to register land along with a plan to establish county courts to a meeting

---

[54] W. Sheppard, *The president of presidents. Or, one general president for common assurances by deeds* (2 edns, 1655, 1656). The book was registered on 4 Sept. 1655 and a copy of the first printing reached George Thomason's hands on 21 Oct.: BL, shelfmark E 855; *Sta. Reg.*, II, p. 10; *TT*, II, p. 130.
[55] Worden, *Rump Parliament*, pp. 108–10, 306, 320.

of the council of state attended by Cromwell. The council's secretary, John Thurloe, reported this development in policy formulation to army headquarters in Scotland.

A new model is lately drawn by Mr Sheppard, an able lawyer, for settling provincial courts throughout the whole nation and a register in every county. It is presented to his highness and council and so well approved that it's thought generally (after some alterations) it will be put in practice before Eastern Term next. This much startles the lawyers and the City.[56]

Thurloe's prediction was wide of the mark as the government had no intention of risking political opposition or alienating the legal establishment as it had when Cromwell and the council adopted and instituted the Chancery Ordinance as a *fait accompli*. They chose instead to follow a more conservative course and it was not until September 1656 that both of Sheppard's recommendations were drafted as bills for consideration by the second protectorate parliament. The government's immediate response in January 1656 was to order the renewal of the £300 salary Sheppard had been paid as Cromwell's legal consultant.[57] As for the plans approved by Cromwell and the council for land registration and county courts, the government empowered Sheppard to take his proposed reforms before the public under his own name.[58] An immediate second printing of the *President* was authorized and the public was made aware of official interest in Sheppard's scheme when the book was recommended in a government newspaper of the same month as a conveyancing precedent 'of singular use and profit to all men'.[59] The publicity drew the desired attention and George Thomason, the book collector, made a point of obtaining a copy of the second printing in February (he had acquired a copy of the first release in October 1655). When Thomason dated the book on the title page, as was his habit, he wrote beside the author's name, *William Sheppard* 'a proper' *Esquire* 'that doth judge himself a fit person to reform the laws'.[60]

[56] Worc. Coll. MS, XXVII, fol. 147v (1 Dec. 1655).
[57] Sheppard's annual stipend was ordered to be continued on 9 Jan. and a committee was appointed to consider the rest of his proposals for legal reform on 8 Feb. That committee returned a favorable report on 19 Feb. 1656: PRO, SP 25/76, fols. 531–2, 552; *CSPD*, IX, pp. 107, 189. The bill for county registers was read in parliament on 23 Sept. and the bill for county courts on 11 Nov. 1656: *CJ*, VII, pp. 427, 452.
[58] For county courts, see below, p. 123.
[59] *Pub. intell.*, no. 17, p. 280.
[60] W. Sheppard, *President* (10 Feb. 1656), title page (BL, shelfmark E 866).

During the three years Sheppard was retained as legal consultant to the protector, the *President* was the only one of his books to be published by the government printer, Henry Hills, and one of two legal studies to be published in more than one edition.[61] Although others were published 'by command' or advertised in government newspapers, Sheppard did not reveal to his readers his position as legal adviser to Cromwell. In each of the first six books he published while he was retained at Whitehall, he intimated in his prefaces that he was writing in the public interest of his own volition although he did occasionally allude to official encouragement. Whether Sheppard himself chose to hide his official connections or the government wanted to mask the political aims of his legal tracts, the public did not learn of Sheppard's position in the administration until the autumn of 1656 when he published *England's balme*.[62]

In the preface of the first printing of the *President*, Sheppard shared with his readers only some general reasons for publishing the volume.[63] For the second printing of January 1656, after his proposals had been reviewed and approved by the council of state and Cromwell, Sheppard added a quite singular comment to his original remarks. He wrote that he had published the work to put right an injustice perpetrated upon the public and himself by the publishers of the *Touchstone*.

The injury that hath been done to you and me by some of the London Stationers touching one of my books formerly printed relating to all common assurances; that they, having received it freely without giving of any money from me, I expected you might have had them [copies of the *Touchstone*] the more reasonably and easily from them. But so far (as I am informed) have they been and done from it as that they have sold them to you at very high rates. Nay, hardly can some of you get them at any rate at all.[64]

[61] See above, n. 17. For the appointment of Hills, see Plomer, *Booksellers*, p. xix; *W & S*, III, p. 258.

[62] See quotation from prefatory remarks 'To the right honorable, the lords and gentlemen assembled in parliament', *England's balme*, at the·beginning of ch. 4.

[63] The reasons Sheppard gave were the favorable reception accorded to his earlier book of precedents and the importance of conveyance precedents, upon which 'men's whole outward estate depend[ed]': Sheppard, *President* (1655), sig. A2r.

[64] W. Sheppard, *President* (1656), sigs. A2r–v. All the ensuing quotations from the *President* have been taken from Thomason's copy of 10 Feb. 1656 (BL, shelfmark E 866). The printed catalogue of the *Thomason Tracts* mentions two copies in the collection, but not that they represent two printings: *TT*, II, p. 130.

Sheppard admittedly had no control over the apparently limited circulation and the overpricing of the *Touchstone* and legal protections for authors' rights, which he specifically advocated in *England's balme*, were not available until the Copyright Act was passed a half-century later. His only remedy was to make a decisive break with the men who had published the *Touchstone*. After the publication four months later of the *Epitome*, in which the entire text of the *Touchstone* was reprinted and which was published by a group that included three of the original *Touchstone* publishers, Sheppard never gave any of the men another of his books to publish.[65] The expanded preface to the second printing of the *President* continued with Sheppard's explanation that he had actually written this book to circumvent the problem presented by his publishers retaining 'right and title' to the *Touchstone*, a somewhat specious argument considering the different natures of the two works.

A little therefore to give remedy herein and to help in a matter of so great importance, I have taken the pains here in this work to contrive and make one great precedent for common assurances by deed in a new and untrodden way and method, and the same very full, short and easy, serving almost to all purposes and cases.[66]

The *President* was, as Sheppard claimed, an entirely new work. But, more importantly, it was written for a completely different purpose. He had recast his knowledge of conveyancing in order to instruct Englishmen how to secure their property claims 'by a common standard' and only his cryptic phrase, 'to help in a matter of so great importance', betrayed his purpose of providing a simplified form for land registration.

Sheppard opened the 361-page *President* with a short description of deeds in general and, in the second chapter, explored various kinds of conveyances. The third and longest chapter supplied 'the great precedent serving for most kinds of conveyances', beginning with directions for preparing the document, continuing with descriptions

---

[65] 'According to sixteenth- and seventeenth-century reasoning, all rights in a manuscript were vested in its present holder': M. Plant, *The English book trade* (1939), pp. 73–4. Lee, Pakeman and Bedell (see above, n. 24) were among the eight publishers of the *Epitome*. These three men also released later editions of Sheppard's works that they had received earlier from the author. They were also among the six publishers of the 1659 *A new survey of the justice of peace*, but that book they acquired by assignment from Thomas Dring in Apr. 1659 and not from Sheppard himself: *Sta. Reg.*, II, pp. 201, 222.

[66] Sheppard, *President*, sig. A2v.

of various types of consideration in eight sections, and followed by thirty-nine sections on covenants. The fourth and last chapter gave precedents for special kinds of deeds described in chapter two.[67] This manual for conveyancers was praised by a later editor for its design, 'certainly a very bold but useful one...as an exercise book for the young student and a general formulary in the conveyancer's office'.[68]

The *President* and the *Touchstone* together comprise Sheppard's most lasting and valuable contributions to English legal literature, yet the full appreciation of these works was left to later generations. More than a century passed after Sheppard's death before the *Touchstone* was republished as a single volume, and the *President* lost its immediate political significance after the failure of the 1656 parliament to establish deed registries. But the republication of the *President* twelve times over the next two centuries proves that Sheppard's creative effort had been well received by succeeding generations of English conveyancers. The first posthumous editions were printed in 1677 and 1684.[69] Five more followed in 1704, 1705, 1712, 1714 and 1725, all containing the full original text as well as an enlarged index and table of regnal years supplied by the editors.[70] During a period of renewed interest in law reform in the early nineteenth century, Sheppard's model for a uniform conveyancing deed caught the attention of three barristers, each of whom was responsible for sending into print a new edition of the *President*. The first editor, F. M. Van Heythusan, deleted some obsolete forms and annotated the text with his own observations, leaving out entirely the fourth chapter on special precedents.[71] Mr Willis produced his own edition under the patronage of Lord Redesdale[72] and T. W. Williams published yet another edition. Williams retained Sheppard's original

---

[67] Ch. 1 (8 sects.), pp. 1–23; ch. 2 (13 sects.), pp. 24–75; ch. 3 (41 sects.), pp. 76–222; ch. 4 (18 sects.), pp. 223–361; Table, pp. 362–74.

[68] *President*, ed. William Browne (1704), sigs. A3r–v.

[69] Both were reprints of the original edition with an added six-page table of regnal years for the correct dating of documents.

[70] All the eighteenth-century editions were edited by William Browne and included 50 pages of precedents. Browne was also the editor of the 1677 and 1685 editions of Sheppard's *Court-keepers guide*: see ch. 2.

[71] Van Heythusan's editions of 1813, 1816 and 1822 were reprints of the original with annotations by the editor. The removal of 'old and obsolete' forms reduced the 361-page original book to 78 pages in the 1813 and 1816 editions and 124 pages in the 1822 edition.

[72] Willis's edition of 1820 was mentioned by Van Heythusan in his introduction of 1822 but no copy has been discovered: F. M. Van Heythusan (ed.), *A reprint of Sheppard's Precedent of precedents* (2nd edn, 1822), pp. iv–vii.

format of four chapters, modernizing the original precedents 'so that the student and conveyancer...may be enabled to prepare the draft of any kind of deed with accuracy and without recourse to other books', thus honoring Sheppard's original objective. Moreover he collated the entire text of the parent work, the *Touchstone*, 'upon which it was originally founded', into his edition.[73] The twelfth and final edition, a reprint of Williams' version, appeared in 1870. Holdsworth thought the *President* to be Sheppard's most valuable work.[74]

Three months after the *President* was released in its second printing Sheppard had a book describing county courts ready for publication, his second reform proposal to have been approved by the council of state in December 1655. *A survey of the county judicatures, commonly called the county court, hundred court and court baron*, published in April 1656, called for the reinvigoration of those ancient assemblies to hear and determine locally all 'suits of small value'.[75] While the *President* had introduced an innovative legal form to simplify land registration, *County judicatures* outlined the jurisdictional competence exercised by local courts in the medieval period in a short, historical study. Although not one of the three local courts in this antiquarian investigation was a court of record, the author argued that by virtue of their traditional powers they shared a promising potential to become integral parts of a national judicial system. Sheppard devoted four-fifths of the text to a description of the county court, allowing only a few pages on the hundred court. The information about the court baron amounted to little more than a definition,[76] but the simultaneous release of the fourth edition of the *Court-keepers guide* which supplied all the necessary information was advertised in a government newspaper that recommended it as 'a piece generally useful and very much approved of'.[77] With both books in print months before parliament was due to convene, a summary of the breadth of jurisdiction claimed by local courts, both historically and currently, was available to the political nation.

In *County judicatures*, Sheppard described the county court as the

---

[73] T. W. Williams (ed.), *Sheppard's President* (1825), sig. A3r, pp. vi–vii.
[74] T. W. Williams (ed.), *Sheppard's President* (1870); *HEL*, V, p. 397.
[75] W. Sheppard, *A survey of the county judicatures, commonly called the county court, hundred court and court baron* (1656), sig. A2v; *Sta. Reg.*, II, p. 49 (11 Apr. 1656).
[76] Sheppard, *County judicatures*, ch. 1 'Of the county court', pp. 1–80; ch. 2, 'Of the hundred court', pp. 81–92; ch. 3, 'Of a court baron', pp. 92–8.
[77] *Pub. intell.*, no. 30, p. 509 (21–8 Apr., 1656); *TT*, II, p. 148 (22 May 1656).

oldest of all English institutions, a reflection calculated to win interest in the conservative political climate of 1656. Incident to the sheriff's office, it had had unlimited administrative and judicial powers in the Anglo-Saxon period until, after a long period of political struggle, Norman and Angevin kings had succeeded in transferring much of its jurisdiction, either to the central courts by writ in civil cases or to the magistrates' authority in criminal matters. The crown's success in strengthening the central courts was so complete by the seventeenth century that the emasculated county court was virtually useless in offering legal remedies apart from the collection of small debts.[78] Sheppard wrote this exposition to arouse interest in reviving the atrophied powers of the county court itself, not of the sheriff, an officer for whom Sheppard had little respect.[79] Acknowledging in his introduction that the court could claim only an extremely limited competence, he urged that the 40s. limit for plaints be raised to £4 to reflect changed currency values.[80]

In the seven-page introduction, Sheppard advocated the re-establishment of county courts on two grounds. The first object would be to lighten the case loads of the central courts, and he contended that if his suggestion were followed a full third of the pleas taken to Westminster could be settled instead in the country. To support his proposal, Sheppard cited as his 'venerable authorities' the ancient practice of the common law and an observation from Coke's *Second Institute* that in times past it had been 'accounted against the dignity and institution of these high [Westminster] courts to hold pleas of small or trifling causes'.[81] The second benefit that would ensue from restoring the county court to its 'pure and primitive institution' would be the advantage brought to suitors since suits heard locally would entail only 'small charge and little or no travel or loss of time', a phrase that was reproduced almost verbatim in *England's balme*.[82] Although Sheppard never mentioned that his proposal for county courts had been approved by Cromwell and the council of state five months earlier, he did allude to the

---

[78] Baker, *Spelman*, II, pp. 51–3; Ingram, 'Communities', pp. 113–14.
[79] In *England's balme* Sheppard questioned the need to retain the ancient office of sheriff at all: Sheppard, *England's balme* (1656), p. 37.
[80] Sheppard, *County judicatures*, sig. A3r, pp. 18–19.
[81] 'A third part of the many thousand actions now depending in Westminster Hall are such trifling actions that might be ended in the county judicatures were these courts duly regulated': ibid., sigs. A2v–3v.
[82] Ibid., sigs. A4v, A2v–3r. For his 1656 proposal for county courts, see *England's balme*, pp. 96–8.

government's resolution to reform along those lines[83] and six months later he presented a more specific proposal to bring county courts into a comprehensive and reconstructed system of justice as courts of record in *England's balme*. In that same month, October 1656, a bill for county courts was introduced to the parliament, but this reform proposal encountered resistance from the membership and England had to wait until 1846 for a coordinated system of local courts.[84]

A month after the appearance of *County judicatures*, Sheppard's sixth new book in two years was released. The printing by 'his highness's special command' of *An epitome of all the common and statute laws of this nation now in force* in May 1656 marks a significant political achievement for Cromwell, the patron to whom it was dedicated. This first English-language encyclopedia of the law satisfied two contemporary goals: to publish translations of the law in the language of the people as the statutes of 1650–1 had ordered,[85] and second, to digest as much English law as possible into a single printed volume. In terms of the latter accomplishment, Sheppard's encyclopedia represented a middle-ground accommodation between the demands of radical groups to reduce the law to 'within the bigness of a pocket-book'[86] and the adamant insistence of the legal profession that the forms and substance of the common law be preserved. Although Sheppard, in his attempt to meet both essential conditions, acknowledged that his 1131-page folio was neither perfect nor finished, the publication of the *Epitome* stands as a major landmark in English legal literature. The public learned of Cromwell's sponsorship through advertisements in a government newspaper that announced the book's release 'by his highness's permission' and from Sheppard's dedicatory remarks, disclosing 'your highness's patronage'.[87] This encyclopedia numbers among the enduring legacies bequeathed to the English people by the first protectorate.

The *Epitome* was Sheppard's most ambitious effort to date to abridge the law or, as the author himself put it, to bring 'an orderly

---

[83] See the quotation from *County judicatures* at the heading of this chapter.
[84] See ch. 4, pp. 196–8.
[85] The Rump's orders for English-language usage in the courts are printed in *A & O*, II, pp. 455, 510 (22 Nov. 1650, 9 Apr. 1651).
[86] A. Woolrych, 'Oliver Cromwell and the rule of the saints', in I. Roots (ed.), *Cromwell, a profile* (New York, 1973), p. 66.
[87] Sheppard, *Epitome*, title page; sigs. A1r–v; *Merc. pol.*, no. 310, p. 6976 (15–22 May 1656).

deduction of our laws from their chaos into methodical form'.[88] Efforts to group case law around heads of legal procedure had begun no later than the fourteenth century and the subsequent invention of the printing press stimulated the production of several abridgments. In the *Epitome*, Sheppard departed from the traditional form by combining statutory authorities with selected case law in a single volume, also adding short definitions of legal terms as might be found in a modern law dictionary. He gathered more than 1500 entries into this reference work, making it one of the most extensive explorations into English law ever undertaken. Following the customary arrangement of abridgments, Sheppard arranged his headings alphabetically. The numerous entries were a combination of selections taken from his own printed works and new material prepared especially for this volume. Almost half the text was material reproduced from the *Touchstone* collated into the encyclopedia in alphabetical order. These essays were printed, for the most part, in their original form, with new explanations, cases and statutes added in a few cases.[89] Excerpts included from other earlier works also conformed to the alphabetical system. Both parts of the *Faithfull Councellor* of 1651 and 1654 were incorporated almost in their entirety[90] as was the full text of the 1654 pamphlet on tithes and the long chapter on copyhold from the 1649 *Court-keepers guide*.[91] He also inserted segments from his *County judicatures* and his manual for constables.[92] This useful encyclopedia was therefore a representative conglomeration of most of the legal works Sheppard had published prior to 1656 interwoven with scores of definitions and new legal headings that he was to develop further in future books.[93]

The *Epitome*, which proclaimed many important legal changes inaugurated by the protectorate, was as much an official manual of

---

[88] Sheppard, *Epitome*, sig. a1v.
[89] The duplication of chapters from the *Touchstone* is complete. Changes were made, for example, in the chapters on 'common recovery', 'gift', 'grant', 'warranty' and 'lease': ibid., pp. 826–34, 625–43, 1083–99, 685–97.
[90] Action of debt, distress and detinue were rewritten for the *Epitome* but other categories from the *Faithfull councellor*, I and II, were incorporated unchanged into the encyclopedia of 1656.
[91] Sheppard added the ordinance of Aug. 1654 to the reprinted text of the *Parson's guide* on pp. 1003–17; the chapter on copyhold appeared on pp. 313–36.
[92] Sheppard, *Epitome*, pp. 365, 791–2.
[93] The *Epitome* contains portions of his later books, *Clerk of the market*, *Corporations*, *Action upon the case for slander* and *Actions upon the case for deeds*: ibid., pp. 363, 718–19, 747, 21–47, 47–77. His own earlier works to which he referred are listed in *Sheppard's Sources*.

the government in power as *Laws concerning religion* had been. The constitutional provisions of the Instrument, the repeal of the Engagement to the Commonwealth, details of the system of triers and ejectors, the new regulations of the 1654 Chancery Ordinance and the powers of the new executive authority all informed the reader of contemporary law and policy.[94] Sheppard also described the jurisdiction of other courts as of 1656, incorporating all the changes made between 1641 and the present, as well as other legal changes, all listed with the date of the order and accompanying provisions.[95] For all the recent material subsumed under the headings, many of the descriptions embodied jarring inconsistencies, indicating that many parts of the book had been composed prior to the meeting of the Long Parliament.[96] The curious mixture of contradictions and omissions interspersed with recent legal changes reveals that the impulse to rush an English-language encyclopedia into print overrode considerations of producing a more finished work.

Overall, the *Epitome* was a great improvement over Sheppard's earliest compilations of law and equity practice, particularly in its design. The 1656 work printed a fairly accurate eighteen-page table of contents with all of the more than 1500 entries listed alphabetically with a page reference. The book's major structural flaw was the arrangement of topics into chapters. Each of the 170 chapters contained several topics, arranged alphabetically but with no consideration for the compatibility of subject matter. The page headings throughout the book printed the topic item which happened to introduce the chapter and, consequently, a major essay of 'forcible

---

[94] For Instrument of Government and constitutional provisions, *Epitome* , pp. 360–6, 780–93, 800–9 *et passim*; repeal of the Engagement, ibid., p. 480; religious settlement, ibid., pp. 895–904; Chancery Ordinance, ibid., pp. 193–226, 782–3.

[95] The following changes were noted in the *Epitome*: court structure, pp. 359–66, 780–93, 862–4, 901; law into English, pp. 683–5; civil marriage, p. 721; probate commissioners, p. 365; abolition of the monarchy and sale of royal lands, pp. 683, 800–9; order for pleading the general issue, p. 782; penalties for abducting heiresses, p. 1117; relief for maimed soldiers, p. 1099; prohibitions against cockfights, maypoles and stage-plays, p. 621.

[96] References to star chamber and the spiritual courts date the composition of part of the book to pre-1641: ibid., pp. 720, 783, 786–7, 921, 941, 1002. Also, the 60-page chapter on testaments was an unedited reprint of the 1648 *Touchstone* essay which described officers and courts of the abolished ecclesiastical system which was obsolete even in 1648: ibid., pp. 931–1002. I am grateful to Father Eric McDermott, S.J., for first calling my attention to this outdated description of probate.

entry' appeared under the heading 'forein and forest', a thirty-page essay on 'condition' fell under the title 'consanguinity, etc.' and a major discussion of 'warranty' was captioned 'waiver, waif, etc.'[97] In addition to these misleading chapter headings the book also suffered from printers' omissions, and many cross-references in the text were left blank.

These flaws and mistakes, not surprising in a volume of such ambitious scope, were recognized by the author who 'doubt[ed] not but the candor of an ingenious reader will find me an excuse from the perplexity which our law (as it confusedly lay) did groan under'. Sheppard informed his readers that his 'labor herein is now grown old, having been the industrious search of thirty-six years' and he challenged others of his profession 'either from my attempts [to] contrive *de novo* something of their own... or that they would bring to perfection what I now offer'.[98] The editorial defects did not detract from the value the Cromwellian government placed on the encyclopedia. That a revolutionary government of the seventeenth century ushered into print such a successful compendium of current laws remains a remarkable feat, and the *Epitome*'s success inspired Sheppard to continue working on an improved version until the year of his death.

The twenty-nine months between June 1654 and October 1656 marked the period of Sheppard's greatest productivity as a legal author. On the latter date his seventh and most interesting book of that short interval, *England's balme*, was published. Before that major work was completed the terms of Sheppard's employment with the government were modified and he was reassigned to work under the direction of the council of state as head of the commission on corporation charters. Another year had not yet elapsed before Sheppard's contract with the government was terminated and he retired from public service. Then, in the late summer of 1659, just months before the restoration of the Stuart monarchy, Sheppard published two new works on legal topics. Both books rightly belong to the period of his employment under the protectorate because the author's introductory notes, the nature of the topics and other internal evidence establish that both were composed prior to

---

[97] Ibid., pp. 281–311, '580'–610, 1083–99.
[98] Ibid., sigs. [A3r–v]. The calculation dates the beginning of his research to 1620, the year he entered the Middle Temple.

September 1658, the month of Oliver Cromwell's death.[99] The lapse of a year or more between the composition and the publication of the works suggests that Sheppard remained in retirement in Gloucestershire during that time and, apart from being named to an assize circuit in the winter of 1659, he seems to have had no active role in Richard Cromwell's protectorate.[100] By the summer of 1659 Sheppard was called back into the political arena when the restored Rump Parliament twice approved his nomination to a provincial bench. Then, at the very time he was sworn to the Welsh bench, his two new books on legal topics were finally released.

A new survey of the justice of peace, his office, which had first been registered with the Stationers' Company in October 1658 was published in August 1659.[101] Like the earlier *Laws concerning religion*, this updated supplement was designed specifically to publicize legal changes made since 1642 and to inform local officials how to enforce current laws. All the enthusiastic reform legislation of the civil-war years and the commonwealth period had created additional responsibilities for justices of the peace and the confusion was compounded by further innovations made by the protectorate. Sheppard's introductory words explained that he had been 'earnestly entreated' (by his protectorate employers?) to revise an earlier handbook that would comprehend all recent changes in duties. Yet seeing no need to produce another full treatise, he had decided instead to compose an abridgment of 'things that are common and of daily use' for the benefit of justices 'who have much other

---

[99] Both works of 1659 describe Sheppard as serjeant-at-law on the title page, an honor he received in Oct. 1656 and which was invalidated by the Rump when that body was restored in the spring of 1659. Sheppard left the government sometime between Aug. and Nov. 1657. His eclipse from political life coincides with the fall from power of both John Lambert and John Owen. There is not enough evidence to connect the political disagreements Cromwell had with his lieutenant and chaplain directly with the termination of Sheppard's contract. However, Sheppard's ties with Owen's religious party and the strength of his commitment to reform cannot be overlooked when the timing of his release from the administration coincides so closely with Cromwell's adoption of a more conservative stance towards the end of 1657.

[100] See ch. 1, n. 194. I am grateful to Prof. Cockburn for verifying the issue of Sheppard's commission.

[101] W. Sheppard, *A new survey of the justice of peace, his office* (1659). This new manual was registered with the Stationers' Company on 12 Oct. 1658, re-registered on 18 Apr. 1659, and the book was in circulation by Aug. when George Thomason received his copy: *Sta. Reg.*, II, pp. 201, 222; *TT*, II, p. 255.

business incumbent on them [and] will not have the leisure to read'
a complete handbook.[102]

The most remarkable characteristic of the *New survey* was the
cautionary approach Sheppard took in his instructions to local
justices. More than three-quarters of the text was devoted to
magistrates' powers out of sessions and the author's directions were
accompanied throughout with warnings that a justice must take great
care not to exceed his authority when acting alone or with one other
magistrate.[103] As he subjected each ordinance and statute to critical
scrutiny, Sheppard exposed countless hindrances to enforcement
and impediments to execution. His overriding concern, an appre-
hension that became the dominant theme of the book, was that a
magistrate might, in ignorant zeal, prosecute his countrymen
wrongly, without the due process to which Englishmen were entitled.
The conclusion to which Sheppard returned time and again in his
discussion of magistrates' duties was that the full authority of the
second *assignavimus* clause of the commission of the peace – to receive
indictments and to hear and determine the same only in general
sessions – was required for the enforcement of many laws. Throughout this work Sheppard warned repeatedly against one or two justices
attempting to enforce a particular law out of sessions. He wrote that
the execution of any law carrying the power of commitment
demanded 'very great care'. He reminded the reader that a magistrate
was liable to a law suit for any power exercised out of sessions. He
admonished justices that they must not attempt to use coercive power
out of their home counties. He cited a Caroline statute that no man
was to be punished twice for the same offense. He cautioned that
justices were not empowered to execute a statute of Edward III which
pertained to fining jailers. He noted the limitations set on the
enforcement of the Blasphemy and Heresy Acts by article XI of the
Humble Petition and Advice that nullified the clause directing
commitment to prison without bail for anyone 'holding that all men
shall be saved, or that man by nature hath free will to turn to God'.
He advised that the statutes regulating alehouses did not empower
justices to fine or imprison offenders out of sessions. A 1657 statute
against persons who 'cheat, deboist, cozen and deceive the young
gentry' was, in Sheppard's opinion, unenforceable out of sessions,
despite its provision empowering one justice to commit the offender

---

[102] Sheppard, *New survey*, sigs. A2v–3v. He cited the recently published reports of
Hutton (1656), Style (1657) and Croke (1657–8).   [103] Ibid., pp. 10–154.

to jail. Violations of the 1652 act for the observance of religious days of humiliation and thanksgiving similarly could not be prosecuted between sessions. The capital penalty for incest precluded enforcement between sessions of the 1650 act against incest and fornication, though the latter crime could be prosecuted.[104] The list of limitations to the justices' powers ran on through the text, accentuating the basic theme of the book: that the prosecution of many contemporary laws must be confined to general sessions.[105]

Points of law about which Sheppard was uncertain also earned caveats. He listed conflicting precedents and remarked, 'There are other statutes, acts and ordinances that...are more doubtfully penned, some appointing a thing to be done and not giving power to anybody to do it or not saying by whom it shall be done...Others are so penned that they do not give a clear power to the justices either to convict the offender of the offense or to do execution of the penalty or pain to be inflicted for the offense.' Elsewhere he cited forty-three examples of statutes in which the authority of the magistrate seemed questionable and, in a separate section of the book, offered his educated opinion about the intention of those statutes, suggesting in each case the best and 'safest' course to follow. Sheppard admitted to uncertainty about the current enforceability of Elizabethan and Jacobean statutes concerning the observation of Lent and fish days. He cautioned magistrates to be sure of facts, persons and 'good titles' before fining for non-payment of tithes. With regard to levying rates for church repair, he withdrew his recommendation of a warrant he had included in the *Clerk's cabinet* because it failed to provide a method for convicting offenders and therefore, 'it must be in the sessions or nowhere'. Towards the end of the *New survey* Sheppard advised more generally, 'where any of the precedents in the *Clerk's cabinet* do differ from the things we have laid down in this work, our advice is that you do not follow' the previously published forms.[106]

---

[104] Sheppard, *New survey*, pp. 58–60, 12, 7–8, 74 (3 Car. I, c. 3), 45, 17–19, 70–1, 20–1, 36, 65.

[105] Cautions to justices about conviction procedures were scattered throughout the book: Sheppard, *New survey*, pp. 11, 12, 15, 16, 18, 26, 29, 33, 34, 39, 43, 50, 58, 65, 69 (twice), 71, 72 (twice), 73, 85, 94, 98, 109, 110, 115, 132, 133, 134, 135, 140, 145, 151, 153, 198.

[106] 'Others set forth how the offender shall be punished...but doth not say how the offender shall be convicted': Sheppard listed 20 such 'uncertainly penned' statutes: ibid., pp. 198–201. The section with 43 questions and answers concluded the book; ibid., pp. 202–30. The remaining references are located ibid., pp. 37, 145, 24, 151.

The most recent laws included in the book were dated September 1657, the very time Sheppard's employment with the government was terminated by a decision of the council of state. The coincidence in timing invites speculation about whether Sheppard's dismissal might have been related to the tenor of the *New survey*'s contents. His uniformly cautious and conservative approach to the lawful exercise of the magistrate's office might well have irritated some of the more impatient members of the council. The rule of the major-generals had been terminated by the second protectorate parliament early in 1657 but the tension lingered on between those in political power who retained an untempered enthusiasm for the stern enforcement of puritan legislation and those with more tender sensibilities towards the letter of the law. Sheppard had always advocated obedience to legal strictures and even in instances where he believed the law to be unjust he had advised compliance until it could be changed. His creative suggestions for law reform had never distorted his strong professional instinct that existing law must be obeyed and enforced according to traditional forms. It remains possible that some members of the council were not sanguine about the distribution of a book that pointed out so many impediments to the rigorous enforcement of laws recently enacted in the interest of godly reformation. Whatever the reason, two years passed from the time the book was completed until it reached the public in the late summer of 1659.[107]

Sheppard's steadfast attitude that laws must be strictly interpreted and properly executed seems to have intensified in the last years of the interregnum. This subtle shift in his legal philosophy was first discernible in the *New survey* and became more apparent in his later legal works. Moreover, his retreat from advocating legal change coincided with the changed political climate in England on the eve of the restoration. Although Sheppard was no less critical of the law's imperfections in his *New survey* than he had been a decade earlier, he seemed to put a finer point on the importance of executing the law strictly according to its letter. He expressed impatience with the nebulous and contradictory phrasing in some statutes on the grounds that the enforcement of badly written law could lead to arbitrary and unjust actions contrary to common-law custom. Every flaw Sheppard discovered in the wording of a statute could become a legal safeguard

[107] See above, n. 101.

against unlawful harassments by local justices. In 1655 Sheppard had made a purposeful effort to limit the application of the Heresy and Blasphemy Acts, confining enforcement to persons whose ideas and behavior were dangerous to the community.[108] Sheppard's inclination to protect his countrymen from persecution by over-zealous magistrates grew during the last troubled years of puritan government. In the unstable political atmosphere of the years following Oliver Cromwell's death, Sheppard assembled a veritable armory of defensive weapons to stave off unrightful prosecutions, particularly with respect to religious laws. This effort culminated in the publication of Sheppard's last handbook for justices of the peace, *A sure guide for his majesties justices of the peace*, printed in 1663, the year after the passage of the stringent Uniformity Act.[109]

In the last year of the interregnum, one month after the *New survey* reached London bookstalls, Sheppard published *Of corporations, fraternities and guilds*, an important and unprecedented study of the laws governing corporate bodies. Much of the material included in this scholarly work had first been assembled by Sheppard when he was chairman of the council of state's commission on charters (1656–7). Although the charters he prepared were fated to be in effect for only a few years, the book that emerged as the product of his studies on this specialized branch of the law remained an important contribution to English legal literature. In the introduction Sheppard acknowledged the patronage Cromwell and the council had provided in sponsoring his initial investigations into the law of corporations. Expressing his admiration for the corporation as a legal device, he described it as 'the best of polities' which 'has a more noble end' than laws 'adapted but for the benefit of individuals'. In conclusion he wrote, 'I thought therefore that nothing would be more acceptable to my countrymen than a discourse in this kind of learning, the rather because no man's pen amongst us has been employed on the subject before: but I have the confidence to think it has something to commend it besides the novelty; and it is the opinion also of those that deserve the greatest credit.'[110]

---

[108] See discussion of *Laws concerning religion*.
[109] See ch. 5.
[110] W. Sheppard, *Of corporations, fraternities and guilds* (1659), sigs. A3r–A4r. George Thomason received his copy in Sept. 1659: *TT*, II, p. 258. Sheppard's innovative contribution to the literature on English corporations was critically evaluated by A. M. Eaton, 'The first book in English on the law of incorporation', *Yale Law Journal*, XII (1903), 259–86, 364–79.

Sheppard's monograph opened with six sections that defined a corporation and its component parts. He provided descriptive details of the name, location, membership and form of government that could be inserted optionally in the incorporative document but then observed that for the initial act of lawful incorporation 'this only is of the substance and must be expressed or strongly implied by the words, that the lord protector doth give leave to make such a corporation'. The letters patent or charter need have only 'apt words; not that there are any certain words for corporations, for they may be made by almost any intelligible words importing the matter intended'.[111] To illustrate the many different types of corporations Sheppard included examples of hospitals and colleges, craft and trade guilds, some dating back to the fourteenth century but most having been established by Tudor monarchs. His samples of lesser corporations existing within a larger body, the Bridewell and the College of Physicians, both within the city of London, had also been founded in the sixteenth century. A different type of precedent was supplied by an expired Elizabethan statute in which parliament had empowered persons seised in fee simple to erect institutions for poor relief without either charter or license of incorporation.[112]

Although the legal device known as a corporation had first been introduced into England through ecclesiastical law, medieval monarchs had made wide use of their prerogative power to incorporate secular and 'mixed' bodies. Powers of self-government were delegated to existing local communities and domestic commerce was controlled by assigning similar self-regulatory powers to guilds of artisans and merchants. From the fourteenth century onwards corporations performed an ever-widening range of services, fulfilling educational, social and philanthropic functions. In each case the king's charter or letters patent represented the link between the central government and the local corporation. Beginning in Elizabeth's reign, there was a surge in charter-making activity as wider powers of self-government were granted to municipalities and more boroughs were created with rights to select their own magistrates and to send representatives to parliament. In the same period the five great trading companies that had formed the base of the nation's

---

[111] The six introductory sections collectively covered only 39 pages of the small octavo. Sheppard, *Corporations*, p. 37–8, 13.

[112] Ibid., pp. 12, 15–16, 26–7, 30, 32. The statute 39 Eliz. I, c. 5 (1597) had expired in 1617: ibid., pp. 7, 31.

overseas commerce all sought and received charters of incorporation. Then, in the first decades of the seventeenth century, a sub-group of these mercantile companies was created when the chartered Massachusetts Bay Company established an overseas settlement in the wilderness of New England. Sheppard did not, however, include either the trading[113] or settlement[114] corporations in his study because by 1659 both had evolved in such different directions in a legal sense that the inclusion of either type would have entailed a very different sort of study. The myriad ecclesiastical corporations that had existed in medieval England were also omitted from consideration since most of them had been abolished by the Long Parliament. Sheppard's concern, as he stated at the beginning of the book, was with existing corporations aggregate only and his particular interest was clearly with contemporary charter activity.[115]

Among the corporations Sheppard included in his study were two erected by the Rump Parliament. The Norwich weavers, first incorporated in 1650, had been entrusted with the responsibility of helping to regulate the cloth trade in their area in order to provide a corrective for the economic dislocations caused by the civil war. The Corporation for the Propagation of the Gospel in New England was established in 1649 as an innovative experiment to proselytize among the native heathen tribes in the New World.[116] In 1656 Cromwell and the council initiated a campaign 'to advance religion and justice' by renewing municipal charters 'to the countenancing of religion and good government and the discouraging of vice in the respective corporations'.[117] At least three of the municipal charters which Sheppard himself prepared for the Cromwellian administra-

---

[113] The Muscovy Company, Merchant Adventurers, Eastland Company, Levant Company and East India Company were all incorporated in the last half of the sixteenth century. By the seventeenth century several had become joint-stock companies. At the time Sheppard wrote the foreign-trade companies had fallen under the control of the Navigation Acts of 1651 and 1654.

[114] The Massachusetts Bay Company, chartered in 1630, had moved outside the pale of laws governing English corporations from the first year of its founding: C. M. Andrews, *The colonial period of American history* (1970), I, pp. 42–3, 432–42; Haskins, *Early Massachusetts*, pp. 26–7, 69, 111.

[115] Sheppard, *Corporations*, p. 3.

[116] The worsted weavers of Norwich and Norfolk had their charter confirmed by acts of 12 Nov. 1653 and 26 June 1657. An act creating a corporation for the Propagation of the Gospel in New England was passed 27 July 1649: *A & O*, II, p. 197, 451, 775, 1137; Sheppard, *Corporations*, pp. 33–4, 35–6.

[117] See ch. 1, p. 52.

tion were reproduced in the text in this pioneer study of the law of corporations, those of Salisbury, Maidenhead and Leeds.[118]

Following the general discussion of what bodies could be incorporated and how, Sheppard continued with a long section entitled 'the charter of incorporation divided into parts and opened' which enumerated the diversified clauses customarily included in contemporary charters. Again he mentioned that the sole, indispensable provision of any charter or letters patent granting incorporation was the name and title of the supreme magistrate under whose authority the corporation was made. Beyond that single essential inclusion, Sheppard recommended strongly that the five powers incident to all corporations since the fifteenth century be listed as well: perpetual succession, a common seal, the power to sue and be sued, the right to hold lands (he mentioned that lands valued up to £200 could be held in mortmain without a license), and the authority to issue by-laws. Although the inclusion of any of these clauses was 'superfluous' and 'needless in law' because all were of the 'essence' of any corporation, Sheppard favored entering them for the sake of spelling out in full all the rights and privileges accorded to and claimed by incorporated bodies.[119]

Sheppard continued his description of contemporary practice by listing the 'usual privileges' the protectorate had granted to corporations. For the remainder of this section and again in the last fifty pages of the book the discussion was devoted to municipalities, the type of charter with which he was most familiar from his work as the government's charter draftsman. The thorough listing of the clauses that a charter might comprehend gave a full picture of the sophisticated development of mid-seventeenth-century civic organization. Over the previous three centuries monarchs had granted liberties of expanding dimensions to existing communities and by Sheppard's generation, when a town was elevated to the status of a legal personality, there was a sizeable number of specific rights the community could expect to have granted, including wide powers of self-government, privileges for holding courts, conducting fairs and

---

[118] See ch. 1, nn. 160, 168, 178. In *Corporations* Sheppard mentioned contemporary charters on pp. 18, 29 and reproduced the texts for those of Salisbury and Maidenhead on pp. 133–72, 173–82 respectively.

[119] Sheppard, *Corporations*, pp. 45, 41–2, 53. Further details of the five powers are found on pp. 4, 23–4, 32–3, 52–5, 82, 87–8. The import of securing these 'five points' as privileges incident to incorporation is discussed by Prof. Weinbaum, *Borough charters*, pp. xxiii–xv.

markets and claiming exemptions.[120] Behind the emerging pattern for uniform grants to municipalities sketched by Sheppard in his directions for the 'best way' to prepare a charter, a fascinating background of local custom and medieval peculiarities was revealed. Sheppard's own preference was for a charter to include a recitation of each town's rights and confirmation of its own traditions. He also listed customs that were held good in law even though they were not mentioned in the charter, rights that a corporation could exercise without special grant and, in a different vein, powers reserved to the crown that could not be claimed by a corporation. Sheppard also suggested inserting a clause that 'had no operation in law' but was 'fit to be put in'. Paraphrasing the instructions given him by the council of state, he advised including a directive 'that the charter be construed in advancement of religion, justice, the public good and to suppress the contrary'.[121]

Following the discussion of clauses 'usually included' in contemporary charters Sheppard explored the body of law governing corporations that had developed from statutes and case law. In section eight he covered ordinances and by-laws a corporation could make, beginning with the precept that ordinances repugnant to the nation's laws were 'void by the very common law'. Several other legal maxims based upon custom and common law completed the general directives and there followed a score of cases to 'prove and illustrate the rules and differences'.[122] The ninth and concluding section of the text was a collection of 'other general rules needful to be known about corporations' and the authorities again were statutes, abridgments and reports. Sheppard's information in this section ranged from such general maxims as 'one corporation cannot create another' to very specific guidelines for leases made by schools and hospitals.[123] In the sections on both ordinances and general rules the majority of the cases cited concerned municipalities and craft and trade guilds, with a few references to colleges, hospitals and alms-

---

[120] Sheppard, *Corporations*, pp. 56–76.
[121] A corporation could erect a town hall, jail and gallows and perambulate its circuits without special grant: ibid., pp. 66–7, 73. Unlawful clauses included those restraining liberty of trade or assuming the 'royal franchise' of pardoning felons: ibid., pp. 43, 79. A version of his recommended clause on 'religion and justice' was found in the Salisbury charter printed at the end of the book: ibid., pp. 75–6, 172.
[122] Ibid., pp. 81–108. His case examples began on p. 88.
[123] Ibid., pp. 109–29.

houses. Cases reported by Sheppard himself and by other contemporaries were cited along with earlier authorities, and Coke's *Institutes* and *Reports* predominated, as was usual in Sheppard's works.

Five Cromwellian charters pertaining to local government were reproduced after the conclusion of the text to illustrate the variety of forms and styles he had cited. One precedent simply named officers to 'be in fact, deed and name one body and perpetual commonality or corporation' endowed with the power 'every year forever...[to] choose and make...some wise and godly man mayor'.[124] A second gave powers of town government to a corporation of tradesmen 'according to the ancient custom within the said town where time out of mind hath been a certain commonality or fellowship of the aforesaid honest men'.[125] The third, responding to a petition from the inhabitants of a town incorporated by Charles I which complained of 'diverse and manifold defects' in their patent, enlarged the body of town governors and ordained the town 'forever a free borough of itself'.[126] The fourth, which can be identified as the charter Sheppard prepared for Maidenhead in October 1656, reincorporated the 'guardians of the bridge' that spanned 'over the water of Thames' and provided officers to maintain the bridge which 'is of great use to our people for carriages'. Cromwell's charter renewal also provided for annual elections and a tollage court to be held every third week.[127]

The fifth and most interesting charter printed at the conclusion of *Corporations* was the thirty-nine-page grant prepared for Salisbury in the spring of 1656.[128] Although the two surviving copies of that city's Cromwellian charter differ in several minor respects from the precedent Sheppard included in his book, there is no reason to doubt that this printed version was the draft originally prepared by Sheppard before it was amended by the council of state and issued to Salisbury.[129] All the characteristics Sheppard had indicated as his own preferences in the variations given in the text were found in this prototype he selected as his full model for a charter of municipal

---

[124] Sheppard, *Corporations*, p. 185.
[125] Ibid., p. 186. [126] Ibid., pp. 183–4.
[127] Ibid., pp. 173ff. to p. 182. The Maidenhead charter was given to Sheppard to revise on 1 Oct. 1656: *CSPD*, X, p. 121.
[128] Sheppard, *Corporations*, pp. 133–72.
[129] A transcription of the original charter issued to the corporation is printed in 'Salisbury charter'. *CSPD*, IX, p. 330.

incorporation. The opening clauses recited the rights and historic 'liberties, privileges, franchises, free customs, jurisdictions...as well by prescription as by sundry charters, letters patent, grants and confirmations of diverse kings and queens of England'. The first revision was the confirmation of the sale to the city of all lands previously held by the bishop and the cathedral and the corollary approval of the city goverment's jurisdiction over all related franchises, a provision which may be taken as a typical charter revision of the interregnum period.[130] The charter continued by confirming all courts and sessions previously granted to the town corporation with a clause providing perpetual protection from future *quo warranto* proceedings. The next clauses dealt with town government and while all the traditional offices and forms of election were retained, the number of officers allowed in the charter of 1631 was reduced by half. The change to a smaller governing body was explained by a general depopulation which in turn was attributed to a 'recent decay in trade and commerce'. As in the better known Colchester charter, all the town officers were named as were the local justices of the peace, and while the former mayor was renamed some of the lesser office-holders were excluded in what undoubtedly was a political purge.[131]

The remaining clauses of the Salisbury draft Sheppard printed in his book listed virtually every detail he had recommended in the text of *Corporations*. Parallels to those provisions he had suggested including were that a jailer, gallows keeper, *custos rotulorum* and clerk of the statutes be named, and that the mayor himself fill both the offices of clerk of the market and coroner.[132] Among the provisions that Sheppard had noted as 'usually granted' were two weekly markets and three annual fairs and a piepowder court, exemptions from tolls, and the establishment of a weekly court of common pleas to hear cases in which debt and damage did not exceed £100.[133] There were also detailed provisions for removing corrupt officials and for governing and taxing the inhabitants of the former bishop's close

---

[130] The secularization of the Gloucester cathedral property by Cromwell and the council was later confirmed by an act of parliament: PRO, SP 25/77, fols. 176–7, 216, 220. *A & O*, III, p. ci (9 June 1657); *CJ*, VII, pp. 464, 552.

[131] The number of aldermen was reduced from 20 to 15 and the assistants from 48 to 24. Sheppard retained the correct initial letters of each officer's name mentioned in the charter, from the re-named mayor, William Stone, to the assistant, Nicholas Beach: Sheppard, *Corporations*, p. 145.

[132] Ibid., pp. 147–57, 164, 151, 168.

[133] Ibid., pp. 168–72.

and, finally, a provision that 'pious and charitable uses be not mis-employed'. The concluding proviso, echoing protectorate policy, read 'that such and no other construction shall be made hereof than that which may tend most to advance religion, justice and the public good'.[134]

As one of the few extant Cromwellian charters, the grant to Salisbury commands our interest for the details it provides of protectorate policy as well as of Sheppard's personal preferences. Apart from the provisions confirming secular jurisdiction over the former bishop's close, the 1656 Salisbury charter was written along very traditional lines. The recital and confirmation of earlier grants, the retention of ancient custom (even to holding elections on St Matthew's day, a feast day which had been abolished by the Rump Parliament), and the inclusion of all the traditional liberties, all were comprehended in the protectorate charter. Moreover the degree of self-government, the autonomy allowed from the county and the sheriff, the range of jurisdictions and the number of town officers all taken together classified this as a document representing the culmination of the range of grants made by monarchs in the medieval period. Sheppard's book, written at the threshold of the modern era in charter-making, remains a period piece marking the highest development of medieval charters, those issued under Oliver Cromwell's protectorate. Within months of the publication of *Corporations* the restored Stuarts introduced a new style in municipal charters and borough charters after 1660 virtually cease to describe municipal history and government. The individual characteristics of town charters which for years had recited local peculiarities and customs were sacrificed for a standardized form.[135]

---

[134] Ibid., p. 172. The council of state's amendments to Sheppard's draft included deletions of the last proviso, 'to advance religion...', and failure to grant a weekly civil court: ibid., p. 169. In May 1656 the council approved the addition of clauses that granted two hospitals: *CSPD*, IX, p. 330: 'Salisbury charter', pp. 192–7. Finally, the council changed two major provisions in Sheppard's draft: the coroner and clerks of the town were to be chosen by the governing body rather than having the offices of coroner and clerk of the market held by the mayor as Sheppard had suggested; and the yearly value of lands permitted to be purchased was reduced from £1000 as Sheppard had included in his draft, to £500: Sheppard, *Corporations*, pp. 157, 166; 'Salisbury charter', pp. 182, 189.

[135] Prof. Weinbaum has written: 'The wholesale policy of ordering municipal affairs by statute after 1660' and the fact that chancery 'deliberately excluded recitals in charters of individual and regional characteristics' together favor '1660 as an historical landmark. The restoration, here as elsewhere, inaugurated a blotting-out of medieval inconsistencies, of which the charter was the very instrument and embodiment': *Borough charters*, pp. xii–xiii.

Sheppard's recital of ancient customs and prescriptive rights not only epitomized the highest development of medieval charters but also supplied a theme that had a strong political edge. The concept of a corporation as 'a body politic that endureth in perpetual succession' was introduced on the first page of the book, and in a score of scattered references to legal principles based on the common law, Sheppard developed a strong argument in support of a community's right to self-government and the liberty of the individual subject. While he had stated unambiguously that the only contemporary source of incorporative power was the authority of the lord protector and that the most inviolable rights of corporations were those confirmed by charter, he simultaneously enlarged upon the counter theme of communities governing themselves 'by mutual consent' according to custom.[136] The notice Sheppard took of prescriptive rights suggests that some of these passages may have been added to the book just before publication.[137] Since the book was published two years after Sheppard left his position as charter draftsman for Cromwell, there was, in the last chaotic year of the interregnum, time enough to contemplate the consequences of the succession of a supreme magistrate unsympathetic to the goals sought by the protectorate. The provisions of the Corporation Act of 1661 and the calling in of municipal charters by Charles II and James II lend credence to the theory that Sheppard anticipated the need for a defense against prerogative powers exercised over municipalities.

In the quest 'to advance religion and justice' Cromwell had selected 'godly men' to hold positions of responsibility in borough corporations, trusting that these political allies would bring the effective leadership needed to achieve the goal of good government.

---

[136] He said a corporation could alternatively exist 'by prescription. That which hath been and continued time out of mind and hath all the incidents and badges of a good corporation, shall continue so, albeit they cannot show any charter for it': Sheppard, *Corporations*, pp. 1, 4, 7.

[137] Sheppard wrote that an election held according to custom or long usage 'is good law, being intended and presumed to begin by common consent, Coke 4.77'. He observed that the crown could not 'take away from any subject any jurisdiction or franchise that he hath well settled in him by former grants of kings or by prescription'. Discussing clauses that restricted the length of leases of land held by the corporation, Sheppard wrote, these laws 'show the prince's desire to have it so. But in law have no operation at all. For the lord protector cannot by law restrain the alienation of their land which is an incident inseparable to the corporation from the very first creation of it.' A general rule was that not only a corporation but 'any town, parish or neighborhood of men by the very common law may make [laws for the]...common good': ibid., pp. 58–9, 68, 72–3, 85.

The protectorate's assertive management of borough government in places like Salisbury and Colchester was a lesson not lost on the later Stuart monarchs. The provisions of the Corporation Act of 1661 allowed for the summary removal of municipal officers whose loyalty to the crown was questioned, and by 1665 cavaliers had replaced puritans in positions of political power throughout England.[138] At the time of the exclusionist movement in the 1680s the Stuarts again used the provisions of that act in another political purge in conjunction with *quo warranto* proceedings against London and other municipalities, calling in their charters for revision under the rubric of loyalty to the crown. The impolitic use of the royal prerogative by both Charles II and James II finally became intolerable for its radical breach of traditional liberties. By 1689 the surrendered municipal charters had been restored and the rights of local communities to govern themselves without interference from the central government had been assured.

Sheppard's monograph was never republished but copies of the 1659 edition remained in use through the restoration period. The passages in *Corporations* that asserted the customary rights and liberties of communities and of individuals exemplified Sheppard's sensitivity to that precarious balance of power between localities and the center that plagued seventeenth-century Englishmen from the first extension of ship money until the passage of the Bill of Rights. His prescient defense of local rights in a book on the laws surrounding the king's powers of incorporation may well have been rooted in attitudes formed in the 1620s and his inclusion of this counter-theme running through *Corporations* was vindicated by the events of 1688–9. Sheppard's published study of 1659 survived as the only enduring residuum of charter-making activity under Cromwell. This pioneer contribution to English legal literature was Sheppard's seventeenth published book since the establishment of the commonwealth ten years earlier and his last to have any connection with interregnum political activities. Within six months of its release Sheppard's career in the service of the state had ended when the Stuart monarchy was restored.

---

[138] The Corporation Act of 1661 (13 Car. II, stat. 2, c. 1) removed from borough offices all men who refused to take two loyalty oaths, two declarations and the Anglican sacrament. Section 5 of the act provided that even those who met all the conditions of the act could be removed from office by royal commissioners in the interest of 'public safety'. See ch. 5, n. 39.

An evaluation of the nine books Sheppard wrote under Cromwell's patronage shows the uneven quality to be expected from so many works produced in the short span of three-and-a-half years. The *Parson's guide, Laws concerning religion* and *County judicatures* were short résumés prepared by a government employee to serve an immediate political purpose. Of these, only the *Parson's guide* was later salvaged by Sheppard to serve as the core of two restoration editions. The two books of precedents, whose contents had less political import, enjoyed longer lives: the *Clerk's cabinet* was republished twice in Sheppard's lifetime and his *President* for conveyances was resurrected by publishers after the author's death to be reprinted eleven times in the next two centuries. The *Epitome*, Sheppard's encyclopedia of law written in the vernacular, continued to be used by lawyers on both sides of the Atlantic for another century. Despite its errors and the obsolete law it contained, it presented so much valuable information in a single volume that members of the legal profession continued to acquire copies for their personal libraries. The *Epitome* also served as the base for *A grand abridgment of the common and statute law of England*, the preparation of which consumed all of Sheppard's remaining years. The *New survey* became obsolete within six months of its printing, but his study of *Corporations*, for all its temporal limitations, remained for many years a valuable text on a specialized topic.

The fate of the remaining book of the protectorate period is as tragic as it is understandable. *England's balme*, Sheppard's proposals for law reform written under Cromwell's patronage, might have become a seminal contribution to English legal literature had it been written under a traditional regime. But the revolutionary character of the government that sponsored the work contaminated its ideas in the eyes of succeeding generations. Charles II's return to the throne brought such a decisive reversal in the political complexion of the nation that Sheppard's works to 1660 fell into disrepute as his reputation and Cromwell's were tarred with the same brush. *England's balme* in particular was dismissed as an intolerably radical scheme promoted by a usurper. The book lay rejected and then forgotten for many generations until finally, more than two centuries after its publication, the value of Sheppard's inventive proposals was vindicated by the passage of the great Judicature Acts of 1873–5.

4

ENGLAND'S BALME

May it please your highness. This piece is composed for a groundwork in order to the regulation of the law, which in truth, is the taking away of heavy burdens and the work of a general reformation; there is none that may more justly challenge a share in the dedication of it than your highness and your council, by whose care it hath been brought forth...At your and the parliament's feet therefore I do lay it down. And (knowing well your resolution to the work) I shall not need to use any quickenings to move you forward therein...It is probable that by this work you may bow the hearts of the people as one man, and unite them to you...To arise for the poor and needy, to set him at liberty from him that doth oppress him, is God's work, well becoming the gods of the earth. If we will be to the rulers that right (as laws) the things which prove grievous to the people, blessing will be upon them which help to take them away. And if there be any way for us to have our fasting and prayer at home accepted, and our works abroad prosperous, surely it will be by loosing the bands of wickedness, undoing the heavy burdens, letting the oppressed go free, and breaking every yoke. For while we speak oppression, and revolt, conceive and utter words of falsehood, the law is slacked, wrong judgment proceedeth. Judgment is turned away backward, justice standeth afar off, truth is fallen in the street, and equity cannot enter...For to do judgment and justice is more acceptable than sacrifice. And now that you be 'up and doing' what you can, and that you may have your heart lifted up with cheerfulness and courage in the work (which is in the ways of the Lord); and therein do worthily and be famous...shall be the prayer of your highness's most humble and faithful servant, W. S.

Dedication, *England's balme* (1656), sigs. A3r–5v

When I was first called by his highness from my country to wait upon him to the end that he might advise with me and some others about some things tending to the regulation of the law...I could not think myself alone (without the help of others) fit, nor durst I presume to attempt more in it than this only: to look them out, and take them up from the mouth and pen of others, and these to contract into heads of grievances and of some remedies annexed...and so by us to have been offered to the consideration of the next parliament. And this rude model being thus prepared, and this parliament now convened and sitting, it hath been advised that it be offered to your honors. And, indeed, I could not do otherwise, but I must acquaint you with what I have seen and heard; which cannot hurt but may, with

144

the blessing of God upon it, contribute something to the work you are
about.

> Prefatory remarks addressed 'To the right honorable, the lords
> and gentlemen assembled in parliament', *England's balme* (1656),
> sig. [a3r]

SHEPPARD'S MODEL FOR REFORM

Sheppard reached the zenith of his political career when he was raised
to the coif a few weeks after he published his masterful compilation
of law-reform proposals, *England's balme*. The book, which came to
be known as *Sheppard's regulation of the law*, was the most comprehensive design for the reform of English law and society published
in the seventeenth century.[1] Sheppard's dedication to his patrons,
Cromwell and the council, 'by whose care it hath been brought
forth', stated that his book had been 'composed for a groundwork
in order to the regulation of the law which, in truth, is the taking away
of heavy burdens and the work of a general reformation'.[2] When,
in the spring of 1654, the protector had charged Sheppard with the
task of collecting the nation's grievances with the law, there was an
embarrassment of rich resource material to be evaluated. Complaints
about deficiencies in the legal system and grievances against the
judicial structure had been accumulating for at least a century and,
over the previous fifteen years, had multiplied. Outcries against
confusion, delay and the expense of law suits were legion and an
earnest desire for legal reform had been a dominant motif in the
public arena even before Sheppard's birth.

---

[1] A confusion in dating the book has arisen from two separate sources. First, the
19 extant copies of *England's balme* all print 1657 as the publishing date on the
title page. The book was, however, actually distributed in Oct. 1656. The
author's introduction was signed at Whitehall on 1 Oct. 1656, the book was
registered with the Stationers' Company on 23 Oct. the same year, and George
Thomason, the book-collector, received his copy on the same day: *Sta. Reg.*,
II, p. 90; Sheppard, *England's balme*, title page: sig. A3v (BL, shelfmark E
1675). The book has also been dated 1651, an error that can be attributed to
the notice, 'Sheppard's Regulation of the Law', printed opposite the first page
of text: sig. A4v. This second title accounts for *England's balme* being confused
with a short pamphlet written by John Shepheard, 'student at law', entitled
Certain proposals for regulating the law, published on 30 Jan. 1652. The
similarities in the authors' names and the two abbreviated titles undoubtedly
account for the mis-dating of *England's balme* to 1651 (i.e. 1651/2) by Allibone,
Critical dictionary; Clarke, *Bibliotheca legum*; *DNB*: *sub* Sheppard; and
Hoffman, *Legal study*, p. 688.

[2] Sheppard, *England's balme*, sigs. A3r–v.

Significant changes in the court structure had been made by the Long Parliament which abolished the conciliar and ecclesiastical courts. Subsequently, parliamentary committees developed further proposals for changes in the legal system and in 1652 the extra-parliamentary law-reform commission prepared more than a dozen proposals that survived as lost bills. Writers of the popular pamphlet literature continued to introduce ideas that ranged over a whole spectrum of plans for improvement and by the time Sheppard embarked upon his project, there was no shortage of suggestions on how to remedy abuses in the legal system. The scope of these proposals for reform extended from the complete abolition of the great courts of Westminster to the more timorous, but time-honored option of posting fee schedules in court rooms.[3] In addition to all the ideas in circulation during the years of the interregnum there were also the efforts made in the pre-civil-war period for Sheppard to consider. Another valuable source for ideas which he weighed carefully was the course followed by another godly commonwealth, the Massachusetts Bay Colony, where the leaders had constructed a legal and judicial system founded on common-law principles. Finally, Sheppard's own professional career had served as a proving ground where he had evaluated empirically defective aspects of the legal system. In the twenty-five years of his legal practice he had become acquainted at first hand with many problems. He was therefore able to apply his own well-considered opinions both to the grievances he chose to include and to the formulation of the various solutions he selected. The aim behind Sheppard's 'regulation of the law' was remarkably single-minded: to adjust archaic, contradictory and undesirable aspects of English law and law enforcement so that every facet would conform to principles of human reason and divine law.

England's balme was a very personal book because, unlike other officially sponsored programs for law reform, it was the work of one man. Recruited by the authority of Cromwell's executive mandate, Sheppard had an enviable flexibility. He was given a small staff of assistants to help him collect grievances 'from the mouth and pen of others' and to consult with him about which remedies would be most suitable.[4] He was not, however, bound to consult with interest

---

[3] The great variety of the proposals appearing in the pamphlet literature has been described by Veall, *Movement for law reform, passim.*

[4] Sheppard, *England's balme*, sig. A7v.

groups, nor was he obliged to negotiate and compromise on each proposed reform, as members of the various parliamentary committees and the Hale Commission had been. He had plentiful resources and more than two years to complete his work. Most important, he had the freedom to incorporate whatever changes he thought most workable into a single, comprehensive plan. It was an independent exercise that yielded a remarkably creative product. As specific grievances were considered, each individual remedy was incorporated into an innovative master design. With diligence and imagination Sheppard framed a model for reform which, if applied, would be as a soothing and healing ointment that would cure England's festering wounds. He had chosen a very ambitious title.

At the time *England's balme* was published there was reason enough to despair of achieving the long-hoped-for settlement. The Long Parliament that had led the war against the king had been torn apart after Pym's death by internal dissension and conflicting aims. Subsequently, the Rump Parliament had mortgaged itself to the army with the potential recourse to military assistance. Brought into being with the help of the sword, its existence was forcefully interrupted by the same blade. The ensuing effort to establish a godly settlement was even less successful, as the mismatched members of the Barebones Assembly struggled in vain to establish a working relationship within the body and to come up with a balanced program. Lambert's constitution and Owen's religious program finally gave Cromwell a hopeful framework for a permanent settlement and it was within these boundaries that Sheppard's reform program was drawn. Then, even while Sheppard was at work on his reform model, Cromwell was persuaded once again to take up the sword and England fell under the rule of the major-generals as, for the third time, expediency seemed to dictate that recourse to armed power was necessary for the safety of the nation. Sheppard voiced his misgivings about the military control of the countryside when he wrote in *England's balme*, 'My fears are that either the sword or some other plague will cleave to us if we thus live in the flames of contention.'[5] He therefore included in his book proposals that amounted to much more than a program of legal reform. *England's balme* presented a formula for a new society, designed with the confident faith that divine providence had led England to the verge

---

[5] Ibid., sig. [a3r].

of a reformation of great promise. With his legal skills, Sheppard aimed to make quick and certain justice available to all Englishmen; and, as a social engineer, he sought to introduce improvements in the quality of life. Sheppard's program also offered viable alternatives to two aspects of protectorate government that several of the political leaders were anxious to improve. These were rule of the countryside by the major-generals and the use of tithes to support the ministry.

The 215-page text of *England's balme* was divided into thirteen chapters with topics grouped generically under categories as, for example, 'certain cases where the law is defective' and 'certain grievances about assurances of men's lands and possessions'. The reader was therefore bound to skip through the pages in order to extract in an organized form the manifest implications of each of Sheppard's proposals. The following passage illustrates the format in which he presented the complaints of delay and expense that had been so frequently expressed by frustrated suitors.

It is objected that suits of law (especially in the great courts at Westminster) are exceedingly troublesome and tedious; that the cure is worse than the disease, insomuch that most wise men will rather lose their right and suffer much wrong than seek their remedy by a suit in law. And a man can hardly there come to obtain the end and fruit of his suit in less time than a whole year at the soonest.[6]

That example typified the sort of problem that had perplexed and daunted would-be reformers for more than a century. Nothing less than a radical reapportionment of the traditional judicial system would bring the healing balm of reform to Englishmen in search of justice. To accomplish this end Sheppard subjected all the customary institutions of government to close scrutiny and evaluated the potential contribution each could make to a redesigned system. He envisioned a new organization in which the disparate courts of the nation would be linked together, each assigned a specific function in an integrated and hierarchical system of authority.

According to Sheppard's plan, each county of England would have a full complement of courts to hear minor law suits. Courts of manors and of borough corporations would join the national network, serving as courts of first instance for suitors under their jurisdictions. Re-established hundred and county courts would take cognizance of all remaining common-law actions except for suits involving title to land which would be heard by newly established county courts of

[6] Ibid., p. 56.

judicature. This latter innovation would, like all courts in the new system, be a court of record, and its jurisdiction would embrace matters outside the ambit of other local courts in order to facilitate the determination of as much legal process as possible within each county. A redistribution of authority and revision of procedures would bring every judicial forum in the land into a unitary framework, still allowing for the preservation of most of the traditional courts of medieval England. Admiralty alone would remain outside the system, exercising its prior jurisdiction as a court of first instance but with the provision that if charged with exceeding its powers, cases could be reviewed by an appellate court of the plaintiff's own choosing. The ecclesiastical and conciliar courts and palatine jurisdictions would remain abolished because their privileged powers distorted the symmetry of Sheppard's coordinated design. All special privileges which proved prejudicial to the common interest would be taken away, including those claimed by special courts and particular individuals.[7]

Sheppard's imaginative reconstruction of the judicial system was based upon the preservation of the twin citadels of English justice, the courts of common law and of equity. Although courts of both types had been established for the benefit of the English suitor, in Sheppard's opinion litigants had been misusing the advantages the double system was meant to impart. He observed that the 'distinction of courts' of law and equity had come to operate 'in opposition... which doth occasion many suits. If the plaintiff be cast at law, he will go to equity; and so with the defendant. [And it is objected] that men have leave and sometimes are sent from one court to another for justice, pretending want of cognizance; and it is hard to know which court hath cognizance of some causes.' His solution to the problem of multiple suits over a single dispute was to give concurrent jurisdiction in law and equity to courts of both types, retaining the two sets of courts as complementary parts of a single system.[8]

[7] Ibid., pp. 62–5, 210, 85. In the interest of economy, page numbers referring to a series of citations from the text have been grouped together in sequential order according to the reference in the text above. Admiralty's jurisdiction had been 'settled' by an act of the Barebones Assembly in July 1653, but three years later the protectorate council of state was receiving complaints from that court about prohibitions issued by common pleas: *A & O*, II, pp. 712–13; *CSPD*, IX, p. 256. The fate of the palatine jurisdictions was a much more troublesome issue and they were abolished and then revived on more than one occasion each between 1646 and 1660.

[8] Sheppard, *England's balme*, p. 58.

Depending upon the nature of a complaint, the plaintiff would select the court he believed most appropriate to his case. If a matter of equity arose in a suit heard by a court of law, the judges would be empowered to render judgment on issues of equity as well as of law, thereby ending the suit in the court of origin. 'And so on the other side. If it be in a court of equity and a matter of law arise, that the same court determine it. But that they call two of the judges of law to the hearing of the cause which shall have voices in the judgment. The matters of law to be tried by rules of law and the matters of equity in a court of law to be tried by petition, witness, or bill and answer, as the judges of the court shall direct.'[9] Sheppard, in his determination to avoid repetitive and multiple suits and to do away with injunctions 'under pretense of equity', elaborated upon the details of this alteration. Equity cases would be broadly defined as any complaint 'where there is no other relief to be found for the party grieved' (including injustices created by acts of parliament); every suit would be resolved in the court to which it first was brought, and a plaintiff would not be permitted to remove his case out of the court to which he had carried it 'upon any pretense whatsoever'. A standardized procedure would be adopted by all courts, both of law and of equity, to simplify adjudication within the dual jurisdiction. Dissatisfied litigants from either type of court would have recourse to an appellate process.[10]

The provisions for appeal which Sheppard incorporated into his master design allowed for a rational and efficient procedure for rehearing cases previously unavailable in the court system. Each shire would have two levels of appellate courts to reconsider cases brought to judgment in the county. With each county endowed with a full complement of courts for minor law suits, lesser equity suits, and for appeals from both types of judgment, Sheppard estimated that a full third of the suits pending in the central courts 'might be ended in the county'. An appellate bench would sit at Westminster to hear appeals of cases outside the county's jurisdiction.[11] The role played at each level by an appellate court can be understood by examining the suggested redistribution of jurisdiction in the counties and at the center.

[9] Ibid., pp. 64–5.
[10] Ibid., pp. 83–4, 99, 64–5, 82, 65.
[11] W. Sheppard, *County judicatures*, sig. A3v; *England's balme*, pp. 20, 47, 51, 64–5, 81–5.

The first step towards resolving a minor dispute involved a mandatory arbitration process. The initial effort to avoid litigation called upon the assistance of local arbitrators, or daysmen, chosen by the adversaries as their representatives in mediation. Like many other of Sheppard's proposals this alternative to going to law was an imaginative adaptation of known practice. From prehistoric times local communities had held *dies amores* (love days) to negotiate amicable resolutions to neighborhood disputes. In Sheppard's generation arbitration was still widely used, particularly in Gloucestershire, sometimes on the initiative of the parties involved, but also in the ecclesiastical courts, in chancery and in requests. It could also be ordered by the privy council and there is evidence that arbitration was imposed by a common-law court in a case originating in Gloucestershire. Parties to civil cases could elect to submit their dispute to arbitration by rule of court on the condition that they agree to accept the decision of the mediators which would be returned to Westminster as the official *postea*.[12] Sheppard's innovation was simply to elevate this familiar process to the status of a required pre-litigation procedure with sworn witnesses. If a settlement were reached, the arbitrators would be empowered to make a binding award. No case of slander would be admitted to court that had not first been heard in arbitration. In cases where agreement was not reached, the arbitrators would submit to the local court a certificate of their findings and their opinions. Sheppard also provided for pre-litigation process in the settlement of boundary disputes and the satisfaction of debts if the alleged debtor lived within a ten-mile radius of the claimant creditor.[13]

When arbitration failed, process for all suits where debt or damage claimed was less than £4 was to be instituted initially in a local court. Manor courts and surviving courts leet would, in these cases, be exercising their customary jurisdictions. In locales not served by either of these customary courts Sheppard would have the ancient hundred and county courts re-established, called at twenty-eight-day

---

[12] A number of arbitration cases in Gloucestershire, 1590–1642, is discussed in W. B. Willcox, 'Lawyers and litigants in Stuart England, a county sample', *Cornell Law Quarterly*, XXIV (1939), 542–3. Mediation prior to common-law actions in two other counties in which Sheppard practised law is discussed in Ingram, 'Communities', pp. 125–7 and T. C. Curtis, 'Quarter sessions appearances and their background: a seventeenth-century regional study', *ibid.*, p. 142, in Cockburn, *Crime in England*.

[13] Sheppard, *England's balme*, pp. 58–60.

intervals and tended by neighboring freeholders. The crucial modifications Sheppard suggested for the customary operation of these local courts were that all were to become courts of record, jury trials would be replaced with a bench hearing testimony from sworn witnesses or wager of law, the decisions of each would be appealable in a superior court, and all local courts were to be supervised by justices of the peace.[14] The newly established county judicature, administered by several justices of the peace sitting with a lawyer, would grant probate, hear poor men's causes and cases involving equity, tithes and legacies in which the claim did not exceed £100. This innovative court would also hear cases involving title to land yielding less than £10 a year. Finally, the county judicature was given appellate jurisdiction over cases referred from local manor, hundred and county courts.[15]

A superior appellate court for each county would hear cases referred from the county judicature and from local borough courts. This superior county bench would be composed of the assembled magistracy exercising an enlarged jurisdiction in sessions. The added dimension of authority given to justices of the peace was a contributing factor of major importance in bringing to each county a self-sufficient judicial system for the vast majority of law suits. The procedure for appeal would be identical to that followed at Westminster and compulsory attendance of the full county bench would ensure that most minor cases of law and of equity would be ended in the county quickly, inexpensively and justly.[16] The county-wide forum of justices gathered together in regular sessions would also hear and determine all but the most serious criminal cases and all suits to title of land yielding between £10 and £20 profit a year. Settlement of the poor and the orphaned, the regulation of masters, apprentices and servants, controls over disruptive persons and disorderly public behavior and all other facets of their traditional judicial and administrative powers in sessions would be discharged efficiently and regularly because each session would continue until

---

[14] Ibid., pp. 49, 63–4, 20, 81.
[15] Ibid., pp. 62–3, 73, 140–2, 98.
[16] Ibid., pp. 81–2, 140–2, 190–1, 98. In 1601 an act 'to avoid trifling and frivolous suits of law in her majesty's courts at Westminster' empowered judges to deprive plaintiffs of full costs if less than 40s. were recovered in an action; it also penalized any plaintiff who brought an action claiming less than 40s. The sheriff who had issued the process was made liable for a £10 fine, damages to the grieved party and a £20 fine to the monarch: 43 Eliz. I, c. 6.

all cases were heard and brought to judgment.[17] By preserving so many familiar parts of English local government Sheppard made his plan both comprehensible and palatable to the population.[18] The officials and suitors of the myriad courts would continue to pursue the customary patterns of litigation in their own locales, conducting their business in borough and manor courts, attending quarter sessions and observing the administration of justice discharged regularly and faithfully by those key officials of local government, the justices of the peace.

The political effect that the jurisdictional adjustments in the lesser courts would have on the population was of no less importance. Sheppard's creative use of arbitrators and of freeholders as judges in the hundred and county courts brought a larger number of subjects into an arena of active participation in the nation's machinery of justice. In effect, the state would be calling upon the assistance of a group of men who had a personal and direct interest in preserving the stability of their local communities and maintaining the peace. Vested property interests of court-keepers, rights Sheppard was always very careful to honor, were to be upheld. The redefined status of manor and borough courts required only that their customary procedures be standardized since the evidence of their suits would become part of the public record, and the courts which were privately held would be required to engage a lawyer to act as a consultant on points of law.[19] The justice of the peace, the most indispensable official in English local government, had the greatest reason to cooperate with the suggested changes because his vast traditional authority would be enlarged. Sitting with his fellow magistrates on the provincial appellate bench, he would serve as the local representative of the national judicial establishment as he presided over the county court of judicature and supervised and regulated all the county's inferior courts of first instance. He was also to be given more extensive law-enforcement powers out of sessions.

In this design of provincial courts Sheppard demonstrated his sensitivity to preserving traditional patterns of local justice, a matter of exceptional significance in this period when the countryside was under the rule of the major-generals. The details propounded in *England's balme* for erecting a godly commonwealth represent not

---

[17] Sheppard, *England's balme*, pp. 35–6, 98, 167–71, 176, 158–9, 77.
[18] For continuation of assizes, see below, n. 22.
[19] Sheppard, *England's balme*, pp. 63, 190.

only Sheppard's best efforts to design a society guided by the
authority of the magistracy and, as will be seen, inspired by the
leadership of the ministry, but his plan also offered a practicable
alternative to the military rule to which Englishmen were subjected
in 1655–6. In his pursuit of a better society he was equally concerned
with resolving problems that had been created by the historical
developments in the judicial system. The determination of most
small suits in the counties would alleviate the hardships of expense,
inconvenience and delay associated with suits taken to Westminster
for adjudication. Having drawn these broad outlines for the local
administration of justice, Sheppard then reconsidered the role to be
played by the great central courts.

The three law courts of Westminster, 'where Englishmen love to
have their rights tried',[20] and the great equity court of chancery
remained at the summit of the judicial structure. Each of these four
major courts would, with few alterations, exercise their customary
jurisdiction but, by hearing only major law suits, the dignity of each
would be considerably enhanced.[21] Law terms were to be kept
according to custom and, with the anticipated reduction in the
number of suits admitted and pending, the case load would be kept
to manageable proportions. The judges of the law courts and the
serjeants would continue their perambulations through the counties
to expedite the settlement of cases under their traditional charges,
but three assize circuits would be travelled each year instead of two.
Each assizes was to be kept in session until all cases came to judgment
in order to eliminate the delays associated with a backlog. Citing the
practice followed in the great sessions of Wales, Sheppard recommended that all cases, both civil and criminal, be heard by two assize
judges sitting together.[22] In chancery, too, the lords commissioners

---

[20] The quotation is from Cromwell's speech to parliament, 4 Sept. 1654: *W &
S*, III, p. 439.

[21] In another work Sheppard had quoted Coke's statement that 'small and
"trifling" causes had been accounted against the dignity and institution of these
high courts': Sheppard, *County judicatures*, sigs. A3r–v. Sheppard was very
specific in his provision that to bring an action a plaintiff must pledge under oath
that his cause was just and 'not feigned', that he set down the substance of the
case and enter into a recognizance to prosecute it to effect and, if the case should
go against him, that he agree to pay costs: Sheppard, *England's balme*, pp. 60–2.

[22] Efforts to persuade assize judges to extend their sessions until all cases had been
heard had been made since the fifteenth century, but there continued to be a
chronic backlog of cases of *nisi prius* as well as cases on the criminal side. I am
grateful to Prof. Cockburn for this information about assize charges and the
accumulation of cases in the seventeenth century. Sheppard, *England's balme*,
pp. 63, 96–7, 77, 198–9.

were to preside together, for Sheppard was adamant in his insistence that no man ever sit alone in judgment. The established jurisdiction of the senior equity court would encompass all equity cases where the claim exceeded £100 as well as matters of contract, marriage and divorce, guardians for minors and estate management for lunatics and idiots. Local chancery commissioners would continue to take depositions in the country to expedite the settlement of cases. In both the employment of local commissioners and the continuation of assize circuits, Sheppard acknowledged the value to the English subject of having a tangible means of identifying with the 'great and remote courts' of Westminster. The retention of these two traditional institutions played an important role in creating a sense of coherence and identification with a judicial system dedicated to bringing justice quickly and visibly.[23]

A superior appellate court, consisting of the judges of the four Westminster courts sitting together, would hear appeals from their own courts with the judges who had heard the case originally disqualified from the rehearing. Other cases heard by this supreme bench would be appeals from the decisions of chancery commissioners, difficult appeal cases referred from the county courts, and cases where the judges of a lower court questioned the justice of a verdict brought by a jury. The central appellate bench would also examine and render decisions on complaints of 'arbitrary power beside and against the law', unjust sentences and excessive fines. A central record office would be administered by the judges of Westminster where records of every case, judgment and fine from every court in the nation would be forwarded for certification.[24] The provision of having judges sit *in banc* at all levels of the judicial system offered safeguards against biased decisions and human error. Finally, Sheppard sought one final guarantee against potential injustice. It was to place an extraordinary judicial power in the hands of the one man whose Christian integrity was, in Sheppard's eyes, above reproach. At the pinnacle of the judicial system the lord protector, Cromwell, assuming a prerogative of his royal predecessors, would preside over a revived court of requests, summoned at his command and held with whichever judges he chose to call. Sheppard envisaged a court of requests as a court

---

[23] Ibid., pp. 45, 143–4, 156–8, 64, 99, 59–60, 107.

[24] These appeal provisions would eliminate the need for bills of review, writs of error and arrest of judgment: ibid., pp. 81–2, 84, 198–9, 47–8, 51, 154, 198, 78–9. The writ of error had already been abolished twice, once by the Rump on 11 Mar. 1650 and again by the Barebones on 4 Nov. 1653: *A & O*, II, pp. 357–8, 773–4.

of last resort to which the protector could remove any case of his choosing. Appeals from any court in the nation still pending after six months or more would be referred there. Principles of equity would prevail not only over common law, but also over acts of parliament.[25] As the guardian of justice, the protector would also receive regular reports about the 'manner and justice of proceedings' at assizes and in the general sessions in the counties. An ombudsman, an 'honest, godly man, though no lawyer', would be appointed to attend the inferior courts 'when he will', reporting directly back to the protector. The protector could also appoint an *ad hoc* commission to settle summarily a group of suits brought by any 'great rich man [who] by his malicious prosecution of many suits at once, will undo a poor man'.[26] With these spot checks on the administration of justice and the protector's option of investigating 'any case he will', Sheppard was confident that no Englishman need fear corruption, error or tyranny from the restructured system of justice.

His determination to see that justice would be done did not end with his provisions for appeal. Like Cromwell, he believed that a society's institutions were no better than the men who administered them.[27] The careful selection and supervision of men involved in every stage of the legal process were factors crucial to the success of the scheme. In Sheppard's opinion, miscarriages of justice were

conceived to come especially from five causes, or ariseth from five sorts of persons: the judges, they sometimes, through simplicity or corruption, do give a wrong sentence; the jury, this sometimes, through ignorance or corruption, doth give a false verdict; the witnesses, they sometimes give false evidence; the lawyers, they sometimes, by their number being all on

---

[25] Sheppard provided no other details about the proposed revival of the sovereign's personal court. From its founding early in the sixteenth century it was a court of conscience whose authority was derived from the residual prerogative. Requests could order specific relief in cases recommended by the king as well as in other areas under its jurisdiction, which included the royal household and the verge, paupers, and institutions that owed their existence to the crown, such as hospitals, corporations and universities. The court of requests had not operated since 1642. For details of its former jurisdiction, see Sir Julius Caesar, *The ancient state, authoritie, and proceedings of the court of requests*, ed. L. M. Hill (Cambridge, 1975), pp. xiv–xxxvi, xl. For Sheppard's proposals, see *England's balme*, pp. 64, 82, 99.

[26] Sheppard, *England's balme*, pp. 45–6, 100.

[27] 'The execution of the office is no better than the man in whose hands responsibilities lie': Sheppard, *Court-keepers guide*, p. 115; 'Attorneys and lawless scriveners practising law and giving advice which is ignorant, wrong and detrimental to their clients and the community at large is an evil fit for the consideration of a parliament': Sheppard, *Touchstone*, sig. A3r.

one side, sometimes by their skill and zeal, overbear a good cause and mislead judge and jury. And the attorneys and other officers of the court, they sometimes knowingly and wilfully, and sometimes negligently or ignorantly, destroy a man's cause. And sometimes it is from the curiosity and multiplicity of pleadings and other proceedings in the suit.[28]

Obstacles to justice created by litigants were of no less importance, but the familiar tactics of delay, harassment and evasion would be prevented by the adoption of Sheppard's new procedural rules. The ignorance and corruption which intruded upon the course of justice from judges, juries, witnesses, counsel and court officers, however, required special attention.

Judges would be chosen from the 'best and wisest' of men, 'lovers of justice'. These men of knowledge and integrity would, like every other officer in the commonwealth, be held accountable for all their actions and decisions so that their 'judgments may be examined and miscarriages punished'. For sentences found to be unjust by another court, the original judge would be ordered to pay damages, and any wilful miscarriage of justice would be punished by loss of office with permanent incapacity. Members of the bench, including justices of the peace on the county benches, would be paid fixed salaries. A legal definition of bribery would establish a firm criterion for evaluating questionable behavior, with severe punishments imposed on those found guilty.[29] The personnel of all courts would be regulated with respect to their numbers, their conduct and their fees. Remuneration would be standardized and officers 'forced to give an exact account of all things received', being liable to severe penalties for accepting more than the posted amount.[30] As for the legal profession, a limit of two lawyers representing each side in a suit would be set in every court, and lawyers and attorneys would be permitted to represent only one client at a time.[31]

The problem of controlling the corrupt practices of jurors and witnesses as well as the conduct of the multitude of men in positions of public responsibility around the country demanded a wide-sweeping and creative solution. Guided by exacting standards for

---

[28] Sheppard, *England's balme*, pp. 43–4.
[29] Judges' salaries had been set at £1000 per annum in 1654. Ibid., pp. 33, 45–8, 53–4.
[30] The penalties for charging higher fees were to pay twice the amount in damages if the transgression was admitted; treble if falsely denied; and loss of office for a second offense: ibid., pp. 97, 40, 61.
[31] Ibid., pp. '54', 98.

honesty and accountability, Sheppard recommended dividing the entire population of the country into those fit to serve the state and those who would be barred from all public posts. The determination of precisely which men of each neighborhood would be qualified for stations of public authority would be made by the justices of the peace, men who themselves had been carefully chosen by the central executive council. The passage in *England's balme* where Sheppard recommended the classification of each individual in every parish of the commonwealth read,

That there be a book in every county settled by the justices of the peace and lying among the session rolls called *A list of names, in ranks and orders*. The first of all, the godly men that are orthodox and declare the power of godliness in their lives and stand well affected to the present government, in two ranks: 1. Of such as are fit to be of grand juries and high constables; 2. Of all the rest that are fit to serve other offices; and that the officers be made of these primarily.

The second rank of all sober and civil men, not pretending more to religion than every man; and that do not declare themselves to be against the present government, divided into two ranks as before. And out of these, the next [remaining] officers be chosen.

The third rank of all godless and wicked men, that frequent not the church or other good meetings; or are dangerous in principles, as Ranters, Quakers and such like; or [are in] any way notoriously wicked or scandalous in their lives: as murderers, thieves, whoremongers, drunkards, alehouse-haunters, bankrupts, cheaters, blasphemers, common swearers, perjured persons and such as are known or vehemently suspected to be such persons; so long as they continue so, be incapable of any office in the commonwealth.

That by this book, the jury book out of the first two ranks be made and settled, to lie also among the rolls of the sessions of the county.[32]

This suggested ranking epitomizes the thrust of the reformed state as envisioned by Sheppard: an oligarchy of moral and God-fearing men filling all positions of responsibility in the state while the dissolute and dishonest were barred from all positions of public

---

[32] Sheppard reiterated his basic criterion in another part of the book: 'that all godless and profane men, scoffers at religion and such-like men be made incapable of all offices in the commonwealth': ibid., p. 54. He also stipulated that jurors be chosen 'of the most substantial men of the country': ibid., p. 50. Sheppard's categories for the 'notoriously wicked and scandalous' appear to have been taken from the Biblical verse he chose for the title page of *Foure last things*: 'but the fearful and unbelieving and abominable; murderers, whoremongers, sorcerers, idolaters and all liars shall have their part in the lake that burneth with fire and brimstone. Revelations. 21. 7–8'. The outlined ranking appears in *England's balme*, pp. 41–2.

authority. While the 'godly' would fill the positions of greatest responsibility and authority, other church-going citizens not opposed to the protectorate government would qualify for positions as petty constables or members of petty juries, serving their community while enjoying the legal protection and liberties the state provided for law-abiding subjects. By excluding the undesirable and untrustworthy from all public duties, Sheppard hoped to eliminate much of the endemic corruption in the realm of public services. For centuries England had suffered from a variety of problems that arose from dependence upon unpaid, local officials, including graft, extortion, bribery and the packing of juries as well as laxness, indifference, partiality and gross ignorance. The collusive behavior of men in public positions and the maze of conflicting and overlapping jurisdictions had given rise to contradictory loyalties and an ill-defined sense of public obligation. By excluding the most untrustworthy, Sheppard anticipated an improvement in the system of justice so that everyone invested with any sort of community responsibility was to be held legally answerable for his actions.[33]

Each local officer, from the constable to the magistrate, would be paid a salary by the parish or the county and anyone discharging a public duty would be remunerated for expenses incurred. Each official would be required to wear a badge identifying himself as a public servant and there was to be continuity of tenure in all offices until successors were sworn. An updated hue and cry enjoined all citizens to assist any officer in the performance of a duty, and officers were to be held strictly accountable for the execution of warrants consigned to them, although an inferior officer could not be sued for executing a warrant issued by a justice of the peace. Negligent officers who failed to collect fines would themselves be fined twice the amount and parishes that did not prosecute offenders would be heavily fined by the county. Bribery, corruption and neglect of office were all to be made heavily penal.[34]

[33] For a description of corruption, negligence and graft in local law enforcement and judicial proceedings, see Cockburn, *Assizes*, pp. 105–9. Royalists and others whose loyalty to the government was questionable caused concern after Penruddock's rebellion in the spring of 1655. Proclamations and ordinances forbidding horse racing and cock fights were issued to discourage conspiratorial plots being formed. By Sept. 1655 the protector issued a proclamation prohibiting delinquents from holding office or voting in elections: *CSPD*, VIII, pp. 53, 232, 296, 343, 409.
[34] Sheppard, *England's balme*, pp. 33, 37–8, 149, 39–40, 28–9, 200.

In Sheppard's plan of reform the justices of the peace were to be the key figures in the government of the countryside, entrusted with increased responsibilities in both administrative and judicial matters. Carefully chosen for their honesty, ability and character, their numbers were to be increased so that there would be at least one magistrate in every hundred to call regular monthly sessions. One magistrate acting alone on the evidence given by one sworn witness would be empowered to convict and sentence all offenses of swearing, perjury, cursing, fornication, bastardy, bawds, unlawful games, unlicensed alehouses, profanation of the Lord's day, vagrants and rogues, idleness, and all laws concerning servants, laborers and apprentices. Two justices of the peace, on the oath of two sworn witnesses, could convict and sentence offenders against laws concerning the poor and the maintenance of highways. Out of sessions, a pair of magistrates could bind to good behavior persons guilty of jesting, fiddling, rhyming, juggling and fortune-telling. Two could award damages for slander, defamation and mocking. Appeals from any of these convictions could be taken to general sessions or to assizes, but then removed no further.[35]

While magistrates would assume a pre-eminent role in the government of the countryside, the sheriff, 'if his office be continued', would be subjected to stringent controls. Demoted from the powerful position the office once commanded, the sheriff would become an official assistant of the courts. He would be forbidden to deputize his duties when executing warrants and, in the same respect, would be freed from liability to private law suits brought against him by individuals. Sheppard's objects in circumscribing the responsibilities of the office and eliminating the ceremonial duties were to reduce the sheriff's vulnerability to corruption.[36]

The success of Sheppard's plan to improve the quality of local government rested upon the careful selection of local officers, all of whom would be held responsible for the execution of their duties. Purchase of office would be forbidden and all county officers were to be compensated for 'their pains' and any expenses incurred in the discharge of their responsibilities. This outlay of public monies

[35] Ibid., pp. 28, 30–1, 163, 161, 35–6.
[36] Ibid., p. 37. On 13 Feb. 1656 the council acted on a report from Lambert's committee for sheriffs ordering that a letter be sent to sheriffs stating that the council was considering how to 'lessen the charges' of his office and forbidding sheriffs to offer gratuities to assize judges or to provide them with food or entertainment: *CSPD*, IX, p. 175.

was tied to a complete reorganization of county finances and public records. Each shire would have a public treasury administered by a salaried county treasurer. All penal fines and forfeitures would be received there, with half the amount forwarded to the exchequer and the remainder to be used by the county for salaries, rewards and public services benefiting the local community.[37] Parishes would be redivided to allow for a more equitable distribution of the tax burden and a consolidated county rate would be collected annually. The tax structure itself would be modified by the following changes: a general survey would readjust land rates to correct existing inequalities; a graduated tax scale would be applied to the new rates to raise the percentage levied on higher income groups; a separate income tax would impose a share of the revenue burden on persons holding 'invisible estates', such as lawyers, physicians, money-lenders, traders and others whose income was derived from services. The more efficient collection of a greater number of fines would help to augment the county's revenues.[38]

In addition to the country treasury, two other types of official repositories would be established throughout the countryside. Each parish would maintain its own archive to enroll births, marriages and burials. A survey of parish lands would yield information about local property rights which would also be entered in that registry. By voluntary arrangement any individual could there enter his claim to a grant of land, common or any other profit of land within the parish boundaries as well as a copyhold right if the controlling manor lay in another parish.[39] Each county was to have a central registry, and all deeds, conveyancing documents, pedigrees, contracts and agreements would be accepted for enrollment after being sealed with the official stamp of the lord protector. Every enrolled document

---

[37] Sheppard, *England's balme*, pp. 22, 33–4, 29–30, 24, 34–5.
[38] Ibid., pp. 145, 170–1, 178–81. The Rump Parliament had authorized a survey to consider the redistribution of parish boundaries in 1649 and Sheppard himself had served as one of the Gloucestershire commissioners making recommendations with a view towards providing ministers with more equitable incomes from tithe collections. Sheppard also proposed that tithes be received into the common county treasury: ibid., pp. 130–1.
[39] The registration of marriages, births and burials was ordered as part of the act for civil marriages passed by the Barebones on 24 Aug. 1653: *A & O*, II, pp. 715–18. Sheppard suggested simplifying the registration process, holding all past marriages good in law even though defective in some particular, and authorizing chancery to void marriages made without the consent of the parents: Sheppard, *England's balme*, pp. 125, 155–8.

would have the force and authority of a court judgment. Each county would be held responsible for building a bridewell next to the county jail as well as an asylum for the insane.[40] With this projected support system of responsible, paid officials and adequate record-keeping facilities, there was promise of an efficiency and reliability previously unknown to English public administration. It remained for Sheppard to introduce simplicity and clarity to the judicial process.

'One and the same method of proceeding in matters of law and equity' would be adopted by all courts, local and central, in the interest of uniformity and coherence. The rules and standardized fees of the courts would be posted publicly for the benefit of suitors and court officials alike. Fines levied on guilty parties would also be standardized and not left to the discretion of the judge. All original writs as well as writs and bills of arrest would be eliminated and all suits would begin with a simple summons. The summons itself would either express the cause of the action or it would be accompanied with a copy of the declaration under the hand of the plaintiff or his attorney. The plaintiff would have the choice of serving the summons himself or having it done on his behalf by the sheriff or coroner. The single exception to the abolition of original writs would be the retention of the action of trespass *de ejectione firmæ* to recover possession of land. If, upon delivery of the summons, the defendant did not appear, a second summons would be served or fixed to his door if necessary and the plaintiff would inform the court under oath that the defendant had been given notice. If the defendant failed to appear, plead and join issue, the court could give the plaintiff judgment by default.[41]

Sheppard established time limits to be honored both by the parties and by the judge. The defendant was given six days to enter his plea in personal and mixed actions. The general issue, 'that the plaintiff hath no such cause of complaint as in his declaration is alleged', was always to be pleaded and the defendant was to submit in writing the facts upon which he planned to stand. The plaintiff then had only

---

[40] Sheppard, *England's balme*, pp. 114–15, 118, 121–3, 36, 170. For details of enrolling land claims, see below, n. 58.

[41] Ibid., pp. 65, 97, 110, 197–8, 68–9, 71, 94, 91, 69, 72, 70–1. Sheppard made provisions for the cursitors of the court to prepare the summons, the declaration and all new process, 'to make amends for their loss of profits on writs and bills'. The use of a summons would eliminate the need for writs of *alias, pluries, exigent* and all outlawries. The rule that the court would proceed in a suit even in the absence of the defendant had also been included in the Chancery Ordinance.

two days to join issue and the trial was to commence within the fourteen days following. If either party did not meet the time limits, the other party would be awarded judgment; and if the judge had been responsible for delaying the trial, he himself would have to pay costs. There were to be set forms for declarations and pleas, pleadings would be short and certain, and no exceptions were permitted in the central courts after three days and, in the case of general sessions, twenty-four hours. Demurrers were to be confined to matters of substance only, not to form, and must be made within the first three days. Any special matters of the case could be presented in evidence so that the case could be settled in the court of origin rather than removed to another court. Arguments by counsel and statements from the bench were to be shortened. At any point in a lawsuit the judge could amend clerical errors. Personal actions which had automatically ended upon the death of one of the parties could continue with the executor of the deceased party assuming the benefit or liability.[42]

As for the trials themselves, juries would be used only in county sessions, at assizes and in the central courts, eliminating the option of jury trial in hundred and county courts and in courts baron. In general sessions small matters would be settled by a grand jury on proof of witnesses alone. In cases where a petty jury was called, the indictor (the bringer of the presentment) would be bound by recognizances to serve as the prosecutor. In cases where a defendant summoned by the clerk of the peace failed to appear, a plea of 'not guilty' would be entered and the case would be tried in his absence. If the defendant were found guilty, he would be punished despite the fact that he had not appeared in his own defense. If the plaintiff did not appear for trial, the defendant would be paid full costs.[43] Sheppard devised many safeguards against corruption, collusion and intimidation at jury trials, not the least of which was the quality of men serving as jurors. Only men assigned by justices of the peace to the first two ranks would be eligible and jury selection would be made either by two magistrates or by lot.[44] No jury would be told beforehand on which case it would serve. Gossip and 'tales told' would be forbidden among jury members. If for any reason there

---

[42] Ibid., pp. 73–6, 54–5, 77–8, 80, 87, 144, 73–4. Sheppard noted that there were three types of pleadings that were so involved that the pleading itself constituted a 'danger' to the cause of justice. [43] Ibid., 49, 32, 70–1, 76.

[44] For qualifications for jurymen see above, n. 32.

were an insufficient number of jurymen, the trial would proceed without a jury. The judge was expected to instruct the jury in the law and if a jury returned a verdict disliked by the judge, either the jury would be asked to reconsider the case or the case would be sent to a superior appellate court. In all cases tried by jury both the plaintiff and defendant would be permitted to have legal counsel and sworn witnesses. If a jury were found guilty by another jury of wilful perjury in the deliverance of a verdict, the grieved party could bring an action on the case against individual jury members.[45] Perjury, which Sheppard took to be endemic in the English system of justice, would in many cases be dealt with summarily by justices of the peace acting alone or in pairs. Wrong judgments knowingly given by judges of the county and hundred courts or courts baron were to be punished by a single magistrate on the proof of one witness, the guilty parties fined and permanently disabled from sitting again as judges. Wilful perjury by witnesses or jurors in sessions could also be punished by two magistrates authorized to award damages.[46]

In order to curtail the number of unnecessary suits and to facilitate quick and just settlements, Sheppard proposed the adoption of the following rules. No suit would be admitted to court if the plaintiff were out of the country or if the accuser were not known. To prevent a suit from being brought in more than one court, the judge could examine the parties under oath to clear all matters in question and the judge's decision would have the force of law (this would pertain to cases where part of a debt had been paid or 'some secret agreement [had been] made between the parties only'). In sessions and in the central courts a pauper could bring a suit after obtaining an affidavit from a justice of the peace or from a lawyer that his possessions were worth less than £5 and that he had good cause to go to the law. If his case

---

[45] Sheppard, *England's balme*, pp. 41, 50, 77, 51. Concern for the quality of jurymen had been on Cromwell's mind in Jan. 1656 when he wrote to Desborough, 'I have written to [the sheriffs] to require their special care in the choice of juries this year, that an attempt may be made of a reformation of the evils of this nature so largely complained of...[It had been reported that] the names of persons to serve on the respective trials are known beforehand, from whence opportunity is given and frequently taken of applications to each one of the jury to pre-engage them on one side or the other, which seldom fails in any cause whatsoever, to the ensnaring...of the weak and the tempting the avarice of the more subtle, which lie in wait for their own advantage...whereby justice is often perverted, the innocent wronged and the wrong-doer prevails and escapes': *W & S*, IV, pp. 87–8 (29 Jan. 1656).

[46] Sheppard, *England's balme*, pp. 47, 150–1, 51–3, 160–1.

was not good and he lost his suit, he would be sent to the workhouse for punishment.[47] At any time before or during a suit the defendant could offer to make amends and if the plaintiff refused good terms he, the plaintiff, would be deprived of recovering costs. In cases where a trespass was trivial or no hurt was sustained in a battery, a plaintiff could retrieve only costs to the amount of damages. In any vexatious suit, large costs would be awarded to the defendant. Any plaintiff who sued out more than one summons against a single defendant would be indicted as a common barrator and the defendant could have an action on the case against him. A plaintiff bringing a previously unsuccessful suit for a third time would be obliged to pay double costs to the defendant.[48] In practical terms the success of Sheppard's new system depended upon strict conformity to the new standardized procedures, the regulation of court fees, the compulsory and systematic keeping of records necessary for the appellate process and, above all, the accountability of all officials serving the public. These requisite conditions sought to bring rationalization to a system known for its obfuscations and absurdities. Sheppard's declared crusade against injustice, delay and confusion led him to propose changes not only in procedure, but in the law itself.

Probate which historically had fallen within the province of the ecclesiastical courts would be brought within the common law. The desire for a swift and fair settlement of estates led Sheppard to propose the establishment of the new county courts of judicature whose judges would be guided by fixed rules of distribution, new inheritance laws and provisions dealing with executors' responsibilities and creditors' interests. These courts would grant probate and letters of administration, charge modest fees for their services and have the coercive power to determine differences. A single appeal from the decisions of these courts could be brought before the next general sessions and creditors would be given public notice of any new trial, with the appeal to be tried by jury.[49] Changes in the

---

[47] Ibid., pp. 108–10, 62, 85.
[48] Ibid., pp. 60, 62, 97, 102, 100–1.
[49] Neither the ecclesiastical courts nor executors had had the power to enforce the proper execution of probate, with the consequence that difficult cases had traditionally been taken to chancery. The abolition of the church courts had further compounded the problems in an already confused branch of the law. In the absence of the adoption of a definitive resolution for probate, the Rump Parliament had named the twenty members of the Hale Commission to serve as probate judges according to the old system: *A & O*, II, pp. 702–3 (8 Apr. 1653); Sheppard, *England's balme*, pp. 62–3, 82, 107–8, 140–2.

inheritance laws included increased benefits in the law of dower, allowing a widow one-third of reversions and rents as well as of lands. Land would descend to half-blood rather than escheat, primogeniture would be replaced by partible inheritance and children born out of wedlock would be legitimatized by a subsequent marriage and included among the legitimate heirs. All of these suggestions derived from Sheppard's impatience with feudal anachronisms as well as his quest to bring the laws of England into harmony with human reason and divine law.[50] There would be new regulations and protections for executors and creditors of an estate. Unwilling to trust a single individual in judgment, Sheppard stipulated that an estate could not be disposed of by one executor acting alone. Executors could call a commission out of chancery for assistance in making a fair and equal distribution of the estate; creditors would be given public notice and those who did not appear to make their claims would lose their debts. If an executor had taken no steps to settle an estate within three months, he would be removed from his position by the court. Any person refusing to accept an executorship would be forbidden to meddle with the estate at a later time. Probate and letters of administration for persons residing in London, Westminster, and the home counties and for Englishmen who died abroad would fall under the jurisdiction of a special court in London.[51]

The process of recovering debts at common law was so unsatisfactory that parliaments since 1641 had made efforts to help creditors recover money due them and to bring relief to poor men imprisoned because they were unable to pay their debts.[52] Two major complications besetting the law of debt can explain the continued frustration despite the sustained interest of reformers. On the one hand, the process at common law for recovering debts was initiated by an action of arrest; the second problem arose from feudal custom which exempted landed wealth from liability for debt. The result of these combined factors was that English jails were filled with debtors, some genuinely and hopelessly indigent while others were men of substance who preferred to remain comfortably confined for years rather than

---

[50] Sheppard, *England's balme*, pp. 199, 213–14.
[51] Ibid., pp. 209–10, 107–8.
[52] See ch. 1, n. 92. A bill of 30 Aug. 1641 for the relief of creditors was rejected, but acts for the relief of poor prisoners and creditors were passed on 4 Sept. and 21 Dec. 1649, 6 Apr. 1650, 5 June 1652 and 5 Oct. 1653. The protectorate suspended the most recent act on 31 Mar. 1654 and issued new ordinances on 9 June and 11 Aug. 1654: *CJ*, II, p. 277; *A & O*, II, pp. 240, 321–4, 378–9, 582, 753–64, 860–1, 888, 911, 943–5.

voluntarily convert their land into liquid assets to satisfy their financial responsibilities. In either case the creditor was no nearer retrieving the money due him, an incongruous situation which drew Sheppard to the heart of both the problems of obligations unmet by imprisoned debtors and the exemption of landed wealth. His proposals for reforming the law of debt were grounded in a resolution to satisfy all rightful debts fully and promptly. The principal thrusts of his approach were to replace imprisonment with confinement in a workhouse where the debtor could work off his debt; and to make all assets, including land, liable for the repayment of debts. These seemingly simple solutions understandably entailed extensive changes. Under Sheppard's plan there would be no imprisonment for any debt amounting to £20 or less, nor in any case where the debtor had sufficient goods or lands to satisfy the debt. In other circumstances there still could be no imprisonment until all the details of the case had been fully investigated by a jury. In all actions of debt the creditor would be required to produce a speciality, a contract under seal, and wager of law as a method of proof was to be abolished. Where a debt was judged valid by a court of law the debtor's entire estate would be held liable for its satisfaction, including entailed and copyhold lands, lands and goods held in trust for the debtor by others and all debts due the debtor.[53] To satisfy debts, goods would be sold first and, 'if that will not do, then that the land, by what estate soever it is held, be either delivered to the plaintiff or counsel to hold til he be paid by the yearly rent; or so much thereof to be sold as to pay the debt; which of these the plaintiff shall desire'. Optionally, an assignment, or transfer, of real or personal property could be made by the debtor to the creditor.[54] In cases of debts mutually owing, a stoppage (a set-off, previously unknown at common law) would be permitted so that both cases could be heard together. A debtor would be responsible for paying accrued interest at the rate of six per cent as well as the principal of the debt. All of these provisions for satisfying debts were to be retroactive, and propertied debtors then in prison would have their estates sold and then be released, while indigent debtors would be transferred to a workhouse.[55]

[53] Sheppard had made provision for the collection of debts under £4 in the county courts: Sheppard, *England's balme*, pp. 90–2, 212.

[54] Ibid., pp. 88–9, 213, 208, 115, 208–9.

[55] In 1651 the Rump Parliament had reduced the interest rate to 6 per cent to promote land sales by the commonwealth: *A & O*, II, pp. 548–50. Sheppard, *England's balme*, pp. 88–92.

To ensure that the new system would work fairly, Sheppard shored up these rules with a number of supporting provisions. After judgment, when the estate was sequestered for partial or full sale to satisfy the debt, execution would be limited to a fixed time. If the creditor had no knowledge of the debtor's visible estate, a justice of the peace, coroner or sheriff would be authorized to seize and secure the estate and to prepare an inventory under court order. An investigation by a grand jury would follow and if it were determined that the debtor 1. had sufficient lands and goods to satisfy the debt; or 2. was a 'loose, prodigal and licentious man who had wasted his estate'; 3. had dishonestly concealed the worth of his estate; or 4. could not prove how his estate had been wasted, the debtor would then be punished.[56] The creditor would be given the option of choosing one of the following penalties: the debtor could either be sent to the bridewell to work for the rest of his life, or be sent to prison for three years, or put himself into service, the creditor taking half the profits of his work. Alternatively, the debtor could arrange for a generous friend to compound with the creditor for the debt. In cases where the debtor was too old or otherwise disabled from work, he would either be kept at the expense of his own parish under confinement or be transported to a foreign plantation. In cases where a jury established that the debtor had deliberately concealed his estate, the estate would be sold, the creditor recompensed to the amount of the debt and the remainder of the profits forfeited to the state. Debtors out of the country could no longer evade their just debts if they had estates in England for, after notification of a suit against them, creditors could proceed to carry a suit through the courts even in the absence of the defendant. Debtors claiming bankruptcy would be ineligible for any public office in the commonwealth. Corporations were to be held liable for their debts just as individuals were. And, as a final protection for creditors, the forfeited estates of felons and traitors would be used to satisfy all claims against them prior to further action.[57]

The numerous conditions of land-holding were among the most complex aspects of English law but it was a field about which Sheppard was particularly knowledgeable. His recommended reforms in this sphere were premised on the establishment of country registries where short, standardized forms for entries of property holdings would be officially enrolled. The form he designed for this

⁵⁶ Sheppard, *England's balme*, pp. 90–2.   ⁵⁷ Ibid., pp. 91–2, 109, 147.

purpose had been published in the *President of presidents* in 1655. Claims properly registered would have the force of a judgment in a court of law, and a statute of limitations would perpetually bar entries not made within twenty days after the agreement of transfer or, in cases of land devised by will, within forty days of the death of the testator. Copyhold estates and claims to rents or encumbrances by custom or prescription would also be entered and any not enrolled would be held fraudulent and void. Sheppard's solution for the case of a man 'whose estate, in reputation, was good' but who could not produce the proper documents to prove his title was to have the claim settled by a suit in equity. The mandatory implementation of this system for registration would allow for the elimination of all fines, recoveries and livery of seisin. The registration of all land would become part of the public record and entries into and claims of land made in secret would be held illegal and void.[58] Sheppard assigned criminal penalties to reinforce and buttress his registration scheme. The counterfeiting of deeds would be punished by forfeiture of half the guilty party's own estate. A seller who resold a piece of land would forfeit his entire estate and be sent to the bridewell for life. If a county officer forged, razed or altered any record in his keeping, he would be turned out of office and forfeit his own estate. Forgery, however, would be removed from the list of capital crimes.[59]

The harsh and horrific aspects of the criminal code had excited cries of protest from reforming pamphleteers throughout the interregnum period. The response from parliaments had, however, been very disappointing, and the Rump Parliament had added incest and adultery to the already long list of capital crimes.[60] The rationalization for assigning penalties of increased severity to these offenses came from Biblical stricture, a favorite authority for many seventeenth-century reformers. Sheppard, too, linked his proposed revisions of the criminal code to his religious beliefs but to an entirely different effect. His suggestions, which were based upon humanitarianism and reason as well as divine law, were to reduce the number of capital crimes,

---

[58] Ibid., pp. 112–19, 212. The Hale Commission had defined encumbrances as 'all conveyances and limitations other than customary rights and duties'. The bill considered by the Rump required that all encumbrances be registered within 12 months of the establishment of the registries and thereafter new encumbrances registered within 40 days of the time they were made: Cotterell, 'Law reform', pp. 114–15.

[59] Sheppard, *England's balme*, pp. 124, 195.

[60] *A & O*, II, pp. 387–9 (Act of 10 May 1650).

not only because many punishments were out of proportion to the offense, but also because many statutory felonies were 'repugnant to the laws of God and evil in themselves'.[61] Scattered throughout *England's balme* were examples of offenses carrying a statutory or common-law death penalty that Sheppard regarded as 'extreme and oppressive to the people'. He voiced no objections to execution for murder, treason or 'horrid blasphemies against the nature of God', but he would have punishments reduced for all other capital crimes. Many of the felonies created by statute, particularly the great number legislated under the Tudors and early Stuarts, seemed to Sheppard so unjust that they had no place in Christian society. Forgers, gypsies, Roman Catholic priests, counterfeiters and sheep-stealers who took their quarry out of England were, by English law, condemned to death. To Sheppard, the most offensive of all criminal statutes was the death penalty for 'a small or trivial theft'.[62] Many proponents of penal reform from the time of Thomas More onwards had singled out the hanging of petty thieves as one of the most barbarous aspects of English law. In *England's balme*, Sheppard underscored his revulsion to the death penalty for crimes of petty theft by contrasting it with another incongruous element of the penal code, benefit of clergy. This privilege of exemption from capital punishment (except in cases of high treason and some other specifically exempted crimes) had originally been accorded only to clergymen in order to determine their eligibility for having a case removed to an ecclesiastical court for adjudication. By Sheppard's day an estimated twenty to twenty-eight per cent of convicted felons or thieves who could read, or indeed had the wit to memorize the 'neck verse', escaped punishment for clergyable offenses before sentencing.[63] Sheppard's solution to the appalling paradox of 'one

---

[61] Sheppard, *England's balme*, p. 7.
[62] Ibid., pp. 191, 195, 134, 204, 196, 16. Self-defenders who merited pardons *de cursu* (as a matter of course) still suffered forfeiture of goods and could spend many months in prison before receiving their pardons. Sheppard would have removed both the forfeiture and the period of waiting for the 'automatic' pardon. For an up-to-date discussion of the English law of homicide, see Green, 'Jury and homicide', pp. 414–99.
[63] The 'neck verse' was Psalm 51.1. After 1623 women were permitted to claim clergy in cases of trivial thefts and by 1693 the full benefits of the privilege were extended to women: J. H. Baker, 'Criminal courts and procedure at common law 1550–1800', in Cockburn, *Crime in England*, p. 41; Cockburn, *Assizes*, pp. 125–9; T. A. Green, 'The jury and the English law of homicide, 1200–1600', *Michigan Law Review*, LXXIV (1976), 493.

[who] escapeth by clergy for manslaughter and another [who] is hanged for stealing because he cannot read' was a double foil: he would abolish the privilege of clergy and, at the same time, remove the death penalty from all but the most heinous crimes.[64]

The procedures followed in criminal prosecutions drew an equally critical eye from Sheppard. The brutal process of *peine forte et dure* (pressing to death) would be replaced by a plea of 'not guilty' entered in the record for those whose refusal to plead came from fear for their families' ruination by the forfeiture of their estates. Sheppard also proposed both granting counsel and having defense testimony on oath when the defendant was charged with a capital crime. Trial by combat would be summarily forbidden because it countenanced men killing themselves. Duels and outlawries would be abolished because they sanctioned murder. The harsh penalties of mutilation and long imprisonment would be abolished. The familial consequences of both forfeiture and corruption of blood would be removed and a felon's estate would be used first to satisfy the legitimate claims of creditors, with the remainder reverting to the family.[65]

With the object of fitting the punishment to the crime, Sheppard suggested reducing many penalties, including the loss of an ear for drawing a weapon and of a hand for striking a blow in the sovereign's palace. Long imprisonment for failing to return a lost dog promptly and the civil disabilities falling on religious dissidents illustrated Sheppard's point about disproportionate punishments. Although Sheppard found those and other aspects of the criminal code 'extreme and oppressive', there were many other 'notorious grievances' where the punishments were not, in his opinion, sufficiently severe. Most of these fell into categories of disorderly behavior, social irresponsibility and, especially, offenses proscribed by the Bible. He called for more extensive laws against swearing and cursing, disobedient children and sexual offenses, all forbidden in the Ten Commandments. Sterner laws were also demanded for the social disruptions caused by drunkenness, bankruptcy and the nefarious activities of rogues and vagabonds.[66] For Sheppard, the answer to

---

[64] Sheppard, *England's balme*, pp. 16, 159.
[65] Ibid., pp. 196–7, 134, 159, 69, 195, 206, 214. An ordinance of 29 June 1654 outlawed duelling as 'unbecoming to Christians' and 'contrary to good order and government' and provided that death as a result of a duel would be adjudged murder: *A & O*, II, pp. 937–9.
[66] Sheppard, *England's balme*, pp. 201, 16, 205, 191, 159–60, 181, 164–7, 173.

the problem of criminal reform was to devise a code that allowed for uniform punishments for common offenses, an ideal sought by reformers of various societies in different ages.[67] He frowned on long, pre-trial imprisonments and favored punishment by constructive public-service work in a house of correction. For minor offenses the public humiliation of the wrong-doer would suffice, and Sheppard preferred having an offender wear a paper collar stating his offense to confinement in the stocks.[68]

Virtually all of the proposals Sheppard incorporated into his design as described to this point had been adapted from ideas put forward by other reformers. He included several specific reforms that had been drafted as bills by early Stuart parliaments or, more recently, by the Long and Rump Parliaments, just as the author of the Chancery Ordinance had incorporated earlier proposals in that reform document. And yet, in this personal selection of grievances as well as in his formulation of specific remedies, Sheppard had brought the general outlines of his judicial and legal reforms into a pattern that bore a striking resemblance to the system established a quarter of a century earlier by the founding magistrates of the Massachusetts Bay Colony. The efforts made by those fellow puritans towards establishing a society in the wilderness had, from most appearances, been remarkably successful and by the 1650s there was enough information available in England so that any interested observer could acquaint himself with how the government and the court system there were intended to work, either by studying the printed laws, sermons and pamphlets or by seeking information from any one of the hundreds of New Englanders who had returned to the mother country since the beginning of the civil war.[69]

[67] Thomas Jefferson's 'bill for proportioning crimes and punishments in cases heretofore capital' which was presented to the Virginia legislature in 1779 bears striking similarities to many of Sheppard's proposed revisions of the English criminal code in 1656. Prof. Kathryn Preyer has documented many of the influences at work in the eighteenth century: K. Preyer, 'Reforming the criminal law in Virginia', paper delivered to the ASLH, Philadelphia, Oct. 1976.

[68] Sheppard, *England's balme*, p. 23.

[69] The only printed laws officially adopted by the general court were contained in *The book of the general lawes and libertyes concerning the inhabitants of Massachusetts*, of which 600 copies sold at 3s. in Oct. 1648. The one known surviving copy, now held by The Huntington Library, was discovered in England, implying that other copies might well have reached the mother country, too. The *Lawes and libertyes* of 1648, reproduced in facsimile and edited with an introduction by T. G. Barnes (San Marino, California, 1975), will hereafter be cited as *L & L*. In 1636 John Cotton published *Moses, his judicials* and the

The influence of Massachusetts polity on Sheppard is most apparent in the structural similarities his plan bore to the unitary and hierarchical court system of the colony, in which each court had jurisdiction in matters of both law and equity and no rival jurisdictions were permitted to exist.[70] A few of the principles followed in Massachusetts had already been adopted in interregnum England, like civil marriage and the conduct of legal proceedings in English, and many of the procedures followed in Massachusetts had, in turn, come from practices that had been known to the settlers at first hand in Holland or in the manor and borough courts of England.[71] There were, too, aspects of New England practice that had been adopted for the sake of expediency, as in the case of simplified procedure, simply because there were few law books and fewer lawyers in the

sub-title, *An abstract of the laws of New England as they are now established*, falsely conveyed the impression that the contents had become law. Cotton's work was published by William Aspinwall in London in 1652 and 1655. In 1642 Thomas Lechford published a tract in London entitled *Plaine dealing* in which he praised the law-making efforts of the puritan colonists. Nathaniel Ward, another colonist who eventually returned to England, compiled a *Body of Liberties* in 1641 that contained 100 clauses of constitutional rights and legal principles, all but 14 of which were incorporated into the *L & L* adopted in 1648. Ward was a barrister of Lincoln's Inn and his *The simple cobbler of Aggawam* (1647) commented further on the laws of New England. In 1651 another returned New Englander, the preacher Hugh Peter, published *Good work for a good magistrate* in London which contained information about colonial laws. The close communication maintained among New England clergy and the English Independents in personal letters and published sermons as well as Sheppard's personal acquaintance with Edward Norris, the Horsley preacher who found a pulpit in Massachusetts, provided additional vehicles for the transmission of information about the colony's legal system. The impressive number of Massachusetts leaders who returned to the mother country during the revolutionary years has been investigated by W. L. Sachse, 'The migration of New Englanders to England, 1640–1660', *American Historical Review*, LIII (1948), 251–78.

70 The major components of the Massachusetts judicial system were clearly apparent in the *L & L* although the published work was not meant to be a comprehensive compilation of all the laws in force. Most of Ward's constitutional provisions were incorporated as was a great deal of statute-law revision.

71 Civil marriage and partible inheritance had been adapted from practice in Holland and the registration of land was known in many English boroughs. The pioneer study of the influence of local and customary law on early Massachusetts legal development is Julius Goebel, Jr, 'King's law and local custom in seventeenth-century New England', *Columbia Law Review*, XXXI (1931), 416–48. The similarities between the 1648 *L & L* and the English proposals of Sheppard and other interregnum law reformers were noticed by T. L. Wolford, 'The Laws and Liberties of 1648', *Boston University Law Review*, XXVIII (1948), 426–63.

new settlement.[72] And yet, no matter where the practices had originated or for what reasons they were applied, in their several distinctive characteristics they combined to form a legal-judicial system unlike any other, and the resemblances of Massachusetts to the proposals in *England's balme* in both outline and detail lends credence to the theory that Sheppard adapted the model of his plans for reform from New England usage.

Most of the extensive legal and judicial reforms Sheppard advocated would have entailed parliamentary sanction under the provisions of the Instrument of Government. The scores of ordinances Cromwell and the council had issued since the establishment of the regime also awaited confirmation. While the agenda prepared for this parliament was extremely ambitious, the political leaders had given no hint of the scope of legal change they intended to sponsor except for the ill-fated Chancery Ordinance.[73] The diversity and magnitude of the government's legislative program did become apparent in the first weeks of the session when a number of bills were introduced or ordered to be prepared.[74] When Sheppard signed the preface to his book at Whitehall on 1 October 1656 he appealed to the parliament 'now convened and sitting' to consider the proposals he had been charged to prepare, urging the members 'to make wholesome laws for the general cure of the whole body' and to 'proceed to a reformation of the whole'.[75] In order to accomplish the comprehensive reform, Sheppard advocated that parliament embark on a project that had awaited legislative attention for generations: the thorough revision of statute law.

The abridgment of English statutes was one dimension of legal reform that had commanded a consensus among administrators and law reformers for nearly a century. Numerous statutes enacted over

[72] The simplifications in procedure are discussed by Haskins, *Early Massachusetts*, pp. 117–18, 168–9, 182, 212–19 and D. T. Konig, *Law and society in puritan Massachusetts. Essex County, 1629–1692* (Chapel Hill, N.C., 1979), pp. 58, 61–2.
[73] In 'Cromwell's ordinances', Prof. Roots has made a valuable contribution to our understanding of the daily occupations and accomplishments of the administration. His conclusions necessarily differ from the interpretation presented here because the material in *England's balme* as well as that in the *President* and *County judicatures* has been taken to be solid evidence that a program of integrated reform was taking shape behind the scenes and that Sheppard's design represented the aspirations for reform of a majority of the council members and the protector himself.
[74] See below, pt II.
[75] Sheppard, *England's balme*, sigs. A1v, A8.

many reigns had produced redundancies and contradictions that were confusing to law-enforcement officers and citizens alike. In the interest of establishing clarity and certainty, Sheppard proposed that parliament specifically repeal all obsolete and 'useless' laws. The next step would be to bring 'all laws about one thing into one law, and to make that law as short and as clear as may be'.[76] His examples of laws that needed to be reduced were those that had been re-enacted with predictable regularity: laws dealing with servants and laborers; the penal disabilities imposed on Roman Catholic laymen and priests; the regulatory legislation concerning the manufacture and distribution of cloth; and the price of bread and beer. Sheppard assured his readers that this process of reducing multiple statutes would strengthen the authority of the law, for 'to take away the weeds will not hurt the wheat'.[77] He also proposed that a cooperative project be undertaken 'to make one plain, complete and methodical treatise or abridgment of the whole common and statute law, comprehending the heads thereof, to which all cases may be referred; and to make those things that are now obscure and incertain, clear and certain. And to have the judges subscribe it for the settled law and to have it confirmed by the parliament.'[78] His conception of the manner in which this general statement of the law could be formulated was grounded in the basic premise of English legal tradition – that the judges alone were responsible for deciding what was good law. Sheppard was not proposing a codification or a statement of rigid principles, but rather in having a comprehensive body of case law assembled which integrated all relevant statutes, legal principles and common-law usages under heads. One of the implicit assumptions

---

[76] The line closes, 'and to have that which is in Latin and French, Englished': ibid., p. 19.

[77] Ibid., p. 19. Revising the statute book had been a concern of government administrators since the reign of Henry VIII. In 1597 Lord Chancellor Ellesmere conveyed the following message from Queen Elizabeth I to parliament: 'And whereas the number of laws already made is very great, some of them being obsolete and worn out of use, others idle and vain, serving no purpose, some again over-heavy and too severe for the offense, others too loose and slack for all the faults they are to punish, and many so full of difficulty to be understood that they cause many controversies and much trouble to arise amongst the subjects. You are to enter into a due consideration of the laws, and where you find superfluity, to prune and cut off, where defect to supply, and where ambiguity to explain, that they be not burdensome but profitable to the commonwealth; which being a service of importance and very needful to be required': Simonds D'Ewes, *Journals...both of the House of Lords and House of Commons*, Paul Bowes, reviser (1682), p. 524 (24 Oct. 1597).

[78] Sheppard, *England's balme*, sigs. A1v, A8r, p. 6.

of the plan was that the compilers of this treatise would search the entire body of statute law, expunging those that had expired and ensuring that the compilation was complete prior to submitting the entire body of law to the judges for approval. It was certainly Sheppard's hope that the project would be undertaken by a capable and experienced group of professionals and that ultimately a Cromwellian parliament or a later legislature would elevate the 'complete and methodical treatise' to statutory authority so that the law that had developed to date would be settled and understood. As a common lawyer, Sheppard realized that a permanent and fixed code of law was neither possible nor desirable within the common-law tradition he hoped to strengthen and preserve. His proposal for the enactment of such a treatise can be reconciled with his awareness of the evolving nature of the law only if it is inferred that the proposed treatise would be the first step in a continuing effort by the compilers and judges to keep the compendium current, adding and extracting both cases and statutes as necessary.

The remainder of Sheppard's proposals in *England's balme* which extended into the fields of commerce, finance and religion distinguish him as a social engineer as well as a law reformer. To supplement deficiencies in the commercial life of the nation he advocated the establishment of new industries and the founding of banks to manage the exchange of money, all to be regulated by the state. To stimulate the economy he would grant to aliens the same free-trade privileges accorded to Englishmen. He also endorsed a radical reform of apprenticeship laws on the grounds that they were unnecessarily rigid. He called for a repeal of the Elizabethan statute that forbade a cottager to build on less than four acres of land. These ideas were developed from his social philosophy that every sector of society should have a sufficient economic base. All able-bodied persons should, in his opinion, be self-supporting and not hindered by legal constraints in the pursuits of their livelihoods. This philosophy of ensuring that the state not carry unnecessary financial burdens had a counterpart in the private sector. His ideas about financial responsibility account for his proposals that debtors be held good for their debts, either by working them off or by selling their lands, and also that bankruptcy be dealt with more harshly to discourage financially irresponsible behavior.[79]

79 Ibid., pp. 201, 203–4, 135. For Sheppard's proposed policies for debtors and bankrupts, see ibid., pp. 90–2, 212, 147. The question of whether to extend commercial and legal rights to foreigners had long been a political as well as an

Other fiscal reforms that Sheppard wanted the state to institute were reassertions of the medieval and Elizabethan policies of state control over industries, prices and wages. The enforcement of old laws and the regulation of new industries through legislation was characteristic of the protectorate's policy of resuming a strong, central control over the countryside after half a century of neglect by the early-Stuart parliaments and the disruptions of the civil war. New laws were needed to establish price ceilings on charges made by country inns. False weights and measures employed in trade would, under Sheppard's plan, be subject to severe prosecution and 'deceitful wares' would be kept off the market. He suggested local enforcement of these controls by two justices of the peace acting together and assuming the full power of the clerk of the market. In corporations these consumer and trade regulations would be enforced by city officials acting in their capacities as justices of the peace.[80]

The public interest would benefit from new legislation for the general improvement of marshes, commons, wastelands and enclosures as well as more stringent laws enforcing the repair of highways and bridges, again delegated to the jurisdiction of local magistrates. Laws against enclosure should be modified, if not repealed, to accommodate those who improved their estates to the profit of the nation. Sheppard suggested that all communal fields might be divided or fenced 'where people desire it'. The serious timber shortage (which affected ship-building and therefore the security of the nation) could be corrected by mandatory reforestation whereby landowners would be legally obliged to plant to woods seven

---

economic issue: see Cooper, 'Social and economic policies', in Aylmer, *Interregnum*, pp. 130–1. The council of state had exempted soldiers from apprenticeship laws and permitted them to exercise any trade they chose by an ordinance of 2 Sept. 1654: *A & O*, II, p. 1006. A study by G. D. Ramsey indicates that few ex-soldiers were able to take advantage of this liberty although the evasion of apprenticeship laws by payments was fairly common even in the early part of the century: G. D. Ramsey, 'Industrial *laisser-faire* and the policy of Oliver Cromwell', in Roots, *Cromwell*, pp. 151–6.

[80] Sheppard, *England's balme*, pp. 184–9, 211–12. Ramsey's article noted above provides many details to support his thesis that during the five-year period of the protectorate a strong and determined government deliberately attempted to enforce the traditional controls and regulations over the nation's economic life. He cites Sheppard's proposals in *England's balme* and his work on the council's corporation-charter committee as the sole philosophical indicators of the return to the traditional and conservative policies of Elizabethan paternalism in regulating the country's commerce and industry. For Sheppard's role in state policy, see Ramsey, '*Laisser-faire*', pp. 141–3; the entire article appears on pp. 136–59.

acres in every hundred or, for smaller holdings, a stipulated number of trees per acre. Enforcement would be entrusted to churchwardens who would report on local compliance under oath to the magistrates at general sessions.[81]

Further fiscal reforms proposed by Sheppard reflected the need to restore order after fifteen years of disruptions caused by the civil wars and the changes in government. He urged that the state guarantee repayment of citizens' loans whether they had been made voluntarily or under coercion. The sale of land purchased from the common-wealth at a fair price would be confirmed by act of parliament but compensation for owners of estates sold at rates lower than the market value would be reconsidered. Buildings that had been destroyed either in wartime or through accidental fire would be rebuilt at the community's expense and compensation would be available for those whose homes had been torn down deliberately to forestall the spreading of fire. Sheppard reckoned that each county would have adequate revenues to cover these responsibilities from the regular income collected into the county treasury.[82] He envisioned the shires of England as self-sufficient entities, each with its own resources for social services. As for the enlarged fiscal responsibilities of the national government, the chronic deficit in revenues was a serious and long-standing problem that had become even more acute when

[81] Sheppard, *England's balme*, pp. 135, 153–4, 174–5, 182–3. The council of state had issued ordinances for the repair of highways and bridges on 31 Mar., 16 May and 2 Sept. 1654 as well as one to reclaim land lost from the sea in Suffolk and Norfolk on 2 Sept. 1654: *A & O*, II, pp. 861, 897, 1013, 1019. The timber shortage was a frequent topic of discussion in council meetings and in Apr. 1654 two council members were asked to prepare a report on forests: *CSPD*, VII, p. 93. Ordinances of Aug. 1654 ordered a survey of timber on former crown lands and reserved forests as collateral security for soldiers' wages: *A & O*, II, pp. 946, 993. At a July 1656 meeting of the council attended by Cromwell a committee of five presented its proposals for the preservation of timber and the report was referred to the council's committee of trade: PRO, SP 25/77, fol. 292.

[82] Sheppard, *England's balme*, pp. 187, 139–40. Compensation by the community for loss by fire was a fairly common English local practice. In 1606 in the North Riding of Yorkshire donations out of the county fund for lame soldiers and hospitals were given to people whose houses and goods had been 'spent by fire'. This practice continued through the seventeenth century and justices of the peace awarded compensation according to the losses suffered: E. Trotter, *Seventeenth-century life in the country parish* (Cambridge, 1919), pp. 186–7, 199–200. Sheppard's enlightened proposal about the state's responsibility to repay loans to private citizens was drafted as a bill for the 1656 parliament and although it failed to pass, land sales were confirmed by act of parliament after the restoration (12 Car. II, c. 12, s. 6): J. I. Thirsk, 'The sale of royalist land during the interregnum', *EcHR*, 2nd ser., V (1952), 188.

the cost of maintaining a standing army and an aggressive navy was added to an already over-burdened national treasury.

The Instrument of Government had called for a 'constant yearly revenue' of £200,000 to defray the regular cost of government as well as additional income sufficient to maintain a 30,000-man army and the navy. The experience of more than two years had proved that the protectorate's economic base was inadequate to support these civil and military commitments. Every salaried officer and employee of the government was well aware of the problems of insufficient revenue because, like Sheppard himself, few were paid promptly or in full. The Instrument had vested all the titles and profits of remaining royal and ecclesiastical property in the protector and his successors but most of the valuable crown and church lands had been sold years before and there was a constitutional provision that no more land could be sold without the express consent of parliament. The great promise of legal, social and religious reform held out by Sheppard's design could not be realized unless the government achieved fiscal viability. The Instrument had provided for the government's receipt of the usual profits of justice and of customs.[83] A series of ordinances for the continuation of the excise tax had been issued as well as several for county assessments and customs, with a new tax on coal levied to finance ship-building. The collection of all monies into a 'public receipt' had been made a constitutional provision and an ordinance of June 1654 established a public treasury.[84] In order to increase the state's ordinary revenues

[83] Cromwell and the council were given the power to raise money 'for preventing the disorders and dangers which otherwise might fall out by sea and land' according to art. XXX of the Instrument, but only until the meeting of the first parliament. Ordinary revenues were to be raised 'by the customs and such other ways and means as shall be agreed upon' by the protector and council: art. XXVII. Art. XXXI provided for the transfer to the protector of former crown and church lands, the lands of delinquents and papists who had not compounded, and the usual profits of justice: *A & O*, II, pp. 820–1. For the chronic shortage in public revenue, see Aylmer, *State's servants, passim.*

[84] The consolidation of public revenues was a continuing concern and in July 1653 the Barebones Assembly had provided for all monies to be brought into one treasury. Art. XXVIII of the Instrument ordered yearly revenues to 'be paid into the public treasury', and an ordinance of June 1654 had implemented the constitutional clause while another ordinance of Sept. 1654 provided once again that all branches of revenue be brought into the exchequer: *A & O*, II, pp. 711, 820, 918, 1016. Prof. Roots has counted 21 ordinances on finance in the early months of the protectorate: Roots, 'Cromwell's ordinances', p. 150. Those concerning the excise were the most frequently issued, but see also those for assessment, customs and coal tax: *A & O*, II, pp. 823, 828, 842, 854, 889, 903, *et passim.*

Sheppard proposed to collect several regular fees in the protector's name. Part of the profits from the official registration of deeds and other enrolled documents in the counties would be forwarded to the national treasury as would a fee from every alienation of land. For every action brought in any of the nation's courts a reasonable fee would be charged as well. Fines would be levied against 'everyone condemned in a [law] suit' as well as on all unsuccessful judicial appeals. Finally, everyone bound to good behavior would be obliged to pay the protector 10s. before release.[85]

In the 215 small octavo pages of *England's balme* Sheppard presented hundreds of distinct suggestions for the reform of the judicial system, revision of the civil and criminal codes, the establishment of mechanisms to secure title to land and a general overhaul in the administrative and fiscal operations of government. All his reforms presupposed government according to the constitutional base of the Instrument. It remains only to describe Sheppard's proposals for the completion of the religious settlement as it had been outlined in the written constitution.

The protectorate's religious settlement was founded on the principle that the civil state assume two responsibilities: first, to provide financial support to preachers who would propagate the gospel; and second, to protect Christian liberty by guaranteeing liberty of conscience. Both were derived from the belief that only the civil magistrate could be entrusted with these duties because, given the lack of an unambiguous scriptural authority for church polity, men should be free to worship as their consciences dictated without the coercive discipline of an ecclesiastical authority. Four articles in the Instrument and three ordinances issued by the protector and council were the authorities upon which this settlement rested.[86] The program represented the philosophy of the conservative Independents, a small group of theologians and lay followers who dominated the formulation of government religious policy from the establishment of the regime until the spring of 1657. Cromwell had consulted with his personal chaplain, John Owen, and three other Independent ministers and it was upon their advice that the settlement was developed. The influence of the Independents was present in the council of state as well. Lambert, the acknowledged author of the constitution, had clearly been guided by Independent principles

[85] Sheppard, *England's balme*, pp. 123, 110–11, 61.
[86] Arts. XXXV–XXXVIII, Instrument of Government: *A & O*, II, pp. 821–2, 855, 922, 968, 1000, 1025.

when he drafted that document. He later became a member of John Owen's church as did two other council members, Desborough and Fleetwood. A fourth councillor, Sydenham, had supported the Independent program as a member of the Barebones Assembly. The influence commanded by the Independents was unrivalled by any other religious group in the council of state and the protector could depend upon conciliar support for the program he developed with the assistance of his chosen religious advisers.[87]

At the time *England's balme* was published this program had been operating successfully for more than two years and yet, in the eyes of some of its advocates, it was neither entirely satisfactory nor complete. Sheppard, who himself subscribed to the principles upon which the settlement was based, took the opportunity to suggest improvements for a system he wished to preserve. The Instrument's statement of constitutional principles asserted 'that the Christian religion as contained in the scriptures be held forth and recommended as the public profession of these nations'. Since the Bible was, for the Independents, the touchstone for both religious truths and spiritual inspiration, Sheppard's first point was to plead for 'a more perfect translation of the scriptures'.[88] The same constitutional clause stipulated that the state would assume responsibility for providing financial support to 'able and painful teachers for instructing the people and for the discovery and confutation of error, heresy and whatever is contrary to sound doctrine'. Sheppard found a deficiency in the settlement on this point, too, because no criteria for 'sound doctrine' had been adopted. Most Independents could agree that there were certain essential truths necessary for salvation, and twice Owen and his colleagues had drawn up a set of basic doctrines: the sixteen fundamentals of 1652 and the twenty of 1654, but neither set had been incorporated in ordinance or declaration. There may have been a fear that any doctrinal test would alienate some portion of the political support the protectorate government wished to garner from other religious groups. Consequently, in the absence of any official standard, the triers had evaluated candidate preachers for their qualities of 'divine grace, exemplary behavior and preaching ability'.[89] Sheppard, believing that there was a great need for some basic doctrinal statement, proposed that 'some moderate,

[87] Cook, 'Congregational Independents', pp. 338–9, 347.
[88] Art. XXXV, Instrument: *A & O*, II, p. 821; Sheppard, *England's balme*, p. 138.
[89] Art. XXXV, Instrument: *A & O*, II, p. 821; Cook, 'Congregational Independents', p. 342.

sweet and wise declaration' of fundamental Christian principles be agreed upon by the protector and the 1656 parliament which they themselves would 'embrace and practice...and persuade all others thereunto'. His idea was to supply a guide against error that would include only the most essential tenets of faith. Matters of less importance could remain open to differing interpretations and individual churches would retain the autonomy they had enjoyed in matters of ceremony and prayer and in the conduct of their own affairs. But it was only fitting that a nation committed to godly reformation should frame a statement of first principles.[90]

A third constitutional principle also required further elaboration through parliamentary action. The Instrument had vowed to protect all peaceable Christians in the exercise of their religion, including those who differed 'in judgement from the doctrine, worship or discipline publicly held forth...so long as they not abuse this liberty to the civil injury of others and to the actual disturbance of the public peace on their parts'. This liberty of conscience was extremely important to the Independents and it accounts in part for their distaste for disciplinary power being exercised by any ecclesiastical authority. The original nucleus of this religious party, the five dissenting brethren, had requested that this freedom be granted by the Westminster Assembly as part of the religious settlement of the 1640s. When the adherents of religious liberty finally acquired positions of pre-eminent influence in the government, the tenet was adopted as a constitutional precept. A fourth article of the Instrument supported this assertion by declaring null and void 'any law, statute or ordinance to the contrary of the aforesaid liberty' and, as a consequence, toleration was extended to groups who chose to remain outside the state-supported system.[91] Again, Sheppard upheld the principle and ventured to suggest some further legal changes that would fortify the spirit of the law. In addition to permitting freedom of worship, Sheppard wanted to repeal a number of civil disabilities and criminal penalties that devolved on violators of the old laws of religious uniformity and were, technically, still enforceable. The laws peripheral to religious worship that he wanted removed from the statute book were that a Roman Catholic be held in *praemunire* for owning a 'Popish picture' and another that he be fined £100 for baptizing or marrying according to his faith; that Baptists were

---

[90] Sheppard, *England's balme*, pp. 137–8.
[91] Arts. XXXVI, XXXVII and XXXVIII, Instrument.

disabled from making wills and from serving as executors. A more recent law carried a fine of from £5 to £50 for saying anything in derogation of the Directory of Worship, while another attached the penalty of imprisonment to anyone holding that the Presbyterian form of government adopted by the Long Parliament was unlawful. Everyone of these laws infringed upon a man's liberty to think and behave as his conscience dictated and violated the philosophies of peaceful coexistence and toleration. All, therefore, required parliamentary repeal.[92]

Sheppard also suggested improvements in the practical operation of the religious settlement. A central body of triers had been appointed in 1654 to select preachers entitled to a state stipend. Thirty-eight commissioners had been named and representatives of the Presbyterian and Baptist ministries had been included as well as Independent clergymen and lay commissioners. The approval of any five triers in attendance was needed for approbation while nine objections were required to exclude a candidate. Meeting at Whitehall four days a week, the triers had performed their duties conscientiously and even critics of the system praised the success of this state-supported selection process. But its flaws were apparent to Sheppard. It was expensive and time-consuming for clergymen to travel to Westminster. More important, there was a dangerous possibility that, with only five votes for approbation needed, an unsuitable person might receive the government's sanction to preach and receive a public salary.[93] Sheppard's proposal to improve the method of operation falls under the rubric of decentralization. He advocated reverting to the plan first proposed in 1652, transferring the responsibility for approval back to 'the proper counties' where local magistrates would supervise a local commission of triers and the allocation of stipends. His theory was that each locale was best able to judge for itself which men were fit to instruct and influence the local community in spiritual matters and to decide where preachers were most needed. Commissions of local triers would make the actual selection of suitable preachers and, guided by the fundamental principles enshrined in the proposed national doctrine, every county of England would apply the same standard to determine basic orthodoxy and to reject error and heresy. County triers would be more likely to have, or be able to obtain personal knowledge about

---

[92] Sheppard, *England's balme*, pp. 202–5.
[93] *A & O*, II, pp. 855–8; Cook, 'Congregational Independents', p. 349.

the local applicants and be better able to judge the qualities of each candidate's character and preaching ability. The shift of control in religious matters from the center to the counties would have the effect of establishing a preaching ministry responsive to the community's religious preferences as well as making the process of approbation more efficient, quicker and cheaper.[94]

The commitment to support a preaching ministry had brought protectorate officials to the reluctant decision that tithe payments must be continued until a substitute source of maintenance was found. The collection of tithes therefore continued into the third year of the protectorate despite the fact that government leaders themselves regarded them as an unfortunate but unavoidable expediency. When Sheppard compiled his statement of the nation's grievances in *England's balme* he understandably included the issue of the widespread opposition to this form of church maintenance. The collection of tithes was linked historically to the parochial form of church government instituted by the medieval Roman church and retained by the Anglican episcopal establishment. Sheppard objected in principle to every remnant of 'Popish practice' and ideally would have banished from England every vestige of the Roman church, including celebration of holy days other than the sabbath, the dating of writs by 'Popish holidays', any set form of prayer, the patronage of churches and even Latinized words used in legal proceedings.[95] As for the maintenance of clergymen, he had a plan to replace tithes with another form of public funding. It was to collect a rent of 20*d.* in every pound-sterling from all land previously chargeable for tithe payment. This rate of approximately eight per cent was lower than the traditional tenth part and the collection of money instead of corn

---

[94] The ejection, or removal, of scandalous ministers was already in the hands of the local communities according to the ordinance of 28 Aug. 1654: *A & O*, II, pp. 968–90; Sheppard, *England's balme*, pp. 131, 142.

[95] Sheppard listed 42 aspects of English religious practice to which he took exception because they 'did and do countenance' what he called the 'heathen' religion. His objections covered all aspects of the parochial and episcopal church structure, tithes, advowsons, benefit of clergy, marriage and burial services conducted by ministers and the use of the names of days dedicated to saints and angels as well as suspensions and ecclesiastical censures. Romish practices or words which had been incorporated into the legal structure were also criticized. These included *deodands* (forfeitures distributed by the high almoner); deliverance to the secular power of heretics for the execution of the sentence of burning; the assize of *darrein presentment*; 'some oaths that have been used'; and the dating for return of writs according to 'Popish holidays': Sheppard, *England's balme*, pp. 128–9.

or other commodities would simplify the distribution of payments to support preachers and their families. These rents would be entrusted to the county treasurers and the triers who, acting under the authority of the justices of the peace, would 'pay it out towards the relief and encouragement of such that give up themselves to the preaching of the gospel, and their wives and children'. The resources of the county treasury would also be used to buy up impropriations of 'spare cathedral and parochial churches' which would be converted to a use suiting the community's benefit.[96] If, however, parliament decided to continue the traditional collection of tithes, all the profits of parsonages and vicarages would still be collected into the county treasury and distributed 'to all [approved] preachers of the gospel that need it and accept it'.[97]

Sheppard's social philosophy was nowhere better exemplified than in his proposals to attain a full and complete religious settlement. He firmly advocated that the local community assume responsibility for orderly government and his proposed religious settlement was not only in the mainstream of the traditional English penchant for local control but it also reflected the congregational inclination of the Independent polity. He believed that if the parish system were kept, preachers in parishes held by lay impropriators should be chosen by the patron from a list of three names submitted by the parishioners themselves, thereby protecting property rights and allowing for local selection of spiritual leadership. Suitable controls over religious practice would be maintained by the commission of triers, supervised by godly magistrates and guided by the national declaration of fundamental principles, still allowing each county, and indeed each neighborhood, the dignity of autonomy and the privilege of selecting its own minister. Of the other advocates of decentralization in the interregnum the Levellers, at one extreme, recommended drastic alterations in the power structure that included the abolition of the central courts of Westminster, and many contemporaries feared that any move towards decentralization would be the first step towards the cantonization of England.[98] Sheppard's program, however, differed decidedly from others in many respects. The design pre-

---

[96] Ibid., pp. 130–1.   [97] Ibid., p. 132.

[98] Chief Justice St John, for one, feared the establishment of county courts. In his charge at the Norfolk assizes in Mar. 1658, he asserted that to preserve the unity of the law, litigants must continue to bring their suits to Westminster: BL, Add. MS, 25276, fols. 7–8.

sented in *England's balme* would have bestowed upon the counties just enough authority to be self-sufficient in caring for their internal affairs. But legally the nation would remain united under a single set of laws promulgated by the protector and approved by parliament, with a comprehensive system of justice that offered an appellate process and a national confession of faith that would maintain the most basic standards of orthodoxy while allowing a flexibility in matters of less importance.

Sheppard had done his job well. He had collected a great number of grievances that had been raised by the people of his beleaguered nation, had sifted and then weighed the complaints against optional solutions. Bearing in mind Cromwell's aspirations for stability, order, security of property and freedom of conscience as well as preserving and strengthening the common law, Sheppard had made recommendations that were woven into a single, comprehensive design and would, in his opinion, have brought reason and justice to the governing of a country dedicated to a godly reformation.

LAW REFORM IN THE PARLIAMENT OF 1656

When the second protectorate parliament met in mid September 1656 it was faced with a sobering amount of imperative public business. There had been no effective legislative gathering for more than three years and pressing problems in many areas awaited resolution. Urgent diplomatic and economic matters claimed its attention and the house was never free of the problem presented by the failure of the 1654 parliament to reach a constitutional settlement, a handicap that continued until the adoption of the Humble Petition in the spring of 1657. An analysis of the statute book alone, however, gives a deceptive picture of the new horizons for reform that were presented for legislative consideration to the parliament for which Sheppard had written *England's balme*. Cromwell's speech of 17 September spelled out the breadth of issues the government hoped to resolve. Law, religion and the reformation of manners predictably earned lengthy expositions, and the protector assured the assembled members that despite foreign threats to the peace of the realm, 'I think your reformation, if it be honest, thorough and just, will be your best security.'[99]

---

[99] *W & S*, IV, p. 270.

It is apparent from the concentration of issues raised in the first six weeks of meetings that there was a government program to match the aspirations for reform voiced by Cromwell in his opening speech. And there is a sufficient degree of correlation between the emergent legislative activity and the proposals outlined in *England's balme* to support the inference that the government was prepared to introduce into practical politics a wide range of reforms. There was not, however, a sufficient amount of coordinated effort to demonstrate that a 'court' policy was consistently pursued through the nine months of meetings. Nor did members of the council of state maintain a unified front in support of a Cromwellian legislative program. But as individual philosophies of reform were expressed in support of or in opposition to specific bills, a general if not altogether consistent alignment of reformers versus detractors emerges.[100] Of the council members who had reviewed and approved of Sheppard's proposals in February 1656, the most active supporters of the reform bills in parliament were Desborough, Wolseley, Strickland, Pickering, Jones and Lambert, while Sidney, Fiennes and Skippon contributed disappointing performances.[101] Conversely, a reluctance to inaugurate any substantive changes characterized the attitudes of the nation's major legal officers. The men responsible for leading resistance to many reform bills were Chief Justice Glynne, Solicitor-General Ellis, Attorney-General Prideaux, Attorney for the duchy of Lancaster Lechmere and Master of the Rolls Lenthall, while Treasury Commissioner Whitelocke typically pursued a vacillating course between support and resistance.[102]

The failure of the council of state to provide steady management

---

[100] Much more would be known about which council members were most active in their support of law-reform bills if a personal memoir from the first weeks of meetings had survived. Thomas Burton began his diary in Dec. 1656 when he was finally admitted to the house from which he had been excluded for the first three months.

[101] Wolseley, Strickland, Pickering, Jones and Lambert were the members of the committee appointed on 8 Feb. 1656 'to receive from Mr Sheppard what he hath to offer about the law and consider thereof': PRO, SP, 25/76, fol. 532. Wolseley and Strickland had also served on the law-reform committee that met with Cromwell in June 1654 to discuss drafting the Chancery Ordinance. Lambert, Desborough and Fiennes were added to the committee that reviewed the ordinance in July 1654, and Pickering to another law-reform committee in Aug.: *CSPD*, VII, pp. 214, 252, 281.

[102] The newsletter writers referred to opposition to several law-reform bills coming from 'the long robe' and the lawyers several times: Worc. Coll., MS xxviii, fols. 88v, 95v–96r, 101v.

or to maintain a unified stance on crucial aspects of the reform program proved to be fatally damaging to those bills that were essential to the reform of the debt law, the establishment of probate courts and several other outstanding matters of unfinished business. But the astonishing incompetence of Thomas Widdrington as speaker was an insurmountable handicap to the effective conduct of business throughout the session. His illness frequently postponed the consideration of regular business and, as he permitted the agenda to slip far behind schedule on occasions when he was present, many bills were lost.[103] The efficient control of this parliament required a capable and firm administrator, if only to handle the great volume of bills that were presented for consideration, and Widdrington's inability to provide the leadership required for management doomed the prospects for the adoption of comprehensive reforms in this session. Even the most forceful and respected political leader would have had problems maintaining the momentum necessary for progress in a house whose members devoted their attention through November and December to a discussion of how to punish James Naylor, the pitiful blasphemer of Bristol. Throughout the spring months the new constitution understandably claimed the attention of the house, with the result that the volume of new legislation passed before the end of the session was disappointingly meager.[104]

The most promising time for reform was therefore in the first six weeks of the session, before these other difficulties intruded upon the pace of activity, and it is important to recognize that during that period there was enough support for many of Sheppard's proposals to permit the introduction and further reading of a number of bills, the appointment of committees to bring in amendments and the

[103] Widdrington ignored the order to hear no private bills in the first month of the session. His inability to keep the house focused on the agenda became more pronounced as his health deteriorated. By 27 Jan. Whitelocke became speaker *pro tem.* when Widdrington's illness forced him to retire for a while: *CJ*, VII, pp. 482, 493 (27 Jan., 18 Feb. 1657).

[104] In the first session Cromwell approved five bills passed by the house in Nov., the Humble Petition on 25 May; 15 bills on 9 June; another on 19 June; and on 26 June 87 ordinances that had been issued between the dispersal of the Rump on 20 Apr. 1653 and 4 Sept. 1654, the day the first protectorate parliament assembled. Also on 26 June the Humble Additional Petition and Advice was approved along with six ordinances issued by the protectorate and eight others that were given conditional approval. All other acts and ordinances not specifically mentioned were to be 'null and void' after 1 July 1657. One of the acts decreed that a second session of the parliament would gather on 20 Jan. 1658: *A & O*, II, pp. 1036–269.

allocation of time for debates in the house. Moreover, there were continuing efforts to keep the attention of the house directed towards the consideration of public business. In the very first week the government succeeded, on a division of 101 to 65, in adopting a resolution to hear no private petitions for a month. On 20 October that order was extended for a month and on 15 November for another fortnight.[105] At the turn of the new year the house resolved that four of every six meeting days would be devoted to public business alone. Similar resolutions passed later in the winter and in the spring, but despite these earnest intentions private bills were brought before the house in each of these periods. Even as parliament was quickly approaching the end of its first session the order for public business only was disregarded by Speaker Widdrington himself 'for the sake of his fees' although, as diarist Thomas Burton caustically noted, 'the house grumbled'.[106]

A government dedicated to reform was observably hard at work in the first two weeks of meetings. The house agreed to hear business left unfinished by the Rump and the Barebones in the initial days of the assembly, and bills for probate, land registration, a new debt law and a new marriage law were all accepted for consideration.[107] A bill to establish registers in every county had been prepared by the government and was read for the first time on 23 September.[108] The official enrollment of documents pertaining to land-holding was one of the earliest and most persistent demands of parliamentary reformers as well as a basic component of Sheppard's reform scheme. The registration of land had first been suggested to the Long Parliament a decade earlier by John Cook and a bill to record conveyances was discussed in detail in the first two months of 1650. Further debates by the Rump on registration had been fruitless and it was not until the extra-parliamentary Hale Commission explored the issue that any progress was made in delineating the particulars of what was to be registered and how. The avowed object was to ensure good title to land through registration, with that record having the force of a judgment in a court of law. After lengthy discussions,

---

[105] *CJ*, VII, pp. 427, 441, 454 (23 Sept., 20 Oct., 15 Nov.); Worc. Coll., MS xxviii, fol. 95v.

[106] 11, 17 Mar, 6, 8, 16 June 1657. Burton, the diarist, had noted earlier that every petitioner for naturalization paid Widdrington a £5 fee to ensure that the case was brought to the attention of the house: *Burton's diary*, I, p. 376; II, p. 192.

[107] *CJ*, VII, p. 427; Worc. Coll., MS xxviii, fol. 77r.

[108] *CJ*, VII, p. 427.

the Hale Commission voted to recommend the registration of encumbrances and also to make the act retroactive. The final version of its draft exempted certain leases, freehold and copyhold and, even more compromising to the bill's effectiveness, registration was not to be made compulsory.[109] In January 1653 when the Hale Commission bills were presented to the Rump the question of county registers provoked heated debates and although the commission had taken care to define with precision all the conditions that were meant to be included, the house spent three months debating the meaning of an encumbrance, a fact not forgotten by an irritated Cromwell four years later.[110] An impasse was temporarily avoided by referring the bill back to a joint committee composed of members of parliament and of the Hale Commission and the redrafted bill was published over the signatures of Bulstrode Whitelocke, John Lisle, Edmund Prideaux (the two chancery commissioners and the attorney-general who all were members of parliament), Chief Baron Lane and commission-member Anthony Ashley Cooper.[111] The April 1653 dispersal of the Rump brought an abrupt end to the eight-year consideration of land registration within parliament, but pamphleteers, arguing both the merits and disadvantages of the scheme, kept the issue alive for the public.[112]

Under the protectorate the establishment of county registers remained a high priority for the government, and in September 1655 Sheppard's model for a short registration form that could be used for all types of land-holdings had been published by the official printer to the council of state, Henry Hills. In December of that year the details of Sheppard's plan for registration were presented to the council of state and early in 1656 his book, *The president of presidents*, was reissued.[113] The remaining details of Sheppard's registration scheme were made available to members of the 1656 parliament when *England's balme* was published in the first weeks of their meetings.

---

[109] Cotterell, 'Law reform', pp. 117, 119; Worden, *Rump Parliament*, pp. 205, 306.

[110] In the spring of 1657 Cromwell said, 'and I remember well in the old parliament that we were more than three months and could not get over the word encumbrances': *W & S*, IV, p. 493 (21 Apr. 1657). The bill had been introduced on 26 Jan. and was still under discussion on 15 Apr. 1653: Worden, *Rump Parliament*, p. 320. See n. 58 for provisions of Hale Commission bill.

[111] *Copy of the draught of an act for registering land* (Whitelocke, Lisle, Prideaux, Lane, Cooper): *Bib. Coop.*, p. 125.

[112] Pamphleteers who published arguments against land registration are noted in Worden, *Rump Parliament*, p. 114.

[113] See ch. 3, nn. 61, 64.

Sheppard's plan followed the Hale Commission's bill in many respects: that a register be established in every county; enrolled documents would have the same authority as a court judgment; that wills and letters of administration also be entered; and that the act be retroactive. There were also major differences between the two proposals: Sheppard would have made registration compulsory; he would have included both copyhold and customary encumbrances; and have instituted parish registers as well as a central office for every county. He also provided for heavy criminal penalties to enforce the system.[114]

Although the establishment of county registers was, according to Sheppard's plan, tied directly to the enrolment of wills and the regional administration of probate in county courts, the registration of land was introduced as a separate bill and the house agreed to hear the second reading in two weeks' time.[115] When it was read again on 10 October the bill was in trouble when the house resolved to debate it in grand committee. With William Lenthall, formerly speaker of the Long and the Rump Parliaments (and currently master of the rolls) in the chair, the house debated the inclusion of registering encumbrances in the bill, the same issue that had been challenged by the Rump in the spring of 1653. General Monck's London correspondent wrote on 11 October that the 'bill being presented for the registering all encumbrances upon real estate has taken up the house these last two days and is appointed on Wednesday next. Truly it is a more weighty business than I could have imagined but I believe it will be pressed so far as shall be practicable.' While the government's determination to see the bill through with substantial support was made clear by that letter, another news-writer noted that upon the second reading the bill 'received a very large debate because of the opposition it received from the long robe'. Despite the sponsors' resolute intentions to 'press' the bill, the objections of the judges apparently carried more weight and on the third day of debate upon the question the house voted that the bill should not be retroactive. One of the major objects of the bill, to register and secure all land title, both presently held and in the future, was thereby defeated.[116] On the last day of debate, 18 October, the fatal

[114] See above, nn. 40, 58; Sheppard, *England's balme*, pp. 112–24, 127.
[115] *CJ*, VII, p. 427 (23 Sept.); Worc. Coll., MS xxviii, fol. 76r.
[116] The quotations are from Worc. Coll., MS xxviii, fols. 89r & 88v. *CJ*, VII, pp. 437, 439 (11, 15 Oct.).

word 'encumbrance' again dominated the contentious discussions and 'with the long robe still [giving] much opposition' the debate was finally adjourned and the matter turned over to a committee whose membership included every major law officer as well as an impressive number of members of the council of state and several major-generals. Whitelocke, Lisle and Prideaux, who had all signed the 1653 printed version of the bill, represented the legal establishment along with Lenthall and Lechmere. Strickland, Rous and Luke Robinson also served on the committee and every one of these men had also participated on the Rump's law-reform committees. While the continuing debate was taken behind the scenes, the arguments presented in the 1656 committee meetings must have carried familiar echoes from the past.[117]

Within a week of that bill's referral to committee, the attention of the house had turned to the related bill of the registration of wills and the establishment of regional probate courts. The question of registering land was dropped until 3 November when the registration committee was ordered to meet in the afternoon.[118] A month passed before a member of the council, Gilbert Pickering, moved that the report on county land registers be heard, but the house rejected his motion and resolved instead to hear a report on the blasphemer of Bristol, James Naylor. The dispute over the word 'encumbrance' had apparently not been resolved by mid December when, in a discussion of the problem of framing a law against blasphemy and avoiding ambiguity in its phrasing, Whitelocke took exception to 'the general words blasphemy and Quakerism. That is like the word "encumbrance"; the more general, the more dangerous for the people of England.'[119] No more was heard of the bill until late April when Major-General Goffe reminded his colleagues in the house that a bill for land registration awaited its third reading, but again the matter was allowed to drop. The evidence seems to indicate that the bill died in committee through a failure to reach agreement on the registration of encumbrances.[120] While the committee of 1653 had been able to reach agreement over a modified bill, the determined council members on the committee of 1656 apparently refused to agree to any sort of compromise that would jeopardize the bill's effectiveness.

[117] Worc. Coll., MS xxviii, fol. 95v; *CJ*, VII, p. 441 (18 Oct.); Worden, *Rump Parliament*, p. 110n.
[118] *CJ*, VII, pp. 445, 449 (24 Oct., 3 Nov.).
[119] *Burton's diary*, I, pp. 24, 170 (5, 18 Dec.).   [120] Ibid., II, p. 36.

A probate bill which was ordered on the same day that the bill for registers was first read was a companion reform because, following the proposals of both *England's balme* and the Hale Commission, it provided for the registration of wills and letters of administration in the same county repositories where land claims would be registered. According to the 1656 bill, probate jurisdiction would be exercised by associated courts of record staffed by professional judges with coercive powers. All wills, including those by which land was devised, would be registered in the appropriate county. It is not known if the bill made any provision for the new inheritance laws in cases of intestacy as had been suggested by both Sheppard and the Hale Commission.[121] The probate bill, for all its innovative provisions, attracted a great deal of support in the 1656 parliament and proved remarkably durable. Despite its ultimate failure after nine months of debate and amendment, the bill came tantalizingly close to enactment. Ordered on 23 September, the bill for regional probate courts received its first two readings in mid October, just at the time the bill for registers met its doom in the debate over encumbrances.[122] At the second reading the bill was referred to a large committee with instructions to alter certain clauses and to introduce amendments. The committee's report, which included a table of fees, was read twice to the house on 1 December and over the course of a lengthy debate eleven amendments were made, most concerned with changing the locations of local probate registers. The following day members took the opportunity to shift the sites of nine more registers, thereby signalling their implicit approval of a new, decentralized system for probate. However, in terms of the substantive provisions for probate administration the bill began to run into trouble as the house modified the clause directing probate judges to hold court at least four times a year. Moreover, the question of returning wills to the parties to whom land had been devised was sent back to the committee for reconsideration.[123]

Three weeks later, on 23 December, the house accepted a petition from Lord Eure, member for the North Riding, which requested among other reforms that courts of probate and of justice be established at York for the benefit of north-countrymen. The following day the committee for probate reported their amendments

---

[121] Ibid., I, p. 226 (24 Dec.); Cotterell, 'Law reform', p. 128.

[122] *CJ*, VII, pp. 427, 445, 446 (23 Sept., 24, 27 Oct.); Worc. Coll., MS xxviii, fol. 76r (23 Sept.).

[123] *CJ*, VII, pp. 462–3 (1, 2 Dec.).

and these were debated the same day. Although an amendment settling a fixed salary of £200 a year on probate judges was approved, the bill was dealt a serious blow when the house voted to remove the clause making county probate jurisdictions courts of record. Even more damaging, the mandatory registration of all wills, including those by which land was devised, brought immediate strong objections from a chief justice, the solicitor-general and the attorney-general who insisted that the registration of wills 'would be the way to encourage forgery' and that anything that 'concerns men's inheritances... cannot be determined but by witnesses before a jury'. Lenthall objected that although a probate seal could be used as evidence for goods in any court, it would never suffice as evidence for lands and that the original will must remain in the hands of the devisee. Debate over various legal ramifications continued until Luke Robinson made the obvious point that unless probate were made a court of record the discussion of mandatory registration was meaningless. Speaker Widdrington offered to amend the bill from the chair in order to delete the clause calling for compulsory registration of all wills but the house resolved to send the bill back to an enlarged committee that was expanded to include 'all the gentlemen of the long robe'. Solicitor-General Ellis and Attorney-General Prideaux who had both objected to compulsory registration were named specifically as new committee members.[124]

Five months elapsed from the time the bill was recommitted on 24 December until the amendments were brought before the house in May, although the committee's report was ordered on five occasions during that period.[125] At this time the house again approved amendments fixing salaries for probate judges and again changed the location of a couple of regional registers; but the central questions of establishing county probate jurisdictions as courts of record and compelling registration of 'every will in writing wherein lands are devised' were both defeated on divisions and the emasculated bill was ordered to be engrossed.[126] In mid June as the session approached

---

124 *Burton's diary*, I, pp. 208–9, 226–7; *CJ*, VII, p. 474 (24 Dec.). Widdrington also wanted to leave out the clause that stated that wills concerning lands must be registered. 'This is an independent clause and may be left out without prejudice to the bill...Make it thus, that where land is devised in the will the court may not keep the will': *Burton's diary*, I, p. 226. Only about 5 per cent of all wills involved land: Cotterell, 'Law reform', p. 128.

125 *Burton's diary*, II, pp. 116–17; *CJ*, VII, pp. 490, 500, 501, 510, 524, 531 (13 Feb., 7, 11, 24 Mar., 28 Apr., 5 May).

126 *CJ*, VII, p. 532. Burton's diary omits accounts between 8 and 12 May.

its concluding days William Strickland and Thomas Wroth, both pleading advanced age, urged passage of the probate bill so that they could settle their own estates. Although motions for a third reading were agreed upon by the house on 15, 23 and 24 June, the volume of business just before adjournment proved fatal. In the last two days of meetings, time was taken to push through private bills and to discuss the ermine-lined robe the protector would wear at the investiture ceremony, and the session closed with the much-debated probate bill abandoned.[127] Instead of the provision for a set of secularized regional probate courts, there was recorded in the statute book yet another continuation of the makeshift arrangement first passed by the hard-pressed but unimaginative Rump in the spring of 1653 which confirmed a secularized probate jurisdiction operating 'as Sir Nathaniel Brent might have done in the late province of [the prerogative court] of Canterbury'.[128]

Another bill that received early attention from the house was related to the attempt to establish a uniform and consistent method for securing land claims. On 29 September a bill was introduced to establish fixed and certain fines to be paid upon the acquisition of copyhold estates claimed either by descent or by alienation. At the second reading the bill was rejected on a close vote, 86 against to 77 for. Although the division was taken on a technical irregularity, the bill's rejection was clearly a political defeat for the government because it was not recommitted for amendment. The clause to which the majority took exception stated that the fine for copyhold was to be fixed at the rate of one year's value of the property. It was objected that any bill which 'charge[d] any of the people of their inheritance...ought to have been left with a blank and left to the judgment of the house'. During this debate a supporter of the bill was challenged for 'mentioning [accusing?] the gentlemen of the long robe' in the debate. He 'was ordered to explain himself, which

---

[127] *Burton's diary*, II, pp. 237, 254, 283; *CJ*, VII, pp. 558, 570, 573 (15, 23, 24 June).
[128] The confirmation of probate was included among the acts and declarations made between the dissolution of the Rump and the convening of the first protectorate parliament that were confirmed on 26 June 1657: *A & O*, II, p. 1131; *CJ*, VII, p. 577. This action specifically confirmed the protector's continuing ordinance of 3 Apr. 1654 which, in turn, merely extended the stop-gap measures taken after Brent's death in Nov. 1652 by the Rump's enactment of 8 Apr. 1653 as well as the protectorate's extension of 24 Dec. 1653: *A & O*, II, pp. 702, 824, 869. Brent, who had served as Laud's vicar-general, had been made sole judge of a secularized probate court by the Long Parliament in 1644 after the abolition of the ecclesiastical courts. He retained the position until his death: Aylmer, *State's servants*, pp. 32–3, 42, 116–17.

he did' and although no other information is available on this sensitive point, it appears that even in the first weeks of the session Cromwell's judges led the resistance to any bill that attempted to impose a regularized system on admittance to land-holding. Regulation of copyhold estates had enough support to be brought up again on 17 December when a bill was referred for amendment to the committee charged with preparing a bill on recusants but that unlikely body apparently took no action and the bill was never heard of again.[129]

The principles of establishing fixed fines on copyhold, securing land claims through registration and administering probate in regional courts of record are all related to a fourth dimension of Sheppard's plan: the establishment of courts of justice in the counties. A bill for 'courts throughout England for justice to people near home' was ordered drawn on 23 September, the same day the bill for county registers was first read and that for county probate ordered.[130] The establishment of local courts of record throughout the countryside was a crucial component of Sheppard's proposed reconstruction of the court system. His county courts and the regional probate courts (which according to the provisions in *England's balme* would hear minor equity cases as well) would together have provided quick and inexpensive justice to all men at no great distance from their homes, and simultaneously have reduced the case load of the central courts at Westminster. The committee responsible for drafting the bill brought in an 'act for laying trials of actions in their respective counties and restraining travelling of jurors out of their proper counties for trial of actions'. It was first read on 11 November and the house agreed to read it a second time within a few days.[131] It was not, however, until 3 December that Desborough moved to have the bill for county courts read a second time in the following week in conjunction with a bill for the recovery of small debts. But it was only after Desborough's insistent prodding that Speaker Widdrington finally recalled that 'there was such a bill indeed, that no action shall be tried at [Westminster] but such as the

---

[129] *CJ*, VII, pp. 429–30, 432, 469 (29 Sept., 3 Oct., 17 Dec.).
[130] Ibid., p. 427; Sheppard, *England's balme*, pp. 96–7; Worc. Coll., MS xxviii, fol. 76r.
[131] *CJ*, VII, p. 452 (11 Nov.). A newsletter writer reported that a bill 'for trial of small causes in the country' was read a second time that week (15 Nov.): Worc. Coll., MS xxviii, fol. 113v.

justices appointed' and the house agreed to a second reading on the following Saturday.[132]

Desborough's interest in the bill for county courts can be explained not only by his membership on the council of state that had approved Sheppard's plan but also by his earlier service on the Hale Commission that had developed a similar scheme. Sheppard's proposals of 1656 and those of the Hale Commission four years earlier provided that these innovative courts of record be made ancillary branches of the central courts where all personal and mixed actions as well as minor criminal cases would commence. Both plans for a restructured judicial system called for the retention of petty sessions and for the abolition of all palatine courts, but there the similarities ended. While the Hale Commission plan would have placed a Westminster judge on the bench of each county court, Sheppard would have staffed the county bench with justices of the peace who would hear appeals from lesser local courts with appeals from their decisions referred directly to Westminster. The county courts projected by the Hale Commission would hear claims arising from probate but no real actions, because all trials concerning title to land would be reserved to *nisi prius* proceedings heard by assize judges on circuit. Sheppard's plan, on the other hand, provided for the county court to hear suits to title of land worth up to £20 a year as well as appeals from a subordinate court of county judicature whose jurisdiction encompassed probate claims, minor equity cases and suits to title of land worth up to £10 annually. Despite the differences in detail, both plans intended the new county courts to be parts of a central system of justice.[133] The 1656 bill for county courts never received a second reading in the house. The establishment of county courts had been opposed for years on the grounds that their establishment would create a 'decentralization of justice' and promote the 'cantonization' of England. These reservations, expressed especially by the judges of the central benches, may explain the lack of sufficient interest in this bill although both Sheppard and the Hale Commission had set clear conditions that the county courts assume a subordinate position in a centralized system of justice. The only time the bill was ever mentioned again during the session was late in April during a

---

[132] *Burton's diary*, II, p. 6; *CJ*, VII, p. 463.
[133] Cotterell, 'Law reform', pp. 66–76; Sheppard, *England's balme*, pp. 35–6, 77, 98, 157, 159, 167–71, 176, 197.

discussion of unfinished business when the house, reminded of the bill for county courts, 'laughed at this'.[134]

Another effort to make justice more accessible was embodied in the bill of 16 October that provided for 'the recovery of small debts and relieving persons in cases of small trespasses within their respective counties'. Small debts traditionally had been recoverable in manor courts and courts leet but in October 1653 the Barebones had, in a reform effort, established new local debtors' courts administered by county commissioners. The novelty introduced by these courts was that the commissioners were empowered to sell debtors' lands to satisfy creditors' claims, and the widespread objections to the summary powers to dispose of land without a jury trial were so great that Cromwell had suspended the act by an ordinance of March 1654. Three subsequent protectorate ordinances had modified the suspension and provided for the act's temporary continuation but with the commissioners' powers severely restricted.[135]

Sheppard's solution to the problems created by the Barebones' small debtors' courts was to return to the traditional method of having existing local courts hear suits where debt or damage claimed was less than £4. These customary courts would be made courts of record and, supervised by a justice of the peace, all decisions would be appealable in a superior county court.[136] The provisions of the 1656 bill are not known, but from the hostility that had been provoked by the summary method devised by the Barebones it can be surmised that the protectorate parliament had under consideration a more traditional process for recovery of debts. At the second reading on 1 November a motion to reject the bill was lost on a division of forty-seven to eighty-nine, a striking indication that two-thirds of the house was willing to consider a new and just way to bring relief to plaintiffs in small causes. The bill was sent to a large committee with instructions to meet on the following Monday but, as happened so frequently in this busy session, the bill never emerged from committee. It was not until 18 June, in the last week of the session, that the house specifically deferred consideration of the bill for the recovery of small debts in an order for the committee to

---

[134] *Burton's diary*, II, p. 36 (24 Apr.).
[135] *A & O*, II, pp. 753, 860, 897, 911, 943 (Oct. 1653; 31 Mar., 16 May, 9 June, 11 Aug. 1654); *CJ*, VII, p. 437 (16 Oct. 1654).
[136] The details of Sheppard's proposals for selling debtors' lands to pay creditors are described above in pt I, nn. 53–5.

present its report in the second session of parliament, scheduled to meet in January 1658. A week after this bill was tabled, the house nullified the Barebones' act for small debtors' courts as well as the related modifying ordinances issued by Cromwell. The only provisions for debt law which were to remain in effect in the intervals between parliamentary sessions were the demonstrably unsuccessful acts for the relief of poor prisoners and creditors passed by the Rump in 1649 and 1650. This regressive step was apparently preferable to continuing the unpopular summary powers for selling land held by the Barebones' commissioners.[137]

On the more general issue of providing alternate courts of justice around the country, it became increasingly clear that this parliament could not be persuaded to take any positive steps towards establishing novel jurisdictions, either as courts of record (as Sheppard had proposed) or as special commissions endowed with summary powers. Interest was, however, demonstrated in reviving some form of the traditional regional courts. On 3 November Lambert, who must have been impatient at the lack of progress on the bills for the county and the probate courts, brought in a bill to establish a court of law and equity at York. Monck's London correspondent wrote that Lambert's bill 'startles the lawyers to see the administration of the law like to be carried into the provinces', a remark that goes a long way towards explaining the failure of the 1656 parliament to enact meaningful reform in the judicial system.[138] The 'opposition of the long robe' was consistent and successfully obstructionist on the issues of regional courts of record for probate and for law, on compulsory land registration and similar innovations. Chief Justice Glynne, Ellis, Prideaux, Lenthall and Whitelocke can all be identified as leaders of resistance to each of those bills. Although there is no record of the details of the law officers' objections to the proposed legal and judicial innovations, it is clear that Lambert found the dilatory response to reform bills intolerable and was determined to take the initiative for providing justice near home for his own fellow north-countrymen.

Representatives from the north had good reason to complain of a denial of justice due to an absence of courts in their proximity. Fifteen years earlier when the Long Parliament abolished the major

---

[137] *CJ*, VII, pp. 439, 449, 561 (16 Oct., 1 Nov., 18 June 1657); Worc. Coll., MS xxviii, fol. 100r; *A & O*, II, p. 1142.
[138] *CJ*, VII, p. 449 (3 Nov.); Worc. Coll., MS xxviii, fol. 101v.

prerogative and conciliar courts, the jurisdiction of the councils of the north and of the Welsh marches had been revoked along with that of star chamber and the palatine courts of Lancaster and Chester.[139] Although the great sessions of Wales continued to dispense justice regularly in the west, no substitute jurisdiction had been provided for the four northern counties. Lambert, Strickland and Lord Eure, all from Yorkshire, and Christopher Lister of Westmorland were the members instrumental in the attempt to persuade parliament to establish some form of substitute court system in the north to hear cases of law, equity and probate.[140] Lambert's bill was given its second reading on 17 November and referred to a large committee that included all the judges. Towards the end of December the house heard, but then ignored a petition requesting further action on the bill for courts in the north. Later that winter the house agreed three times to order a reading of the amendments to the bill for York courts but the session closed with the amendments unheard and the matter dropped from consideration.[141]

Efforts to restore regional justice through the re-establishment of palatine jurisdictions fared better. The palatine liberties of Lancaster had been revived in 1646 and although the Barebones had temporarily abolished the duchy jurisdiction, by September 1653 Lancaster's jurisdictional privileges had been restored and were confirmed by two protectorate ordinances.[142] A bill to confirm the palatine liberties of Durham received two readings in the spring of 1657 but the appointed committee never returned a report. A similar petition for Ely had been read on 21 November but the order for the second reading of the bill was not followed. Cromwell's inclination to return to the traditional patterns of English ways after 1657 resulted in his restoring the palatine liberties of Chester by proclamation in June 1658.[143]

Sheppard's proposed reconstruction of the judicial system entailed a very logical hierarchical arrangement of courts of record established

---

[139] *Statutes*, V, p. 110 (16 Car. I, c. 1).

[140] Eure: *Burton's diary*, I, pp. 208–9; Lambert: Worc. Coll., MS xxviii, fol. 101v; Lister: *CJ*, VII, p. 427; Strickland: *Burton's diary*, II, p. 237.

[141] *Burton's diary*, I, pp. 208–9; II, p. 237; *CJ*, VII, pp. 427, 474.

[142] The palatine liberties of Lancaster had been revived on 17 July 1646 and although the Barebones abolished the duchy jurisdiction, in Sept. 1653 the jurisdictional privileges were restored by two protectorate ordinances: *A & O*, I, p. 885; II, pp. 722, 844, 921.

[143] *CJ*, VII, pp. 456, 511, 538 (Nov. 1656, 25 Mar., 23 May 1657); *W & S*, IV, p. 836 (June 1658).

through the countryside with provisions for appeal to the courts of Westminster. Owing to parliament's failure to establish county courts for law and for probate, both of which were pre-conditions for the appellate system, there was no effort to introduce the remaining jurisdictional adjustments spelled out in *England's balme.* Nor was the establishment of a high court of appeal brought to the attention of this legislature, although the erection of such a high court had been advocated both by Sheppard and by the Hale Commission of 1652.[144] The only discussion of central-court jurisdiction considered by the 1656 parliament concerned the court of chancery. Cromwell's ordinance of 1654 had not yet been confirmed by a parliament although the provisions of the reform had been in effect since June 1655. Every principal figure that had been involved with this controversial reform was a member of this parliament and the two former commissioners, Whitelocke and Widdrington, had an important political investment in engineering an outright repeal of the ordinance. But although both men commanded influential positions of leadership in the assembly there was also a small but determined party dedicated to saving Cromwell's most important reform. The differences that certainly must have been aired in the meetings of the committee assigned to consider the ordinance can only be surmised, because on 19 February the house rejected a motion to hear the committee's report. The identity of the tellers on the division, however, provides an indication of the report's recommendations because Desborough and Colonel Purefoy took the count for rejection and Desborough's record for supporting reform motions throughout the session was remarkably consistent.[145] Since the other teller was one of Cromwell's supporters from the army, it can be safely assumed that the report did not endorse a confirmation of the Chancery Ordinance. The presumption that the report recommended a suspension (as had the 1654 parliament), if not an abrogation of the ordinance is even more convincingly demonstrated by the political reputations of the tellers in favor of reading of the report, Nicholas Lechmere and Denis Bond. Lech-

---

[144] The Hale Commission had provided that appeals from the county courts proposed in its plan would, in civil cases, be heard by common pleas and in criminal cases by the upper bench. The court of exchequer was to be abolished according to that scheme: Cotterell, 'Law reform', pp. 66–76. Sheppard's plan advised only that appeals from the county courts go to the 'appropriate' central court.

[145] Desborough's record as reformer was the best of all the councillors.

mere, as attorney-general for the duchy of Lancaster, aligned himself
with the legal establishment in this parliament and, by virtue of his
office, would have had a strong interest in preserving a traditional
legal structure. The activities of the Rump's law-reform committees,
of which both Lechmere and Bond were members, formed a pattern
of coordinated resistance to reform bills in the years from 1649 to
1653. Bond, although not a lawyer, had been a close associate of the
current attorney-general, Prideaux, his Dorset neighbor, since the
days of the Rump. Blair Worden, in his study of that parliament,
noted eight occasions upon which Bond resisted reform bills 'at
critical moments'. It does not take much imagination to conclude
that the report Lechmere and Bond voted to have presented contained
a repudiation of the reforming ordinance Cromwell had insisted be
implemented.[146]

Throughout the spring of 1657 the house had a great deal of
business to settle, including the new constitution and issues of finance
as well as the preparation of new bills and the review of earlier
legislation. The decision taken by the house on 29 April to extend
the controversial Chancery Ordinance only until the end of the
current parliament appears to be a compromise taken to avoid a
time-consuming reappraisal that would be bound to stir up dissension
and resurrect old arguments. The major opponents of the ordinance,
Whitelocke and Widdrington, as well as its supporters, the current
commissioners of the great seal, Lisle and Fiennes, all assumed low
profiles as the resolution was adopted without debate.[147] But while
the decision to allow the ordinance to expire apparently represented
a consensus that this was the most politic move at this sensitive time
when the new constitution was being negotiated with Cromwell,
Lisle and Fiennes may already have decided to extend its provisions
beyond its statutory life in defiance of parliament's decision.[148]

On the very next day, 30 April, the irrepressible Desborough
moved that a new bill for the regulation of chancery be brought in
by a committee 'if they see cause'. A weary house in a placating mood
agreed to appoint a large committee, taking care to include every
major official of the judiciary in its membership and instructed them
to meet in a few days' time. On 5 May, as some of the more restless

[146] Worden, *Rump Parliament*, pp. 35, 110, 116, 203–4.
[147] *CJ*, VII, p. 527 (29 Apr.) Burton makes no comment on the resolution and it
seems to have passed without debate: *Burton's diary*, II, pp. 77–8.
[148] Lisle and Fiennes continued to enforce the provisions of the ordinance after Feb.
1658, the date of its statutory expiration.

members of the house called for adjournment, the committee for the regulation of chancery was again instructed to meet. The conservative committee, however, never reported back to the house and the session ended with Cromwell agreeing to the expiration of the Chancery Ordinance at the closing of that parliament.[149]

Desborough also took part in an attempt to make admiralty a court of record with a declared jurisdiction over foreign contracts. The bill was rejected on its first reading and although the question was debated again in the spring, the house could agree only to confirm the continuation of the act passed by the Barebones Assembly.[150] Sheppard's proposal to revive the judicial functions of the court of requests was not brought before the 1656 parliament. The office of requests had been revived in the first month of the protectorate and although the two masters of requests were sitting as members of parliament, neither displayed any interest in sponsoring a bill to re-endow requests with its former judicial functions.[151]

Two attempts to regulate personnel serving in the courts were frustrated even more easily than the efforts to introduce reforms into the judicial structure. On 18 September a bill which proposed to pare down the interest and rewards of clerks of the courts was given its first reading but was then dropped. A month later a large committee was appointed to consider the number and quality of attorneys and solicitors as well as any abuses for which they were responsible. After some discussion, unprincipled practices of manorial stewards and under-sheriffs and their bailiffs were added to the committee's assignment. But no bill of regulation was returned to the house and there is no evidence that the committee formulated any recommendations.[152] The orders issued in 1654 by the judges of the

---

[149] Desborough's motion was seconded by Thomas Wroth who, according to Worden, had been a radical in the Rump Parliament: *CJ*, VII, p. 528; *Burton's diary*, II, p. 80; Worden, *Rump Parliament*, p. 130. For the resolutions, see *CJ*, VII, p. 531 (5 May); *A & O*, II, p. 1140 (26 June).

[150] *Burton's diary*, II, pp. 57–60 (28 Apr. 1657); *CJ*, VII, p. 461 (29 Nov. 1656); *A & O*, II, p. 1132 (26 June 1657).

[151] In Mar. 1656 the brothers Nathaniel and Francis Bacon were appointed masters of requests and their primary duties seem to have been assisting the protector in handling the petitions that were sent to the head of state in great volume. Both sat in the 1656 parliament, and Nathaniel Bacon also served as an admiralty judge. The masters of requests administered the oaths to the members of parliament before the second session: Aylmer, *State's servants*, pp. 46, 71; *CJ*, VII, p. 578; Underdown, *Pride's purge*, p. 251n; *W & S*, III, p. 167; IV, pp. 120, 580, 703–4, 711.

[152] *CJ*, VII, p. 438 (13 Oct. 1656); Worc. Coll., MS xxviii, fol. 73r (18 Sept.).

upper bench and common pleas for the regulation of their own courts were still in effect[153] but the conduct of officials in all other courts, which was of such great concern to Sheppard, failed to stimulate any interest in the parliament of 1656.

In the realm of procedural reform, there were efforts to introduce new bills as well as a willingness to reconsider measures taken by previous governments. On 25 September the house appointed a committee to consider abuses in granting writs of *certiorari* and to make recommendations for limiting their use. This prerogative writ which removed an action from a lower court to either chancery or the upper bench had the practical effect of delaying prosecution of a suit. The bill was never drafted, but the use of *certiorari* was expressly forbidden in the act for sabbath observance passed on 26 June 1657.[154] On 16 October a bill to restrain unnecessary suits on bonds and bills was read for the first time and a month later the house ordered its second reading on the following day. The order was, however, disregarded and the bill was dropped.[155] A third move towards legal reform was made almost as an afterthought. On the last day of the session, just before adjournment, the house resolved to recommend that Cromwell and his council in consultation with the judges 'take some effectual course' in the interval between sessions towards reforming the inns of court, to revive readings, 'keeping up the exercise of students there' and to provide for the maintenance of 'able and godly ministers' at the inns.[156] In summary, little was attempted and nothing accomplished in procedural innovations by this parliament, a disappointing record in view of the extensive reform proposals formulated by Sheppard. The parliament did, however, review procedural reforms that had been enacted earlier: one by the Rump and another passed by the Barebones. The 1650 act for pleading the general issue was brought into question on 25 September when the solicitor-general and the attorney-general were requested to bring in a bill to prevent the general issue from being pleaded in the prosecution of certain statutes. Six months passed before the third reading of the bill was ordered but, as in so many

---

[153] Both sets of orders also regulated attorneys and other officials as well as abuses by sheriffs and bailiffs.
[154] *CJ*, VII, p. 428 (25 Sept.); Act disallowing *certiorari*: *A & O*, II, p. 1169 (26 June).
[155] *CJ*, VII, pp. 439, 456 (16 Oct., 18 Nov. 1656).
[156] Ibid., p. 578 (26 June 1657).

other cases, the house ignored its own order and the bill was lost. On 24 April after a lengthy debate the house decided that all statutes enacted prior to the dissolution of the Rump in April 1653 would remain in full force unless specifically repealed, and this decision had the effect of confirming the Rump's act for pleading the general issue. The writ of error had been abolished by both the Rump and the Barebones and the latter assembly had also discontinued the use of *supersedeas*. Both these limitations were ratified and confirmed on 26 June 1657.[157] The Barebones' act to eliminate fines on bills, declarations and original writs was modified to exclude fines for alienations on writs of covenant and of entry, but in all other respects the act was confirmed.[158]

Reconsideration and revision of other earlier legal reforms drew more attention from the house. The ordinance of 1646 abolishing the court of wards and liveries was felt to require confirmation and the house ordered the preparation of three related bills on 23 September: one to abolish the court, a second to provide for the care of orphans and the preservation of their estates, and a third to care for idiots and lunatics.[159] The bill to abolish the court of wards required recommittals, debates and amendments which stretched over two months and by the end of November the bill was one of five presented to Cromwell for his consent.[160] By this act feudal tenures were converted to free and common socage and the act was passed again in the second year of the restoration. The Barebones Assembly had provided for the care of idiots and lunatics by the court of chancery but in March 1654 Cromwell had reclaimed the sovereign's custodial rights over these wards of the state; the bill ordered in September 1656 for the care of idiots and lunatics was never drafted and parliament took no further action on the matter.[161] Purveyance, another remnant of feudalism Sheppard sought to abolish, had been suspended in the

---

[157] *A & O*, II, p. 443 (23 Oct. 1650); *Burton's diary*, II, pp. 42–4; *CJ*, VII, pp. 428, 513, 523 (25 Sept. 1656, 27 Mar., 24 Apr. 1657).

[158] *A & O*, II, pp. 357, 773, 1140 (11 Mar. 1650, 4 Nov. 1653, 26 June 1657).

[159] Ibid., I, p. 833 (1646); *CJ*, VII, p. 427 (23 Sept. 1656). The committee appointed to draft the three bills included Ellis, Prideaux, Lenthall, Glynne and Whitelocke.

[160] *A & O*, II, p. 1043 (Nov. 1656); *CJ*, VII, pp. 439, 445, 450, 453, 456, 457, 459–60 (16, 25, 29 Oct., 6, 14, 20, 22, 27 Nov. 1656).

[161] The Cavalier Parliament abolished the court of wards for the third time in 1661: 12 Car. II, c. 4. See also Cromwell's ordinance of 20 Mar. 1654 which amended the Barebones' act of 13 Dec. 1653: *A & O*, II, p. 834.

early days of the Long Parliament but it was not until the meeting of the 1656 parliament that legislative action was taken and purveyance abolished by statute.[162]

Reform of the law of debt which had attracted more attention than any other branch of the law during the interregnum continued to retain the interest of parliamentary reformers in 1656. The reforms enacted by the Rump Parliament had proved to be both unsatisfactory and incomplete; and the method established to recover small debts by the Barebones excited justifiable protest for its flagrant disregard of due process because of the commissioners' summary powers to sell the lands of debtors.[163] The carefully reasoned proposals Sheppard had formulated in *England's balme* had incorporated strict controls to protect the interests of debtor and creditor alike and the complexities of incorporating all of his provisions with the proper safeguards would have required a very detailed bill that would undoubtedly have provoked controversy. On 25 September a committee of six was ordered to draft a bill 'to compel those who are of ability and lie in prison to pay their debts' as well as to provide relief 'for those unable to pay'. The assertive language of the order was a strong indication that the government was determined to pursue a genuine and complete reform of debt law, correcting the injustice whereby rich men had avoided satisfying their just debts. Desborough's presence on the small committee suggests that the council of state had a detailed bill in mind for this committee's consideration, and that Desborough's task was to garner some extra-conciliar support from the other five members of the committee before the bill was presented to the house.[164] A month passed before the bill was presented, and it was rejected on the first reading. The house ordered a new bill prepared and added thirty-four new members to the original committee.[165] By 3 December a new bill 'for the recovery of certain just debts' received its first reading and the second was ordered for the following week. On the appointed day the house was embroiled in debate concerning the blasphemer, James Naylor, and nothing more was heard on the bill for two months.[166] On 19

---

[162] *CJ*, VII, pp. 447, 449, 467 (19 Oct., 3 Nov., 12 Dec. 1656); *A & O*, II, p. 1057 (9 June 1657). This was passed again by the Convention Parliament in 1660: 12 Car. II, c. 24. See G. E. Aylmer, 'The last years of purveyance, 1610–60', *EcHR*, 2nd ser., X (1957), 84, 90.

[163] See above, pt I, n. 52.   [164] *CJ*, VII, p. 428 (25 Sept. 1656).

[165] Ibid., pp. 445, 447 (25, 29 Oct. 1656); Worc. Coll., MS xxviii, fol. 100r.

[166] *CJ*, VII, pp. 463, 465 (3, 6 Dec. 1656).

February the house ordered that the bill be read a second time on the twenty-third, but on that day when the question was put to the house that the bill be read, the members voted in the negative. The second postponement of the second reading can, like the first, be explained by the intrusion of a matter of greater interest to the majority of the members. On this occasion it was Christopher Packe's initial presentation of an alternate constitutional settlement, the Humble Petition and Advice, that displaced the reading on 23 February of the bill to reform the debt law. Council-member Desborough and a fellow major-general, Berry, took the count of the sixty-two members who favored hearing the debt bill while two conservatives, John Reynolds and Sheppard's Gloucestershire neighbor, George Berkeley, served as the tellers for the eighty-three members who preferred to set the bill aside in order to hear the petition requesting Cromwell to take the title of king.[167] Towards the end of March a third and new bill for the 'recovery of certain just debts' was read and the house resolved to give this bill a second reading in a week's time.[168] But the failure of the house to act on its own order was only the first in a series of procrastinations over the following two months,[169] and as the end of the session approached the house could agree only to revive and continue for another year the extremely unsatisfactory acts of the Rump Parliament for the relief of poor prisoners.[170] The temporary nature of these extensions held out the promise that this parliament would, in its second session, reconsider both the problems of creditors unable to recover their money and the distress of poor prisoners; but the problems of English debt law lingered on well into the nineteenth century.

Although reform of the law and of the judicial structure made little headway in the 1656 parliament, questions pertaining to 'the

---

[167] The Gloucestershire royalist George Berkeley was an acquaintance of Sheppard: ch. 1, n. 206; *Burton's diary*, I, p. 377; *CJ*, VII, pp. 493, 496 (19, 23 Feb. 1657).

[168] *CJ*, VII, p. 513 (27 Mar. 1657).

[169] Council-members Desborough, who had been on the original committee, and Wolseley, who continued to request the third reading, were the most active supporters of the bill: *Burton's diary*, II, pp. 100, 245; *CJ*, VII, pp. 524, 531, 534, 537, 546, 549 (29 Apr., 1, 5, 14, 21 May, 5, 6 June).

[170] On 13 & 16 June 1657 resolutions were made to revive and continue the acts of 21 Dec. 1649 and 6 Apr. 1650 until 24 June 1658: *Burton's diary*, II, p. 245; *CJ*, VII, pp. 557–8; *A & O*, II, p. 1140. As it became clear that no satisfactory reform would be enacted, many members brought in private bills requesting permission to sell or convey their lands to satisfy their debts: *Burton's diary*, I, p. 81 (9 Dec. 1656); *A & O*, II, p. 1137. Others heard from Feb. through Apr. are found in *CJ*, VII, pp. 489, 496, 498, 500, 501, 514, 515, 520.

settlement of the nation' in matters of economy, religion and manners did attract support. A number of issues raised in *England's balme* having to do with commercial and economic improvement were introduced as private or public bills. Two of Sheppard's more important proposals were timber conservation and the regulation of land held in common. Cromwell and the council had been concerned with the first question since November 1654 when they issued a warrant noting that 'no provision hath of late years been made for the preservation and growth of timber and trees within the said forest [of Dean], the due care whereof hath ever been esteemed of special concernment to the public interest of this nation'. In that order the protector empowered eight Gloucestershire gentry to enforce the laws in the Forest of Dean to protect the common woods and halt 'the great wastes and spoils committed to the prejudice of the commonwealth'.[171] On 25 September 1656 Whitelocke brought in a bill for the 'increase and preservation of timber' and upon its second reading two days later a committee of forty-five was instructed to consider the bill that afternoon.[172] On 16 October the grievances of the inhabitants of the Forest of Dean were referred to the same committee and on 23 October the broader question of timber preservation for shipping as well as the fines due from the destruction of wood and timber since 1640 were added to the committee's assignment. The revised bill received its first reading on 18 November, its second on 6 December and on 25 December the bill was amended and ordered engrossed. The day of the third reading, 14 March, another general bill was ordered to be drawn by Chief Justice Glynne to ensure that forest perambulation returns would be confirmed to protect the boundaries of all state timber lands.[173] The bill for the Forest of Dean was not taken up again until 9 June when the act was approved, allowing for the enclosure of one-third at a time of the forest to preserve the 'growth and thriving of young wood' for a period of up to twelve years. The act also restored the traditional rights of the forest's inhabitants and repealed grants made by Charles I for the sale and destruction of wood. Ten days later the surveyors of other forests were directed to give special attention to 'all thriving timber of oak and elm'.[174] A week later, as the house tangled with

---

[171] W. Sheppard, *England's balme*, pp. 182–3; *W & S*, III, pp. 514–15 (29 Nov. 1654).

[172] *CJ*, VII, pp. 428–9 (25, 27 Sept.); Worc. Coll., MS xxviii, fols. 77r, 78r.

[173] *CJ*, VII, pp. 439, 444, 456, 465, 475, 501 (16, 23 Oct., 18 Nov., 6, 25 Dec. 1656, 14 Mar. 1657).

[174] Ibid., p. 552 (9 June 1657); *A & O*, II, pp. 1114, 1121 (9, 19 June 1657).

the problem of repaying loans that had been made to the state, it was suggested that the forest lands of England and Wales be sold immediately to satisfy public debts. Desborough objected, warning the house, 'if you sell your forests you will destroy your navigation'. His point was taken and the matter of selling forest lands was dropped.[175] In a related question the house resolved to confirm an earlier ordinance reserving forest lands as collateral security for soldiers' needs.[176] During the third reading of the bill that Glynne had drafted naming and empowering forest commissioners around the country, the decision was taken to establish an appeal committee to hear complaints against prosecutions of forest laws.[177] Although Sheppard's suggestion that regulations for timber preservation be imposed on privately held lands was not introduced, the parliament did act upon preserving timber in state forests in these several far-sighted moves.

A bill for the 'improvement of waste-grounds and regulating of commons and commonable lands and preventing depopulation' might well have been written by Sheppard himself. The bill was brought in by Major-General Whalley on 19 December and Lenthall attacked it immediately 'for he never liked any bill that touched on property'. Whalley defended the bill as being for the general good because it prevented depopulation and encouraged the increase of cultivated land, 'which is the very support of the commonwealth'. But the house apparently was convinced by the argument that the bill would threaten property rights and the house resolved that the bill be rejected and not read again.[178] Two bills concerning the drainage of the fens in Lincolnshire and Hampshire were ordered to be read in late November but the house's concern with Cromwell's consent to its first five bills occasioned a postponement and both bills were subsequently lost without ever being read. The following spring, during the review of earlier ordinances, the house recommended confirmation of an order to preserve the work being done in the fens and the revival and continuation of an act to recover and preserve lands in East Anglia 'surrounded by the rage of the sea'.[179] A bill to make the River Ouse navigable was engrossed on 1 June

---

[175] *Burton's diary*, II, p. 238; *CJ*, VII, p. 556 (13 June 1657).
[176] *A & O*, II, p. 1138 (26 June 1657).
[177] Desborough, Lambert and Sydenham, all council members, were named as appeal commissioners among others: *CJ*, VII, p. 561 (18 June 1657).
[178] *Burton's diary*, I, pp. 175–6; *CJ*, VII, p. 470 (19 Dec. 1656).
[179] *CJ*, VII, pp. 455, 523–30 (20 Nov. 1656, 24–30 Apr. 1657); *A & O*, II, pp. 1131–2 (26 June 1657).

and forwarded for the protector's consent on the 26th; inexplicably, it never reached the statute book.[180] A bill for maintaining and repairing highways was given two readings before it was dropped for lack of interest or of time.[181] The house was told of a bill to regulate the commission of sewers that had already been prepared, but the bill was never read.[182] Sheppard had objected to the harshness of the law of wreck and sought a remedy whereby the law could be changed so that owners could more easily retrieve their lost goods. On 28 October a large committee including members from all the port towns was ordered to draft such a bill but it was April before the bill was ordered to be read the following week and, once again, more urgent issues crowded out a less compelling matter and the bill was never heard.[183] One of the most neglected areas of national regulation was the cloth trade and the matter was taken up on a regional basis. Separate bills were prepared for the textile industries in Norwich, Yorkshire, Devon and for western serges, but only the Norwich bill passed[184] along with the Rump's act restricting tobacco planting and the 1654 ordinance to correct abuses on the Thames and Medway rivers.[185]

The apprenticeship laws were another aspect of the nation's commercial life that had concerned Sheppard. He had proposed altering the traditional regulations on two counts: first, that some men naturally possessed more skill in a craft or trade than others who had fulfilled the seven-year training obligation; and second, an accommodation should be made for the many fully trained craftsmen who found it impossible to produce the credentials they had earned many years earlier. Parliament, however, did not see fit to alter the traditional laws and agreed only to confirm an ordinance exempting returned soldiers, permitting them to exercise any trade.[186] On the other hand, Sheppard's concern about establishing price ceilings for charges made by country inns was brought to the attention of the house in the first weeks of meetings. On 29 September a large committee including all the judges was instructed to meet on the next

[180] *CJ*, VII, pp. 543, 575, 577 (1, 26 June 1657).
[181] Ibid., pp. 464, 478 (4 Dec. 1656, 2 Jan. 1657); W. Sheppard, *England's balme*, p. 174.
[182] *CJ*, VII, p. 463 (2 Dec. 1656); Sheppard, *England's balme*, pp. 198–9.
[183] *CJ*, VII, pp. 446, 516 (28 Oct. 1656, 1 Apr. 1657); Sheppard, *England's balme*, pp. 192–3.
[184] *A & O*, II, pp. 775, 1137; *CJ*, VII, pp. 455, 459, 467, 514.
[185] *A & O*, II, 1137, 1140.
[186] *A & O*, II, p. 1132 (26 June); Sheppard, *England's balme*, pp. 203–4.

day 'to consider the great abuses in inns as to their unreasonable prices, both for horse-meat and man-meat' as well as abuses in alehouses, tippling-houses, inns and taverns, tobacco shops and strong-water houses and gaming houses, taking into consideration at the same time a revised reduction of all statutes concerning alehouses and drunkenness. A week later the same committee was given the additional charge of appraising the laws concerned with profane swearing and correcting any defects that could be discovered.[187] A bill establishing one general post office for England, Scotland and Ireland passed its third reading on 9 June, but only after two hours of debate. It received the protector's consent the same afternoon.[188] On the same day an act was passed providing that aliens were to pay twice the amount levied on English subjects for licenses to transport fish, thereby defeating one of Sheppard's goals that foreigners be given the same free-trade privileges as citizens. The benefits of English citizenship were manifest in the dozens of petitions for naturalization that the house heard as private bills.[189] Sheppard's proposal to establish a national bank was never introduced as a legislative bill although as early as January 1654 the council of state had appointed a committee to consider forming such an institution at the request of a London merchant.[190] The regulation of printing and the establishment of copyright were discussed with reference to three separate cases, but no general statute was enacted and Sheppard's hope that 'the right of every man's copy be preserved' in a general copyright statute was not fulfilled until 1709.[191] The related issue, raised in *England's balme*, of government control over printing houses and the publication and importation of 'dangerous books' was not considered by the parliament but was taken up on executive initiative in 1658 when Cromwell and the council ordered the enforcement of earlier statutes against the publication of 'un-

---

[187] *CJ*, VII, pp. 430, 435 (29 Sept., 7 Oct.); Sheppard, *England's balme*, pp. 46–7; Worc. Coll., MS xxviii, fols. 83r, 84r. See below, nn. 221, 222, 225, for discussion of consolidating statutes.

[188] *A & O*, II, p. 1110; *Burton's diary*, II, p. 201; *CJ*, VII, pp. 551–2 (9 June).

[189] *A & O*, II, p. 1099; *CJ*, VII, p. 552 (9 June); Sheppard, *England's balme*, p. 201.

[190] *CSPD*, VI, pp. 365–6; Sheppard, *England's balme*, p. 135; *W & S*, III, p. 167.

[191] The house appointed a committee to 'consider of a way to suppress private presses', and another to investigate the printing of 'false Bibles': *Burton's diary*, I, p. clxxxix (21 Nov.); *CJ*, VII, p. 442 (20 Oct.). The next spring the copyright to Croke's *Reports* was awarded to Harbottle Grimston by order of parliament: *CJ*, VII, p. 551 (9 June 1657).

licensed, scandalous and seditious books' without the assistance of any new legislation.[192]

In *England's balme* Sheppard had voiced the plea for 'a more perfect translation of the scriptures',[193] and early in November 1656 the government awarded its official printer, Henry Hills, the right to publish a version of the Bible 'with hundreds of gross errors corrected'. Two weeks later parliament's grand committee on religion was asked to present a report on the printing of false Bibles and a month later the Bible committee was still holding meetings. In mid January the committee resolved to investigate all versions of the Bible that had been printed in the previous two years and to forbid the importation of Bibles printed outside England.[194] A group of theologians met with some members of parliament to discuss mistakes that had appeared in English translations, and by 16 February Dr Brian Walton's polyglot Bible was published, thereby satisfying Sheppard's demand for a 'more perfect translation'. In June parliament confiscated 7900 copies of 'imperfect translations' that had been distributed by publishers between 1653 and 1657.[195]

With respect to other matters touching religion, Cromwell had opened the parliament by asking its members to confirm the ordinances of his religious settlement. 'That which had been our practice since the last parliament hath been to let all this nation see that whatever pretensions be to religion, if quiet and peaceable, [all may enjoy] conscience and liberty to themselves [so long as they do] not make religion a pretense for arms and blood...I confess that I look at [the liberty and protection in the worshipping of God according to their own judgments] as the blessedest thing which hath been since the adventuring upon the government that these times produce.'[196] While the conditions of freedom for all to worship under the protection of a tolerant government was Cromwell's proudest accomplishment, this parliament ultimately enacted measures that were in fact regressive when compared to the conditions that had

---

[192] *CSPD*, XII, p. 71 (warrant of 22 June 1658 to the masters and wardens of the Stationers' Company to execute the acts of 1643, 1647, 1649 and 1653); Sheppard, *England's balme*, p. 182.

[193] Sheppard, *England's balme*, p. 138.

[194] *Burton's diary*, I, pp. clxxxix, 258, 348 (21 Nov., 26 Dec.); *CSPD*, VI, p. 289; *Thurloe State Papers*, IV, p. 584; *W & S*, III, pp. 27–8, 769–70; IV, pp. 114–15, 145, 327–8.

[195] *Burton's diary*, I, pp. 351–2; II, p. 221; *CJ*, VII, pp. 554–5; Whitelocke, *Memorials*, IV, p. 285.

[196] *W & S*, IV, pp. 271–2.

been fostered and advanced by the protectorate since its establishment. On 25 May 1657 the house adopted a new written constitution,
the Humble Petition and Advice, in which article XI explicitly
promised the adoption of a confession of faith, to be agreed upon by
the protector and parliament, but under conditions that did not
satisfy Sheppard's behest for 'some moderate, sweet and wise
declaration' of doctrine.[197] While this constitutional precept allowed
the same protection to those who could not in conscience subscribe
to a national doctrine as had the provision in the Instrument, the
specific restrictions were more limiting. Reflecting the rising fear of
Quakerism, those 'who publish horrid blasphemies, or practise or
hold forth licentiousness or profaneness' were excepted from the
provision as were those followers of Popery and prelacy named in the
original protectorate constitution. Moreover, the further elaboration
of article XI specifically denied state support to any minister who
could not agree to subscribe to the national doctrine. This curtailment of toleration to part of the clergy in the interest of religious
uniformity was the beginning of a movement that reached its apex
with the adoption of the restoration Act of Uniformity. Although
Sheppard had proposed extending state support even to lay preachers
and allowing for the establishment of a loose confederation of
congregationalist churches, the actions taken by this parliament had
the reverse effect. And the legal disabilities Sheppard had wanted to
remove from Papists and Baptists were issues that were never
brought before this parliament.[198]

The principal elements of Cromwell's religious settlement that
had been accomplished by ordinance were the establishment of the
two commissions, of triers and of ejectors, the first a group of laymen
and ministers representing several disciplines and faiths, centralized
in London. The second ordinance, establishing commissions to eject
'scandalous, ignorant and insufficient ministers', had delegated the
responsibilities of removing unfit preachers to the local communities.
The 1656 parliament confirmed unconditionally Cromwell's ordinance for the triers as well as the third ordinance of the religious
settlement, 'for the better maintenance and encouragement of
preaching ministers and for uniting of parishes',[199] but Sheppard's
suggestion that the triers' commission be decentralized was never

---

[197] *A & O*, II, pp. 1053–4 (25 May 1657); Sheppard, *England's balme*, pp. 137–8.
[198] Sheppard, *England's balme*, pp. 192, 202–5.
[199] *A & O*, II, pp. 1132, 1136.

raised in the parliament, nor was his proposal that magistrates be authorized to equalize parish endowments by altering local boundaries. Moreover, the 1654 ordinance that had established ejectors was specifically limited to a life of only three years beyond the adjournment of parliament's first session.[200] As for the question of ministerial support, the Instrument had provided for tithe collections 'until a provision less subject to scruple and contention' was found, and Cromwell had told the assembly at the beginning of its meetings that he intended to keep tithes 'until I see a legislative power to settle maintenance to them another way'.[201] Sheppard's innovative plan to collect local taxes for ministerial support in lieu of tithes was never brought before the body and the idea of collecting a tax based on any sort of land-holding was such anathema to the house that it was expressly forbidden by article VII of the Humble Petition and Advice.[202] The general question of financing preachers did come to the attention of the house on the last day of October when a committee of forty-eight was instructed to meet the following day to consider settling and providing for ministers and also to investigate tithe collections in Wales and in four northern counties.[203] On 4 November a committee was directed to bring in a bill to raise the incomes of ministers in cities and towns but the winter passed with no report made from either of these committees.[204] In April the bill for ministerial support still had not received its first reading and after seven separate orders a bill was finally read on 1 June 'for confirming and reviving several ordinances of parliament for the recovery of tithes, with alterations and additions'.[205] Two council members, Desborough and Strickland, urged at this time that the bill be given a second reading but their motion, which was opposed by Whitelocke and Lenthall among others, failed and all chances for a general reform or adjustment in the collection of tithes was lost.[206] Another of Sheppard's ideas was embodied in a bill permitting trustees to purchase impropriations

[200] Ibid., p. 1139; Sheppard, *England's balme*, pp. 131, 142.
[201] Instrument of Government, art. XXXV; *W & S*, IV, p. 272.
[202] Art. VII which called for a constant yearly revenue specified, 'no part thereof to be raised by a land tax': *A & O*, II, p. 1052. Heated debates over a tax on land can be found in *Burton's diary*, II, p. 24.
[203] *CJ*, VII, p. 448 (31 Oct.); Worc. Coll., MS xxviii, fol. 105v.
[204] *CJ*, VII, pp. 449–50 (4 Nov.).
[205] Ibid., pp. 519, 523–4, 531, 535, 538, 540, 543 (2, 24, 27 Apr., 5, 20, 23, 26 May, 1 June).
[206] *Burton's diary*, II, p. 165–6.

for the support of ministers in several parishes, but the bill died in committee after only two readings.[207] At least twelve bills to augment ministers' livings in specific parishes received one or more readings, but only an earlier act for the Isle of Wight was confirmed at the end of the session.[208] Five towns did benefit from acts passed to provide either for increased salaries for ministers or the promotion of more frequent preaching, but there were no general acts to supply preachers to parishes in need of resident or itinerant clergy as Sheppard had proposed.[209] In the last week of the session Lambert and Strickland were instrumental in appointing a committee to bring in a bill to improve ministerial maintenance in their own northern counties, but the bill never materialized.[210] At the second reading of a bill to increase maintenance for Northampton ministers, one member objected to any increase on the grounds that 'ministers had never so large a maintenance in England as they have at this day. They have £20,000 a year of dean and chapter lands besides the tithes of delinquents.' William Strickland, brother of the council member, rejoined, 'notwithstanding that allowance I know of many that have not £20, not £5 a year. If there be scandalous maintenance, there must be scandalous ministers. How can we expect the lamp should burn without oil? We honor God by honoring his messengers. I desire it [the bill] may be committed.'[211] But despite the determined efforts of many dedicated reformers, virtually no progress was made on the important question of making sufficient provision for a competent preacher in every English and Welsh parish.

Another reform tangential to the religious question that Sheppard had wanted improved was the act for civil marriages that had first been passed in 1653 by the Barebones Assembly. He had objected to the rigid and complex provisions of the act and the 1656 parliament did mitigate the most unreasonable and harsh provisions when they annulled the clause providing for the invalidation of all marriages that were not legally correct in every particular. The act

---

[207] *CJ*, VII, pp. 503, 515 (13, 31 Mar.).
[208] The places were Totnes, Preston, Savernack, Romford, Havering, Holborn parish, Hornchurch, Portsmouth, Exeter, Northampton, Plymouth, Bristol and the Isle of Wight: *CJ*, VII, *passim*.
[209] *A & O*, II, pp. cii (Plymouth, Great Yarmouth, Exeter, Northampton and Isle of Wight); Sheppard, *England's balme*, pp. 133, 138–9.
[210] *CJ*, VII, p. 561 (18 June).
[211] This bill for Northampton received its third reading on 12 Feb. and passed in June: *Burton's diary*, I, pp. 159–61 (17 Dec.).

itself was, however, confirmed only for the six months following the end of that session of parliament, with no provisions for the future made.[212] Two new acts, on recusancy and on sabbath observance, were passed by this parliament that also presaged the restoration settlement as the laws reverted to a spirit characteristic of the enactments of Tudor and early Stuart parliaments. The recusancy act compelled suspected Roman Catholics to subscribe to a lengthy oath that denied the principles of transubstantiation and salvation by works and the existence of purgatory as well as abjuration of Papal authority. The statute concluded with the provision that any suspected person failing to take the oath 'shall be adjudged a Popish recusant, convict to all intents and purposes whatsoever', thereby forfeiting two-thirds of their real and personal property.[213] The Act for the Better Observation of the Lord's Day, first read on 7 January, was a lengthy and detailed act that included among other provisions a protection to ministers from disturbances and provided for the act's enforcement at general sessions, with conviction by either confession or on the oath of one sworn witness. The strict prohibitions of activities on the sabbath were spelled out in detail and heavy penalties for violations were assigned. The most significant provision of the act was a clause that enjoined compulsory church attendance, providing 'that all...persons shall...upon every Lord's day diligently resort to some church or chapel where the true worship and service of God is exercised, or shall be present at some other convenient meeting place of Christians, not differing in matters of faith from the public profession of the nation'.[214] The Rump had passed a similar act in 1650, but the object at that time had been to repeal the Elizabethan laws compelling attendance in the established church. While both the acts of 1650 and 1657 allowed a degree of latitude in the choice of worship, at least to the extent that Independent and Presbyterian churches would fall within the permissible limits, this statutory restatement of compulsory church attendance was another indication of a return to a less tolerant atmosphere. The combined effect of this statutory regulation and the constitutional provision calling for the adoption of a national confession of faith that would more closely define 'true worship' and

---

[212] *A & O*, II, pp. 715, 1139 (24 Aug. 1653, 26 June 1657); Sheppard, *England's balme*, p. 155.
[213] *A & O*, II, p. 1170.
[214] Ibid., pp. 1162–70 (the quote appears on p. 1167); *Burton's diary*, I, p. 310.

'matters of faith' was of a much more circumscribed religious settlement than that which had prevailed for the first three years of the protectorate.

On the related issue of liberty of conscience, Cromwell and his council had repealed the Rump's loyalty oath, the Engagement to the Commonwealth, as one of the first acts of state.[215] By rescinding that most recent in a series of political oaths that had been imposed on various groups of the population since the reign of Henry VIII, Cromwell and the council had asserted the principle that a man's conscience must not be enchained by oaths, a maxim Sheppard had included in *England's balme*.[216] When the 1656 parliament met, a bill against customary oaths was introduced on 4 October and received its second reading just three days later. On 6 November the committee to which the bill had been assigned was ordered to meet, but that directive was the last that was heard of repudiating oaths until the following spring.[217] Late in May the new constitution was adopted and a month later the house took up the question of article XVIII which provided that the protector 'will be pleased to take an oath... to govern these nations according to the law'. On 23 June the question of whether to impose a similar oath on the new council and the members of parliament raised the possibility that some sort of oath might ultimately be extended to the entire population. The question provoked a heated debate that lasted for two days, with members of the council of state taking active roles against the adoption of any sort of comprehensive oath. Sydenham asserted, 'I had rather live under a magistrate that is under no oath' while Wolseley strenuously objected to the consideration of extending any oath to the nation at large. Strickland reminded the house that 'of late we have had a very great weight of oaths upon us', and when the vote was taken on the question of a nation-wide oath, Lambert and Sydenham served as tellers for the negative.[218] On the following day the house confined its discussion to the oath the protector would

---

[215] *A & O*, II, p. 830 (19 Jan. 1654).
[216] Sheppard, *England's balme*, p. 210. The Hale Commission had drafted an act against customary oaths that provided no person be compelled to do homage or to take an oath to do fealty; or any oath on matriculation in the universities or on taking any degree; or on entrance into the freedom of any corporation, society or company, but with the proviso that office-holders could take an oath concerning the execution of the office: *CSPD*, VI, p. 338 (1653).
[217] *CJ*, VII, pp. 434–5, 450 (4, 7 Oct., 6 Nov.).
[218] *A & O*, II, p. 1056; *Burton's diary*, II, pp. 274–82 (23 June 1657).

take, and when the addition of a clause about religion was suggested Desborough objected, 'the oath is full enough without it. To put in such a clause about the protestant religion will be a snare in regard of the great disputes about what [precisely] shall be the protestant religion.' Sydenham again objected on principle to adopting any oath and reminded the house that the repeal of the Engagement had included a 'declaration against all oaths as burdens and snares to tender consciences'. Despite all the objections put forward by council members and others, the house approved not only an oath for the protector and his successors to swear, but also one for members of the council of state and a third for members of parliament, adopting all three as constitutional amendments.[219]

As for Sheppard's urging that this parliament finally consider embarking on the long overdue project of abridging the statutes of the realm, the energetic and promising start made in the first weeks of the session again belied the accomplishments recorded in the statute book. At the seventh meeting of the new parliament the house appointed a large committee, which included all the judges, to review all the laws passed since the dismissal of the Rump Parliament to determine which should be continued and which revised or repealed. The members were directed to meet in two days' time, but there is no indication that the committee ever met that autumn.[220] Instead, the revisions of specific categories of statutes were assigned to several smaller committees with orders to reduce and 'supply the defects', and the broader question of statutory review was temporarily laid aside as the house focused attention on laws pertaining only to the overlapping areas of social control and economic regulation. On the very day the general review committee was first supposed to meet, the house reassigned the judges and other committee members 'to consider of the abuses in alehouses, tippling-houses, inns and taverns, tobacco shops and strong-water houses and gaming houses …and to revise the laws touching alehouses and made against drunkenness', revising and reducing each to one law. The same day 'indecent fashions' and 'other excesses in apparel' were debated in the house and a bill was ordered brought in.[221] At the end of the week a small committee was appointed to revise and reduce 'into one law'

---

[219] The Humble Additional and Explanatory Petition and Advice was adopted on 26 June 1657: A & O, II, pp. 1184–6; Burton's diary, II, pp. 274–96.
[220] CJ, VII, p. 429 (27 Sept.).
[221] Ibid., pp. 430, 435 (29 Sept., 7 Oct.).

the acts concerned with bastardy, adultery and fornication.[222] The following week the committee for alehouses was ordered to enlarge the laws against profane swearing, while a new committee was charged with the preparation of a bill to cover the wages and 'habits and fashions' of servants, laborers and apprentices.[223] Laws concerning beggars, rogues and vagrants came under the scrutiny of the house on 16 October when another small committee was ordered to reduce all earlier legislation pertaining to those elements of society as well as acts concerning 'wandering, idle, loose and dissolute persons'. The same committee was asked to consider drafting a bill for a previously unnoted group of suspect persons, 'those who live at very high rates and have no visible estates, profession or calling suitable thereunto'.[224] The question of weights and measures, which first had been raised in a meeting of the grand committee of the whole house for trade on 29 September, was referred to a committee appointed to consider price regulations for inns, but it was not until 3 November that a bill was ordered to revise and supply defects in all the statutes concerned with weights and measures, the clerk of the market and the assizes of bread and beer.[225]

Efforts made by the committees charged with revision of the statutes pertaining to the government's socio-economic policy were, for the most part, lost in the flood of more urgent business. Although further directives were given to the committees – as in mid October when the alehouse committee was instructed to provide in its bill that penal fines for alehouse violations be set aside for the use of the poor and a new bill be prepared to set the poor at work building stocks[226] – by the end of the session only three of the nine categories of statutes had been acted upon by the house. The 1654 ordinance on drunkenness and profanity among customs workers was simply confirmed with no alterations.[227] A new statute against rogues was not much more ambitious. Although there was some debate in December about the redeeming charms of music, the act of 9 June 1657 simply added musicians performing in alehouses to the list of offenders covered by the Elizabethan act against rogues, vagabonds

---

[222] Ibid., p. 433 (4 Oct.); Worc. Coll., MS xxviii, fol. 83v.
[223] CJ, VII, p. 435 (7 Oct.).
[224] Burton's diary, I, p. clxxxiii; CJ, VII, p. 439; Worc. Coll., MS xxviii, fol. 92r.
[225] CJ, VII, pp. 449, 511. On 5 Feb. 1656 Cromwell had ordered the execution of the 1642 act regulating uniformity of weights and measures as a temporary measure: PRO, SP 25/76, fol. 521.
[226] CJ, VII, p. 439 (16 Oct.).   [227] A & O, II, p. 1132.

and sturdy beggars.[228] There was only one genuinely new piece of legislation passed at the end of the session. Its purpose was to punish by confinement in a house of correction persons who lived 'at very high rates and great expenses, having no visible estate, profession or calling (answerable thereunto) [and] maintain themselves in their licentious, loose and ungodly practices'. The preamble explained that its purpose was to restrain those who 'make it their trade and livelihood to cheat, debauch, cozen and deceive the young gentry and other good people of this commonwealth'.[229] The program to revise and abridge many aspects of social legislation was therefore a failure.[230]

Towards the end of the session the house turned again to the project that had been abandoned since the first weeks of meetings: the consideration of all statutes and ordinances issued since the April 1653 dispersal of the Rump. Two months later the recommendations of the committee assigned to this review were adopted and eighty-eight acts and ordinances were unconditionally confirmed as well as all legislation pertaining to customs and excise. Fourteen others were ordered to continue in force under provisional conditions or specific time limits.[231] Several important areas in Sheppard's design for reform were never brought to the attention of this parliament. These were his proposals to reform criminal law and procedure,[232] the inheritance laws, and his innovative plan to restructure the court system with provisions for superior courts of appeal and concurrent jurisdiction in law and equity.

[228] Act of 39 Eliz. I, c. 4 with amendments on fiddlers and minstrels, confirmed on 9 June 1657: *A & O*, II, p. 1098.

[229] *A & O*, II, p. 1249.

[230] Although no earlier acts were repealed or reduced, a few new acts in related fields did pass: Act for preventing the multiplicity of buildings in and around the suburbs of London; Act for the better suppressing of theft upon the borders of England and Scotland, and for the discovery of highwaymen and other felons: *A & O*, II, pp. 1223, 1262.

[231] The committee was appointed on 29 April and the acts were confirmed on 26 June with the provision that all other acts and ordinances not included in the list be 'absolutely null and void': *Burton's diary*, II, p. 39; *A & O*, II, pp. 1131–42.

[232] Cromwell, too, had hoped that parliament would attend to alterations in the criminal code. On the opening day of the session the protector had exhorted, 'there are wicked, abominable laws that will be in your power to alter. To hang a man for sixpence, threepence, I know not what; to hang for a trifle and [to] pardon murder, is in the ministration of the law through the ill framing of it. I have known in my experience abominable murders quitted; and to see men lose their lives for petty matters! This is a thing God will reckon for': *W & S*, IV, p. 274 (17 Sept. 1654).

One of the most successful areas of accomplishment for this parliament was the post-war settlement of the nation. The greatest number of bills passed or confirmed in the first session related to the necessary business of legalizing the revolution and assuring the nation that the problems following in the wake of fifteen years of war, civil disruption and changes of government would be secured for the peace and tranquillity of the nation. The legitimacy of the regime was quickly established by acts renouncing Charles Stuart's claim to the throne and providing for the safety and security of Cromwell, the nation's acknowledged leader. A third act, also confirmed in November 1656, asserted parliament's role as a partner in the present government by the declaration that the passage of bills would not determine the length of the session.[233] A new indemnity act and a statute for the attainder of Irish rebels were drawn and finally passed on the last day of the session.[234] The 1654 ordinance for union with Scotland was simply confirmed after a much-debated new bill was lost,[235] and the session closed with the confirmation of twelve acts pertaining to Scotland and eight concerning Ireland.[236] A general act to relieve persons who had acted in parliament's service was also passed, along with many private bills for compensation and acts authorizing investigations into tithe collections and accounts of the army and sequestration committees.[237]

Sheppard had proposed that parliament take action in three specific areas to benefit the 'settlement of the nation': to provide compensation for private homes destroyed in the wars, to repay loans made to the state by citizens, and to confirm the sale of lands to individuals by parliament.[238] By the end of the session all three of Sheppard's suggestions had been taken up, but with varying degrees of success. The state's willingness to assume responsibility for compensating individuals for property loss was confined to the citizens of the war-torn city of Gloucester. In a December debate on that bill Lenthall proposed that Irish lands worth £10,000 be assigned to the use of the citizens of Gloucester who had 'suffered their houses to be burned down for your service'. Other members

---

[233] *A & O*, II, pp. 1036, 1038 (26 Nov. 1656).
[234] Ibid., pp. 1180, 1250 (26 June 1657).
[235] *CJ*, VII, pp. 445, 450, *et passim*.
[236] *A & O*, II, pp. 1100, 1110, 1131–41. All were confirmations of earlier acts and ordinances with the exceptions of an act of 9 June to settle Irish lands and the post-office act which extended to both Scotland and Ireland.
[237] Ibid., p. 1131.
[238] Sheppard, *England's balme*, pp. 139, 140, 187.

wanted to include compensation to the citizens of Colchester, Hull and Lyme, but their motions did not carry.[239]

The repayment of loans that had been made to the state was a much more difficult problem for a parliament summoned to provide new supply to a financially hard-pressed government. The scarcity of funds to meet present and future fiscal needs presented a difficulty in itself. In mid December the house was reminded of its moral obligation to repay money borrowed by the state and one speaker made the point that many citizens who had 'lent money freely in 1642 [were now] reduced to great need and extremity'.[240] In January new members were added to the committee considering the repayment of 'loans made on the public faith' but no real progress was made until March when a member, John Arthur, submitted a private petition requesting the repayment of his own loan of £3697 12s. 4d. The question was sent to committee but no more action was taken until June.[241] On the penultimate day of the session with the serious matter of the state's debts to private citizens still unresolved, the house recommended that Cromwell and the council appoint county commissioners 'for ascertaining the monies due upon the public faith... with such restrictions and limitations to prevent fraud as they shall think fit', reporting back to the next session of parliament.[242] On the final day of the session the house did approve acts to repay three individuals and the last part of clause XII in the Humble Petition and Advice solemnly vowed to honor all debts made 'upon the public faith'.[243] The final resolution to the issue of repayment was only deferred, as was the case with so many of the other issues considered by this parliament.

The third problem, the confirmation of land sales made by parliament, naturally attracted the greatest amount of interest from the property-holding gentry sitting as members of this house. In the first week of October an army reporter wrote to Scotland that the house had appointed a committee 'to examine falsehoods in buying and selling forfeited lands', adding, 'I know knaves will be discouraged and the commonwealth a gainer'.[244] The confusion arising

[239] *Burton's diary*, I, p. 203 (22 Dec.); *CJ*, VII, p. 530 (5 May).
[240] *Burton's diary*, I, p. 93 (10 Dec.).
[241] *CJ*, VII, pp. 503, 546, 559, 563.   [242] *Ibid.*, p. 575 (25 June).
[243] *A & O*, II, p. 1054 (Humble Petition, 25 May); *CJ*, VII, p. 577 (26 June, bill number 16).
[244] Worc. Coll., MS xxviii, fol. 83v (week preceding 7 Oct.). The committee was appointed on 3 Oct.: *CJ*, VII, p. 432.

from the great amount of lands that had changed hands over the past fifteen years invited both investigation and confirmation if a true settlement for the nation were to be achieved. Although the sale by the Long and the Rump Parliaments of lands once owned by bishops, deans and chapters as well as the sale of delinquents' lands had been almost completed prior to the establishment of the protectorate, the present government was bound to assume responsibility for assuring good title to lands that had been sold under honest and fair conditions. In November, Lambert brought in a bill for the confirmation of church lands sold by parliament that received two readings. The matter was referred to a committee of the whole house.[245] This action had the effect of tabling other bills on this matter and it was not until the new constitution was being drafted in the following spring that all land sales were confirmed by a provision in clause XII.[246]

The session therefore ended with more promises than accomplishments. Before the second session assembled in January 1658 two of Cromwell's most loyal adherents, John Lambert and John Owen, had fallen from political favor for their opposition to the constitutional settlement that, when it was adopted in May and June 1657, replaced the Instrument Lambert had written and the tolerant religious settlement of which Owen had been the architect. Of the other Cromwellian supporters who had advocated reform, a majority were named to membership in the other (upper) house of the new bicameral legislature, and with little government leadership left in the lower house, the session ended as a practical failure. The parliament was dissolved just weeks after it assembled with no acts at all entered into the statute book. Sheppard, whose contract with the government had been terminated, had retired to his Gloucestershire home late in the summer of 1657, his usefulness to the government ended after the new constitution had been adopted. A shift back to more traditional and familiar patterns was followed as the new philosophy of government brought in its wake an increased number of supporters of more conservative inclinations than those adhering to any other government since 1649. With revolutionary experiments in government effectively ended, there was no further need for a law-reform consultant to design innovative improvements.

Sheppard's accuracy in identifying the grievances of the nation

[245] *CJ*, VII, pp. 453, 455 (13, 19 Nov.); Worc. Coll., MS xxviii, fol. 108v.
[246] *A & O*, II, p. 1054 (25 May).

was ultimately vindicated by the reforms enacted by nineteenth-century parliaments. There was, however, one component of the reforms embodied in *England's balme* that was so unrealistic it was never seriously contemplated by future legislatures. This was Sheppard's assumption that parliament might agree to have local magistrates undertake to rank the entire population of the countryside, allocating a monopoly of political rights and privileges to an exclusive minority. Although distinctions between the godly and ungodly still prevailed in Massachusetts, with the 'elect' exercising a similar claim over both political privilege and public responsibility, the assumptions upon which that covenanted community had been founded were being questioned even within the first generation of the settlement, and rule by the godly was moving towards a more precarious footing. Sheppard was as interested in preserving the fabric of social stability as was Cromwell, but his suggested substitution of the 'elect' replacing the traditional ruling families was never a viable option for the English commonwealth.[247]

Another of Sheppard's hopes was that it would be possible 'to make one plain, complete and methodical treatise, or abridgment of the whole common and statute law...and therein to make these things that are now obscure and uncertain, clear and certain. And to have all the judges subscribe it for the settled law, and to have it confirmed by parliament.'[248] It is possible that he may have had in mind a compilation of constitutional guarantees, similar to those incorporated into the 1648 *Lawes and libertyes* adopted by the Massachusetts general court; a modernization, as it were, of Magna Carta, that reservoir of rights and liberties that served so many purposes for seventeenth-century lawyers in search of an irrefutable precedent. It can, however, be convincingly argued that Sheppard had in mind a project of much broader proportions, one upon which he himself had been working for a quarter of a century: an encyclopedic abridgment containing cases and statutes, with definitions and descriptions of customary law and common-law and chancery practice. This challenging enterprise had fascinated Sheppard since he first began his legal education and by the time he was asked by Cromwell to prepare recommendations for legal improvement, he had already prepared two such collections.[249] He

---

[247] Sheppard, *England's balme*, pp. 41–2.
[248] Ibid., p. 6.
[249] See ch. 2 for *Faithfull councellor*, I & II, and ch. 3 for the *Epitome*.

had acknowledged in the introduction to the second, his *Epitome*, that while he knew himself to be inadequate to do justice to a project of such magnitude, he hoped that a parliament would authorize and sponsor a similar undertaking, delegating the work to a committee of competent lawyers who, in a coordinated effort, would complete and perfect a task he felt himself unequal to finishing. Inasmuch as this parliament had been unable to complete projects of much less ambitious scope, proving for example, to be unable even to reduce and revise the group of statutes pertaining only to apprenticeship laws, there could be no expectation that this legislature could ever seriously consider undertaking such a project.

Sheppard himself did, however, return to this very project that he had hoped would be done under parliamentary auspices and while he disclaimed his own abilities for the task, he continued working on *A grand abridgment of all the common and statute laws of England* from the time he left the protectorate administration until the end of his life. His efforts were improved upon by the great abridgers of the eighteenth century and, by the nineteenth century, parliamentary commissions did embark upon projects to 'make the law more clear and certain', charging committees to review aspects of both substantive law and procedure. Many of the recommendations that emerged were adopted in reforming statutes that brought both the clarity and simplicity that Sheppard and other reformers had long advocated.

A great proportion of the remaining proposals in *England's balme* ultimately were enacted, although at an erratic pace over the ensuing two hundred and fifty years. Sheppard's goal had been the legal unification of England, but the incorporation of all the nation's courts into a single, hierarchical judicial structure was chronologically almost the last of Sheppard's proposed reforms to be accomplished. The major restructuring of the court system according to the provisions of the Judicature Acts of 1873–5 required years of study before the changes could be carried out, and the bold measures Sheppard had proposed were never seriously contemplated until after the statute-making body had itself been reformed. Prior to the nineteenth-century Reform Acts that extended the franchise, there was neither the inclination nor the bureaucratic machinery of parliamentary committees needed for the enactment of comprehensive reforms in the judicial structure.

Sheppard's suggestion that local courts be established as part of a coordinated system for the convenience of suitors seeking justice near their homes was one issue that remained alive after the restoration. Matthew Hale, who had opposed the plan when he worked on the 1652 extra-parliamentary committee, later proposed in his *Considerations touching the amendment or alteration of the lawes* the innovative establishment of local courts much like those of Sheppard's plan. In 1675 and 1696 parliament considered bills to regulate local courts but neither effort was successful. Bills to establish courts of record for suits claiming small damages passed the commons in three parliaments of William III, but each one was rejected in the house of lords.[250] In the mid eighteenth century Middlesex was given its own courts by parliamentary enactment but efforts to establish local courts of record elsewhere failed. Finally, in 1846 an entirely new set of courts was established throughout England to deal with cases where debt or damage claimed was under £20.[251] These courts were so successful that subsequent statutes enlarged their jurisdiction to encompass any common-law action that had the consent of both parties, most cases of contract, tort, replevin and bankruptcy as well as cases of equity and probate involving only moderate sums.[252] Probate jurisdiction remained vested in the ecclesiastical courts until 1857 when the state established a new court to hear testamentary cases that used common-law rules of evidence with the provision that contested issues could be sent to a law court for trial. Lesser cases of probate were later transferred to the county courts.[253]

The movement towards a unified court system which culminated in the Judicature Acts of 1873–5 began half a century earlier, in the same decade that the membership in the house of commons was itself modified. In 1832 a general simplification of common-law procedure provided for a uniform writ of summons, just as Sheppard had suggested adopting for all the courts in 1656.[254] Over the next three decades, additional statutes abolished all real actions but three, attempted to secure uniform and more flexible procedure in all the

[250] Cotterell, 'Law reform', pp. 73–4; *HEL*, I, p. 189.
[251] The courts actually had no connection with the historical shires but rather divided England and Wales into 500 districts with 59 circuits: Middlesex, 23 Geo. II, c. 33 (1750); County Court Act, 9 & 10 Vict., c. 95 (1846).
[252] 51 & 52 Vict., c. 43 (1888); 3 Edw. VII, c. 42 (1903); 24 & 25 Geo. V, c. 53 (1934).
[253] *HEL*, XV, p. 127; 20 & 21 Vict., c. 77.
[254] *HEL*, XV, p. 104; 2 & 3 Will. IV, c. 39.

courts, and granted judges greater discretionary powers, allowing as well for amendments to be made at any time, as Sheppard had proposed in *England's balme*.[255] The Common-law Procedure Acts of 1852 and 1854 allowed plaintiffs to join several complaints into one action; abolished outlawry and the writs of *alias* and *pluries*; established an arbitration system that was so successful that the powers of the office were enlarged by the 1889 Arbitration Act; and corrected some of the problems that arose from law and equity being adjudicated in separate courts. An act of 1854 empowered chancery to conduct trials by jury and have evidence presented in open court as well as to deliver decisions in all cases of common law.[256] But the law courts remained unable to deliver equitable remedies until the Judicature Acts finally established a unitary court system, with law and equity administered concurrently in every court, with the provision that equity would prevail in cases where the two came into conflict. This act consolidated the courts of chancery, king's bench, common pleas, exchequer and admiralty as well as the recently established courts of probate and divorce. Joined together, the courts formed the new supreme court of judicature with two branches: a high court of justice with original jurisdiction and a high court of appeals to crown a series of superior courts.[257] At the same time the complete reconstruction of the court system allowed for the adoption of a simplified and uniform code of procedure, as Sheppard had proposed two hundred years earlier, with subsequent statutes clarifying the new system and providing that judges could make new procedural rules when necessary.[258]

The Judicature Acts also made possible the adoption of Sheppard's plan to limit the number and regulate the responsibilities of court officials, a proposal that until then had defied implementation because of the complex and entrenched system of tenures, fees and perquisites. Some significant efforts to reform the officials of the courts had been realized forty years earlier when parliamentary commissions had analyzed and reported on staff positions in the central courts that resulted in the abolition of several positions and fixed salaries for the remaining officials.[259] The six-clerks office in

---

255 *HEL*, XV, p. 109.
256 *HEL*, XIV, p. 198; 15 & 16 Vict., c. 76; 17 & 18 Vict., c. 125.
257 36 & 37 Vict., c. 66; 38 & 39 Vict., c. 77.
258 *HEL*, I, p. 646; 36 & 37 Vict., c. 68; 39 & 40 Vict., c. 59; 44 & 45 Vict., c. 68; 56 & 57 Vict., c. 66; 57 & 58 Vict., c. 16.
259 *HEL*, I, pp. 262–4, 647–8; 6 Geo. IV, c. 82; 7 Will. IV & 1 Vict., c. 30.

chancery was finally abolished in 1843.[260] Two reports issued by a commission in 1874 led to the establishment of a central office of the supreme court by an act of 1879 that regulated the duties and tenures of all officials serving on the merged staff.[261]

The seventeenth-century aim to make title to land more certain through the establishment of registries was unrealized for almost three centuries. An 1862 act to establish a general registry for England and Wales was a practical failure, and another attempt in 1875 that provided for the voluntary registration of freehold land also failed to solve the problem. It was not until 1925 that the Land Registration Act established an effective system to secure land claims.[262]

Sheppard had realized that rational and just methods of proof and procedure required the abolition of many archaic judicial customs. The writ of attaint, although rarely applied after the seventeenth century, could still be used to punish jurors who gave false verdicts until it was abolished by section 60 of the Juries Act in 1825. Wager of law, that had called upon neighborhood compurgators to serve as character witnesses since the Anglo-Saxon period, continued to be employed by defendants at Westminster in cases of debt and detinue as late as 1824. Nine years later it was specifically abolished by the Civil Procedure Act.[263] The writ of error was used as an appeal procedure until it was abolished by the 1852 Common-law Procedure Act.[264] Benefit of clergy, that had been attacked repeatedly in *England's balme* and criticized by Cromwell in his 1656 speech opening parliament, continued to be employed for generations by convicted defendants seeking exemption from punishment. After Sheppard's death, the full benefits of the privilege were extended to women and although the reading test was discontinued in 1706, the privilege itself was not abolished until 1827.[265]

Most of the reforms of the criminal code were delayed until the nineteenth century. *Peine forte et dure* was rendered obsolete by the

---

[260] 5 & 6 Vict., c. 103.
[261] 42 & 43 Vict., c. 78.
[262] 25 & 26 Vict., cc. 42, 53; 38 & 39 Vict., c. 87.
[263] Baker, *Legal history*, pp. 88, 223; *HEL*, I, p. 308; 3 & 4 Will. IV, c. 42.
[264] 15 & 16 Vict., c. 76 (1852).
[265] The privilege was extended to women in 1693. When the privilege was abolished in 1827, an act of Edward VI extending the privilege to peers was overlooked until 1841 when the question arose during the trial of Lord Cardigan. A second act of the latter year abolished clergy definitively: 7 & 8 Geo. IV, c. 28; 4 & 5 Vict., c. 22.

1772 Felony and Piracy Act which made refusal to plead to a felony equivalent to a guilty plea; but it was not until the Criminal Law Act of 1827 that a plea of 'not guilty' could be entered in the court record for prisoners refusing to plead. The penalty of forfeiture of estate was not abolished until 1870 when it was enacted that no forfeiture should ensue from convictions of either treason or felony. That act also mitigated many of the traditional punishments, including death by quartering for traitors.[266] Sheppard's proposal to abolish trial by battle was not realized until 1819,[267] and the three Tudor statutes prescribing the death penalty for gypsies, to which he had objected, were not amended until 1820, and the statutes themselves were not repealed until 1856.[268] Between 1826 and 1832 a group of consolidating statutes amended the criminal law and repealed all or parts of 256 statutes, ranging in date of enactment from the twelfth to the nineteenth century.[269] In 1836 the Prisoners' Counsel Act permitted defendants accused of felony to be represented by counsel, allowed accused persons to examine all depositions submitted to the court, and by 1848 an act provided that witnesses for the prosecution were to be examined in the presence of the accused.[270] In 1837 the death penalty was removed from most cases of forgery as well as crimes of burglary, robbery and piracy if no violence or assault had been committed. In 1861 a consolidating act removed capital punishment from robbery convictions even when the crime had been accompanied with violence.[271]

The reform activities in the parliaments that met between 1660 and 1820 present a disappointingly different picture. The reactions against the fertile period of reform proposals during the interregnum were so strong and negative that little was attempted and even less was accomplished for many generations after Sheppard and his fellow law-reformers had published their suggestions for legal improvement. The repudiation of puritan accomplishments began immediately in 1660 when the languages used in the courts and for

---

[266] Felony and Piracy Act (1772); Criminal Law Act (1827); Forfeiture Act, 33 & 34 Vict., c. 23 (1870).
[267] 59 Geo. III, c. 46 (1819).
[268] Death penalty removed from statutes against Egyptians of 1530, 1554 & 1563 by 1 Geo. IV, c. 116 (1820); statutes repealed by 19 & 20 Vict., c. 64 (1856).
[269] 7 Geo. IV, c. 114 (1826); 7 & 8 Geo. IV, cc. 27–31 (1827); 9 Geo. IV, c. 31 (1828); 11 Geo. IV & 1 Will. IV, c. 66 (1830); 2 & 3 Will. IV, c. 34 (1832).
[270] 6 & 7 Will. IV, c. 114 (1836); 11 & 12 Vict., c. 42 (1848).
[271] 2 & 3 Will. IV, c. 62 (1832: death penalty removed from horse and cattle stealing); 7 Will. IV. & 1 Vict., cc. 84–8 (1837); 25 & 26 Vict., c. 96.

legal records reverted to the medieval Latin. It was not until 1731–2 that parliament restored the use of English as the language of the law as had been done for a brief decade eighty years earlier.[272] The contrasts between the energetic efforts of the brief five-year protectorate and the long, fallow period that followed are most dramatically illustrated by the dissimilar degrees of interest in regulating the courts of justice. Under Cromwell's mandate a comprehensive ordinance of specific provisions had been prepared to reform the largest, most expensive and most dilatory court in the nation; having seen its provisions enforced, Sheppard had then prepared the clear guidelines published in *England's balme* to reform the entire system of justice with proposals of dimensions comparable to the scope of changes decreed by the nineteenth-century Judicature Acts. Conversely, in the period of reaction that followed the protectorate, neither Charles II nor James II had displayed any interest in reforming their courts and it was not until 1689 that a parliament turned its attention to an enquiry into the fees of officials in the law courts and chancery. The bill that was drafted was not enacted; nor was the bill of 1691–2 for the prevention of abuses in the six-clerks office. Forty years then passed before a commons committee prepared recommendations for remedies against extortion by chancery officials and prohibitions against offices being executed by deputies. Although that report was signed by the chancellor in office none of the proposed reforms were undertaken, and between 1737 and 1801 there was not one set of rules, orders or regulations issued for the court of chancery by any of its officers.[273]

[272] 4 Geo. II, c. 26 (1731).
[273] *HEL*, I, pp. 435–6. Holdsworth noted that no orders were issued by any chancellor from Hardwicke to Loughborough (1737–1801).

5

LATER CONTRIBUTIONS TO LEGAL
LITERATURE, 1660–1674

It is not improbable that we are fallen into the last age of the world, foretold by our blessed Savior, wherein the love of many shall wax cold and iniquity shall abound. And among the abounding iniquities of this age the iniquity of the tongue, that little member set on fire by hell, is not the least; and among the evils of the tongue, is there any more pernicious and deadly, and yet more common and epidemical than back-biting and slander?... It is true that in former times we find actions on the case for slanderous words very rarely brought, which speaks thus much, that such words were then very rarely spoken. But in these days they are become almost as natural to men as their language and discourse. And therefore the disease, so deeply rooted and over-spreading calls for the application of the remedy which our law doth abundantly furnish us withal.

'To the reader', *Action upon the case for slander* (1662), sig. a1r

For who knows not how frequent and foul the deceits of men in their trades by weights, measures and the like... are amongst us here today; and how much we suffer by it? And who knows not that these frauds are not only against the law of the nation, but against the law of God.

Introduction, *The clerk of the market* (1665), sig. A2r

When I applied my thoughts to this study I presently received encouragement from the word *justice* which drew my curiosity to a new search, to wit, why any man should call anything rather his own than another's? And when I found that it proceeded not from nature, but consent, I conceived the reason. Because from a community of goods there must needs arise contention, and from that all other kinds of calamities ensue, which by nature every man is taught to avoid. From whence I observed the absolute necessity of assurances and contracts, the learning on which subject I have gathered out of the scattered volumes of our laws.

Dedication to the judges of the Westminster courts, *Law of common assurances* (1669), sigs. [a4r–v]

Sheppard's public career had ended by the time Charles Stuart returned to England to claim his crown. Although a number of men who had been named judges and serjeants by interregnum governments were reappointed to serve the Stuart monarchy,

Sheppard was not among them.[1] Once he had discharged his services to Cromwell and the protectorate administration, he was quite satisfied to return to his provincial life, rejoining his family in the parish of Hempstead near Gloucester. He had never been, nor did he seem inclined to become part of the legal fraternity at Westminster and, approaching his sixty-fifth birthday in the year of the restoration, he remained in retirement in the country and devoted his energies to scholarly pursuits. In the remaining fourteen years of his life he wrote seven new books, all designed to expand a general knowledge of English legal practice. The change of regime ended his hopes for substantive reform and, abandoning his creative ideas for simplifying legal procedure and restructuring the judicial system, he confined his efforts to compiling orderly arrangements of contemporary law. These later books dealt with subjects on which he had previously written: local law enforcement, property law and an abridgment. His only departure from those familiar topics was an innovative two-volume study of actions on the case, published just after the restoration.

The first of the two books was *Action upon the case for slander*, published in 1662. An earlier monograph on this specialized topic had been published by John March in 1647 and while the higher quality and greater scope of Sheppard's work was a decided improvement, it is noteworthy that slander was singled out from the numerous forms of actions on the case by two legal authors as the subject of these pioneering contributions to legal literature.[2] Both March and Sheppard deplored their countrymen's intemperate habits of speech and as early as 1651 Sheppard had prefaced a short discourse on actions on the case for slander with an explosive diatribe against 'those wicked and slanderous tongues [that] do certainly soil men's reputations' and called for 'the false tongue [to be] cut out'. Reversing his customary advice about going to law only as a last resort, Sheppard urged men who had been slandered to take their complaints to court, even though 'it hath been said of old by some that these actions are not favored in the law'. He continued, 'I cannot see any reason why these suits should be discouraged or suppressed,

---

[1] See above, ch. 1, n. 222.
[2] March's book, *Actions for slaunder* (1647, 1648, 1655, 1679; the Second Part, 1649), was written in essay form, had no categorical divisions, no table and no index. The study was of such limited scope that the book's significance lies principally in the author's pioneering effort.

rather than actions of trespass done to men's bodies and estates. The wound given to the name is worse and more mischievous; and therefore (for my part) I think it would bring more dishonor to the law and the professors thereof if men should remain remediless herein.'[3]

In his comment about actions on the case being 'not favored in the law' by some, Sheppard was referring to the traditionalists among the legal writers of the early part of the century, particularly Lord Ellesmere, Henry Finch and Francis Bacon, who had been critical of the increased use of this and other novel forms of litigation. These men had believed that the procedural modifications and the increased employment of fictions, the use of which had escalated in the late sixteenth century, threatened the survival of the medieval forms of action and the very traditions of the common law. While Ellesmere wanted to return to the status quo of the mid sixteenth century and Finch favored a retreat to the state of the law in the late fifteenth century, Bacon advocated a reconstruction of the old forms of action in order to achieve certainty.[4] The changes that were taking place were, on the other hand, heralded as advantageous developments by others, including William Fulbeck and John Davies 'who believed that the common law had reached its greatest hour'. The expansion of actions on the case gave the law courts the flexibility to provide remedies for wrongs done that were not available in the medieval writs and, as a consequence, the law itself was changing. Sheppard was just beginning his legal education when this dialogue took place and two of the leading advocates of the changes in legal process were Edward Coke and John Dodderidge, the two scholars who had exerted the strongest influence on the development of Sheppard's legal philosophy. Coke and Dodderidge held that the increasing complexity of the common law when applied with 'a proper attention to method and reason could reveal the richness and relevancy of this ancient institution'.[5] Forty years later, when Sheppard wrote his pair of books, actions on the case were being used even more widely in the courts. Moreover, at the time they were published, the educational facilities of the inns of court

---

[3] W. Sheppard, *Faithfull councellor*, I (1651), p. 41.
[4] Ibid., pp. 40–1. L. A. Knafla has discussed the various legal philosophies current in that remarkable generation of legal scholars: *Law and politics*, pp. 106–7, 116–22, 128.
[5] Knafla, *Law and politics*, pp. 106–7.

were in a state of extreme deterioration.[6] Consequently his two guides came to be used as legal textbooks, supplying information not otherwise available on this specialized branch of the law to a generation of students and practitioners. Both *Action upon the case for slander* and its companion volume of 1663, *Actions upon the case for deeds*, were republished in 1674 and 1675 respectively.[7]

In the 1663 volume Sheppard's introductory definition of actions on the case was quite properly cast as a negative statement where he wrote 'this action is given for a remedy against a wrong in a case where no other action is to be had'.[8] In the medieval period the courts had dispensed justice by redressing grievances that had been set forth in writs (complaints) purchased by plaintiffs to initiate law suits. If there was no existing writ appropriate to the grievance, the wronged party had no recourse to royal justice. And yet within a generation of the period in which distinct new forms of writs ceased to be created, an accommodation for remediless complaints was found.[9] This adaptation began in the fourteenth century when random cases of special circumstances not involving violence or breach of the king's peace were admitted to the courts. Sheppard explained that these were known as actions on the 'special' case 'because the whole cause or case [of the complaint], so much as is in the declaration (save only the time and place) is set down in the writ'. It therefore became possible for a wronged party to bring an action on the case that was based simply upon the allegation that a wrong had been committed for which damages were claimed.[10]

Throughout the middle ages this miscellaneous body of law

[6] W. Holdsworth, 'Disappearance of the educational system at the inns of court', *Univ. of Pennsylvania Law Review*, LXIX (1921), 201–18; Prest, *Inns of Court*, pp. 44–6, 59, 133–8, 237, Appendix 1.

[7] *Actions upon the case for deeds* was entered in the Stationers' Register under a different title on 3 June 1662. See below, *Chronological Bibliography of Sheppard's Books*. A nineteenth-century bibliographer listed a 3rd edition of that work but it appears to be a ghost edition as no copy has been located: Marvin, *Legal bibliography*, p. 643.

[8] W. Sheppard, *Actions upon the case for deeds*, p. 2.

[9] The adaptation of old 'original' writs to fit new grievances hinged on the writ (or action) of trespass which was first framed about 1200. By the later fourteenth century new variations of writs of trespass which made no mention of force and arms and which set out the details of the plaintiff's case were accepted by the judges at Westminster: Maitland, *Forms of action*, pp. 39–40, 53–8; Milsom, *Foundations of common law*, pp. 244–70.

[10] W. Sheppard, *Actions upon the case for deeds*, p. 2. Non-forcible writs of trespass separated from trespass with force and arms and came to be recognized as a new and distinct branch of common-law actions.

increased in volume slowly but steadily. By Elizabeth's reign a number of factors were contributing to a greatly expanded use of actions on the case. Both the cultural climate and the economic milieu were becoming increasingly sophisticated and, with a plentiful supply of legal advisers seeking clients, a factor which added more yeast to a society already in ferment, a growing number of men carried their complaints against adversaries into court, asking for damages.[11] At the same time the common-law courts were acquiring more business, chancery and the prerogative courts of star chamber and high commission offered the plaintiff alternative tribunals for redress of grievances. Star chamber, in particular, had the flexibility to fashion new law by refining the definition of serious criminal misdemeanors. As Professor Barnes has written, in the first quarter of the seventeenth century that controversial forum was principally a court for private litigants who brought criminal charges of sophisticated crimes of cunning rather than crimes of violence. Cases of slander, forgery, perjury, deceit, malfeasance and libel that were adjudicated in star chamber became models for cases with similar charges brought on actions on the case in the law courts. This adaptation occurred easily and naturally because the common-law judges who participated in star-chamber proceedings were quite willing to hear civil cases in their own law courts in which circumstances paralleled the criminal actions heard by the conciliar tribunal. The body of case law on actions on the case grew steadily until it assumed a dominant role in Westminster proceedings and made up about one-quarter of the *nisi prius* cases on assize circuits.[12]

By the mid seventeenth century a paradoxical situation had arisen. Actions on the case whose distinction had rested initially with the singularity of each complaint had grown in number and variety to the extent that it was possible to subdivide this amorphous body of law. This was precisely what Sheppard hoped to accomplish in his two books. Written in a transitional period of legal development, these works have historical importance for their definitions of the contemporary state of the law when actions on the case were still unclassified complaints unattached to a theoretical system. By the eighteenth century the fields of contract and tort were recognized to

[11] Baker, *Legal history*, pp. 58–60; Knafla, 'Inns of court', pp. 234–41, *Law and politics*, pp. 7, 105–6; Milsom, *Foundations of common law*, pp. 256–61.
[12] T. G. Barnes, 'Star chamber and the sophistication of criminal law', *Criminal Law Review* (June 1977), 316–26; Cockburn, *Assizes*, pp. 99–102, 140.

have a coherence independent of the old forms of action and in the generation before that modern organization of the law was accomplished, Sheppard wrote these two books on slander and assumpsit, the two most frequent causes of complaints brought to the courts on actions on the case.[13] In both books Sheppard endeavored to separate complaints of wrongful words and deeds that had been adjudged actionable by the courts from others that remained of questionable actionability or had been held to be not actionable. Sheppard gathered his cases from the three central law courts and arranged them by subject matter. He also called upon the supporting authorities of the Year Books, legal treatises, books of entries and more than a score of printed law reports, sifting through his material to find authoritative illustrations to demonstrate legal principles.[14]

In *Action upon the case for slander* Sheppard divided his categories into eighteen chapters and his selections were drawn from thousands of precedents that had been established since the common-law courts had begun to accept actions on the case for words early in the sixteenth century.[15] Two other chapters explored areas of slander falling outside the scope of the common law.[16] Other precedents were described in four more chapters and the study concluded with a final chapter of 354 case illustrations that filled a third of the book. The usefulness of this monograph was enhanced by an introductory table

---

[13] Holdsworth wrote, 'Very few books upon special branches of the common law have as yet made their appearance. Two published by Sheppard...illustrate the growth of the modern law of contract and tort round the actions on the case': *HEL*, VI, p. 606.

[14] See below, *Sheppard's Sources.*

[15] Remedies for defamation had been available in the church courts since the eleventh century but these tribunals had no power to award damages. Eminent persons of high rank (e.g. peers of the realm, bishops) had been protected from slander by a series of statutes *de scandalum magnatum* beginning with 3 Edw. I, c. 34 (1275). Sheppard's chapter topics were slander of title to land; of *scandalum magnatum*; slander for treason; for murder; for witchcraft; for rape, sodomy, buggery and houseburning (all four taken together in one chapter); slander for theft; slander that may bring a man in danger of corporal punishment and slander for petit larceny; of perjury; of forgery; words of slander for incontinency; slander for imputing some transgression of a penal law; words that hinder one's preferment; words charging deceit or cozening; slander that related to men in their offices, professions and places of trust; scandalous words that relate to men in their trades and way of living; and action on the case for conspiracy and libel.

[16] Chapters 16 and 17 dealt briefly with 'spiritual words' that were actionable only in the church courts (such as whore, bastard, fornicator, heretic, miscreant and schismatic) and 'passionate and vain words' that the courts had adjudged to be not actionable because the words were held to be 'trivial' or 'of no import' (e.g. to call a person a rogue, a varlet or a pocky knave).

of contents and a concluding cross-referenced alphabetical table.[17]
Virtually all of the cases Sheppard cited had been heard between 1570 and 1660. Examples of cases where a man's professional reputation was slighted were scattered throughout the eighteen chapters. Of those cases where local officials had been disparaged or charged with incompetence, slanders against justices of the peace were most numerous, but there were also many cases involving minor officials in which constables, jailers, churchwardens, town clerks and chancery commissioners had not hesitated to haul their adversaries into king's bench by means of an action on the case for slander or perjury.[18] Suits brought by lawyers and attorneys charging impugnment of professional reputation were the second most numerous to those brought by magistrates.[19] Thus the law of slander owed part of its development to the willingness of the nation's judicial arm to protect from disparagement the reputations of men who commanded positions of local authority or who participated in legal-judicial activities. The general rule that covered the protection of officials' reputations had emerged from the principle that slanderous words were actionable and that damage could be presumed by a charge of incompetence or unfitness in a profession or a trade. The other two categories of actionable words, also presuming damage, were accusations of crimes that carried legally sanctioned punishments or imprisonment and imputations of venereal disease, the plague or leprosy. As the courts had ruled on the defamatory nature of various words or phrases in these three categories, an ever lengthening list of words had been held to be actionable or non-actionable.[20] Sheppard

---

[17] The illustrative cases filled 66 of the book's 183 pages.
[18] For 15 cases brought by justices of the peace, see Sheppard, *Action upon the case for slander*, cases 4, 5, 6, 7, 56, 77, 155, 182, 200, 201, 203, 263, 278, 292, 334. Suits brought by constables, cases 66 & 193; by a jailer, case 291; by a churchwarden, case 193; by a town clerk, case 118; by a chancery commissioner, case 202; by a sheriff, case 295; by an undersheriff, case 64. All these cases are found in ch. 15, pp. 117–83.
[19] Cases brought by lawyers and attorneys were cases 28, 36, 159, 169, 182, 186, 192, 199, 234, 280, 286, 297, 316, 330. J. H. Baker has found a high proportion of lawyers and court officials bringing actions on the case for slander in the early sixteenth century: Baker, *Spelman*, II, p. 243, n. 6.
[20] In the same period the ecclesiastical courts were kept busy adjudicating upon cases of defamation while star chamber heard practically any suit brought. The abolition of those two courts at the beginning of the civil-war period resulted in the common-law courts absorbing most of the types of litigation they had handled. For the enduring contributions of star chamber, see Barnes, 'Star chamber', pp. 322–3.

included all the popular words of opprobrium in his work as well as local terms of derogation and regional variations of meanings, the latter examples illustrating the continuing strength of provincialism in seventeenth-century English society. And it is not surprising that many disparaging remarks pertaining to the Welsh were included in a book compiled by a lawyer who had spent most of his life in the western marches.[21]

The companion volume, *Actions upon the case for deeds*, published in 1663, was twice the length of its predecessor. In the introduction Sheppard wrote, 'You shall have herein the performance of the promise I made in my last piece: the second part of actions upon the case.'[22] In structure, the book followed the earlier work. A table of contents listed the topical chapters by page number, and the text began with three short introductory chapters. The wider range of cases in this second volume invited a more discursive approach to the historical development and the first chapters on actions in general presented in outline form definitions of concepts and terms used by the legal profession in establishing actionability in the courts. In the second chapter Sheppard set out fourteen basic rules that governed all proceedings at common law. The third dealt in a general way with actions on the case and again the author extracted legal principles from the precedents of three hundred years. The convention for initiating a suit in this form was based upon the legal fiction that both malice in the defendant and damage to the plaintiff must be shown. Second, Sheppard noted the 'frequent practice...at this day', established by *Slade's case* (1602), that a 'special action of the case will lie in very many cases wherein there is another remedy by a formed action in the register'.[23] That is, the existence of an older remedy did not preclude initiating a suit on the more recently developed action of case. Third, all actions but those on the case upon an assumpsit must be brought in the lifetime of both parties. And fourth, the curious paradox whereby some actions on the case could,

[21] For example, in London it was actionable to call a woman a whore or a bawd because public humiliation and criminal penalties devolved on women of those designations. In the north of England actionable words included daffidowndilly (a double-dealer) and out-putter (horse stealer).

[22] W. Sheppard, *Actions upon the case for deeds* (1663), sig. B1r. The printer noted that the author was 'sometimes of the Middle Temple': ibid., sig. B4v.

[23] Ibid., p. 10. He cited Coke's report of *Slade's Case*, Fitzherbert's *Natura Brevium* and Croke's *Reports*. Plaintiffs preferred to sue in case to avoid wager of law: see J. H. Baker, 'New light on *Slade's Case*', *CLJ*, XXIX (1971), 51–67, 213–36.

by the seventeenth century, be brought alleging force and arms, thus reversing the principle by which case had first broken away from trespass.[24] The final sections of this chapter presented guidelines that had been used for bringing actions on the case and with them Sheppard cited many conflicting authorities. His unwillingness to suggest which criteria might prevail in a court of law was entirely consistent with his intended purpose for in the introduction he had written, 'you will find nothing of mine here but the method, or labor of putting together and setting out the grave and learned judgments, resolutions and opinions of the eminent and learned judges, both of former and present times'.[25] Sheppard's failure to give his readers his own opinions of good law was more than compensated for by the hundreds of cases and the information he had gathered and arranged by topic for publication. The inclusion of many discrepancies in the law made this a valuable manual for practitioners in order to guide them to fuller reports on this branch of the law and to any legal principles that had emerged from the cases.

The fourth and longest chapter of the book dealing with contract and assumpsit was more germane to subsequent legal developments than any other part of the two volumes. From an historical perspective, the evolution of the writ of trespass in the development of actions upon an assumpsit in this and the earlier period was of the utmost importance in the growth of contract actions. Sheppard began this chapter by defining various types of contract and continued with statements of general principles pertaining to both actions of debt and of assumpsit. The requirements of contractual obligations were found among scattered reports and Sheppard's exercise was to present whatever rules might be discovered, separating those that could be grounded in actions on the case from those that could not.[26] In a recent study of the common law of contract A. W. B. Simpson commented that Sheppard's *Actions upon the case for deeds* was a 'somewhat rambling and disorderly work' and that passages of it were 'confused and muddled'. Simpson acknowledged, however, that Sheppard did define the contemporary law and credited him with attempting to impose some order on the development of assumpsit. Sheppard's 'disorderly' description of the extremely complicated history of contracts is more a reflection of the disorderly

---

[24] This was more fully explored in ch. 14 under 'process'.
[25] Sheppard, *Actions upon the case for deeds*, sig. B1r.
[26] Ibid., pp. 33–5.

state of the law than of the author's ineptitude and his book was not, nor could it be a complete and final statement of the law of contract.[27] In *Slade's case* the judges had ruled that 'upon every executory contract there is an assumpsit implied, and therefore upon this the party to whom it is made may upon it have an action of debt or action upon the case at his election'.[28] With the ability to use the action of assumpsit for any type of contract or covenant, the modern law of contract began to develop. There were various types of actionable assumpsit or agreement but the common law began to form principles applicable to all and, in identifying actionable agreement, Sheppard noted that the consideration was 'the material cause of the engagement, by which it [the contract] is made obligatory'. The consideration, to be good, could be 'never so small a matter, as a penny or a penny's worth, or a pint of wine to induce the promise'. But without consideration the contract was only a 'naked promise and void in law, and no action will lie upon it'. Throughout the chapter on assumpsit Sheppard specified the consideration of each case in the margin, noting whether or not it had been held to be good. Sheppard set out five requirements for an action to be brought on a matter of contract: the thing promised to be undertaken must be lawful; it must be possible to be done; it must be clear and certain; it must be coherent and agreeing in itself and with the consideration; and it must be serious and weighty. He also described the differences between real and personal, express or implied, parole or in writing that had been developed by the time he wrote.[29]

The remaining chapters in *Actions upon the case for deeds* examined in less detail other non-forcible wrongs that could be brought in case. Discussions of actions of nuisance, deceit, breach of trust, trover and conversion, bailment of goods, detinue, vexatious suits of law and examples of nonfeasance, misfeasance and malfeasance not mentioned in earlier chapters completed the topical portions of the book. The final three chapters explained how actions might be ended, what constituted a bar to litigation, and rules pertaining to process and pleading, with a list of further references. The fifteenth and concluding chapter constituted about half the book, presenting 553 'choice cases' to illustrate each category of the preceding chapters.

[27] A. W. B. Simpson, *A history of the common law of contract* (Oxford, 1975), pp. 485, 506–34, 612–13.
[28] Sheppard, *Actions upon the case for deeds*, p. 202.
[29] Ibid., pp. 18, 84. For a discussion of the requirement of consideration in assumpsit, see Baker, *Spelman*, II, pp. 286–97.

The vast majority of cases cited had been heard in the seventeenth century, including fifty-four from the interregnum period.[30] Both of Sheppard's volumes on actions on the case were reprinted within twelve years of their first issuance. The publishers omitted the final chapters of case illustrations from both works, and the editions of the 1670s appeared in quartos rather than folios, but the texts were essentially unchanged.

In 1663, the year in which Sheppard published the second volume on actions on the case, he also sent into print a book he had completed within the previous year. *A sure guide for his majesties justices of the peace*, his third entirely new manual for that officer, was a sharp critique of the restoration religious settlement that was still being forged by the Cavalier Parliament.[31] The legal and constitutional changes of the restoration settlement were so sweeping that his own two earlier works for magistrates were, by his own estimation, 'deficient and will frustrate your expectations if too much confided in'. Since 'the change of times, repeal of old and addition of new laws have rendered necessary' a completely new guide, he had compiled this summary of recent legislation with particular emphasis on the laws pertaining to the re-established Church of England, 'a subject in which no man hath yet dipped his pen'.[32] Sheppard recognized, however regretfully, that the restoration of the Stuart monarchy was the final act in the disruptive political drama of his generation and his shrewd analysis of how the law was being applied by the triumphant forces of Anglicanism was a forceful denunciation of the political abuses and technical shortcomings in the operation of contemporary law.

Parliament had re-established the national church under conditions that were to breed constitutional conflicts for the next three decades and to circumscribe the political structure for the next two centuries. The lack of generosity in the legislation passed by the Cavalier Parliament elicited an embittered reaction from the puritan lawyer who had so recently served the more tolerant Cromwellian adminis-

---

[30] Chapter 15 filled 185 of the book's 387 pages. The case examples reflected the proportionate emphases of the book's contents: contract and assumpsit, 395 cases, pp. 202–330; nuisance, 39 cases, pp. 330–42; deceit, 18 cases, pp. 342–55 [sic: pp. 343–50 missing]; trover and conversion, 23 cases, pp. 355–62; malicious and vexatious suits of law, 40 cases, pp. 363–74; feasance and non-feasance, 37 cases, pp. 374–87.

[31] See chs. 2 and 3 for discussion of his other manuals.

[32] W. Sheppard, *A sure guide for his majesties justices of peace* (1663), sigs. A2r–v.

tration and Sheppard's stern objections to the way new and old laws were being used to foster a witch hunt led him to apply the most strict interpretations to all the legislation pertaining to religious practices in order to protect nonconformists from undue harassment. Conflicting statutory authorities, the ambiguous and nebulous wording of statutes and abuses in enforcement provided him with a wealth of material to analyze as he explored the civil and religious consequences of the restoration settlement. The course of events by which puritan authority was systematically crushed by militant Anglicanism and communicants of the Church of England came to enjoy a complete monopoly of political power invites a brief review.

The decisive changes wrought so quickly in the English political structure were not anticipated by most Englishmen in April 1660. On the contrary, the prospects of reaching a fairly generous resolution to the thorny religious issues that had plagued the nation for more than a century had looked promising when the exiled Stuart announced from the Dutch town of Breda,

And because the passion and uncharitableness of the times have produced several opinions in religion...we do declare a liberty to tender consciences, and that no man shall be disquieted or called in question for differences of opinion in matter of religion which do not disturb the peace of the kingdom; and that we shall be ready to consent to such an act of parliament...for the full granting of that indulgence.[33]

Charles II's stated intentions seemed to hold in October of that year when the restored king issued a royal 'Declaration concerning ecclesiastical affairs' offering concessions to non-Anglicans, at least until such differences as existed could be resolved by a synod. But several problems connected with this gesture did not augur well for a universally acceptable settlement. In the first place, the declaration, which was probably drafted by Lord Chancellor Clarendon and merely assented to by the king, aimed at a more comprehensive membership in the national church and ignored the extension of toleration offered by the still-exiled Charles months earlier from Breda. Second, of the many non-Anglican religious groups in England, only Presbyterians could accept the terms of compromise set forth. And of that group, those inclined to a strict persuasion found even the limited episcopacy suggested by the plan authoritarian and therefore unacceptable. Third, the sectarians and Independents

[33] 'The declaration of Breda' (4 April 1660) as quoted in J. P. Kenyon, *The Stuart constitution 1603–1688* (Cambridge, 1966), p. 358.

were offered no doctrinal or institutional concessions at all and their resentment at being ignored in the royal declaration was heightened by the rough handling their preachers were receiving that very autumn. With the non-Anglican groups more divided than they had been in the 1650s, there was no unified force to resist a vigorous reinstitution of the Church of England. Finally, and most important, the royal declaration failed to receive the approval of the Convention Parliament even though the Presbyterian and other non-Anglican representatives could have, in strategic agreement, commanded a majority of the votes.[34]

The difficulties in reaching a tolerant settlement were compounded by the reality that the unofficial re-establishment of the Anglican church had already begun at the grass-roots level even before the king returned. Without waiting for official enactments or proclamations, Anglicans around the country began to restore their neglected church on their own initiatives in every way within their powers. The Book of Common Prayer was used again in services both in humble parish churches and in the house of lords as early as May 1660. A spontaneous movement towards reconstruction gained strength and momentum through the intervention of local magistrates. Those justices of the peace, appointed for their royalist sympathies in the first months of the restoration, began prosecuting ministers who failed to follow the traditional form of worship and Anglican ministers, long sequestered from their livings, were returned by lay patrons as puritan incumbents surrendered to local pressures and resigned their benefices.[35] In Hempstead, Sheppard witnessed the resignation under pressure of his own parish preacher whose puritan views were unacceptable to the local Anglican establishment.[36] Laymen, too, fell victim to Anglican revenge, particularly in Gloucestershire with its heavy concentration of puritans. Hapless puritans were indicted on charges of sedition on the strength of Edwardian and Elizabethan statutes and during the autumn of 1660

[34] R. S. Bosher, *The making of the restoration settlement* (New York, 1951), pp. 146, 187–98, 202; G. R. Cragg, *Puritanism in the period of the great persecution 1660–1688* (Cambridge, 1957), pp. 5–7.
[35] Bosher, *Restoration settlement*, pp. 100–1, 163–4, 199–207; Cragg, *Puritanism 1660–88*, pp. 31–7.
[36] For the preacher of Hempstead, Jonathan Smith, see ch. 1, n. 204. The estimated number of ministers displaced between 1660 and 24 August 1662, the enforcement date of the Act of Uniformity, was 724: Bosher, *Restoration settlement*, p. 266; Matthews, *Calamy*, pp. xii–xiii.

the persecution of non-Anglicans took on a vindictive character. The deliberate misapplication of old conventicle and recusancy statutes by magistrates led Sheppard to marshal whatever protection the law could provide as he prepared his new guide for justices of the peace.

While the royalist sector of the population indulged themselves by all available means in repudiating non-Anglican practices and personnel, the representatives at the Convention assembly avoided grappling with the unresolved and thorny religious issues.[37] In January 1661 an insurrection in London involving some fifty Fifth Monarchists added fuel to the fire of militant Anglicanism. A nervous nation fearful of any threat to stability overreacted to news of the event and, as with the Popish Plot two decades later, suspicions of conspiracy and treason raised panic. Religious dissent *ipso facto* was reckoned to constitute a threat to national security and the note of anxiety in the nation's mood was directly reflected in the results of the parliamentary elections later that spring when the moderates of the Convention were not returned. The inter-faith synod of clergymen that the king had promised to call finally assembled in April 1661, but its effectiveness was doomed from the outset by the greater authority of the two solidly Anglican bodies of parliament and convocation that were meeting concurrently. The stature of those two traditional assemblies robbed the Savoy Conference of all political leverage and the synod was terminated in July with nothing accomplished.

It was left to the men sitting in the aptly named Cavalier Parliament to determine the nature of the church settlement. Moved by a spirit of revenge, the group ordered the public hangman to burn the Solemn League and Covenant and required every member of the house of commons to take holy communion according to Anglican rites. One of its first acts was to restore the bishops to their seats in the house of lords, thus permitting the spiritual peers to resume their legislative roles after a hiatus of twenty years. With the princes of the church sitting again in the upper house, the Anglican character

---

[37] The Convention which sat from Apr. to Dec. 1660 was told by the king's councillors that a national synod would be called in the near future to attempt to settle religious differences. The single decision the convention could not postpone was the question of providing for parish clergy. The Act for Settling Ministers (12 Car. II, c. 17) protected all but commonwealth 'intruders' from deprivation of their livings, but that standard was soon replaced by the much more stringent conditions of the Act of Uniformity passed by the Cavalier Parliament.

of parliament became even more pronounced. In July 1661 the ecclesiastical courts were revived and by late summer the administrative machinery of the Church of England was well along the way to a complete re-establishment through the concerted efforts of parliament and the officers of the church.[38] After a summer recess parliament reassembled in November and passed the Corporation Act which placed local political power firmly in the hands of the Anglican laity.[39] By December, convocation had completed a revised Book of Common Prayer into which more than 600 changes had been incorporated, and this was sent to parliament for approval.[40] Through the winter, parliament pressed on in its relentless drive to make England safely and staunchly Anglican. Quakers fell victim to punitive laws for their refusal to take 'lawful oaths'.[41] The capstone of this phase of the religious settlement finally passed both houses in May when the Act of Uniformity definitively repudiated the sentiments of tolerance expressed by Charles II two years earlier.[42] Through a series of enactments between May 1661 and May 1662 the Cavalier Parliament had established a state church in which the clergy and members of the teaching profession were subordinated to parliamentary regulations based on religious requisites; had imposed civil disabilities on English subjects who refused to conform to the re-established church; had entered into the statute book the orthodox doctrine of the Thirty-nine Articles and the Revised Book of Common Prayer; and had buttressed the entire religious settlement

[38] The ecclesiastical courts were reinstated conditionally by 13 Car. II, c. 12.

[39] The preamble explained that the object was to remove from corporation offices those who had assumed authority 'during the late troubles' and replace them with 'persons well affected to his majesty and the established government'. Royal commissioners were to remove and exclude from office all who were not communicants of the Church of England and all who refused the Oaths of Supremacy and Allegiance as well as those refusing to swear to the unlawfulness and treason of taking arms against the king. There was also a fourth oath, renouncing the Solemn League and Covenant. Furthermore the royal commissioners were authorized to remove from office at their own discretion and in the interest 'of public safety' even persons who had met all the conditions set by the act: 13 Car. II, stat. 2, c. 1.

[40] F. Proctor and W. H. Frere, *New history of the Book of Common Prayer* (1949), p. 195.

[41] 14 Car. II, c. 1.

[42] Parliament moved the date of enforcement back from Michaelmas to Midsummer Day in a drive of sheer enthusiasm, but because of delays in passage the enforcement date was finally pushed forward to St Bartholomew's Day (24 Aug.). The act passed the second house on 8 May and received the king's assent on 19 May: Bosher, *Restoration settlement*, pp. 250, 254; 14 Car. II, c. 4, ss. 1–27.

with penal legislation enforced by the civil power. This legislation was of such an uncompromising and comprehensive nature that Sheppard realized that the only refuge from an accelerated pace of persecution which the letter and spirit of the laws invited was to explore in detail the conditions and limits of each section of the punitive statutes. His *Sure guide* was ready for distribution within months of the Act of Uniformity's enforcement date.

Sheppard accepted the undoubted legality of the parliamentary legislation and, in accordance with his personal standards and legal philosophy, recommended compliance with the law. But he was quick to notice that strict legal obedience to every section of the acts passed was, in fact, impossible because of technical flaws, contradictory directives, and the problems raised by the confusion in the multitude of earlier laws was now compounded by a new batch of statutory provisions. His appraisal of how the settlement could be enforced was alternately questioning, condemnatory and, in some places, satirical. In a sense the book's very title, the *Sure guide*, was a sarcastic reproach to the Cavalier Parliament for having bestowed statutory authority on so much badly written law. The most comprehensive statute of all, the Act of Uniformity, certainly required an immediate interpretation that could be understood by the justices of the peace who were to be responsible for much of its enforcement. The preamble, conditions and penalties of the act made clear that parliament expected stringent enforcement, yet one of the twenty-seven sections left the legislators' meaning wide open for misunderstanding. Section twenty provided that 'the several good laws and statutes of this realm which have been formerly made and are now in force for the uniformity of prayer and administration of sacraments...shall stand in full force and strength...[and] be joined and annexed to this act'.[43] That provision alone was enough to put an inveterate law reformer on his guard. The need to abridge repetitious laws and to edit expired laws out of the statute book had been recognized by statesmen and law reformers for generations and in the previous century Queen Elizabeth I, when speaking of the redundancy of legislation, had charged her parliament 'to prune, and cut off' superfluous acts.[44] Sheppard's investigation of the mischief that would ensue from the indiscriminate revival of all previous laws of religious practice served as one of the major themes of his *Sure*

[43] 14 Car. II, c. 4, s. 20.
[44] See above, ch. 4, n. 77.

guide. The contradictions, ambiguities and deficiencies in the statutes governing religious conduct gave Sheppard the opportunity to complete a project he had long advocated, to edit and abridge one section of the statutes of the realm in order to determine with as much precision as possible which of the laws could be held to be in force, to whom they applied, and the proper procedures of enforcement. The exercise was irresistible to a man of Sheppard's interests and there is a certain irony in the circumstances surrounding this accomplishment. His efforts to reform the law under the protectorate had been thoroughly discredited by the change in regime and yet finally, when his public career was in eclipse, he achieved a significant portion of his long-standing goal, a critical summary of all the laws relating to English religious practice.

In the *Sure guide*, Sheppard arranged the laws pertaining to religious practice into thirteen topics, allowing a chapter to each. His discussion of Quakers was the only chapter that dealt exclusively with restoration legislation, all others reaching back to review legislation of previous reigns that had been revived by section twenty of the Act of Uniformity. Five chapters included analyses of both recently passed acts and the statutes of earlier periods while seven chapters dealt only with laws enacted by medieval, Tudor and early Stuart parliaments.[45] In theory, the scope of each statute passed by a king and parliament had been adequately spelled out in the preamble which explained its purpose, and in the sections that described particulars of application and enforcement. In practice, however, many statutes had defined offenses without specifying how the law was to be enforced. Moreover, at the time Sheppard wrote, many magistrates were twisting some laws to suit their own ends and he cited three groups of statutes in which the letter and the spirit of the law were being flagrantly perverted as part of the campaign to crush puritanism: the Elizabethan Act of Supremacy, the legislation against recusants, and statutes prohibiting conventicles. The Elizabethan oath of supremacy imposed onerous financial penalties and the dangers of *praemunire* and treason on ministers, teachers, lawyers and all public officials who failed to comply. When Sheppard wrote, a hundred years later, the same statute was being tendered illegally to persons whose loyalty to the restored crown was suspect. He therefore gave instructions for its proper administration, including

---

[45] Ch. 6, 'About coming to church', for example, discussed four Tudor and one Jacobean statutes: W. Sheppard, *Sure guide*, pp. 132–43.

what persons were bound to take it, who could administer it (justices of the peace were not so authorized), the conditions under which it must be tendered and the manner of indictment and trial to which the accused offender was entitled, warning of the penalties for abuses in its application, including liabilities that would be incurred by magistrates for illegal imprisonment of individuals refusing to take the oath.[46]

'An act for the better discovering and repressing of Popish recusants' which had been enacted in the year after the Gunpowder Plot and whose very title explained its purpose had re-activated the harsh penalties of the Elizabethan recusancy laws and encouraged informers with generous rewards. In 1610 another statute had extended the provisions of the 1606 act to apply to the population at large.[47] These Jacobean statutes, too, were being used as weapons against nonconforming puritans and Sheppard cited law reports, resolutions from the bench and details of procedure listed in the statute in his effort to define the proper boundaries of this genre of laws against recusants.[48] The Elizabethan act prohibiting conventicles drew a similar discursive commentary from the author. He defined a conventicle first as Lambarde had, likening it to an unlawful assembly or riot, and second, according to its meaning in canon law wherein persons met to plan the 'impeachment or deprivation' of any part of the doctrine or government of the Church of England.[49]

---

[46] There were a number of statutory conditions governing the imposition of the oath (e.g. the presence of two witnesses) and Sheppard spelled out each detail, cautioning magistrates not to exceed their jurisdiction: ibid., pp. 151–4.

[47] 3 Jac. I, c. 4; 7 Jac. I, c. 6. It was Sheppard's opinion that the latter statute had expired: ibid., p. 159.

[48] Sheppard devoted two chapters to the problems of enforcing recusancy statutes in addition to the section mentioned in n. 47 on the Jacobean statutes: chs. 8 and 14, pp. 155–63, 192–4. Citing the authority of Coke, Sheppard admonished that 'it doth not become the justices to go to seek the parties' to administer the Jacobean oath and 'the constable may not upon this warrant break [into] the house to apprehend the party til he hath refused to take the oath before them who have authority to tender it to him, or commit some contempt to the king, for he is not yet an offender, nor indicted, nor charged by any matter of record': ibid., p. 160. He added that the judges assembled at Serjeants' Inn in 1612 had resolved that the oath could not be tendered to any individual for a second time, nor could an individual be punished for his refusal to take it a second time: ibid., p. 159.

[49] Sheppard, citing Lambarde and Wingate, defined a conventicle as 'a meeting under color of exercise of religion, to oppose the king's authority in causes ecclesiastical or against the laws and statutes of the realm': 35 Eliz. I, c. 1; Sheppard Sure guide, pp. 163–70, 173.

Sheppard questioned whether the meetings held 'to preach, pray and speak to one another for the edification of one another, in the holy faith...are against this branch of the statutes'. Informal religious gatherings were extremely important to him. In 1652 he had written a convincing plea to legalize lay prophesying[50] and by 1663 he argued convincingly that the Elizabethan statute was meant to apply only to seditious sectaries and persons who impugned the king's authority. He also noted that in 1623 the judges had questioned the validity of the statute and, according to their ruling, any grieved party prosecuted under its provisions could have an action of false imprisonment and, by writ of *habeas corpus*, have his case removed to king's bench.[51] The publicity Sheppard gave to the 'many knotty doubts' and deficiencies of the sixteenth-century Conventicle Act may have had the unintentional effect of bringing further distress to the beleaguered puritan community because in the very next year, 1664, parliament passed a new act carrying the same title which prohibited meetings of five or more persons held for 'any exercise of religion'.[52]

In the chapters covering the ramifications of the 1662 Act of Uniformity Sheppard provided extensive information about the duties and liabilities imposed on the clerical and teaching professions. Although a host of older statutes regulated the qualifications of a practising minister,[53] the act of 1662 added an unprecedented number of oaths and abjurations.[54] Once installed in office the minister was bound by a baffling array of charges and proscriptions under threat of fines, imprisonment, suspension and deprivation of office, forfeiture of goods, *praemunire* and treason by the revival of older laws under the directive of section twenty. Sheppard pointed out that this accumulation of duplicate directives with different

---

[50] W. Sheppard, *The people's priviledge* (1652).

[51] Sheppard suggested that since magistrates were not named in the statute, its enforcement could not be said to fall to their charge; nor could they bind a man to good behavior or require sureties: Sheppard, *Sure guide*, pp. 169–70. He noted that Wingate had interpreted the statute to apply only to Popish recusants: ibid., p. 163. He cited Hutton's *Reports* (1656) which had noted that the majority of the judges in 1623 had doubted the validity of the statute's enforceability since it had never been implemented: ibid., p. 169.

[52] Ibid., p. 169. The Conventicle Act of 1664 (16 Car. II, c. 4) imposed a fine of £5 for the first offense and transportation to the colonies after the third conviction. It expired in 1668 and in 1670 another act with more severe penalties was passed (22 Car. II, c. 1).

[53] Ibid., pp. 76–8, 97–111. The 13 earlier statutes he cited dated from 21 Hen. VIII to 21 Jac. I.

[54] 14 Car. II, c. 4, ss. 2, 4, 6, 8, 13, 15.

assigned penalties meant that a minister could be punished twice for a single offense.[55] He also listed several responsibilities for which ministers were held legally liable under pain of criminal penalties, including the regular reading of old statutes from the pulpit, supervision of the paraphernalia used in churches and visiting the sick.[56] Additionally, twenty-six new provisions were superimposed by the 1662 act and although this capstone of the Anglican church's re-establishment was modelled on its Elizabethan precursor, there were several important variations that made its application more severe. Applying to university personnel, schoolteachers and private tutors as well as the clergy, the act required full compliance under penalty of deprivation from office. All the earlier oaths of supremacy and allegiance were revived along with a new declaration of non-resistance to the king, the abjuration of the Solemn League and Covenant, subscription to each of the Thirty-nine Articles and 'unfeigned assent and consent to all and everything contained and prescribed in and by' the Revised Book of Common Prayer.[57] Moreover, a 1661 statute warned that a minister would be subject to *praemunire* if 'he preach or print that the king is a heretic or a Papist...so if he preach or maintain that the Long Parliament is yet in being...or that the two houses of parliament have a legislative power without the king'.[58] The short-range consequence of these statutory conditions was the ejection of an estimated 936 ministers between May and August 1662. By computing an additional 724 preachers who had been forced out of their livings after 1660, the total number of victims in this purge of puritans (c. 1760) amounted to almost one-fifth of the English clergy. The immediate loss of so many trained clergymen was a high price to pay for Anglican hegemony and it will never be known how many of the 'godly party' followed their preachers out of the established church into religious and political ostracism.[59]

[55] For example, if a minister used anything but the Book of Common Prayer he could suffer the collective penalties of 2 & 3 Edw. VI, c. 1; 1 Eliz. I, cc. 1, 2; 5 Eliz. I, c. 2 as well as 14 Car. II.

[56] Sheppard, *Sure guide*, pp. 71, 103, 105–8, 126–7, 143–5.

[57] Ibid., pp. 99–102 (14 Car. II, c. 4, ss. 4, 6, 7, 13, 20). Elizabethan clergy had been required to assent only to those Articles 'which concern the confession of the true Christian faith and the doctrine of the sacraments': Bosher, *Restoration settlement*, p. 250.

[58] Sheppard, *Sure guide*, pp. 107–8 (13 Car. II).

[59] Most of the information about the effect of the Act of Uniformity on the English clergy has come from Bosher, *Restoration settlement*, *passim*; the number of ejections, p. 266; Matthews, *Calamy*, pp. xii–xiii.

For those ministers and laymen of puritan inclinations who, like Sheppard, chose to stay within the national church, the terms of conformity were extremely exacting. Among the provisions that demonstrated parliament's adamant intention to enforce the letter of the law was the order that 'sealed copies' containing the full text of the Acts of Uniformity of 1559 and 1662 and the Revised Book of Common Prayer be used in all ecclesiastical and common-law courts as legal documents. Furthermore, 'true and printed' copies of the Prayer Book were to be obtained for every church and college in the country, the cost to be borne by parishioners or officials.[60] Sheppard noticing a loophole in this statutory provision concluded that upon failure to supply the book, ministers and parishioners alike would be exempted from all provisions in the Prayer Book and could not be punished for breaches of duty.[61] The new laws also provided that at every public service the ministers were to read and the people to follow the entire liturgy of the Prayer Book, heeding each rubric and allowing for no deviations in prayers, vestments or ornaments. Sheppard pondered the consequences of attempts to enforce strictly this statutory injunction and concluded,

There being so many things by the Book of Common Prayer required in the gestures of the minister and the people; that some things they are to read with a loud voice, some things the priest is to say standing...other things he is to read kneeling...and all the Prayer [Book] to be read and ceremonies to be observed every day. Whether for any omission herein the minister or people be not, *rigore juris*, in extremity indictable for it and so liable to all the penalties appointed to be inflicted...And if the law shall be literally taken, how men shall endure to kneel so long as the whole Common Prayer time.[62]

Although the final remark was certainly a criticism of the formalism of Anglican rites,[63] Sheppard's assertion that the Cavalier Parliament had enacted an unenforceable law when it annexed the Book of Common Prayer to the Act of Uniformity was later vindicated by two

---

[60] 'Sealed copies' were those revised copies approved and passed under the great seal.

[61] Sheppard, *Sure guide*, p. 124.

[62] Ibid., pp. 146–7. Elsewhere Sheppard noted that ministers were bound by statute to read all the Common Prayer and the Litany on Sundays, Wednesdays and Fridays, 'which is that which few do': ibid., p. 115.

[63] He later wrote, 'these laws are not to be taken literally: for if so, then every public prayer made by a minister before or after sermon seems to be against them [the laws], and all that are present thereat seem liable to all the great penalties of the statutes for the same': ibid., p. 124.

centuries of litigation in the central courts about such issues as the legality of a procession and the placing of flower vases in a church.[64]

The complete reading of the liturgy not only took absolute precedence over sermons but the minister was also directed to 'faithfully tell the people of their duty of subjection and obedience' to Anglican doctrine[65] and not 'spend [his] time and study in search of speculative and abstruse notions, especially about the deep points of election and reprobation and...not presume...doctrinally to determine anything concerning the same'.[66] As for the provision that the Thirty-nine Articles must be read in public by every preacher called to a pulpit, Sheppard warned that they must be read verbatim and only from a true copy of the Book of Common Prayer, underscoring the point by citing a case in which a minister had been deprived of his benefice through the patron's trickery.[67]

---

[64] A canon lawyer has written, 'The attempt to give the Book [of Common Prayer] a monopoly in the field of public worship and to allow no deviations from it...have proved impracticable...It is probably true to say that there is not a single minister who uses the Book without some deviations from it and not a single church where the Book, the whole Book, and nothing but the Book is used in the manner intended.' And, 'the unfortunate tendency of the courts in the nineteenth century to construe the rubrics as they would construe acts of parliament led to a rigidity which may now be softened by the provisions in the new Ecclesiastical Jurisdiction Measure 1963'. Finally, 'For two centuries [1663–1863] no deviations from the forms prescribed in the Prayer Book were permitted, though the addition of hymns was held to be lawful': E. G. Moore, *An introduction to English Canon law* (Oxford, 1967), pp. 61, 90, 108. Both processions and flower vases were at issue in *Elphinstone* v. *Purchas* (1870): ibid., pp. 109, 113.

[65] Sheppard, *Sure guide*, p. 67.   [66] Ibid., pp. 67–8.

[67] Sheppard told the story, 'it is held unsafe for a minister to read them out of Rogers' *Exposition* of these Articles as they are there transcribed or the like; for it happened that a minister, being to read the Articles, took the right book with him and laid it by him on the desk till he had read the Common Prayer, intending then to read it. And in the mean time, by the patron's means, that Book was privately taken away and another book, which was not a true copy, foisted into the place thereof: which he took up and read. And this was adjudged no good reading within the statute, whereupon he lost his living: reported by Justice Jones' (J.C.P., d. 1640): ibid., pp. 97–98, 107. Rogers' exposition was one of the most authoritative sources on the Thirty-nine Articles. Thomas Rogers (d. 1616), chaplain to Bishop Bancroft and bishop of London 1590–1604, had been an outspoken opponent of puritanism. Rogers wrote *The faith, doctrine and religion professed and protected in the realme of England...expressed in Thirty-nine articles* in 1585–87, with subsequent editions published in 1607, 1621, 1625, 1629, 1633, 1639, 1658, 1661. Deviations in wording between the Book of Common Prayer and Rogers' commentary were slight: e.g. in Article 9 Rogers uses the words 'against the spirit' while the Book of Common Prayer reads 'always contrary to the spirit': T. Rogers, *The faith, doctrine and religion* (1621), p. 39; Sheppard, *Sure guide*, p. 82.

Sheppard also explored the limits of the ecclesiastical laws as they pertained to the citizenry. Since the Revised Book of Common Prayer had been elevated to statutory authority, Sheppard held that the contents of earlier versions had been superseded and informed his readers that offenses against charges and proscriptions in earlier versions were not indictable.[68] As for the provisions of the new book, a layman could be indicted only for failing to have his child christened with the sign of the cross or for failure to follow the rubrics of kneeling and standing, and neither of these offenses fell under the authority of the secular arm.[69] In another chapter of the *Sure guide*, Sheppard made a mockery of the confusions in the multiple statutes governing church attendance[70] and, in particular, of the nebulous wording of an Edwardian act.[71]

In his comments on canon law Sheppard noted that parliament, being the instrument of the statutory revival of the church's judicial arm, assumed a pre-eminent authority over the scope of powers exercised by the church courts. Their jurisdiction had been specifically restricted to the status quo of 1639 and the courts were henceforward forbidden to impose the *ex officio* oath or any other 'whereby the party swearing may accuse or charge himself in any criminal matter'. Additionally, the king was forbidden to appoint a tribunal invested with extraordinary powers like those bestowed on the former high commission.[72] Yet even with these specified limitations Sheppard was wary of the jurisdictional claims of the rival

[68] Earlier versions of the Book of Common Prayer had appeared in 1549, 1552, 1559 and 1604. Sheppard, *Sure guide*, pp. 17, 74, 141–2, 146–7.
[69] Ibid., pp. 146–7.
[70] Ch. 6, 'About coming to church', discussed conflicting statutory obligations based on 5 & 6 Edw. VI, c. 1; 1 Mary, c. 2; 1 Eliz. I, c. 2; 23 Eliz. I, c. 6; 29 Eliz. I, c. 6; 3 Jac. I, c. 4; and 14 Car. II, c. 4: ibid., pp. 132–43. Sheppard queried whether section 20 of the 1662 act bound every man to follow all previous directives concerning attendance at regular and holiday services, 'for, if so, there will scarce be found a man that may not be found faulty in one thing or another, and so indictable and punishable for it': ibid., p. 140.
[71] This sixteenth-century law stated that a person 'endeavoring himself to go to his parish church [should] abide there soberly', and Sheppard remarked that a 'deceit' against the intent of this statute could not be prevented because 'if one that in heart is against the thing shall come to church and stand under the wall or sit in the porch...but doth no more join in the service than a child or a dog that is present...or one come thither and sleep there', the objective of the act would be completely defeated and yet grounds for prosecution would be virtually impossible to discover: ibid., p. 139 (5 & 6 Edw. VI, c. 1).
[72] The church courts were conditionally re-established by 13 Car. II, st. 1, c. 12. Sheppard, *Sure guide*, p. 65 (13 Car. II, st. 1, c. 4). See also pp. 64–9, 184–91.

system and he cited seventeen statutes and four legal authorities to support his assertion that a party aggrieved by a suit in an ecclesiastical court could 'have his relief in the courts of Westminster'.[73] His chapter on canon law also noted that the Cavalier Parliament had specifically disallowed the seventeen Laudian canons of 1640, novelties in ceremonials and ornaments that the late archbishop had introduced in the 1630s.[74] He also asserted as a common-law rule that no law could be held binding on the laity without the sanction of parliamentary authority, and maintained that the canon-law-making powers of convocation were constitutionally dependent upon royal writ and subsequent parliamentary approval.[75] His discussion of the canons then recognized to be in force was of particular value since the pertinent laws dated back to 1604 and the most recent printed collection had been published thirty years earlier.[76] The great overlap of canon and statute law in matters of doctrine and rules governing church officers was recognized by Sheppard and he contended that in cases of conflict, statute law always carried the greater authority.

Sheppard's purpose in preparing this guide was to explain the changes made by the restoration settlement so that justices of the peace would better understand the redistribution of their duties. He therefore listed the recently annulled laws of the interregnum period that 'are now of no use to us' along with his explanation of the new statutes and his identification of half-forgotten laws.[77] Controls over heresies, blasphemies and religious errors had been removed from the jurisdiction of magistrates and returned to that of the church courts, as was the enforcement of all canon law and the punishment of the 'deadly sins' of fornication and adultery.[78] Conversely,

73 The statutes dated from 1297 to 1571, and his authorities included Coke, Croke, Keilwey (Caryll) and Plowden: ibid., p. 190.

74 The innovative canons of 1640, passed by convocation and approved by Charles I after the dissolution of the Short Parliament, included such controversial issues as the position of the communion table. The Long Parliament deemed them illegal in Dec. 1640 and eight months later impeached 14 bishops for the part they had played in the passage of the canons: Moore, *Canon law*, p. 24; J. Parker, *Introduction to the history of the successive revisions of the Book of Common Prayer* (Oxford, 1877), p. lxx, n. p; Sheppard, *Sure guide*, pp. 187–8.

75 Sheppard, *Sure guide*, p. 191. He also noted that the 39 Articles of 1562 had not been held to be binding until they were confirmed by 13 Eliz. I, c. 12; ibid., pp. 188, 191. This theme ran through the entire chapter on canon law: ibid., pp. 184–91. See also Moore, *Canon law*, p. 25.

76 This was the only major collection of approved canons from the sixteenth-century reformation to have received the official approval of both houses of convocation and of the crown: Moore, *Canon law*, p. 24.

77 W. Sheppard, *Sure guide*, pp. 38, 71, 108, 109, 113, 115, 150, 176, 396.

78 Ibid., pp. 38, 71, 108, 115, 150, 186, 188–9.

section twenty of the 1662 act which provided for the re-adoption of all pre-1642 legislation had revived many repetitive, ambiguous and contradictory laws concerning observance of the sabbath, holidays and feast days, disturbances of church personnel and property, obligations and prohibitions and the numerous laws against recusancy,[79] all of which Sheppard scrutinized for the provisions of proper enforcement.[80] In addition to those cognizable in quarter sessions, justices could prosecute out of sessions a layman's absence from church and a minister's failure to obtain a license to preach or to use the Book of Common Prayer.[81] To this arsenal of old laws the 1662 act added a provision empowering justices to fine and imprison schoolmasters and ministers for various newly defined breaches.[82] Sheppard's information about the limits of these laws was provided in an attempt to prevent some of the most flagrant abuses in enforcement, warning justices of the legal liabilities of wrongfully tendering oaths or unlawfully imprisoning suspected offenders. Many of the nonconformists who were prosecuted in quarter sessions and assizes were faced with rigged testimonies, hostile benches, confusing rules of evidence and intentional breaches of correct procedure. Given the onerous penalties of immense fines or distraint of possessions, extended periods of imprisonment and the possibility of being transported out of England, a non-Anglican's only chance for survival in a system intent upon breaking his resistance to the Church of England lay only with a sympathetic jury, a technical error in a *mittimus* or the assistance of legal counsel to challenge any illegal procedures.[83] In Sheppard's efforts to curtail the political campaign against dissident groups, he called upon whatever defenses English law could provide. When advising that the law itself

---

[79] Sabbath observance: ibid., pp. 7, 19, 125, 132–43; holidays and feast days: ibid., pp. 7, 174–80; recusancy: ibid., pp. 7, 19, 128, 196–201; disturbing a minister: ibid., pp. 112–13, 116–17, 123; sacraments: ibid., pp. 7, 128–9; behavior in churchyards: ibid., pp. 7, 183; churchwarden's office: ibid., p. 183; swearing, cursing and wilful perjury: ibid., pp. 19, 149–50.

[80] An Elizabethan church-attendance law which was being used improperly against nonconformists (23 Eliz. I, c. 1) called for a penalty of £20 a month fine for persons not attending church regularly and yet made no provisions for convictions of the offense: Sheppard, *Sure guide*, pp. 138–42.

[81] Jurisdiction of justices of the peace out of sessions: ibid., pp. 7, 124–5, 142.

[82] 14 Car. II, c. 4, ss. 5, 7, 10. The Five-Mile Act (17 Car. II, c. 2) which was drafted a couple of years later was also aimed at the leadership and prevented nonconformist preachers from pursuing the alternative occupation of teaching under a penalty of £40.

[83] Cragg, *Puritanism 1660–88*, pp. 36–65. Sheppard's commentary on the enforcement was interspersed with his descriptions of old and new laws: *Sure guide*, pp. 64–201.

in some instances offered protection against harassment, he was reviving arguments like those that had been used by John Hampden and John Eliot in the years when he was first learning and applying his legal craft.[84] Although the persecution of puritans did not end until the national mood shifted away from its fears of protestant sedition, Sheppard's guide may have had a moderating effect on some over-zealous justices who had been misapplying the law.

A third of the way through the *Sure guide* Sheppard finally turned from his discussion of religious laws to descriptions of traditional duties belonging to the office of the justice of the peace, beginning with a general statement on 'the peace of the county', sureties and good behavior along with forty-three examples of 'disturbances of the peace'.[85] In the thirty-four subsequent chapters he combined discussions of magistrates' powers in and out of sessions according to topic. All the customary charges pertaining to the prosecution of crime, regulation of local commerce, levying of rates, appointment of subordinate officers and responsibilities for the poor, the disabled and the labor force won separate chapters. Sheppard reached back to medieval legislation in search of a continuum for these officers' obligations, and his long experience as an author and a magistrate helped towards constructing a balanced portrait of the justice's role in local society. Reports of cases, resolutions of the judges and citations to Coke's *Institutes* embellished his account and several times he referred the reader to his own earlier books on justices of the peace.[86] He included several pages of directives about the magistrate's use of warrants and printed the texts of thirty-seven of the most commonly used forms.[87] In closing, he attached an explanatory guide to the enforcement of two recent statutes.[88] The *Sure guide* was re-published in 1669 with corrections made by the author. Fourteen additional statutes dating from 1660 to 1664 were appended in short chapters and the dating of warrants was modernized from 1662 to 1669.[89] This excellent book continued to be used by English magistrates through the eighteenth century.[90]

[84] The legal and constitutional challenges to Charles I's rule coincided in time with the years of Sheppard's legal training and his early law practice.
[85] W. Sheppard, *Sure guide*, pp. 202–11.
[86] Ibid., pp. 338, 428, 432–3, 435.   [87] Ibid., pp. 465–510.
[88] Ibid., pp. 511–24 (highway repair and unlawful cutting of wood).
[89] Of the new statutes included in the 2nd edition, only the Conventicle Act of 1664 (16 Car. II, c. 57) dealt with religious issues.
[90] In 1774 Thomas Howbalt purchased a copy from John Farnell (Folger Shakespeare Library, copy 134783); in 1770 W. W. Ashford of Birmingham acquired a copy from the library of Henry Joyce (author's personal copy).

In 1665, two years after the first printing of the *Sure guide*, Sheppard published his last manual on local law enforcement choosing the clerk of the market as his subject.[91] Traditionally the clerk of the market had headed a local bureau of standards for trading and selling but, through the centuries, enactments of new and revised rules had redistributed the responsibility for enforcement among a number of authorities. By the seventeenth century the clerk's powers had been 'much lessened' by the diffusion of warrants to other officers, particularly to justices of the peace and assize judges. Yet, as Sheppard pointed out, the clerk's office 'doth still remain and he hath a jurisdiction still'.[92] His duties were to keep a court, bring charges and impose fines, while more severe punishments for infractions were by this time left to officials of higher status. This manual was not strictly a guide for the officer named in the title but rather a collection of data and a summary of standards, both national and regional, for the use of any of the officials charged with the enforcement of regulations.

The text of the *Clerk of the market* was divided into seven sections and supplemented by cases and charts from a score of authorities. One major theme of the manual was the supervision of public markets, including details of the assize of bread and beer and guidelines for the quality of meat and fish sold. These duties alone amounted to a considerable responsibility in towns where several daily markets were held and Sheppard also included standards and measures set by the exchequer for bartered items like paper, soap and candlewax. Regulations for the weight and composition of the coin of the realm and statutes governing regional variations in the manufacture and measure of cloth were described as were units of land, important inclusions in a nation that retained so many local customs. Sheppard noted discrepancies of definition for an acre and a hide and left his reader to rely upon 'the estimation of the country' for an acceptable local meaning.[93]

Sheppard's persistent concern with honesty, especially where public duties were involved, was once again given full rein, beginning on the title page which carried the stricture, 'A false weight is an abomination of the Lord, but a just weight is His delight.'[94] In his introductory words to the reader Sheppard wrote, 'Now if by this work we may by any means provoke the offenders themselves to repentance and amendment; or, though they continue to offend, if

[91] W. Sheppard, *Of the office of the clerk of the market* (1665).
[92] Ibid., p. 118.   [93] Ibid., pp. 23, 18–26.   [94] Ibid., title page.

we may persuade such as have power to punish them for their
offenses, and so do anything for the cure of this great evil, we shall
account our pains well bestowed.'[95] In Sheppard's lifetime a scandal
had occurred in his own city of Gloucester when the privy council
discovered that the mayor, who filled the office of the clerk of the
market, was using bushels larger than the standard size by two and
three quarts for measuring corn brought to town by local farmers.
In that case the council had ordered the false measure destroyed and
the prevention of similar fraudulent practices was the very motive
that had inspired Sheppard to prepare this detailed handbook.[96] His
high-principled temperament was expressed for the last time in print
in the editorial remarks of this book, published when he was in his
seventy-first year. The *Clerk of the market* was never reprinted. Its
distinction may rest principally with what its publication tells about
the author, that dishonesty offended him and that his habits of
industry, perseverance and attention to detail never failed him. In
his septuagenarian years he had been persuaded by the 'importunate
request of a friend' to send this 'small and rude treatise' into print
with the hope that 'some good might accrue to the public by it'.[97]
Even at a time when his failing energies were directed to enlarging
his treatise on conveyancing and completing his abridgment, no law
of the land was too minor to escape his attention.

In the first decade of the restoration period Sheppard completed
six books. In addition to the studies on actions on the case and the
two on local law enforcement, he also prepared a two-volume
enlargement of his conveyancing monograph, the *Touchstone*.
London's great fire of 1666 destroyed the nearly completed first
volume in press, delaying its release by several years, and volume two,
The law of common assurances, reached the bookstalls first, in 1669.
The new impression of the first part, *The practical counsellor in the
law*, which was not completed until 1671 contained eight chapters
in its 500 pages. Several of them duplicated topics that had been
covered in the *Touchstone* and one described other areas of the law.
Cases to illustrate the topics of each chapter filled more than half
the pages of the book.[98] The second volume, the *Law of common*

[95] Ibid., sigs. A2v–3r.
[96] Willcox, *Gloucestershire*, p. 206.
[97] W. Sheppard, *Clerk of the market*, sig. A2r.
[98] W. Sheppard, *The practical counsellor in the law* (1671). Sheppard wrote, 'This
volume, although at present it appears new to you, yet is a second impression;
the first, not quite finished in the press, totally lost in the late, dreadful

assurances, was a nineteen-chapter study of deeds and charters, again with several chapters duplicating those of the *Touchstone* and more than a third of the book listed 700 cases.[99] The combined length of the two volumes was more than three times the length of the original book of 1648 and yet Sheppard did not approach his goal of improving upon his first effort when he supplanted the readable monograph with two bulky volumes that included more than 1500 cases.[100]

Both volumes were dedicated to the judges of the Westminster benches and Sheppard wrote in one, 'As the many growing and increasing evils of the present age require, and are the cause of accumulating new laws which in some manner abrogate or alter the old, so there is a constant necessity requiring new books that may give suitable information touching all necessary points fit for the younger sort of *tyros* to be instructed in.'[101] His recognition that students and practitioners needed up-to-date compilations of cases at this time when legal education was dependent upon textbooks rather than exercises at the inns of court had led him to gather precedents from many recently published reports[102] and while he acknowledged that both were works 'of more labor than ingenuity', he contended that 'the subject matter is of great consequence' and 'I shall not apologize for the work'.[103] The many recent decisions that Sheppard had 'gathered out of the scattered volumes of our laws'[104] were undoubtedly consulted by practitioners, but for all the prodigious efforts he had expended in preparing the *Practical counsellor* and the *Law of common assurances*, both volumes had only contemporary value and neither approached the merit of the parent work, the *Touchstone*, which retained its usefulness for two centuries.

Sheppard's final publication appeared in April 1675, just a year

---

conflagration of the City of London': sig. A2v. Duplicated chapters were those on common recoveries, fines, and bargain and sale. New topics introduced in this volume were usury and fraudulent conveyances. The cases filled 262 of the book's 500 pages.

[99] W. Sheppard, *The law of common assurances* (1669). Duplicated chapters were those on condition, warranty and covenant. The 763 cases filled 262 of the 898 pages.

[100] The folio editions of the two enlargements together had 1398 pages of text while the *Touchstone*, published in quarto, had only 529 pages.

[101] W. Sheppard, *Practical counsellor*, sigs. A2r–v.

[102] See *Sheppard's Sources*.

[103] W. Sheppard, *Law of common assurances*, sig. A1r; *Practical counsellor*, sig. A2v.

[104] W. Sheppard, *Law of common assurances*, sig. [a4v].

after his death at the age of seventy-eight. His four-part *Grand abridgment* was, in conceptual scheme, a lineal descendant of his *Faithfull councellor*, I and II, of 1651–3 and the *Epitome* of 1656.[105] Following the traditional alphabetical arrangement of English abridgments, he again added legal definitions, descriptions and short treatises under separate headings. Many parts of the *Grand abridgment* were adapted from the two earlier works, some passages reproduced as they first appeared while others were rewritten, many with the commentary shortened and the references and citations expanded. This final work typifies in many respects both the strengths and weaknesses of Sheppard's many contributions to legal literature. Written in English, as all his books were, it was a useful guide for students and practitioners with its inclusion of recent cases from contemporary law reports, as well as references to Rolle's *Abridgment* which had been published seven years earlier. In the fourteen years of his retirement that Sheppard spent perfecting it, he added a significant number of new entries that made this, the last of his encyclopedias, the most comprehensive of the three. The index was fuller and more carefully compiled and the editors made minor additions to the text to bring the entries up to date in the months that elapsed between Sheppard's death and the book's release.[106] Yet, for all the labor Sheppard expended upon it, his last book was by no means his best. Its major limitation was the quality of the entries which did not approach the excellence of the other great comprehensive works of the seventeenth century, Coke's *Institutes* and Rolle's *Abridgment*, the latter edited for publication by Matthew Hale. Moreover, many of Sheppard's additions suffered in comparison to those sections that had been reproduced from his earlier works, particularly the extracts from the *Touchstone*.

A comment written in a copy of the *Grand abridgment* in 1762 compels consideration. The note, which appears in the fly-leaf of Volume I of the copy now held by Lincoln's Inn reads, 'N[ote]: 11 November 1762, at the rolls. Sheppard's *Abridgment* having been cited with some apology for the book, Sir Tho. Clarke, master of the rolls, said that it was one of the best of the abridgments; but he said

---

[105] Sheppard died on 26 Mar. 1674: GRO, P 173, Acc. 3077, IN 1/1, fol. 43v. The imprimatur's permission for publication that appeared opposite the title page was dated 28 Apr. 1675.

[106] For example, in pt I one section concluded, 'bearing date in 1674', after which the editors added '& 1675': Sheppard, *Grand abridgment*, pt I, p. 427.

that Mr Shep the author had been thought a great plagiary and in particular that many parts of this abridgment were taken from the notes of Sir William Jones [J.].'[107] This observation was made at the same time that Booth of Lincoln's Inn had written in his copy of the *Touchstone* that the work had actually been written by Justice Dodderidge, a contemporary of Jones.[108] If, as was alleged, there were cases cited in Sheppard's *Grand abridgment* that could be attributed to or correlated with reports made by Jones, that occurrence has two possible explanations. The *Reports* of William Jones, J.C.P. and J.K.B., were published by an unknown editor thirty-five years after the judge's death, a fairly common practice in the field of seventeenth-century law reporting.[109] Given the lapse of so many years before Jones's reports were finally sent into print, it is extremely probable that at least one manuscript copy of the judge's notes had been in circulation for some time before publication. It would therefore be possible for Sheppard to have seen a copy of the manuscript at some point during those years and, if he had done, may have taken citations of cases from it for use in his own abridgment. The continuing work of Sheppard's life had been to translate and bring into print as much of the law as he could discover, and he is known to have cited cases from unpublished reports in order to make his references as full as possible.[110] Jones's *Reports* were not published until 1675, the year after Sheppard's death. Therefore any material Sheppard might have used from Jones's reports would have had to have been taken from an unpublished manuscript that may have been unidentified at the time Sheppard consulted it.

Another explanation for the allegation of 1762, one that is even more plausible, is that both Sheppard's abridgment and the posthumous publication of Jones's personal papers contained reports

---

107 Lincoln's Inn, shelf number 123.a. In 1932 a legal bibliographer quoted the notation in the Lincoln's Inn Library copy, commenting, 'Sheppard's works have been very much disparaged in modern times, but the following remark [as quoted above in text]...shows that his *Abridgment* had at least some reputation in the eighteenth century': J. D. Cowley, *A bibliography of abridgments, digests, dictionaries and indexes of English law to the year 1800* (Selden Society, 1932), p. liii.

108 See ch. 2 for full discussion of Booth's charge against Sheppard concerning the authorship of the *Touchstone*. Dodderidge, J., died in 1628. William Jones served as J.C.P. 1621–2 and J.K.B., 1624 until his death in Dec. 1640: *DNB*: *sub* Jones; Foss, *Judges*, VI, pp. 338–41.

109 W. Jones, *Les reports de divers special cases* (1675). Wing J 1003–4.

110 For Sheppard's use of unpublished reports, see *Sheppard's Sources*, *sub* Noy (1656) and possibly the Readings of Callis and Risden.

of identical cases, a likely possibility since Jones, in the last sixteen years of his life, 1624–40, rode exclusively on the Oxford circuit, the assize circuit that Sheppard himself frequented.[111] Furthermore, the cases reported by Jones covered only the years 1621–40, the very time that Sheppard began his personal collection of cases. In fact, Sheppard specifically cited decisions handed down by Jones at the Gloucester assizes in his first publication that cited cases.[112] With this contiguity in both time and place one would expect a duplication of cases reported by the two men. In all of Sheppard's works the majority of cases that appear to be of his own report are those handed down by judges on the Oxford and Western circuits and in the Welsh marches, the area of his private law practice. If Jones's reports had come into print while Sheppard was compiling his abridgment, he certainly would have cited his source by name if he had used them, as he always did when referring to recently published reports. Sheppard's source citations were one of the most valuable characteristics of his encyclopedic abridgments. But since Sheppard died a year before the publication of Jones's *Reports*, we can only conjecture that either there was a duplication of cases reported by the two men or that Sheppard had included in his abridgment cases discovered in a manuscript that was later attributed to Jones. The eighteenth-century charge of plagiarism against Sheppard must therefore be set in the context of the contemporaneous accusation that the Cromwellian adherent was not the true author of the *Touchstone*.[113]

The seven new books Sheppard composed in the last fourteen years of his life along with his enlarged version of the *Parson's guide* demonstrate his remarkable perseverance in his quest for legal improvement. While his works of the protectorate period were more interesting with their presentation of innovative reforms – particularly *England's balme* and the *President of presidents* – the books of his last years were valued by contemporaries to varying degrees. The importance of his two-volume enlargement of the *Touchstone* rests principally with the 1500 cases he gathered and arranged for publication.[114] His other two-volume work with its systematization of actions on the case (for which he collected more

---

[111] Cockburn, *Assizes*, pp. 57, 141, 270–2, 289; Foss, *Judges*, VI, p. 340.
[112] Jones's reports were of cases from 18 James I to 15 Charles I. In the 1648 *Touchstone* Sheppard cited a decision by Jones and Whitelocke, JJ, at the Lent assizes in Gloucester in 1631 on p. 282; Jones at Gloucester (n.d.) on p. 271. For further decisions by Jones see ch. 2, n. 50.
[113] See ch. 2, n. 23.   [114] See above, p. 259.

than 900 cases) was the more original contribution. Sheppard's enlargement of his 1654 book on tithes and the republication of his handbook on warrants as well as his short guide for the clerk of the market indicate that there was a continuing audience for those specialized books on the law. The only one of Sheppard's later legal works to include any political comment was his new manual on local law enforcement, the *Sure guide*. His critical review of the instruments of Anglican hegemony did not, however, detract from the valuable descriptions Sheppard supplied of the duties and responsibilities of the justices of the peace and the book remained in use into the eighteenth century. The enduring contribution of the *Sure guide* lies in Sheppard's review and appraisal of the legal ramifications of section twenty of the Act of Uniformity. In this, the author fulfilled his life-long ambition of subjecting to critical examination a portion of the statutes of the realm, identifying redundancies, contradictions and problems of enforcement in all the legislation concerning religious practice. Sheppard's last work, the *Grand abridgment*, was the culminating product of his half-century study of English law. It was perhaps fitting that his life ended before he could pronounce the work complete. His major professional goal had been to methodize and to translate into the vernacular the laws of his country so that they would be known to the people they were meant to serve. By the author's admission, his two earlier encyclopedias were faulty and incomplete and so, with unflagging energy, Sheppard continued to the end of his life to pursue his objective of demystifying the law and organizing its content. His determination and tenacity in continuing to work on this project exemplifies as well as any other accomplishment of the seventeenth century the dedicated and disciplined character of the puritan spirit.

6

CONCLUSION

At the core of Sheppard's continuing concern with legal improvement was the presumption that every man had the right to expect justice to be done. The two compelling forces in his life, the law and religious practice, were both subjected to public scrutiny during the years in which he was approaching his professional maturity. When the heated debates in the Long Parliament gave way to civil war Sheppard, believing that the political changes of his generation brought with them the possibility and even the assurance of improvement, did not hesitate to offer his services to parliament's cause. Several years of active involvement as a county committeeman had brought him into contact with the disruptive activities of radical groups as well as with the disturbing proposals for social change that were being circulated in political and religious pamphlets. Responding to those revolutionary proposals, Sheppard had by the early 1650s written tracts reaffirming his support for the traditional class structure, particularly the professions of the law and of the ministry, and for the protection of property rights. But while he remained a strong advocate of retaining the social cement of law and religion, he continued to publish criticisms of contemporary legal practice, asserting his optimism that improvement was possible and that deficiencies in the legal system could be corrected.

The master design for reform that Sheppard created was commissioned by a head of state in a unique period of English history when the constitutional revolution made it possible to consider carrying out genuine innovations in the very structure of the institutions of law and of government. The Long Parliament had set a precedent for legislating changes in the judicial structure when it abolished the prerogative, palatine and ecclesiastical courts; and the regicides and the Rump had carried England further along the road of innovation when they abolished the monarchy itself and established the commonwealth. When the protectorate was established, Cromwell's strong moral commitment to reform was matched by his recognition of the political need to respond to the wide-ranging grievances that had contributed to the constitutional collapse. Recognizing that the members of his determined and hard-working council were deficient in legal skills, he hired an expert with professional experience and a known interest in reform to design an overall remedial plan. Sheppard began his assignment by taking the public pulse, making every effort to learn all the grievances then current. Designing workable reforms for all the complaints he judged worthy of attention, he fashioned them into an interlocking design that would have definitively resolved most of the long-standing grievances within the context of the traditional common-law setting. The comprehensiveness of Sheppard's plan was, however, the very factor that doomed its acceptance as a totality by a seventeenth-century parliament.

The success of Sheppard's plan presupposed the passage of all its interdependent parts, but the numerous details that ensured its effectiveness provoked hesitations and outright objections from the membership. If Cromwell had won a greater degree of political cooperation from his parliaments, more piecemeal reforms might have been enacted, but no consensus on the adoption of Sheppard's plan could be expected from representatives of a nation so fearful of the radical ideas propounded by sectarian and anti-establishment groups. The dangerous attacks on several fundamental assumptions concerning the legal, social and religious institutions had elicited a defensive attitude from members of the propertied class and of the legal profession. A genuine fear of social anarchy and loss of property brought the natural leaders of society to view the customary operation of the law and of the courts as shields which protected their traditional interests. Even such modifications as the registration of land appeared to be unnecessarily risky to a nation that had just undergone fourteen years of constitutional disruption, civil war and demonstrations of religious radicalism. While Sheppard must be credited with the foresight to anticipate which components of the judicial institutions would have to be altered in order to facilitate a complete reform, neither the approval nor the implementation of his plan were politically realizable in 1656.

A second political impediment to the enactment of the legal and judicial reforms Sheppard proposed was the absence of a definitive constitutional settlement. By the time political compromise on the adoption of the Instrument of Government had been reached in the spring of 1657, the government had forfeited the support of its most ardent advocates of reform. Most members of the political nation who ultimately cooperated with the protectorate government both in the country and at the center opposed many of the reforms Cromwell had hoped to achieve. Cromwell had recognized as early as 1650 that 'we cannot mention the reformation of the law but they presently cry out, we design to destroy propriety [property]'[1] and, realizing that the success of his government depended upon the support of the propertied classes, Cromwell had chosen Sheppard to devise a reform that would ensure security of property while it sought to institute legal equality. But the propertied classes of the nation remained apprehensive, and this reluctance to sanction further changes partly explains both the failure of constitutional ratification and the lack of interest in the enactment of specific reforms. The religious attitudes held by both Cromwell and Sheppard were also too radical for a majority of the political nation. Cromwell's goal of establishing liberty of conscience and toleration for all peaceable Christians, and his emphasis on the quality of the clergy rather than on the form of church government (to which Sheppard had given legal articulation in *Laws concerning religion*) were too far out of the mainstream of accepted conventions. Cromwell and Sheppard had also hoped to impose effective standards over the selection of all officials serving the state, but objections from members of the ruling establishment who feared the prospect of sharing authority with new men from outside the traditional ranks brought the question of the tolerance extended by the religious settlement to the center of the general reform issue. At the restoration, Anglicanism became the unifying force in politics. Although this opposition to the English revolution was not consolidated until 1660, the Cavalier Parliament definitively repudiated Cromwell's entire rationale for a reformed government when the old order was restored around the rallying point of the reconstructed Church of England.

Another explanation for the failure of law-reform efforts in the seventeenth century lies with administrative impediments, particularly the institutional conventions of the judicial system with its self-perpetuating freehold offices and perquisites. G. E. Aylmer's important studies in the administrative history of the period 1625–60 have contributed immeasurably to a comprehension of how the offices of government actually functioned. Professor Aylmer con-

---

[1] As quoted by Ludlow in C. H. Firth (ed.), *The memoirs of Edmund Ludlow, 1625–1672* (Oxford, 1894), I, p. 246 (26 June 1650).

cluded that the Caroline administration was unreformable because the patronage system that was an entrenched part of the bureaucratic structure invited abuse, and that reform was not possible until a professional civil service, quality controlled and with loyalty to the state itself, was established. In his study of the state's administration after 1640, he found that although higher standards obtained among government officials, 'the sector least affected' by the administrative reforms 'was the legal side of government: the common-law courts and (despite the 1655–8 changes) chancery'.[2] This and other studies of the operation of government bear out Holdsworth's earlier conclusion that many reforms that 'deserved to be carried out...were opposed by almost all those who had had a technical training in the system which it was proposed to reform'.[3]

Resistance to law reform by members of the profession has been the most commonly presented explanation for the failure to adopt more changes during the protectorate period and throughout the interregnum in general. Evidence of the legal community obstructing reform is supplied in an appraisal of the men filling Cromwell's benches. Of the judges 'inherited' by the protectorate government who were retained under new patents, neither of the chief justices can be considered proponents of the type of reform Cromwell recognized was necessary and Sheppard proposed. Oliver St John, C.J.C.P., who was appointed two months before Pride's purge and served until the restoration, feared, for example, that the establishment of county courts and the adjudication of suits away from Westminster would adversely affect the unity of the law.[4] Henry Rolle, C.J.K.B., who had also been elevated in October 1648, resigned in June 1655 over the issue of the legality of customs' collections raised in Cony's Case. Three of Cromwell's serjeants arguing for the defendant in the same case claimed that the ordinances promulgated by the protector and council had no binding effect because the constitution had not been ratified. The validity of Cromwell's Treason Ordinance was similarly questioned by Baron Thorpe and Serjeant Newdigate, who were consequently dismissed from their respective office and rank in the spring of 1655.[5] Cromwell's insistence on implementing the only major judicial

---

[2] Aylmer, *State's servants*, p. 328.
[3] *HEL*, I, p. 434.
[4] Oliver St John, 'The introduction to my charges at the assizes at Thetford in Norfolk' (21 Mar. 1658): BL, Add. MS, 25276, fols. 7–8.
[5] Cockburn, *Assizes*, pp. 290, 292; *Thurloe State Papers*, III, pp. 359, 385; *W & S*, III, pp. 719, 733, 739–40. See also ch. 1, n. 133.

reform of his administration, the Chancery Ordinance, provoked the resignations under pressure of two of the chancery commissioners. The ordinance was subsequently enforced by two other commissioners,[6] but the prospects for legislative reform were much reduced when the two former commissioners, Bulstrode Whitelocke and Thomas Widdrington, assumed positions of leadership in the 1656 parliament. Although Cromwell, to his credit, filled his benches with the most qualified men he could find, few of his judges displayed any interest in formulating or implementing structural and procedural reforms of the nature Sheppard had designed. The protector, who genuinely desired to institute meaningful law reform, recognized that 'the great grievance [with the law] lies in the execution and administration'.[7] And yet all of his judges disclaimed authorship of the single innovative reform of his administration, the Chancery Ordinance of 1654.[8] The surviving evidence indicates that William Sheppard, author of *England's balme* and Cromwell's personal legal adviser, was almost certainly the draftsman of that controversial reform.

Another law-reform issue of the seventeenth century that failed to be realized was the abridgment of the statutes of the realm. Sheppard had proposed that the number of acts be reduced to remove redundancies and contradictions, and that parliament repeal those that were archaic or offensive. He had also hoped to consolidate all the statutes of one genre, re-ordering the legislative law into a rational and understandable form. Elizabethan and early-Stuart administrators, too, had recognized that there were just too many statutes to keep track of and to enforce. Professor W. J. Jones has pointed out that the Book of Orders issued in 1630 which attempted to assign priorities in local law enforcement was, in fact, an indication of what was not being done. Jones rightly concluded that 'The ability to enunciate policy was well ahead of administrative capacity', an astute evaluation that covers many aspects of the issues falling under the purview of law reform.[9] The commendable but daunting task of

---

[6] Chancery Commissioners John Lisle and Nathaniel Fiennes enforced the Chancery Ordinance for at least three years, well beyond the date of expiration as proscribed by the 1656 parliament.

[7] *W & S*, IV, p. 274 (Cromwell's speech to parliament of 17 Sept. 1656).

[8] Christopher Hill has noted that Cromwell's achievements in the field of law reform 'were limited by the men with whom he had chosen to work': Hill, *God's Englishman*, p. 164.

[9] Jones, *Politics and the bench*, p. 92.

reducing the statute book to manageable proportions was of a dimension beyond the capacity of seventeenth-century parliaments. While Cromwell's administration made some important adjustments in particular acts to 'remedy defects', no legislative body or committee succeeded in preparing a comprehensive reduction or abridgment for consideration until the nineteenth century. The single permanent accomplishment in Sheppard's lifetime of bringing together earlier statutes of one genre and incorporating new provisions was the Cavalier Parliament's passage of the Act of Uniformity, a glaring example of a missed opportunity to review all previous relevant legislation. Instead of repealing statutes that had expired or had been recognized by the courts to have serious enforcement problems, the assembly of 1663 re-endowed with statutory authority an unwieldy body of half-forgotten, badly written and contradictory statutes.[10]

Despite the failure of Sheppard's innovative proposals, his other contributions to legal literature over the course of his thirty-three-year writing career are considerable. The wide experience he gained from his country practice enabled him to comment on many aspects of the law as it actually operated in his generation and to recognize problems in its administration. His critical faculties were sharpened by the perspective he gained from his diverse professional activities. In his first book, for example, he expressed his criticism of the quality of men appointed to the office of constable. A concern with the training, conduct and character of men entrusted with the administration of the law was to become a recurrent theme throughout his writing career and in his second work he noted the hazards of entrusting property transactions to lay conveyancers. In his third work he called for the same standards governing public officials to be extended to stewards of manor courts, noting that the lack of controls over that officer invited serious breaches of justice. In a later work he lent his support to the contemporary trend towards an increased professionalization of the administration of the law when he strongly endorsed the appointment of recorders to borough corporations.[11] His first-hand observations of problems arising from untrained or self-serving persons handling technical legal transactions and procedures, resulting in maladministration at best and

---

[10] For a discussion of the 1662 Act of Uniformity, see ch. 5.
[11] *Constables* (1641), *Touchstone* (1648), *Court-keepers guide* (1649), and *Corporations* (1659).

expensive and lengthy law suits at worst, prompted him to encourage the imposition of quality controls over all officers with responsibilities for law enforcement or matters of property right. His own dedication to the cause of legal improvement through the dissemination of accurate information about the direction of common-law substantive developments and his suggestions ·for mandatory controls in the administration of the law characterize the entire corpus of his legal works.

Sheppard's comments on problems in the contemporary operation of the law were most marked in his handbooks for justices of the peace, the officer Sheppard viewed as the mainstay of local government. The changing problems that he observed in local law enforcement led him to compose three different manuals for magistrates, two of which he re-edited for new printings. The first, published in 1650 and re-issued three times, addressed the question of law reform directly by calling attention to the unwieldy number of statutes justices of the peace were expected to enforce. His second effort, written towards the end of the protectorate period, provided a resume of changes that had been made in the law since the beginning of the civil war. In that work, the focus of his concern was the potential abuse of authority by magistrates. By 1663 Sheppard had prepared his third entirely new guide in which he noted abuses then occurring in the enforcement of religious laws as a consequence of the restoration settlement. The misapplication of many older statutes impelled Sheppard to review the entire body of legislation pertaining to religious practice, delineating the intention, provisions and limits of enforcement for each. His discussion of the disparity between the law as it had been enacted and as it was then being enforced provided valuable information for contemporaries, offering advice on protections against illegal prosecution to religious dissidents and strong caveats to over-zealous magistrates on the penalties for abuse of authority.[12]

Sheppard's most interesting contributions to legal literature were his proposals for making the law more efficient and more responsive to the needs of his society. The nine works he produced for Cromwell in the middle period of his writing career elaborated upon the protector's goals for law reform and clarified the intentions of the

---

[12] Full references for his manuals on justices of the peace are listed in the *Chronological Bibliography*.

regime for introducing reform into practical politics. All the familiar
guideposts of Cromwell's stated aspiration for reform are found in
Sheppard's writings, particularly honesty in law enforcement, a
more humane criminal code, certainly in property rights and a quest
for godly government. As for the reforms of the judicial structure,
the proposals in *England's balme* have a fascinating consistency with
what is known of Cromwell's goals for general reform, providing
details, previously unrecognized, of what Cromwell hoped might be
accomplished. Sheppard, having been charged to discover the
'grievances of the nation', faithfully assembled hundreds of popular
complaints, recording them with an astute insight into the underlying
causes of the problems that had provoked criticisms. In the text of
England's balme Sheppard touched on legal, judicial, administrative,
economic and social problems, and his ability to identify the most
serious hindrances to justice enabled him to design a workable
model for comprehensive reform. One of his most noteworthy legacies is certainly the value his design is now recognized to have. The
parliaments of the nineteenth century, vindicating his appraisals
of the problems in the legal and judicial systems, enacted the reforms
he had suggested in his imaginative work of 1656, from the Common
Law Procedure Act and the reforms of the criminal code to the
institutional reforms of the Judicature Acts. Holdsworth and other
legal historians recognized Sheppard's prescience when noting the
similarity of ideas propounded in *England's balme* to the course of
reform ultimately taken by modern English parliaments.

Sheppard's works have a particular value to legal historians
because he lived and wrote in a period of change, a time of transition
in English law when procedural modifications and judicial alterations
were transforming the law in fundamental ways. Although the
modern structure of law did not acquire coherence until the eighteenth century, Sheppard recorded the direction of legal developments
in his generation, leaving as his legacy a contemporary account. He
did not comment on the constitutional issues of the interregnum even
though he was connected with the final and most interesting
constitutional experiment of that period. He did, however, write
about the effects of the abolition of the prerogative and ecclesiastical
courts. His publications clarified for his readers the legal consequences of those alterations in the judicial structure, both during
the civil war and interregnum and after the restoration, providing

current information about which courts were available to adjudicate grievances.[13] Cases of slander, perjury, forgery, libel and other criminal actions that had been heard in star chamber were accepted by the law courts after 1641 as misdemeanors and torts. The simultaneous increase in the number of actions upon the case upon an assumpsit contributed to the growing body of unclassified case law on contracts, and Sheppard can be credited with collecting and methodizing the many varieties of this popular form of litigation in his two-volume study.[14] The great number of cases he included was a significant contribution in publicizing the progress that was taking place in the fields of contract and tort in the period just prior to the time each was recognized as a separate field. While Sheppard was not a theoretician of either contract or tort, he was an alert and productive technician with prodigious energy who, by noting the empirical development of the law of his day, supplied the profession and the public with up-to-date compilations and summaries of recent changes in many aspects of the law.

Sheppard's life-time accomplishments as a law reformer are considerable. Over the span of his thirty-three-year writing career he produced twenty-three books on the law which appeared in forty-nine different releases or new editions, covering most of the major fields of law of his generation. In his works his continuing concerns were manifest in three areas: the accessibility of the law, its effectiveness in bringing justice, and the changes that were occurring. While his focus on reform and his suggestions for improvement are most pronounced in his books of the protectorate period, evidence of his critical concern can also be found in his writings of the earlier and later periods. Acknowledging the evolving, organic nature of the law, Sheppard sought to identify changes that had been made by statute and ordinance and, more important, to record additions to the body of case law. With unflagging devotion to his principles of professional responsibility, Sheppard produced a remarkable body of published information and comment upon the content and practice of English law of his day and age.

---

[13] *Faithfull councellor* I (1651) & II (1654); *Epitome* (1656); and *Grand Abridgment* (1675).

[14] *Action upon the case for slander* (1662) and *Actions upon the case for deeds* (1663).

BIBLIOGRAPHICAL COMMENT

The durability of Sheppard's works over the last three centuries can be estimated quantitatively only from sketchy and incomplete evidence. Accurate figures that would indicate the number of copies printed of a particular seventeenth-century book, tract or pamphlet are virtually impossible to discover. The few exceptions are cases when parliament records show an order for a certain number of copies to be printed, as in the case of the Hale Commission bills. Indications of a book's contemporary importance therefore depend either upon the evidence of several editions appearing in quick succession or from a marked popular response to a particular work in answer or refutation to the original publication. Sheppard's books on manorial courts and his manuals for local officers fall into the former category while his religious tracts concerning lay preachers and questions of faith belong to the latter.

In the years of Sheppard's political activity, 1641–59, he published nineteen different works of which George Thomason, the London bookseller, collected eleven. Most of his legal works continued to be available in London for more than fifty years after his death. Despite the political discredit that attached to Sheppard's reputation at the restoration, sixteen of his legal books were still being sold at bookstalls in 1663, as well as one of the four religious works.[1] In 1666 the Great Fire took an appalling toll of booksellers' stocks and subsequent catalogues took care to list those volumes that had escaped the conflagration. A 1672 list of bookseller Henry Twyford's stock included six legal works by Sheppard.[2] Between 1671 and 1714 another London bookseller, Thomas Bassett, published at least three catalogues of available law books, noting their prices. Bassett's index listed most of Sheppard's legal publications and the most valued items, to judge by their prices, were the *Abridgment*, the *Touchstone* and its enlargements and the *President*, while the local guides and case-law books all sold for far less.[3] The *Term catalogues*, another bibliography taken from contem-

---

[1] Only the out-dated *Laws concerning religion* was unavailable. The single religious work still in the bookstalls was *Sincerity and hypocrisy*. The listings of Sheppard's books were printed in *Action upon the case for slander*, *Actions upon the case for deeds* and the 1662 edition of the *Court-keepers guide*.

[2] Twyford's list was appended to R. Vaughan, *Practica Walliæ* (1672), pp. [213–15].

[3] Bassett offered eighteen of Sheppard's books in 1671, twenty-one in 1694 and twenty in 1714. The *Abridgment*, *Touchstone* and *President* were 20s., 6s., and 5s., respectively, and all the others were either 1s. or 2s.: T. Bassett, *A catalogue of the common and statute law-books of this realm ;...collected by Thomas Bassett and are to be sold at his shop* (1671, 1694, 1714).

273

porary records, reflected the same proportionate market values for Sheppard's works. Of his seven works found in the quarterly lists of new books and reprints after the Great Fire, the *Touchstone* and its enlargement were again the most expensive, selling for 12s. and 14s., while the local manuals sold for 1s. and 2s.[4]

The availability of Sheppard's works throughout the remainder of the eighteenth century is more difficult to trace. Publishing records suggest that all but one of his books were out of print between 1704 and 1780. The exception was the *President of presidents* which was re-issued in 1712, 1714 and 1725.[5] However, a court decision of 1757 citing the *Touchstone* prompted the printing of a new edition of that book in 1780 which was followed by five subsequent British editions as well as one in Ireland and two in America.[6] By 1768 the bibliographer John Worrall had acquired nineteen of Sheppard's books that had been published in the seventeenth century as well as copies of the eighteenth-century editions of the *President*. Early editions of the *Touchstone* were priced at more than three times the amount asked for any other of his books.[7] In 1788 Worrall's successor, Edward Brooke, sold the 1780 edition of the *Touchstone* for £1 5s.[8] This revival of interest in Sheppard led to the re-publication of the *Court-keepers guide* in 1791 and the *President* in 1813, 1822, 1825 and 1870.

At the turn of the nineteenth century R. W. Bridgman compiled a critical bibliography for lawyers interested in assembling private collections. Among the thousands of treatises recommended for a personal library, only the *Touchstone* of Sheppard's legal works was included.[9] A few years later John Clarke, a later successor to Worrall's bookshop, published a catalogue of his stock listing all but one of Sheppard's twenty-three legal works. The most recent editions of the *Touchstone* sold for 18s. while all his other books were priced from 1s. to 6s.[10] In 1834 when W. T. Lowdnes compiled his *Bibliographer's manual of English literature* he included only the *Touchstone* of all Sheppard's works, referring to it as a 'much esteemed work'.[11] In 1856 the antiquarian Charles Purton Cooper

---

[4] Arber, *Term catalogues*, I, pp. 14, 40, 45, 59, 175, 193, 263, 279; II, p. 52; III, p. 405.   [5] See ch. 3 n. 70, and *Bibliography*.

[6] Both the Dublin edition and the first American edition were pirated from Hilliard's 1791 London edition. Isaac Riley of New York was the first American publisher in 1808–10 and J. S. Littell published a reprint in Philadelphia in 1840–1. I am grateful to Morris L. Cohen for sharing with me the information he has collected on the bibliography of early American law.

[7] Worrall's catalogue included various editions of law books printed up until Eastern term 1777 and the preface was signed Michaelmas term 1768. The *Touchstone* was offered at 18s. and all the others at 6s. or less: J. Worrall, *Bibliotheca legum : or, a catalogue of the common and statute law books of this realm* (1777), p. 64 *et passim*.

[8] E. Brooke, *Bibliotheca legum* (1788), pp. 156–7.

[9] Bridgman, *Legal bibliography*, pp. 343–4.

[10] Clarke, *Bibliotheca legum, passim*. Only the *New survey of the justice of peace* (1659) was not available.

[11] Lowdnes, *Bibliographer's manual*, IV (1672). The same held true for the 1863 edition of that work: H. G. Bohn (ed.) (1863), VIII, 2378.

offered five of Sheppard's books at a public sale and eight others 'which the owner wishes to dispose of to some Public Library by private agreement'.[12]

Library holdings of the four inns of court indicate that Sheppard's reputation in the legal community had recovered considerably by the nineteenth century. In 1833 the Inner Temple published a catalogue of the printed books and manuscripts in their library. Their relatively modest collection included ten different books by Sheppard with two copies each of the *Touchstone* and the *President*.[13] Lincoln's Inn printed a similar catalogue in 1859 which listed ten books by Sheppard, with three editions of the *Touchstone* and duplicate copies of the *President*.[14] In 1888, when Gray's Inn issued their catalogue, eleven of Sheppard's legal works were inventoried, again with extra copies of both the *Touchstone* and the *President*.[15] The register of Sheppard's own inn, the Middle Temple, which was published in the early twentieth century listed only five of his publications. A new edition of that catalogue a decade later recorded the acquisition of one more of the former student's works.[16]

Several of Sheppard's legal works were carried across the Atlantic for use in the American colonies. In 1664 Dr Luke Barber, a physician living in Maryland, cited the authority of Sheppard's *Faithfull councellor*, I, on his own behalf in court.[17] The books listed in the 1699 will of Capt. Arthur Spicer, a lawyer and justice of the peace in Richmond County, Virginia, mentioned an 'old and broken copy' of Sheppard's *Epitome*.[18] In eighteenth-century colonial America at least seventeen private libraries held copies of Sheppard's books. Six Virginians owned copies of the *Abridgment*.[19] William Byrd II (d. 1744) had acquired a copy of the *Epitome* as well as one of *Corporations*.[20] There were at least three copies of the *Faithfull councellor* in eighteenth-century Virginia, two copies of the *Touchstone* and one of *Action upon the case for slander*.[21] Robert 'King' Carter, one of the most influential men in colonial Virginia, left a 1652 copy of Sheppard's *Whole office of the country justice of peace* when he died in 1732 and Edmund Berkeley of that colony (d. 1718) left a book on

12 *Bib. Coop.*, pp. 21, 41–3, 85, 90.
13 *A catalogue of the printed books and manuscripts in the library of the Inner Temple* (1833), pp. 77–8.
14 W. H. Spilsbury (ed.), *Catalogue of the printed books in the library of the honourable society of Lincoln's Inn* (1859), p. 722.
15 Douthwaite, *Gray's Inn*, pp. 532–3.
16 C. E. A. Bedwell (ed.), *A catalogue of the printed books in the library of the honourable society of the Middle Temple* (Glasgow, 1914), II, p. 1116; Supplement (1925), p. 172.
17 L. M. Friedman, *A history of American law* (New York, 1974), p. 83.
18 'Libraries in colonial Virginia', *WMQ*, III (1894–5), 133.
19 W. H. Bryson, *Census of law books in colonial Virginia* (Charlottesville, Va., 1978), p. 175, number 562: 'Libraries of colonial Virginia', *WMQ*, IV (1895–6), 94.
20 Bryson, *Census*, p. 74, nos. 558, 560.
21 *Ibid.*, pp. 74–5, nos. 561, 566, 557, in that order.

constables' duties and another for justices of the peace as well as an abridgment of English law, all three of which might have been Sheppard's books.[22] In 1746 an inventory of the library of a Philadelphia lawyer listed four of Sheppard's books, the *Court-keepers guide*, the *Whole office*, the *Epitome* and the *President*.[23] Samuel Peachey, a third-generation Virginia justice of Richmond County, was bequeathed all the books left by his grandfather in 1712. When the younger Peachey's will was proved in November 1750 three of Sheppard's books were mentioned, the *Faithfull councellor*, the *Abridgment* and *Action upon the case for slander*.[24] Thomas Jefferson owned at least two law books by Sheppard, the *Abridgment* and the *President*.[25]

In the early nineteenth century when the American legal community was studying seriously the problems created by the expanding and disparate development of federal and state law with a view to possible codification, David Hoffman, a Baltimore lawyer, included *England's balme* in a bibliography of English sources on that topic. All the other pre-nineteenth-century sources he listed had been taken from the eighteenth-century *Law tracts* of Bacon and of Hargrave. Hoffman's notice of Sheppard's most interesting book would seem to imply that he either owned or had seen a copy of Sheppard's collection of law-reform proposals.[26] In 1846 an anonymous law-reporter recommended Sheppard's *Touchstone* to aspiring lawyers as necessary reading on real property for those who meant to become accomplished in their profession.[27]

Sheppard's religious tracts have not enjoyed the same durable success. None was ever republished and no post-restoration references to them have been found. Copies of three have been located in libraries specializing in either renaissance collections or in religious tracts.[28] Only one copy of

[22] L. B. Wright, *The first gentlemen of Virginia* (San Marino, Calif., 1940), p. 261; 'Library of Edmund Berkeley, Esq.', *WMQ*, II (1894), 250–1.

[23] E. Wolf, II, 'The library of Ralph Assheton: the book background of a colonial Philadelphia lawyer', *Papers of the Bibliographical Society of America*, LVIII (1964), 345–79.

[24] Bryson, *Census*, pp. 74–5, nos. 561, 562, 557; 'The Peachey Family' and 'Libraries in colonial Virginia', *WMQ*, III (1894–5), 11–13, 132–3.

[25] E. M. Sowerbury, *Catalogue of the library of Thomas Jefferson* (Washington, D.C., 1953), pp. 220–1, 278–9. I am indebted to Morris L. Cohen for his assistance in helping trace Sheppard's influence in America. Professor Cohen attests to 'a strong conviction that [Sheppard's] works were widely distributed in this country' in the seventeenth and eighteenth centuries: correspondence from Cohen to Matthews, Nov. 1974.

[26] Hoffman, *Legal study*, p. 688. I am grateful to Dr Charles M. Cook for drawing my attention to this and to other American references to Sheppard's works. His research into the early-nineteenth-century codification movement in the United States has made me aware of the striking parallels in grievances as well as proposed remedies between that period and mid-seventeenth-century England.

[27] 'Law Studies', *Law Reporter*, VIII (1846), 435.

[28] Most notably The Folger Shakespeare Library, Washington, D.C.; the McAlpine Collection at Columbia University, New York; Dr Williams's Library and the British Library, London.

Sheppard's *Catechism* for the people of Gloucester has been discovered, and that in the nearby Bodleian Library of Oxford University.

Sheppard's most original book, *England's balme*, has been found to survive in at least nineteen copies. These have been located in private, public and institutional libraries.[29] Donald Wing's manuscript for the *Short-title catalogue* listed fourteen copies[30] and this writer has discovered only five additional holdings, although other copies may survive in private hands.

[29] United Kingdom: two copies in the British Library (one from the Thomason Collection), and one each at the Bodleian Library, Oxford University; at Caius and Trinity Colleges and the Cambridge University Library, Cambridge University; Lincoln's Inn, London; and the Edinburgh University Library. In the United States: three copies at the Library of Congress, Washington, D.C.; and one each at The Folger Shakespeare Library, Washington, D.C.; Bowdoin College Library, Brunswick, Maine; the Houghton Library and the Harvard Law School Library, Harvard University, Cambridge, Massachusetts; Columbia University Law Library, New York; Beinecke Rare Book and Manuscript Library, Yale University, New Haven, Connecticut; Biddle Law Library, University of Pennsylvania, Philadelphia; and the Union Theological Seminary Library, New York.

[30] Wing's manuscript information was provided by J. S. Smith, assistant in the Wing Revision Staff, Beinecke Rare Book and Manuscript Library, Yale University, letter of 16 Oct. 1973. The *National Union Catalogue* listing includes copies held by the Los Angeles Law Library and Princeton University. Responses to enquiries to those two institutions however were disappointingly negative. The former library was unable to locate either the book or the catalogue card after an extensive search in the rare book collection and the latter library possesses only a microfilm of a copy at Harvard University.

CHRONOLOGICAL BIBLIOGRAPHY OF
SHEPPARD'S BOOKS

Sheppard prepared for publication forty-nine editions of the twenty-seven books he wrote. Forty-seven were published in his lifetime and two, the *Grand abridgment* and the second edition of *Actions upon the case for deeds*, were released in the year following his death. At least twenty-one, and possibly twenty-two editions of his works were published posthumously.

In the chronological list below the following conventions have been adopted. The figures printed after the title refer to the number of pages in at least one copy of the book. The first number designates the number of pages preceding the text, beginning with the title page and including the dedication, preface and, in some instances, a table of contents. The second figure indicates the number of pages in the text itself. The third refers to the sum of pages in the index or table following the text. These numbers do not, however, apply to every copy of the work in question but are included to provide one example of each work to illustrate its comparative length. One difficulty with reporting the pagination of seventeenth-century books is that contemporary purchasers had their books bound to their own specifications, and the index and/or table might either precede or follow the text. Another complication arises from the surviving copies in which dedicatory pages and prefaces have been cut out of bound volumes by owners who objected to Sheppard's political statements and his laudatory comments about Cromwell and other public figures of the interregnum. Finally, there are cases where pages have simply been lost from unbound or re-bound copies. The sample copy cited here is meant only to illustrate the relative length of Sheppard's introduction and the text. Some of his writings, like the thirty-one-page pamphlet *The parson's guide*, were composed to provide information about a single aspect of contemporary law. At the other extreme his 1131-page *Epitome* and the 1162-page *Grand abridgment* admittedly embraced as much information as Sheppard could discover about the English legal system.

The size designation which follows the pagination has been determined by the foliation recorded in the book's signature. Discrepancies from other catalogues and bibliographies are due to errors made by earlier bibliographers who, on occasion, categorized small quartos as octavos or duodecimos or, conversely, identified a large quarto as a folio.

The date of publication follows the citation to the book's size. Disputed dates are discussed in the text. With one possible exception[1] ghost editions cited by bibliographers have been eliminated.

[1] *President of presidents* (1820), ed. Mr Willis.

The final entry in the principal citation, appearing in round brackets, is the number assigned to the work in Donald Wing's *Short-title catalogue 1641–1700*.
In the second part of each entry an attempt has been made to date each book as closely as possible. Arber's *Term catalogues*, the registers of the Stationers' Company and the holographic notes made by George Thomason on the title pages of the books in his collection have all been used as aids. Dates recorded by other contemporary collectors have been used for *Sincerity and hypocrisy* and the *People's priviledge*. Evidence of licensing or official patronage has also been included in the second part of each entry.
Posthumous editions are listed last. Only the editor's name and the place and date of publication have been included.

The offices and duties of constables, borsholders, tything-men, treasurers of the county-stock, overseers for the poore, and other lay-ministers. Whereunto are adjoyned the severall offices of church-ministers and church-wardens. 32 + 359 pp., 8vo, 1641 (S 3200); 4 + 218 + 7 pp., 8vo, 1655 [?] (S 3202); 20 unpaginated chs. + 5 pp., 8vo, 1657 (S 3203).

The touchstone of common assurances. Or, a plain and familiar treatise, opening the learning of the common assurances or conveyances of the kingdome. 12 + 529 + 6 pp., 8vo, 1648 (S 3214); 12 + 529 + 6 pp., 8vo, 1651 (S 3215). Some 1648 edns were entitled *The learning of common assurances.*
26 Mar. 1648 (*TT*, I, 603); 12 July 1648 (*Sta. Reg.*, I, 298).
E. Hilliard, ed., 1780, 1784, 1791; R. Preston, ed., 1820–1, 2 vols.; E. G. Atherly, ed., 1826, 2 vols.; Hilliard, ed., Dublin, 1785; New York, 1808–10, 2 vols. (vol. 3, appendix of United States law by John Anthon); Hilliard & Preston, eds., Philadelphia, 1840–1, 2 vols.

Of the foure last and greatest things : death, judgement, heaven and hell. The description of the happinesse of heaven, and misery of hell, by way of antithesis. With the way or means to passe through death, and judgement, into heaven, and to avoid hell. 6 + 66 pp., 4to, 2 edns 1649 (S 3196–7). 20 Apr. 1649 (*TT*, I, 739).

A new catechism, or, the grounds of Christian religion. 8 + 56 pp., 4to, 1649 (S 3193).

The court-keepers guide : or, a plaine and familiar treatise, needful and usefull for the helpe of many that are imployed in the keeping of law dayes or courts baron. Wherein is largely and plainly opened the jurisdiction of these courts, with the learning of mannors, copyholds, rents, harriots and other services and advantages belonging unto mannors, to the great profit of lords of mannors, and owners of these courts. 4 + 254 + 4 pp., 8vo, edns identical for 1649, 1650, 1654, 1656, 1662 (S 3177–81).

4th edn, 22 May 1656 (*TT*, II, 148).
W. Browne, ed., 1676, 1685 (S 3181A–2); 1791.
6th edn, 22 Nov. 1676 (*Term cat.*, I, 263).

The whole office of the country justice of peace. Wherein is plainly set down all their power and duty both in and out of the quarter sessions. The second part of the office of the countrie justice of peace. Wherein is plainly set down their power and duty in the sessions. Pt I, 12 + 205 + 10 pp.; pt II, 2 + 197 + 8 pp., 8vo, 1650 (S 3216A); 1652 8vo, listed by Wing. No surviving copy located. BL copy now lost (S 3217–18); pt I, 16 + 268 + 11 pp.; pt II, 4 + 212 + 8 pp., 8vo, 1656 (S 3219).
4 Mar. 1650 (*Sta. Reg.*, I, 339).

The office of a justice of peace. Wherein is plainly set down their power and duty, both in and out of general and special sessions. Heretofore published by William Sheppard, Esq.; And now enlarged...by a lover of justice. 12 + 232 + 6 pp., 8vo, 1662 (S 3199A).

The second part of the office of the countrey justice of peace. Wherein is plainly set down their power and duty in the sessions. The 4th edition corrected and enlarged by William Sheppard, Esquire. 2 + 243 + 37 pp., 8vo, 1661 (S 3219A).

The faithfull councellor : or the marrow of the law in English. In two parts. The first, methodically and plainly shewing, how any action may be warrantably laid in the common law, for relief in most causes of wrongs done : in which is handled many of the special and most usefull heads of the law now in practice. The second, by way of appendix, in what cases, and for what injuries relief is to be had in the high court of chancery ; wherein is set forth very much of the learning touching the jurisdiction and method of proceedings in that court. 6 + 519 + 11 pp., 4to, 1651 (S 3186); 6 + 484 + 10 pp., 4to, 1653 (S 3187).
'Published by authority' (1651 edn).

The people's priviledge and duty guarded against the pulpit and preachers' incroachment. And their sober justification and defence of their free and open exposition of scriptures. Wherein is briefly and very plainly shewed that Christians, that are not preachers in office, not onely may, but ought freely to expound scriptures one to another : and this without any prejudice to the preacher's office. 12 + 87 pp., 4to, 1652 (S 3207).
23 Mar. 1652 (*TT*, I, 865); 14 Apr. 1652 (J. Collinges, *Vindiciæ ministerii evangelici*, 1652, p. 47).

The offices of constables, church-wardens, overseers of the poor, supravisors of the highwayes, treasurers of the county-stock : And some other lesser country officers, plainly and lively set forth. In two books. The first book being of the office of high-constable, petit-constable, borsholder, tything-man, etc. 106 + 6 pp., 8vo, 1652 (S 3201).

The office and duty of church-wardens, overseers of the poor, supravisors of the high-wayes, governor of the house of correction. As also the treasurer of the maimed soldiers, the prisoners in the king's bench and marchalsea, and the prisoners in the common gaol. The second part. 73 + 3 pp., 8vo, 1652 (S 3199).
28 May 1652 (*TT*, I, 872).

The second part of the faithfull councellour. Or, the marrow of the law in English. In which is handled more of the usefull and necessary heads of the common law. With an alphabetical table of the most materiall things therein contained. 4 + 364 + 15 pp., 4to, 1654 (S 3209).
16 Mar. 1654 (*Sta. Reg.*, *I, 444*). Signed over to new publishers on 5 Dec. 1655 (*Sta. Reg.*, II, 21).

The justice of peace, his clerk's cabinet. Or, a book of presidents, or warrants, fitted and made ready to his hand for every case that may happen within the compasse of his master's office ; for the ease of the justice of peace, and more speedy dispatch of justice. 16 + 127 pp., 8vo, 1654 (S 3189); 15 + 127 pp., 8vo, 1660 (S 3190); 2 + 126 pp., 8vo, 1672 (S 3191).
15 June 1654 (*Sta. Reg.*, I, 449).
1672 edn, '*Cum gratia & privilegio regiæ majestatis*' (title page).[2]

The parson's guide : or the law of tithes. Wherein is shewed, who must pay tithes, and to whom, and of what things, when, and how they must be paid, and how they may be recovered at this day, and how a man may be discharged of payment thereof. 6 + 31 pp., 4to, 3 edns 1654 (S 3204–5; 3rd edn not listed by Wing, copy S 3205.2 held by The Folger Shakespeare Library); 20 + 99 pp., 12mo, 1670 (S 3206); 6 + 96 pp., 12mo, 1671 (not listed by Wing. Copy held by Harvard Law Library, Treasure Room).
15 June 1654 (*Sta. Reg.*, I, 449): 23 June 1654 (*TT*, II, 71). 21 June 1670; 1671 edn, 'In the right of his majesties grant of sole priviledge for the printing of law books' (*Term cat.*, I, 40, 45).

A view of all the laws and statutes of this nation concerning the service of God or religion. 7 + 84 pp., 12mo, 1655 (S 3216).
'Published by command' (title page).

The president of presidents. Or, one general president for common assurances by deeds : wherein is contained an extract or abridgment of all the readings and presidents thereof extant. Of singular use and profit to all men. 6 + 361 + 12 pp., 4to, 2 edns 1655–6 (S 3209; 2nd edn not listed by Wing. Copy held by BL, shelfmark E 866).

[2] In compliance with a clause in a 1662 statute, 13 & 14 Car. II, c. 33, law books of the restoration period were to have noted on or near the title page that royal allowance had been granted for the book to be printed. Notice of this official grant was also printed in the 1671 edition of the *Parson's guide*, the 1669 *Law of common assurances* and the 1675 *Grand abridgment*.

4 Sept. 1655 (*Sta. Reg.*, II, 10); 21 Oct. 1655; 10 Feb. 1656 (1st & 2nd edns dated by George Thomason: BL, shelfmarks E 855, E 866). 1677, 1684; W. Browne, ed., 1704, 1712, 1714, 1725; F. M. Van Heythusan, ed., 1813, 1822; T. W. Williams, ed., 1825, 1870; [Willis, ed., 1820; possible ghost[3]].
28 May 1677; [Nov.] 1683; [May] 1704 (*Term cat.*, I, 279; II, 52; III, 405).

A survey of the county judicatures, commonly called the county court, hundred court, and court baron. Wherein the nature and use of them, and the way and order of keeping them is opened ; for the great ease and profit of all such as have occasion to keep, or use them. 10 + 98 + 3 pp., 8vo, 1656 (S 3213).
11 Apr. 1656 (*Sta. Reg.*, II, 49).

An epitome of all the common & statute laws of this nation, now in force. Wherein more than fifteen hundred of the hardest words or terms of the law are explained ; and all the most useful and profitable heads or titles of the law by way of common place, largely, plainly, and methodically handled. 24 + 1131 + 13 pp., 4to, 1656 (S 3184).
15 May 1656 (*Merc. pol.*, 310, 6976).
'Published by his highness special command' (title page).

England's balme ; or proposals by way of grievance & remedy ; humbly presented to his highness and the parliament : towards the regulation of the law, and the better administration of justice. Tending to the great ease and benefit of the good people of the nation. 22 + 215 + 8 pp., 8vo, 1656 (S 3183).
11 Oct. 1656 (*Sta. Reg.*, II, 90); 23 Oct. 1656 (*TT*, II, 163).

Sincerity and hypocrisy. Or, the sincere Christian and hypocrite in their lively colours, standing one by the other. Very profitable for this religion-professing time. Together with a tract [by Thomas Barlow] *annexed to prove : that true grace doth not lye so much in the degree as in the nature of it.* 16 + 416 pp., 4to, Oxford 1658 (S 3210).
Apr. 1658 (*TT*, II, 205); 31 Mar. 1658 (R. Baxter, *Of saving faith*, 1658, sig. A2v).

A new survey of the justice of peace, his office. Wherein is briefly, yet clearly opened the severall parts thereof : and what one or more justices of the peace may do therein, in, or out of the sessions of the peace, by all the laws made to this day ; and now in force. With the names, or times, of the statutes, acts, and ordinances themselves, relating to this office. Alphabetically set down under apt titles. 8 + 230 + 14 pp., 4to, 1659 (S 3194).

---

[3] See n. 1.

12 Oct. 1658; 18 Apr. 1659 (*Sta. Reg.*, II, 201, 222); Aug. 1659 (*TT*, II, 255).

Of corporations, fraternities and guilds. Or, a discourse, wherein the learning of the law touching bodies-politique is unfolded, shewing the use and necessity of that invention, the antiquity, various kinds, order and government of the same. Necessary to be known not only of all members and dependants of such bodies; but of all the professours of our common law. With forms and presidents, of charters of corporation. 6 + 187 pp., 8vo, 1659 (S 3195).
Sept. 1659 (*TT*, II, 258).

Action upon the case for slander. Or, a methodical collection, under certain heads, of thousands of cases dispersed in the many great volumes of the law; of what words are actionable, and what not. And of conspiracy, and a libel. Being a treatise of very great use and consequence to all men, especially in these times, wherein actions for slander are more common then in times past. 5 + 183 + 10 pp., fol, 1662 (S 3173A); 6 + 287 + 16 pp., 4to, 1674 (S 3176).
2nd edn, 26 May 1674 (*Term cat.*, I, 175).

Actions upon the case for deeds, viz. contracts, assumpsits, deceipts, nusances, trover and conversion, delivery of goods, and for other male-feasance and mis-feasance. Collected out of many great volumes of the law already extant. A learning of very great and common use for all degrees of men. 5 + 377 + 19 pp., fol, 1663 (S 3174); 8 + 815 + 24 pp., 8vo, 1675 (S 3175). 1680 [possible ghost].[4]
Entered 3 June 1662 as *Actions upon the case about contracts of disceipt, nusams* [sic], *&c. Or, a methodicall collection under certeyn heads of thousands of cases dispersed in the many great volumes of the law, of the wrongs done to men about breach of agreements, breach of trust, deceipt & other things, with the remides touching the same; being a most excellent and proffitable learning, and of dayly use & practise in the law as conteyning all sorts of actions upon the case, except for slander, before publisht by the same authour W. S. Esq.* (*Sta. Reg.*, II, 309); 2nd edn 25 Nov. 1674 (*Term cat.*, I, 193).

A sure guide for his majesties justices of peace : plainly shewing their duty, and the duties of the several officers of the counties, hundreds, and parishes, (viz.) sheriffs, county-treasurers, bridewell-masters, constables, overseers of the poor, surveyors of the high-wayes, and church-wardens, &c. With the heads of the statutes, concerning the doctrine and cannons of the Church of England. 8 + 524 + 7 pp., 4to, 1663 (S 3211); 6 + 493 + 5 pp., 4to, 1669 (S 3212).

---

[4] A third edition of 1680 was listed by J. G. Marvin, *Legal bibliography* (Philadelphia, 1847), p. 644, but no copy has been discovered.

Of the office of the clerk of the market, of weights and measures, and of the laws of provision for man and beast, for bread, wine, beer, meal, &c. 8 + 123 + 10 pp., 4to, 1665 (S 3198).

The law of common assurances, touching deeds in general. viz feoffments, gifts, grants, and leases. 15 + 898 + 17 pp., 4to, 1669 (S 3192).
28 June 1669 (*Term cat.*, I, 14).
'*Cum gratia & privilegio regiæ majestatis*' (title page).

The practical counsellor in the law. Touching fines, common recoveries, judgements, and the execution thereof; statutes, recognizances, and bargain and sale. Collected out of the many great volumes of the law. 4 + 500 + 6 pp., 4to, 1671 (S 3208).
22 Nov. 1670 (*Term cat.*, I, 58–9).

A grand abridgment of the common and statute law of England : alphabetically digested under proper heads and titles. Very usefull and beneficiall for all persons whatsoever that desire to have any knowledge in the said laws. In four parts. 12 + 580 + 511 + 344 + 250 pp. (tables differ according to variation of binding, from 1 to 4 vols.), 4to, 1675 (S 3188).
28 Apr. 1675 [sig. a3v].
'*Cum gratia & privilegio regiæ majestatis*' (title page).

* * *

The work listed below has been attributed incorrectly to Sheppard.[5]

An exact collection of choice declarations, with pleas, replications, rejoynders, demurrers, assignment of errours : and the entries of judgments thereupon affirmed. Collected by W. S., one of the clerks of the upper bench office: in the reignes of Queene Elizabeth, King James, and the late King Charles. 1653 (S 3185).

The name of William Small was entered as the collector in the register of the Stationers' Company on 9 November 1652. The editor and translator of the *Exact collection*, J. W., stated in the introduction that Small, an attorney who had been a clerk of king's bench since the 1590s, had begun to assemble the material during the reign of Elizabeth, 'not imagining that these ensuing precedents, collected for his own private use, should ever have worn an English garment, or be seen without a court character'.[6] When, in 1650, the Rump Parliament ordered that all court records be kept in English, the aged Small agreed to have his personal collection of entries translated and published to be used as a guide by younger clerks in order to avoid errors in court procedure.

George Thomason made no attempt to identify W. S. by name when he corrected the publication date in his copy of the book[7] although he had

[5] *British Museum general catalogue of printed books* (1964), CCXXI, p. 236; *TT*, II, p. 7; Wing S 3185.
[6] W. S., *Exact collection* (1653), ed. J. W.: *Sta. Reg.*, I, p. 405.
[7] Date corrected from 1653 to 28 Feb. 1652 [i.e. 1653 New Style]: BL, Shelfmark E 210 (1).

correctly identified Sheppard when only his initials had appeared on the title page of *Sincerity and hypocrisy*. A catalogue of law books printed in 1662 did, however, ascribe the *Exact collection* to William Small.[8] Some eighteenth- and nineteenth-century legal bibliographers correctly attributed the book to Small[9] and the error of ascribing the book to Sheppard was apparently first made in the later nineteenth century. Since that time historians who have mistakenly credited Sheppard as the author of the *Exact collection* have concluded incorrectly from the information on the title page that Sheppard was made a clerk of the upper bench in 1653, the year the book was published.[10] In that year, however, Sheppard was still living in Gloucestershire, attending to his duties as a member of the county committee and occupied with the demands of his country practice. Moreover, while Sheppard did publish two books of precedents – one on warrants issued by justices of the peace and the other on a simplified conveyancing form – there is no internal evidence to suggest that he compiled this book of entries used in the central courts.

[8] Bound with W. Sheppard, *Action upon the case for slander* (1662), sig. Eee2r (copy held by The Folger Shakespeare Library).

[9] J. Worrall, *Bibliotheca legum* (1777), pp. 83, 88; Clarke, *Bibliotheca legum*, pp. 282, 289.

[10] *DNB : sub* Sheppard; Niehaus, 'Law reform', p. 216; Veall, *Movement for law reform*, p. 93; *W & S*, IV, p. 314; Winfield, *Chief sources*, p. 240.

SHEPPARD'S SOURCES

Sheppard called upon an extensive range of source material in the preparation of his books on legal topics. In addition to the legal texts listed below, he frequently referred to decisions from the bench, to statutes and Year Books, and to various Books of Entries, a few of which can be identified. He was also wont to cite a Biblical verse in support of a legal stricture. Because most of these works were composed during the years Sheppard resided in Gloucester, it is tempting to assume that he personally owned many, if not most of the volumes in this rich collection of books on English law. His inclusion of recently published reports confirms that he kept abreast of legal publications, and older books cited in his later works but not in earlier ones suggests that he continued to enlarge his personal collection of reference books. On occasion he specified that his reference was to the 'last published' edition of the source. In some cases his citation was apparently to a yet-unpublished manuscript in circulation; for example, Noy's *Reports*, published in 1656, was cited in the 1650 edition of his *Court-keepers guide*. When he cited the Readings of Callis and Risden, it is not clear whether he used a manuscript in circulation or the published version.

Only those editions of his sources which antedate Sheppard's citation have been noted. Unless otherwise indicated, all references to Sheppard's works are to his own first edition. Posthumous editions of Sheppard's books by later editors have not been included. Sheppard's sources are listed in alphabetical order and his own works in which they were cited have been abbreviated according to the following key:

ACD	*Actions upon the case for deeds* (1663, 1675)
ACS	*Action upon the case for slander* (1662, 1674)
C	*Constables* (1641, 1652, 1655, 1657)
CFG	*Corporations, fraternities and guilds* (1659)
CKG	*Court-keepers guide* (1649, 1650, 1654, 1656, 1662)
CM	*Clerk of the market* (1665)
E	*Epitome of all the common & statute laws* (1656)
EB	*England's balme* (1656)
FC I	*Faithfull councellor*, first part (1651, 1653)
FC II	*Faithfull councellor*, second part (1654)
GA	*Grand abridgment* (1675)
JPCC	*Justice of peace, clerk's cabinet* (1654, 1660, 1672)
LCA	*Law of common assurances* (1669)
LCR	*View of all the laws concerning religion* (1655)

NSJP   *New survey of justice of peace* (1659)
PCL   *Practical counsellor in the law* (1671)
PG   *Parson's guide, or the law of tithes* (1654, 1670, 1671)
PP   *President of presidents* (1655–6)
SCJ   *Survey of the county judicatures* (1656)
SGJP   *Sure guide for justices of peace* (1663, 1669)
T   *Touchstone* (1648, 1651)
WOJP   *Whole office of the country justice of peace* (1650, 1652, 1656, 1661)

Anderson, E., *Les reports...des mults principals cases* (1664, 1665). Wing A 3085–6.
> GA, LCA

Assize of bread and ale (1496, edns to 1636). STC 864–83.
> CM

Aston, R., *Placita Latine redivia: a book of entries* (1660, 1661). Wing A 4069–70.
> ACS

Bacon, F., *Apophthegmes new and old* (1624, 1626). STC 1115–16.
> GA, LCA

The historie of the raigne of King Henry the seventh (1622, edns to 1641). STC 1159–61. Wing B 299.
> GA

The use of the law (1629). STC 1175 [attributed to J. Dodderidge by Sheppard].[1]
> E, FC I, GA, T

Bagshaw, E., *The rights of the crown of England* (1659). Wing B 393.
> GA

Two arguments concerning canons and praemunire (1641). Wing B 401.
> SGJP

Bancroft, R. (Abp), 'Articuli cleri' (1605). Printed in Coke's *Second Institute*.
> E

Benloe, W. & Dalison, W., *Les reports de...des divers resolutions* (1661). Wing B 1871.
> ACD, ACS, GA, LCA, PCL

Book of Common Prayer (1549, edns to 1662). STC 16267–422. Wing B 3612–25.
> C, E, GA, SGJP, WOJP

Book of orders [*Orders and directions for the better administration of justice*] (1630). STC 9252.
> C (1641, 1655, 1657)

Bracton, H., *De legibus & consuetudinibus Angliae libri quinque* (1569, 1640). STC 3475–6.
> GA, LCA, SGJP

---

[1] Although this work is attributed to Bacon in STC 1175, the nineteenth-century editors of the works of Francis Bacon did not believe it to be his. See J. Spedding, R. L. Ellis & D. D. Heath (eds.), *The works of Francis Bacon*, VII (1879), pp. 453–7.

Bridgman, J., Personal opinions cited.
   ACD, E, FC I, FC II, GA, LCA, T
Reports of (1659). Wing B 4487.
   ACD, ACS, GA, LCA, PCL
Britton, J., Britton [On the laws of England] (1540, 1640). STC 3803–4.
   CM, GA
Brooke, R., La graunde abridgment (1573, edns to 1586). STC 3827–9.
   ACS, ACD, C, CFG, CKG, E, FC I, FC II, GA, LCA, PCL, PG,
   SGJP, WOJP
Brownloe, R. & Goldsborough, J., Reports of divers choice cases (1651,
   1654). Wing B 5201 [or] Reports, a second part (1652). Wing B 5198–9.
   ACD, ACS, E, FC I, FC II, GA, LCA, LCR, PCL, PG
Bulstrode, E., The reports of...divers resolutions (3 pts, 1657–9). Wing B
   5444, 5446, 5448.
   ACD, ACS, GA, LCA, PCL, PG (1670, 1671), SGJP
Callis, R., The reading...upon the statute of sewers, 32 Hen. VIII, c.1
   (1647). Wing C 304.
   E
Calthorpe, C., The relation between the lord of a mannor and the copy-holder,
   his tenant (1635, 1650). STC 4369. Wing C 312.
   CKG, E, GA
Camden, W., Brittania (1586, edns to 1607). STC 4503–8 [or] Britain
   (1610, 1625). STC 4509–10.
   SGJP
Carew [Carey], G., Reports on causes in chancery (1650, 1665). Wing C
   555–6.
   E, FC I, GA, LCA
Caryll, J., Reports of (1602, 1633), ed. J. Croke. STC 14901–2. Also known
   as Keilwey reports.[2]
   ACD, ACS, C (1641, 1655, 1657), CKG, E, FC I, FC II, GA, LCA,
   PCL, SGJP, T
Clayton, J., Reports & pleas of assises at Yorke (1651). Wing C 4610.
   GA
Coke, E., The compleate copy-holder (1641, edns to 1650). Wing C 4912–4.
   CKG, E, FC I, GA
Institute, I (1628, edns to 1670). STC 15784–9. Wing C 4924–7.
   ACD, CFG, CKG, CM, E, FC I, FC II, GA, LCR, NSJP, PCL,
   PG, SCJ, SGJP, T, WOJP
Institute, II (1642, edns to 1671). Wing C 4948–52A.
   ACD, ACS, CKG, E, GA, LCR, NSJP, PCL, PG, SCJ, SGJP,
   WOJP
Institute, III (1644, edns to 1671). Wing C 4960–5.
   E, GA, LCA, LCR, PCL, WOJP
Institute, IV (1644, edns to 1671). Wing C 4929–32.
   CKG, CM, E, GA, SGJP, WOJP

[2] See L. W. Abbott, Law reporting in England 1485–1585 (1973), pp. 39–44;
Baker, Spelman, II, p. 171; A. W. B. Simpson, 'Keilway's Reports', LQR,
LXXIII (1957), 89.

Little treatise of bail and mainprize (1635, 1637). STC 5489–90.
ACD
Reports (11 pts, 1600–16; 12th pt, 1656; 13th pt, 1659, edns to 1672).
STC 5493–5524. Wing C 4944–5, 4969–70.
ACD, ACS, C, CFG, CKG, E, FC I, FC II, GA, LCA, LCR,
NSJP, PCL, PG, SGJP, T, WOJP
The compleat attorney (1654). Wing C 5628.
E
*The complete justice. A manuall or analecta. Being a compendius collection
out of such as have treated of the office of justices of the peace, but
principally out of Mr Lambert* [Lambarde], *Mr Crompton & Mr
Dalton...formerly styled The complete justice : but now corrected with
diverse and sundry new additions* (1638, 1642, 1656). STC 14888. Wing
C 5643–3A. Also 1641, not in Wing, Folger Shakespeare Library, copy
M 545A.8.
WOJP
Constitutions and canons ecclesiastical (1603, edns to 1633). STC 10068–79.
C (1641), SGJP
Cowell, J., *The interpreter : or booke containing the signification of words*
(Cambridge, London, 1607, 1637, 1658). STC 5900–3. Wing C 6644.
E, GA, PCL, SGJP
Croke, G., *The reports of* (3 vols., 1657–61, edns to 1669). Wing C 7014–19.
ACD, ACS, GA, LCA, NSJP, PCL, PG (1670, 1671), SGJP
ed. *Keilwey reports.* See Caryll, J.
Crompton, R., *L'authoritie et jurisdiction des courts* (1594, 1620). STC
6050–1.
ACS, CKG, CM, E, FC I, FC II, GA, LCR, PCL, PG, SGJP,
T, WOJP
ed. *Fitzherbert's justice enlarged* (1583, edns to 1620). STC 10978–83.
CM, SGJP, WOJP
Curriehill, Sir John Skene, *De verborum significatione* (1641, 2 edns). Wing
C 7681–2.
T
Dalton, M., *Officium vicecomitum : the office and authority of sheriffs* (1623,
1628). STC 6212–13.
CKG, E, GA
The countrey justice (1618, edns to 1666). STC 6205–11. Wing D 143–6.
C, CM, E, FC II, GA, JPCC, NSJP, SGJP, WOJP
Davies, J., *A perfect abridgment of the eleaven bookes of* [*Coke's*] *reports*
(1651). Wing D 406.
FC II, LCA
A directory for the publique worship of God (1644, edns to 1660). Wing D
1543A–53A.
E, EB, LCR, NSJP, WOJP
Dodderidge, J., *A compleat parson* (1630, 1641). STC 6980. Wing D 1792.
GA
The English lawyer (1631). STC 6981.
E, FC I, FC II, GA

The lawes resolutions of women's rights (1632). STC 7437.

E, FC I, FC II, GA, LCA, T

The lawyer's light : or a due direction for the study of the law (1629). STC 6983.

E, FC I, T

The office and dutie of executors: or, a treatise of wills and executors, directed to testators (1641). Wing W 1358 (also attributed to Thomas Wentworth: *DNB*: *sub* Wentworth).

E, FC I, FC II

[*The use of the law*]. See Bacon, F.

Dyer, J., *Abridgment des reports de* (1585, edns to 1620). STC 7385–7.

ACD, ACS, C (1641, 1655, 1657), CFG, CKG, E, FC I, FC II, GA, LCA, LCR, PCL, PG, SGJP, T, WOJP

Finch, H., *Law, or a discourse thereof* (1613, edns to 1661). STC 10870–2. Wing F 931.

ACD, ACS, C, CKG, E, FC I, FC II, GA, LCA, T

Nomotechnia : un description del common leys d'Angleterre (1613). STC 10870.

ACD, E, FC I, FC II, GA, LCA, T

Fitzherbert, A., *La graunde abridgement* (1514–17, edns to 1577). STC 10954–7.

ACD, ACS, C, CKG, E, FC I, FC II, GA, LCA, PCL, T

The newe boke of justices of peace (1538, edns to 1566). STC 10970–7. See also Crompton, R.

C, SGJP, WOJP

New natura brevium (1534, edns to 1666). STC 10958–67. Wing F 1096–8.

ACD, ACS, C (1641), CKG, E, FC I, FC II, GA, LCA, LCR, PG, SGJP, T

Fleta, or a commentary upon the English law, written by an anonymous author (a prisoner in the Fleet) in the time of King Edward I (1647). Wing F 1290–90A.

CM, GA

Fortescue, J., *De laudibus legum Angliæ* (1616). STC 11197. Also published as *A learned compendium of the politique laws of England* (1567, edns to 1599). STC 11194–6.

E, GA

Glanville, R., *Tractatus de legibus et consuetudinibus regni Anglie* (1555?, 1604). STC 11905–6.

E, GA

Glisson, W. & Gulston, A., *A survey of the law* (1659). Wing G 866.

ACD, GA

Goldbolt, J., *Reports of certain cases* (1652, 1653). Wing G 911–12.

ACD, ACS, GA, LCA, PCL

Goldsborough, J., *Reports of* (1653). Wing G 1450.

ACD, ACS, E, GA, LCA, PCL, PG, SGJP

Hetley, T., *Reports and cases* (1657). Wing H 1627.

ACD, ACS, GA, LCA, PCL

Hobart, H., *The reports of* (1641, edns to 1671). Wing H 2205–8.
ACD, ACS, CFG, CKG, E, FC I, GA, LCA, PCL, PG
Horne, Andrew, *The mirrour of justices* (1642, 1646). Wing H 2789–90.
GA
Howes, E., ed., *John Stow's The Annales of England* (1615, 1631). STC 23338, 23340.
E
Hughes, W., *Grand abridgment of the law* (3 vols., 1660–3). Wing H 3324.
ACS, GA, LCA, PCL
Reports of certain cases (1652, 1653). Wing H 3330–1.
ACD, C (1655, 1657), E, GA, PCL
Hutton, R., *The reports of* (1656). Wing H 3843.
ACD, ACS, GA, LCA, NSJP, PCL, SGJP
Instrument of Government (1654).
E, LCR
Jenkins, D., *Eight centuries of reports* (1661). Wing J 606.
ACD, ACS, GA, LCA, PCL
Justice restored : or, a guide for his majesties justices of peace (2nd edn, 1661). Wing J 1252.
SGJP
Keilwey reports.[3] See Caryll, J.
Kitchin, J., *The aucthoritie of al justices of peace ... whereunto is added a verie perfect fourme for kepinge of court leetes ... and the boke called Returna brevium* (1580). STC 14886–7.
C, T
Le court leete et court baron ... and Returna brevium (1580, edns to 1620). STC 15017–25.
ACD, ACS, C, CKG, E, FC I, FC II, GA, LCA, T
Lambarde, W., *Duties of constables, borsholders and tything-men* (1583, edns to 1633). STC 15145–62.7.
C (1652), E
Eirenarcha (1581, edns to 1640?). STC 15163–76.5.
C, CM, E, GA, SGJP, WOJP
Lane, R., *Reports in the court of exchequer* (1657). Wing L 340.
ACD, GA, LCA, PCL, SGJP
Latch, J., *Plusieurs tres-bons cases* (1661, 1662). Wing L 537–8.
ACD, GA, LCA, PCL, SGJP
Leonard, W., *Reports and cases of law* (1658). Wing L 1103.
ACD, ACS, GA, LCA, PCL, SGJP
Ley, J. See Marlborough.
Littleton, T., *Of tenures* (1482, edns to 1671). STC 15719–83. Wing L 2586–8.
CKG, E, FC I, FC II, GA, LCA, PCL, T
Manwood, J., *A brefe collection of the lawes of the forest* (1592, edns to 1615). STC 17290–2.
E, GA, SGJP

---

[3] See n. 2, *sub* Caryll.

March, J., *Actions for slaunder* (1647, edns to 1655). Wing M 571–2A.
  ACD, ACS, GA
Reports : or, new cases (1648). Wing M 576.
  ACD, ACS, C (1655, 1657), CKG (1662), E, FC I, GA, LCA, LCR,
  PCL, PG (1670, 1671), SGJP, WOJP
Marlborough, James Ley, Earl, *Reports of divers resolutions in law* (1659).
  Wing M 688.
  ACD, ACS, GA, LCA, PG (1670, 1671)
Minshew, J. *The guide into tongues* (1617, edns to 1627). STC 17944–7.5.
  CM
Moore, F., *Cases collect and report* (1663). Wing M 2535.
  GA, LCA, PCL, PG (1670, 1671)
Noy, W., *The compleat lawyer* (1651, edns to 1674). Wing N 1441–7.
  E, FC I, LCA
Reports and cases (1656, edns to 1669). Wing N 1449–50.
  ACD, ACS, CKG, GA, LCA, SGJP
Owen, T., *Reports of* (1650, 1656). Wing O 831–2.
  ACD, ACS, GA, LCA, PCL, PG (1670, 1671), SGJP
Perkins, J., *Incipit perutillis tractatis magistri Johis Parkins* [*A profitable
  book treating of the laws of England*] (1528, edns to 1658). STC
  19629–45. Wing P 1543–4A.
  ACD, CFG, CKG, E, FC I, FC II, GA, LCA, PCL, T
Plowden, E., *Les comentaries ou les reportes de dyvers cases* (1571, edns to
  1659). STC 20040–7.5. Wing P 2606.
  ACD, ACS, C (1641, 1655, 1657), CFG, CKG, E, FC I, FC II,
  GA, LCA, LCR, PCL, PG, SGJP, T, WOJP
Popham, J., *Reports and cases* (1656). Wing P 2942.
  ACD, ACS, GA, LCA, PCL, SGJP
Powell, R., *A treatise of the antiquity, authority, uses and jurisdiction of the
  ancient courts of leet* (1641, 1642). Wing P 3066–7.
  CKG
Powell, T., *The attourneys academy, or the manner and form of proceeding
  practically upon any suit whatsoever, in any court of record whatsoever,
  within this kingdom* (1647). Wing P 3068.
  FC I
Pulton, F., *De pace regis et regni* (1609, edns to 1623). STC 20495–8.
  C, E, FC I, FC II, GA, WOJP
Rastell, J., *Abridgment of the statutes* (1519, edns to 1533). STC 9517.7–18,
  9520–1a, 9536.
  CM, GA, SGJP
Les termes de la ley : or certain difficult words (*c.* 1523, edns to 1642). STC
  20701–18. Wing R 286–8.
  E, T
Rastell, W., *Registrum omnium brevium* (1531, edns to 1634). STC 20836–9.
  ACD, CM, LCR, PCL, PG, SGJP
Risden, T., Reading 'On forcible entries, 8 Hen. VI, c. 9' (MS, 12 Eliz.
  I or 10 Jac. I. May have been printed in 1648. Cited by E. Brooke,

Bibliotheca legum Angliæ (1788), II, p. 193).
WOJP
Rogers, T., *The faith, doctrine and religion professed and protected in the realm of England* (1584, edns to 1661). STC 21226–33. Wing R 1832–3.
SGJP
Ryves, T., *The poore vicars plea* (1620). STC 21478.
C (1641)
St Germain, C., *Doctor and student* (1528, edns to 1673). STC 21559–82. Wing S 312–13.
ACD, CKG, E, FC I, FC II, GA, LCA, PCL, PG, T
Sheppard, W., *Actions upon the case for deeds* (1663). Wing S 3174.
GA
Action upon the case for slander (1662). Wing S 3173A.
GA
The court-keepers guide (1649, edns to 1662). Wing S 3177–81.
E, GA
An epitome of all the common & statute laws (1656). Wing S 3184.
GA, LCA
The faithfull councellor, I (1651, 1653). Wing S 3186–7.
E, GA
The faithfull councellor, II (1654). Wing S 3209C.
E
The justice of peace, his clerk's cabinet (1654). Wing S 3189.
E, NSJP, SGJP
The law of common assurances (1669). Wing S 3192.
GA
A new survey of the justice of peace (1659). Wing S 3194.
GA, SGJP
The offices and duties of constables (1641, 1655, 1657). Wing S 3200, 3202–3.
E, GA
The offices of constables, pt 1; *Of churchwardens*, pt 2 (1652). Wing S 3201, 3199.
LCR (pt 2 cited)
The parson's guide : or, the law of tithes (1654, 3 edns). Wing S 3204–5.
LCR
The practical counsellor in the law (1671). Wing S 3208.
LCA
A sure guide for his majesties justices of peace (1663, 1669). Wing S 3211–12.
GA
The touchstone of common assurances (1648, 1651). Wing S 3214–15.
E, FC I, FC II, GA
A view of all the laws... concerning religion (1655). Wing S 3216.
E
The whole office of the country justice of peace (1650, 1652, 1656, 1662).

Wing S 3199A, 3216–3219A.
> E, GA, LCR, NSJP, SGJP

Skene, J. See Curriehill.

Smith, T., *De republica Anglorum* (1583, edns to 1640). STC 22857–67.
> C, E, GA

Spelman, H., *H. Spelmanni archaeologus ; in modum glossarii* (1626, 1664). STC 23065. Wing S 4925.
> GA

Standford, W., *An exposicion of the kinges prerogative* (1567, edns to 1607). STC 23213–18.
> ACS, E, FC I, FC II, GA, LCA, SGJP, T, WOJP

Les plees del coron (1557, edns to 1607). STC 23219–24.
> E, GA, SGJP

Style, W., *Narrationes modernæ, or modern reports* (1658). Wing S 6099.
> ACD, ACS, CFG, GA, LCA, NSJP, PCL, SGJP

Regestum practicale (1657). Wing S 6102.
> ACD, ACS, GA, NSJP, PCL, SGJP

Swinburne, H., *A briefe treatise of testaments and last willes* (1590, edns to 1640). STC 23547–51.
> E, FC II, GA, T

Tothill, W., *Transactions of the high court of chancery*, ed. R. Holborne (1649). Wing T 1952.
> E, FC I, GA

West, W., *Symboleography* (1590, edns to 1647). STC 25267–79.7. Wing W 1394.
> CKG, CM, E, FC I, GA, LCA, PCL, T

Whitelocke, B., Keble R. & Lenthall, W., *A collection of such orders heretofore used in chancery* (1649). Wing W 3021.
> FC I

Wilkinson, J., *A treatise collected out of the statutes concerning the office of coroners and sherifes* (1618, edns to 1638). STC 25648–51.
> CKG

Winch, H., *Reports of* (1657). Wing W 2964.
> ACD, ACS, GA, LCA, PCL, SGJP

Wingate, E., *Maximes of reason* (1658). Wing W 3021.
> GA, PCL

Statuta pacis : or, a perfect table (1644). Wing W 3023.
> CM, E, SGJP

Yelverton, H., *Les reports de divers speciall cases* (1661). Wing Y 25.
> ACD, ACS, GA, LCA, PCL

Young, W., *Vade mecum and cornucopia : or, a table of the statutes concerning justices, with an epitome of Standford, Pleas of the crown* (1643, 1650). Wing Y 94–94A.
> WOJP

INDEX

Note: The *Bibliographical Comment* and *Sheppard's Sources* have not been indexed.

CAMBRIDGE STUDIES IN ENGLISH LEGAL HISTORY

The Law of Treason in England
in the Later Middle Ages
J. G. BELLAMY

The Equity Side of the Exchequer
W. H. BRYSON

The High Court of Delegates
G. I. O. DUNCAN

Marriage Litigation in Medieval England
R. H. HELMHOLZ

The Ancient State, Authoritie, and
Proceedings of the Court of Requests
by Sir Julius Caesar
EDITED BY L. M. HILL

Law and Politics in Jacobean England:
The Tracts of Lord Chancellor Ellesmere
LOUIS A. KNAFLA

The Legal Framework of English Feudalism
S. F. C. MILSOM

The Judicial Committee of the Privy Council
1833–1876
P. A. HOWELL

The Common Lawyers of Pre-Reformation England
Thomas Kebell: A Case Study
E. W. IVES

Marriage Settlements 1601–1740
LLOYD BONFIELD

Printed in the United Kingdom
by Lightning Source UK Ltd.
101035UKS00002B/26